Accelerate DevOps with GitHub

Enhance software delivery performance with GitHub
Issues, Projects, Actions, and Advanced Security

Michael Kaufmann

BIRMINGHAM—MUMBAI

Accelerate DevOps with GitHub

Copyright © 2022 Packt Publishing

Group Product Manager: Rahul Nair
Publishing Product Manager: Vijin Boricha
Senior Editor: Athikho Sapuni Rishana
Technical Editor: Nithik Cheruvakodan
Copy Editor: Safis Editing
Project Coordinator: Ashwin Kharwa
Proofreader: Safis Editing
Indexer: Tejal Daruwale Soni
Production Designer: Sinhayna Bais
Marketing Coordinator: Nimisha Dua
Senior Marketing Coordinator: Sanjana Gupta

First published: September 2022

Production reference: 2180822

Published by Packt Publishing Ltd.
Livery Place
35 Livery Street
Birmingham
B3 2PB, UK.

978-1-80181-335-8

www.packt.com

To my family, who had to spend many weekends and nights without me. To my colleagues from Xpirit and the DevOps community for giving me feedback, challenging my ideas, and giving me the opportunity to learn.

– Michael Kaufmann

Foreword

In 2011, entrepreneur Marc Andreessen famously claimed in the *Wall Street Journal* that "Software is eating the world," predicting that the rise of software would digitally metamorphose every industry and every sector of the world as we know it. As I sit here writing this a decade later, there is nothing to say except "Marc was right." Software has transformed our lives, and with that, it has also transformed every company and organization. Look at how it has fundamentally changed entertainment with Netflix, or travel and hospitality with Airbnb, or quite nearly everything purchasable under the sun with Amazon. Grocery stores now have a digital experience, parking meters are being replaced by phone apps, the oldest and most traditional banks have moved to the cloud, and cars get over-the-air updates more frequently than your mobile phone.

Every company is becoming a software company. Millions of lines of code already represent the foundation of the global economy. Software developers are the architects of this new, digital world. No longer can any organization, no matter the size or the industry, compete and thrive without software and developers.

And this trend isn't showing any sign of slowing down. According to the *World Economic Forum*, an estimated 70% of new value created in the economy over the next decade will be based on digitally enabled platform business models. To harness this opportunity, every organization will need to tap into the power of open source. Without open source, they won't stay competitive. Companies will also need to adopt DevOps practices to help refresh and strengthen their internal culture and continuously enhance software delivery performance. Naturally, as GitHub's CEO, I believe that GitHub is the best place for every organization to achieve this.

When Marc wrote his article in 2011, GitHub was still in its early days, focused on the hosting of git repositories. Today, GitHub has evolved to a full DevOps platform with features that support developers in every step of the developer lifecycle. With more than 83 million developers using our platform, we provide *the* home for the world's developers. GitHub is the place where every project - open source, cloud native, mobile, or enterprise - can be created, modernized, and deployed to its destination. It's the place where the interconnected community of developers builds the world of tomorrow.

I am thrilled that somebody as experienced as Michael has penned *Accelerate DevOps with GitHub*. Whether you are a professional software developer, computer science student, solutions architect, or site reliability engineer, this book is for you. *Accelerate DevOps with GitHub* provides clear, concise, and practical ways for you and your organization to harness the power of DevOps and GitHub. I think it will help you in the years to come, preparing you for the golden era of software development.

I am so proud of the long hours of hard work that you spent writing this book, Michael, but beyond this, I'm even more proud of all the meaningful change and progress I know it will help create for others.

Thomas / @ashtom

CEO GitHub Inc.

Foreword

Michael and I first met at a conference where we were both speaking on DevOps. We bonded over our shared passion for DevOps, and met often on the speaking circuit. It became a tradition for us to take selfies together each time we met. Our friendship and his passion for DevOps are why I was so excited to see that he was going to share his knowledge with the world by writing this book.

As time passes, the tools we use may change. However, the information shared in this book applies universally to organizations embarking on their DevOps transformation.

With COVID driving the world to remote, I really appreciated Michael covering asynchronous work. This has quickly become our new normal and teams must develop this muscle to stay agile and productive on remote and distributed teams.

It was great to read about the use of feature flags, which can be a game changer. Feature flags separate delivery from releasing and enable more advanced deployment strategies. It also reduces the need to rollback and drastically reduces the time to recover from bad code. However, as with anything, there is a cost. Michael does a great job covering the cost of using feature flags and how to mitigate it. This allows the reader to make an informed decision about whether feature flags are right for them.

Many teams I meet assume that going faster means cutting corners, but Michael explains the importance of infusing quality and security into your process. Additionally, he provides practical guidance about how to accomplish this. When DevOps is implemented correctly, you deliver secure, higher-quality code faster.

Often, to harness the true power of DevOps, your application must be refactored. Michael covers software architecture and the impact it has on your process and your team. He also covers the trade-offs of each option to help teams decide which is best.

I am confident that the readers of this book will find it to be an indispensable tool to support their DevOps transformation.

Donovan Brown

Partner Program Manager, Azure Incubations, Azure Office of the CTO

Contributors

About the author

Michael Kaufmann believes that developers and engineers can be happy and productive at work. He loves DevOps, GitHub, Azure, and modern work – not only for developers.

He is the founder and CEO of Xpirit Germany, a consulting company of the Xebia group, and he has been working in the IT sector for more than 20 years. Michael helps his clients to succeed through cloud and DevOps transformation and the implementation of new ways of working.

Microsoft awarded him with the titles **Microsoft Regional Director (RD)** and **Microsoft Most Valuable Professional (MVP)** – the latter in the DevOps category and GitHub since 2015.

Michael shares his knowledge through books and training, and is a regular speaker at international conferences.

"I want to thank the people who have been close to me and supported me, especially my wife, Gladys, and my parents."

About the reviewers

Mickey Gousset is a staff DevOps architect at GitHub. He is passionate about DevOps and helping developers achieve their goals. Mickey speaks on DevOps and cloud topics at various user groups, code camps, and conferences around the world, and is also the author of several books on **Application Lifecycle Management (ALM)** and DevOps.

Stefano Demiliani is a Microsoft MVP and **Microsoft Certified Trainer (MCT)**, a Microsoft Certified DevOps Engineer and Azure Architect, and a long-time expert on Microsoft technologies. He works as a CTO for EID NAVLAB, and his main activities are architecting solutions with Azure and Dynamics 365 ERPs. He's the author of many IT books for Packt and a speaker at international conferences about Azure and Dynamics 365. You can reach him on Twitter, LinkedIn, or via his personal website.

Unai Huete Beloki has been working as a DevOps expert for the last 5 years. He started in 2017, working as a customer engineer at Microsoft, providing support and education related to DevOps (mainly GitHub and Azure DevOps) and Azure around the EMEA region. In July 2020, he moved on to the Azure technical trainer role at Microsoft, where he provides Azure and DevOps training to customers worldwide and is one of the global leads for the *AZ-400: Designing and Implementing Microsoft DevOps Solutions* course/exam. He received a BSc in electronic and communications engineering and a master's in telecommunication engineering, both from the University of Navarra.

Table of Contents

2

Plan, Track, and Visualize Your Work

3

Teamwork and Collaborative Development

4

Asynchronous Work: Collaborate from Anywhere

5

The Influence of Open and Inner Source on Software Delivery Performance

Part 2: Engineering DevOps Practices

6

Automation with GitHub Actions

7

Running Your Workflows

8

Managing Dependencies Using GitHub Packages

9

Deploying to Any Platform

10
Feature Flags and the Feature Lifecycle

11
Trunk-Based Development

Part 3: Release with Confidence

12
Shift Left Testing for Increased Quality

13
Shift-Left Security and DevSecOps

14
Securing Your Code

15
Securing Your Deployments

Part 4: Software Architecture

16
Loosely Coupled Architecture and Microservices

17
Empower Your Teams

Part 5: Lean Product Management

18
Lean Product Development and Lean Startup

19
Experimentation and A|B Testing

Part 6: GitHub for your Enterprise

20
GitHub – The Home for All Developers

21
Migrating to GitHub

22
Organizing Your Teams

23
Transform Your Enterprise

Preface

We are in the 2020s and research has shown us for more than 10 years that companies with high developer performance not only outperform their competitors in velocity and throughput, they also score higher in quality, innovation, security, employee satisfaction, and most importantly, customer satisfaction.

And yet, besides some *unicorn* companies, the majority of traditional businesses struggle to transform themselves. Established rigid structures and slow processes, monolithic application architectures, and long release cycles for traditional products make it hard for companies to change.

This, however, is not a new phenomenon. Transformational changes are always hard and take many years to succeed, if the companies do succeed at all. The probability of failure is also very high. This is because transformation has to happen on so many levels – and if these changes are not aligned, the transformation is bound to fail. This book will help you with your transformation - not only by providing the research for high developer performance but also by providing practical examples on how you can accelerate your software delivery.

This book is a practical guide to DevOps. It helps teams that are already on their DevOps journey to further advance into DevOps and speed up their software delivery performance by providing simple solutions to common problems. It will help teams find the right metrics to measure their success and learn from other success stories without just copying what these teams have done themselves. The book uses GitHub as the DevOps platform and shows how you can leverage the power of GitHub for collaboration, lean management, and secure and fast software delivery.

By the end of this book, readers will understand what influences software delivery performance and how they can measure delivery capabilities. They will therefore realize where they stand and how they can move forward in their journey with transparency and simple solutions for cross-team collaboration. Equipped with simple solutions for common problems, they will understand how they can leverage the power of GitHub to accelerate: by making work visible with GitHub Projects, measuring right metrics with GitHub Insights, using solid and proven engineering practices with GitHub Actions and Advanced Security, and moving to an event-based and loosely coupled software architecture.

Who this book is for

This book is for developers, solution architects, DevOps engineers, and SREs, as well as for engineering or product managers who want to enhance software delivery performance. They may be new to DevOps or already have experience but struggle to achieve maximum performance. They may already have experience with GitHub Enterprise or come from a platform such as Azure DevOps, Team Foundation Server, GitLab, Bitbucket, Puppet, Chef, or Jenkins.

What this book covers

Chapter 1, Metrics That Matter, explains the theory behind lean management and how you can measure performance and cultural change. It looks into developer productivity and why this is so important to attract talent and achieve outstanding customer satisfaction.

Chapter 2, Plan, Track, and Visualize Your Work, is about work insights: accelerate your software delivery performance by applying lean principles. You'll learn how to plan, track, and visualize the work across your teams and products using GitHub Issues, Labels, Milestones, and Projects.

Chapter 3, Teamwork and Collaborative Development, explains the importance of collaborative development of software and how GitHub can be used for collaboration across teams and disciplines.

Chapter 4, Asynchronous Work: Collaborate from Anywhere, explains the benefits of asynchronous ways of working and how you can leverage them for improved and shared responsibilities, distributed teams, better quality, and cross-team collaboration. It shows how you can use GitHub Mobile, Microsoft Teams, Slack, and GitHub Pages, Wikis, and Discussions to collaborate from any location and any device.

Chapter 5, Influence of Open and Inner Source on Software Delivery Performance, describes the history of free and open source software and the importance it has gained over the recent years and in the context of cloud computing. It will teach you how to leverage open source to speed up your software delivery. Moreover, it will explain how open source practices applied to inner source will help you transform your organization, and the impact open and inner source can have on your in- and out-sourcing strategy.

Chapter 6, Automation with GitHub Actions, explains the importance of automation for quality and speed. It introduces you to GitHub Actions and how you can use them for any kind of automation – not only continuous delivery.

Chapter 7, Running Your Workflows, explains how you can tackle hybrid-cloud scenarios or hardware-in-the-loop tests using the different hosting options for the GitHub Actions workflow runners. It shows how to set up and manage self-hosted runners.

Chapter 8, Managing Dependencies Using GitHub Packages, describes how you can use GitHub Packages and semantic versioning together with GitHub Actions to manage dependencies between your teams and products.

Chapter 9, Deploy to Any Platform, shows how you can easily deploy to any cloud and platform with simple hands-on examples for Microsoft Azure, AWS Elastic Container Service, and Google Kubernetes Engine. It shows how you can perform staged deployments with GitHub Actions and how to use Infrastructure as Code to automate the provisioning of your resources.

Chapter10, Feature Flags and the Feature Lifecycle, explains how Feature Flags – or Feature Toggles – can help you to reduce complexity and manage the lifecycle of features and your software.

Chapter 11, Trunk-Based Development, explains the benefits of trunk-based development and introduces you to the best Git workflows to accelerate your software delivery.

Chapter 12, Shift Left Testing for Increased Quality, takes a closer look at the role of quality assurance and testing on developer velocity and shows how you can shift left testing with test automation. The chapter also covers testing in production and chaos engineering.

Chapter 13, Shift Left Security and DevSecOps, takes a broader look at the role of security in software development and how you can bake security into the process and practice DevSecOps, zero-trust, and how you can shift left security. The chapter looks at common attack scenarios and how you can practice security and create awareness using attack simulations and red team | blue team exercises. The chapter also introduces you to GitHub Codespaces as a secure development environment in the cloud.

Chapter 14, Securing Your Code, describes how you can use GitHub Advanced Security to eliminate bugs, security, and compliance issues by performing static code analysis with CodeQL and other tools, successfully manage your software supply chain with Dependabot, and eliminate secrets in your code base using Secret Scanning.

Chapter 15, Securing Your Deployments, shows how you can secure deployments to your environments and how you can automate your complete release pipeline in a secure, compliant way to also meet regulatory requirements. The chapter covers **Software Bills of Materials (SBoM)**, code and commit signing, dynamic application security testing, and security hardening your release pipelines.

Chapter 16, Loosely Coupled Architecture and Microservices, explains the importance of loosely-coupled systems and how you can evolve your software design to achieve this. The chapter covers microservices, evolutionary design, and event-based architectures.

Chapter 17, Empower Your Teams, is about the correlation of the communication structure of your organization and your system architecture (Conway's law) and how you can use this to improve architecture, organization structure, and software delivery performance. It covers the two-pizza team, the Inverse Conway Maneuver, and a mono- versus multi-repo strategy for your code.

Chapter 18, Lean Product Development and Lean Startup, is about the importance of lean product management at a product and feature level. It shows how you can incorporate customer feedback into your product management, create Minimal Viable Products, and how you can manage your enterprise portfolio.

Chapter 19, Experimentation and A|B-Testing, explains how you can evolve and continuously improve your products by conducting experiments to validate hypotheses through evidence-based DevOps practices like A|B-testing. It also explains how you can leverage OKR to empower your teams to conduct the right experiments and to build the right products.

Chapter 20, GitHub: The Home for All Developers, explains how GitHub can serve as the holistic, open platform for your teams. It explains the different hosting options, pricing, and how you can integrate it in your existing toolchain.

Chapter 21, Migrating to GitHub, will discuss strategies to migrate from different platforms to GitHub and integration points for other systems. It explains how you can find the right migration strategy and how you can use the GitHub Enterprise Importer and Valet to perform the heavy lifting.

Chapter 22, Organize Your Teams, talks about best practices to structure your repositories and teams into organizations and enterprises to foster collaboration and facilitate administration. The chapter covers role-based access, custom roles, and outside collaborators.

Chapter 23, Transform Your Enterprise, puts all the pieces together. This book gives you a lot of tools that you can use to drive a successful transformation and to gain developer velocity. But only if all pieces are put together will the transformation succeed. The chapter will explain why many transformations fail, and what you should do to make your transformation a success.

To get the most out of this book

Software covered in the book	System requirements
GitHub	Any operating system. You will need an account on `https://github.com`.
Git	All operating systems. You should have an up-to-date version of git installed (at least version 2.23).
GitHub CLI and GitHub Mobile	Optional – but you might want to install GitHub CLI (`https://cli.github.com/`) or GitHub Mobile (`https://github.com/mobile`).

If you want to follow the hands-on labs to deploy to Azure, AWS, or Google you will need an account for the given cloud environment.

If you are using the digital version of this book, we advise you to type the code yourself or access the code from the book's GitHub repository (a link is available in the next section). Doing so will help you avoid any potential errors related to the copying and pasting of code.

Download the example code files

The examples and hands-on labs of this book are on GitHub at `http://github.com/wulfland/AccelerateDevOps` and `https://github.com/PacktPublishing/Accelerate-DevOps-with-GitHub`. If there are updates to the code or labs, the GitHub repository will get updated.

We also have other code bundles from our rich catalog of books and videos available at `https://github.com/PacktPublishing/`. Check them out!

Download the color images

We also provide a PDF file that has color images of the screenshots and diagrams used in this book. You can download it here: `https://packt.link/vzP6B`

Conventions used

There are a number of text conventions used throughout this book.

`Code in text`: Indicates code words in text, database table names, folder names, filenames, file extensions, pathnames, dummy URLs, user input, and Twitter handles. Here is an example: "You can customize the dialog to choose the issue template by adding a file `config.yml` to `.github/ISSUE_TEMPLATE`."

A block of code is set as follows:

```
name: 💡 Custom Issue Form
description: A custom form with different fields
body:
  - type: input
    id: contact
    attributes:
      label: Contact Details
```

When we wish to draw your attention to a particular part of a code block, the relevant lines or items are set in bold:

```
blank_issues_enabled: true
contact_links:
  - name: 👥 Discussions
    url: https://github.com/wulfland/AccelerateDevOps/discussions/new
    about: Please use discussions for issues that are not a bug, enhancement or feature request
```

Any command-line input or output is written as follows:

```
$ gh secret set secret-name
```

Bold: Indicates a new term, an important word, or words that you see onscreen. For instance, words in menus or dialog boxes appear in **bold**. Here is an example: "Open the following repository and create a fork by clicking **Fork** in the top-right corner of the repository."

> **Tips or important notes**
> Appear like this.

Get in touch

Feedback from our readers is always welcome.

General feedback: If you have questions about any aspect of this book, email us at customercare@packtpub.com and mention the book title in the subject of your message.

Errata: Although we have taken every care to ensure the accuracy of our content, mistakes do happen. If you have found a mistake in this book, we would be grateful if you would report this to us. Please visit www.packtpub.com/support/errata and fill in the form.

Piracy: If you come across any illegal copies of our works in any form on the internet, we would be grateful if you would provide us with the location address or website name. Please contact us at copyright@packt.com with a link to the material.

If you are interested in becoming an author: If there is a topic that you have expertise in and you are interested in either writing or contributing to a book, please visit authors.packtpub.com.

Share Your Thoughts

Once you've read *Accelerate DevOps with GitHub*, we'd love to hear your thoughts! Scan the QR code below to go straight to the Amazon review page for this book and share your feedback.

https://packt.link/r/1801813353

Your review is important to us and the tech community and will help us make sure we're delivering excellent quality content.

Part 1: Lean Management and Collaboration

In *Part 1*, you will learn how to reduce ballast in your development process and move to a lean and collaborative way of working that allows your teams to accelerate their value delivery. You'll learn how to use GitHub to work together from everywhere effectively and use work insights and the right metrics to optimize your engineering productivity.

This part of the book comprises the following chapters:

1
Metrics That Matter

The hardest part when implementing **DevOps** is a shift in conversations with management. Management is used to asking the following questions:

- How much will it cost?
- How much will we earn from it?

From a management perspective, these are reasonable questions. But in a DevOps world, they can be toxic and can lead to a large amount of planning upfront if they are answered at the wrong time and in the wrong way. In this chapter, I'll show you metrics that can shift discussions with management away from efforts toward general engineering velocity and developer productivity.

I'll explain how to measure engineering velocity and developer productivity and how to make your DevOps acceleration measurable.

The following topics will be covered in this chapter:

- Why accelerate?
- Engineering velocity
- High-performance companies

- Measuring metrics that matter
- The **SPACE**) framework for developer productivity
- Objectives and key results

Why accelerate?

The expected lifespan of companies is decreasing rapidly. According to Richard Foster from the Yale School of Management, the average lifespan of a **Standard & Poor's (S&P) 500**-listed company 100 years ago was 67 years. Today, it is 15 years. Every 2 weeks, an S&P-listed company goes out of the market, and by 2027, it is expected that 75% of the top 500 companies will be replaced by new companies. Another study from the Santa Fe Institute (*The Mortality of Companies*) concludes that the average lifespan of a **United States (US)** company across all industries is about 10 years.

To remain competitive, companies must not only solve a customer problem; they also need to deliver products and services that delight their customers, and they must be able to engage with the market and respond quickly to changing demands. **Time to market** is the most important driver for business agility.

Software is at the heart of every product and service in every industry, not only because the digital experience has become as important as (or maybe even more important than) the physical experience. Software touches every part of a product life cycle, for example:

- **Production:**
  - Supply chain management
  - Cost optimization/predictive maintenance/robotics
  - Product individualization (lot size 1)
- **Sales, after-sales, and service:**
  - Webshop
  - Customer service and support
  - Social media
  - Digital assistant

- **Digital product:**

  - Companion app

  - Integrations

  - Mobile experience

  - New business models (pay-by-use, rent, and so on)

These are just examples to illustrate that most interactions your customers have with your company are digital. You do not just buy a car today—you are already aware of the brand from social media and the press. You buy and configure a car on a website or in a store with a salesperson, but also by looking at the screen of a tablet. The price of the car is influenced by the optimization of your assembly line by robotics and **artificial intelligence (AI)**. The first thing you do with the car is to connect your phone. While driving you listen to music, make a phone call, or respond to a text message using your voice. The driving assistant keeps you safe by braking for you if something is in your way and by making sure you stay in your lane; and soon, cars will do most of the driving autonomously. If you have a problem with a car or an app, the chances that you'll use the app or email to contact after-sales are high, especially for the younger generations. A car is mainly a digital product. Not only are there millions of lines of code that run in a car, but there are also millions of lines of code that power cars' apps, websites, and the assembly line, (see *Figure 1.1*).

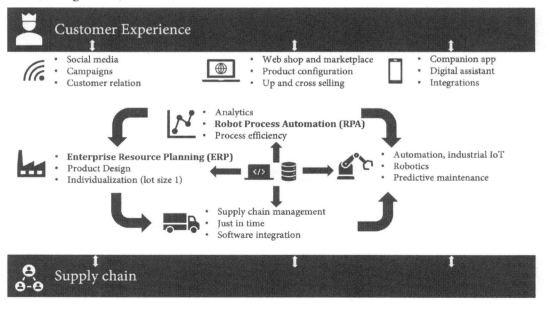

Figure 1.1 – Software and data at the heart of the customer experience

The good thing is that software can be changed much faster than hardware can. To accelerate your time to market and your business agility, software is the key driver. It is much more flexible than hardware components and can be changed in days or weeks, not months or years. It also allows a much better connection to your customers. A customer that is using your app is more likely to respond to a survey than one in a physical shop. Also, hardware does not provide you with telemetry of how your products are being used.

To be one of the companies that stay in business for longer than 10 years, your company must leverage the power of software to accelerate its market response and delight customers with a great digital experience.

Engineering velocity

How does your company measure developer velocity? The most common approach is effort. There used to be some companies that used metrics such as lines of code or code test coverage, but those are obviously bad choices, and I'm not aware of any company today that still does this. If you can solve a problem in one line of code or in 100 lines of code, one line is obviously preferable since every line comes with a maintenance cost. The same goes for code test coverage. The coverage itself says nothing about the quality of the tests, and bad tests also introduce additional maintenance costs.

> **Note**
>
> I try to keep the wording agnostic to the development method. I've seen teams adopt DevOps practices that use Agile, Scrum, **Scaled Agile Framework (SAFe)**, and Kanban, but also Waterfall. But every system has its own terminology, and I try to keep it as neutral as possible. I talk about requirements and not user stories or product backlog items, for example, but most of the examples I use are based upon Scrum.

The most common approach to measure developer velocity is by estimating requirements. You break down your requirements into small items—such as user stories —and the product owner assigns a business value. The development team then estimates the story and assigns a value for its effort. It doesn't matter if you use story points, hours, days, or any other number. It's basically a representation of the effort that is required to deliver the requirement.

Measuring velocity with effort

Measuring velocity with estimated effort and business value can have side effects if you report the numbers to management. There is some kind of *observer effect*: people try to improve the numbers. In the case of effort and business value, that's easy—you can just assign bigger numbers to the stories. And this is what normally happens, especially if you compare the numbers across teams: developers will assign bigger numbers to the stories, and product owners will assign bigger business value.

While this is not optimal for measuring developer velocity, it also does no big harm if the estimation is done in the normal conversation between the team and the product owner. But if the estimation is done outside your normal development process, estimates can even be toxic and have very negative side effects.

Toxic estimates

The search for the answer to the question *How much will it cost?* for a bigger feature or initiative normally leads to an estimation outside the normal development process and before a decision to implement it. But how do we estimate a complex feature and initiative?

Everything we do in software development is new. If you had done it already, you could use the software instead of writing it anew, so even a complete rewrite of an existing module is still new as it uses a new architecture or new frameworks. Something that has never been done before can only be estimated to a limited certainty. It's guessing, and the larger the complexity, the bigger the *cone of uncertainty* (see *Figure 1.2*).

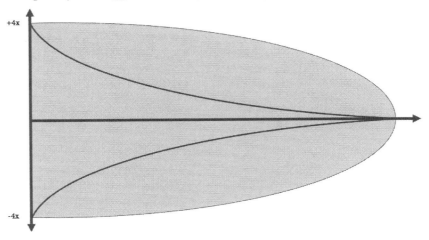

Figure 1.2 – The cone of uncertainty

The cone of uncertainty is used in project management and its premise is that at the beginning of a project, cost estimation has a certain degree of uncertainty that then is reduced due to rolling planning until it is zero at the end of the project. The x axis is normally the time taken, but it can also relate to complexity and abstraction: the more abstract and complex a requirement is, the bigger the uncertainty in estimation.

To better estimate complex features or initiatives, these are broken down into smaller parts that can better be estimated. You also need to come up with a solutions architecture as part of the work breakdown. Since this is done outside the normal development process and in time upfront and outside the context, it has some unwanted side effects, as outlined here:

- Normally, the entire team is not present. This leads to less diversity, less communication, and therefore *less creativity* when it comes to problem-solving.

- The focus is on *finding problems*. The more problems you can detect beforehand, the more accurate your estimates probably are. In particular, if you treat estimates later to measure performance, people learn fast that they can buy more time if they find more problems and can therefore add higher estimates to the requirements.

- If in doubt, the engineers who are assigned with the task of estimation take the *more complex* solution. If, for example, they are not sure if they can solve a problem with an existing framework, they might consider writing their own solution to be on the safe side.

If these numbers were only used by management to decide upon the implementation of a feature, it would not do that much harm. But normally, the requirements—including the estimates and the solution architecture—are not thrown away and later are used to implement features. In this case, there is also a less creative solution visible that is optimized for problems and not for solutions. This inevitably leads to less creativity and outside-the-box thinking when implementing features.

#NoEstimates

Estimates are not bad. They can be valuable if they take place at the right time. If the development team and the product owner discuss the next stories, estimates can help to drive the conversation. If the team plays, for example, planning poker to estimate user stories and the estimates differ, this is an indication that people have different ideas on how to implement it. This can lead to valuable discussion and may be more productive, as you can skip some stories with a common understanding. This is also true for the business value. If the team does not understand why the product owner assigns a very high or very low number, this can also lead to important discussions. Maybe the team already knows a way how to achieve a successful outcome, or there are discrepancies in the perception of different personas.

But many teams feel more comfortable without estimating the requirements at all. This is often referred to under the hashtag **#noestimates**. Especially in highly experimental environments, estimation is often considered a waste of time. Remote and distributed teams also often prefer not to estimate. They often take discussions from in-person meetings to discussions on issues and **pull requests** (**PRs**). This also helps when documenting the discussions and helps teams to work in a more asynchronous way, which can help to bridge different time zones.

With developer velocity off the table, teams should be allowed to decide on their own if they want to estimate or not. This also might change over time. Some teams gain value from this, while some do not. Let teams decide what works for them and what doesn't work.

The correct way to estimate high-level initiatives

So, what is the best way to estimate more complex features or initiatives so that the product owner can decide if these are worth implementing? Get the entire team together and ask the following question: *Can this be delivered in days, weeks, or months?* Another option is to use an analogy estimation and compare the initiative to something that has already been delivered. The question is, then: *Is this initiative smaller, equal, or more complex than the previous one delivered?*

The most important thing is not to break the requirements down or to already lay out a solution architecture—what is important is just the *gut feeling* of all engineers. Then, have everyone assign a minimum and a maximum number for the unit. For the analogy estimation, use percentages relative to the original initiative and calculate the results using historical data.

The easiest way to report this would look like this:

```
Given the current team,
if we prioritize the initiative <initiative name>,
the team is confident to deliver the feature in between
<smallest minimum> and <highest maximum>
```

Taking the smallest minimum and the highest maximum value is the safest way, but it can also lead to distorted numbers if the pessimistic and optimistic estimates are far apart. In this case, the average might be the better number to take, as illustrated here:

```
Given the current team,
if we prioritize the initiative <initiative name>,
the team is confident to deliver the feature in between
<average minimum> and <average maximum>
```

But taking the average (the *arithmetic mean*; in Excel, =AVERAGE() is used for this) means having a higher or lower deviation, depending on the distribution of the single estimates. The higher the deviation, the less confident you really can be that you can deliver that feature in that period. To get an idea of how your estimates are distributed, you can calculate the *standard deviation* (=STDEV.P() in Excel). You can look at the deviation for the minimum and the maximum, but also the estimate of each member. The smaller the deviation, the closer the values are to the average. Since standard deviations are absolute values, they cannot be compared with other estimations. To have a relative number, you can use the **coefficient of variation (CV)**: the *standard deviation divided by the average*, typically represented as a percentage (=STDEV.P() / AVERAGE() in Excel). The higher the value, the more distributed the values from the average; the lower the value, the more confident each team member is with their estimates or the entire team is with regard to minimum and maximum. See the example in the following table:

Team Members	Minimum	Maximum	Arithmetic Mean	Standard Deviation	CV
Member 1	1	4	2.5	1.5	60.0%
Member 2	4	8	6.0	2.0	33.3%
Member 3	3	6	4.5	1.5	33.3%
Member 4	2	4	3.0	1.0	33.3%
Member 5	1	4	2.5	1.5	60.0%
Member 6	5	12	8.5	3.5	41.2%
Average	2.7	6.3	4.5	1.8	43.5%
CV	55.9%	46.2%			65.7%

Table 1.1 – Example for calculating estimations

To express uncertainty in the deviation of the values, you can add a confidence level to the estimation. This can be text (such as low, medium, or high) or a percentage level, as illustrated here:

```
Given the current team,
if we prioritize the initiative <initiative name>,
the team is <confident level> confident to deliver the feature
in <arithmetic mean>
```

I don't use a fixed formula here because this would involve knowing the team. If you look at the data in the example (*Table 1.1*), you can see that the average of the minimum (**2,7**) and the maximum (**6,3**) are not so far away. If you look at the individual team members, you can see that there are more pessimistic and optimistic members. If past estimations confirm this, it gives you very high confidence that the average is realistic, even if the minimum and maximum values have a pretty high CV. Your estimate could look like this:

```
Given the current team,
if we prioritize the initiative fancy-new-thing,
the team is 85% confident to deliver the feature in 4.5 months"
```

This kind of estimation is not rocket science. It has nothing to do with complex estimation and forecasting systems such as the three-point estimation technique (`https://en.wikipedia.org/wiki/Three-point_estimation`), PERT distribution (`https://en.wikipedia.org/wiki/PERT_distribution`), or the Monte Carlo simulation method (`https://en.wikipedia.org/wiki/Monte_Carlo_method`), and they all depend upon a detailed breakdown of the requirements and an estimation on a task (work) level. The idea is to avoid planning upfront and breaking down the requirements and relying more on the gut feeling of your engineering team. The technique here is just to give you some insights into the data points you collect across your team. It's still just guessing.

From developer to engineering velocity

Effort is not a good metric for measuring developer velocity, especially if it is based upon estimates, and in cross-functional teams, velocity does not only depend upon developers. So, how do you shift from a developer velocity to an engineering velocity?

High-performance companies

Organizations with a high engineering velocity outperform their competitors and disrupt markets. But what exactly are high-performance companies?

The Developer Velocity Index

In April 2020, McKinsey published their research about the **Developer Velocity Index** (**DVI**) (*Srivastava S., Trehan K., Wagle D. & Wang J. (2020)*). This is a study taken among 440 large organizations from 12 industries that considers 46 drivers across 13 capabilities. The drivers are not only engineering capabilities—they also contain working practices and organizational enablement such as the company culture. The study shows that the companies in the top quartile of the DVI outperform other companies in their market by four to five times, and not only on overall business performance. Companies in the top quartile score between 40 and 60% higher in the following areas:

- Innovation
- Customer satisfaction
- Brand perception
- Talent management

The study conducted interviews with more than 100 senior engineering leaders at 440 large organizations across 12 industries. The interview contained 46 drivers across 13 capabilities in 3 categories, outlined as follows:

- **Technology**: Architecture; infrastructure and cloud adoption; testing; tools

- **Working practices**: Engineering practices; security and compliance; open source adoption, agile team practices

- **Organizational enablement**: Team characteristics; product management; organizational agility; culture; talent management

The DVI, therefore, goes way beyond pure developer velocity. It analyzes the engineering velocity and all the factors that influence it and relates them to business outcomes such as revenue, shareholder returns, operating margin, and nonfinancial performance indicators such as innovation, customer satisfaction, and brand perception.

The state of DevOps

The findings align with the results from the **DevOps Research and Assessment (DORA)** *State of DevOps* report (`https://www.devops-research.com/research.html#reports`) but take them one step further by adding the business outcomes. The *DevOps Report 2019* states how elite performers compare against low performers (*Forsgren N., Smith D., Humble J. & Frazelle J. (2019)*), as outlined here:

- **Faster value delivery**: They have a 106-times faster **lead time (LT)** from commit to deploy.

- **Advanced stability and quality**: They recover 2,604 times faster from incidents and have a 7-times lower **change failure rate (CFR)**.

- **Higher throughput**: They do 208 times more frequent code deployments.

High-performance companies not only excel in throughput and stability but are also more innovative, have higher customer satisfaction, and greater business performance, (see *Figure 1.3*).

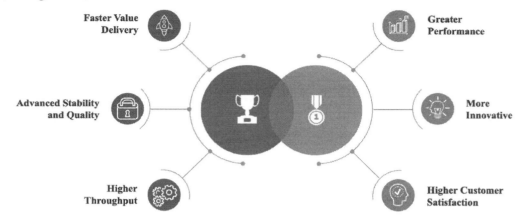

Figure 1.3 – High-performance companies

Focusing on the measures that highlight the capabilities that set apart high-performance companies from medium and low performers, you can make your transformation visible and provide management with metrics that hopefully matter more to them than lines of code or estimation-based velocity.

Measuring metrics that matter

"The key to successful change is measuring and understanding the right things with a focus on capabilities."

– Forsgren. N., Humble, J. & Kim, G. (2018) p. 38

To measure where you are on your transformation journey, it's best to focus on the four metrics that are used in DORA—two for performance and two for stability, as follows:

- **Delivery performance metrics:**
  - Delivery lead time
  - Deployment frequency
- **Stability metrics:**
  - Mean time to restore
  - Change fail rate

Delivery lead time

The delivery lead time (DLT) is the time from when your engineers start working on a feature until the feature is available to the end users. You could say *from code commit to production*—but you normally start the clock when the team starts to work on a requirement and changes the state of it to *doing* or something similar.

It is not easy to get this metric automated from the system. I will show you in *Chapter 7, Running Your Workflows*, how you can use GitHub Actions and Projects together to automate the metric. If you don't get the metric out of the system, you can set up a survey with the following options:

- Less than 1 hour
- Less than 1 day
- Less than 1 week
- Less than 1 month
- Less than 6 months
- More than 6 months

Depending on where you are on the scale, you conduct the survey more or less often. Of course, system-generated values would be preferable, but if you are on the upper steps of that scale (months), it doesn't matter. It gets more interesting if you measure hours or days.

> **Why not lead time?**
>
> From a **Lean management** perspective, the LT would be the better metric: how long does a learning from customer feedback flow through the entire system? But requirements in software engineering are difficult. Normally, a lot of steps are involved before the actual engineering work begins. The outcome could vary a lot and the metric is hard to guess if you must rely on survey data. Some requirements could stay for months in the queue—some, only a few hours. From an engineering perspective, it's much better to focus on DLT. You will learn more about LT in *Chapter 18, Lean Product Development and Lean Startup*.

Deployment frequency

The deployment frequency focuses on speed. How long does it take to deliver your changes? A metric that focuses more on throughput is the DF. How often do you deploy your changes to production? The DF indicates your batch size. In Lean manufacturing, it is desirable to reduce the batch size. A higher DF would indicate a smaller batch size.

At first glance, it looks easy to measure DF in your system. But at a closer look, how many of your deployments really make it to production? In *Chapter 7, Running Your Workflows*, I will explain how you can capture the metric using GitHub Actions.

If you can't measure the metric yet, you can also use a survey. Use the following options:

- On-demand (multiple times per day)
- Between once per hour and once per day
- Between once per day and once per week
- Between once per week and once per month
- Between once per month and once every 6 months
- Less than every 6 months

Mean time to restore

A good measure for stability is the mean time to restore (MTTR). This measures how long it takes to restore your product or service if you have an outage. If you measure your uptime, it is basically the time span in which your service is not available. To measure your uptime, you can use a smoke test—for example, in Application Insights (see `https://docs.microsoft.com/en-us/azure/azure-monitor/app/monitor-web-app-availability`). If your application is installed on client machines and not accessible, it's more complicated. Often, you can fall back on the time for a specific ticket type in your helpdesk system.

If you can't measure it at all, you can still fall back to a survey with the following options:

- Less than 1 hour
- Less than 1 day
- Less than 1 week
- Less than 1 month
- Less than 6 months
- More than 6 months

But this should only be the last resort. The MTTR should be a metric you should easily get out of your systems.

Change fail rate

As with DLT for performance, MTTR is the metric for time when it comes to stability. The pendant of DF that focuses on throughput is the change fail rate (CFR). For the question *How many of your deployments cause a failure in production?*, the CFR is specified as a percentage. To decide which of your deployments count toward this metric, you should use the same definition as for the DF.

The Four Keys dashboard

These four metrics based upon the DORA research are a great way to measure where you are on your DevOps journey. They are a good starting point to change your conversations with management. Put them on a dashboard and be proud of them. And don't worry if you're not yet an elite performer—the important thing is to be on the journey and to improve continuously.

It's very simple to start with survey-based values. But if you want to use automatically generated system data you can use the Four Keys Project to display the data in a nice dashboard, (see *Figure 1.4*).

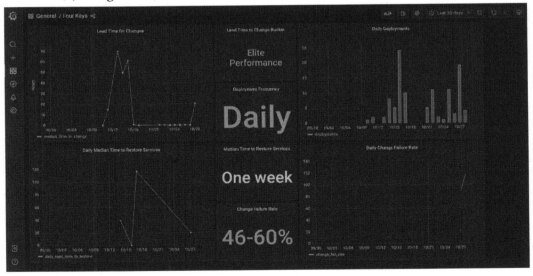

Figure 1.4 – The Four Keys dashboard

The project is open source and based upon Google Cloud (see `https://github.com/GoogleCloudPlatform/fourkeys`), but it depends on webhooks to get the data from your tools. You will learn in *Chapter 7, Running Your Workflows,* how to use webhooks to send your data to the dashboard.

What you shouldn't do

It is important that these metrics are not used to compare teams with each other. You can aggregate them to get an organizational overview, but don't compare individual teams! Every team has different circumstances. It's only important that the metrics evolve in the right direction.

Also, the metrics should not become the goal. It is not desirable to just get better metrics. The focus should always be on the capabilities that lead to these metrics and that we discuss in this book. Focus on these capabilities and the metrics will follow.

The SPACE framework for developer productivity

The DORA metrics are a perfect starting point. They are easy to implement and there is lots of data to compare. If you want to take it one step further and add more metrics, you can use the **SPACE framework for developer productivity** (*Forsgren N., Storey M.A., Maddila C., Zimmermann T., Houck B. & Butler J. (2021)*).

Developer productivity is the key ingredient to achieving a high engineering velocity and a high DVI. Developer productivity is highly correlated to the overall well-being and satisfaction of developers and is, therefore, one of the most important ingredients to thrive in the war of talents and attract good engineers.

But developer productivity is not just about activity. The opposite is often the case: in times of firefighting and meeting deadlines when activity is normally high, productivity decreases through frequent task switching and less creativity. That's why metrics that measure developer productivity should never be used in isolation, and never to penalize or reward developers.

Also, developer productivity is not solely about individual performance. As in team sports, individual performance is important, but only the team as a whole wins. Balancing measures of individual and team performance is crucial.

SPACE is a multidimensional framework that categorizes metrics for developer productivity into the following dimensions:

- **Satisfaction and well-being**
- **Performance**
- **Activity**
- **Communication and collaboration**
- **Efficiency and flow**

All the dimensions work for individuals, teams, and the system as a whole.

Satisfaction and well-being

Satisfaction and well-being are about how happy and fulfilled we are. Physical and mental health also fall into this dimension. Some example metrics are given here:

- Developer satisfaction
- **Net promoter score** (**NPS**) for a team (how likely it is that someone would recommend their team to others)
- Retention
- Satisfaction with the engineering system

Performance

Performance is the outcome of the system or process. The performance of individual developers is hard to measure. But for a team or system level, we could use measures such as LT, DLT, or MTTR. Other examples could be uptime or service health. Other good metrics are customer satisfaction or an NPS for the product (how likely it is that someone would recommend the product to others).

Activity

Activity can provide valuable insights into productivity, but it is hard to measure it correctly. A good measure for individual activity would be focus time: how much time is a developer not spending on meetings and communication? Other examples for metrics are the number of completed work items, issues, PRs, commits, or bugs.

Communication and collaboration

Communication and collaboration are key ingredients to developer productivity. Measuring them is hard, but looking at PRs and issues gives you a good impression of how the communication is going. Metrics in this dimension should focus on PR engagement, the quality of meetings, and knowledge sharing. Also, code reviews across the team level (**cross-team** or **X-team**) are a good measure to see what boundaries there are between teams.

Efficiency and flow

Efficiency and flow measure how many handoffs and delays increase your overall LT. Good metrics are the number of handoffs, blocked work items, and interruptions. For work items, you can measure total time, value-added time, and wait time.

How to use the SPACE framework

> *"One way to see indirectly what is important in an organization is to see what is measured, because that often communicates what is valued and influences the way people behave and react."*
>
> – *Forsgren N., Storey M.A., Maddila C., Zimmermann T., Houck B. & Butler J. (2021) p. 18*

All the dimensions are valid for individuals, teams, groups, and on a system level, (see *Figure 1.5*).

	Satisfaction & Well-being	**P**erformance	**A**ctivity	**C**ommunication & Collaboration	**E**fficiency & Flow
Individual	• Developer Satisfaction • Retention	• Code Review Velocity	• Focus Time • # Commits • # Issues / PBIs • Lines of Code	• Code Review Score (quality) • PR Merge Times	• Knowledge Sharing • X-Team Reviews
Team	• Developer Satisfaction • Retention	• Velocity (shipped) • Delivery Lead Time	• Cycle Time • Velocity (done) • # Issues / PBIs	• Code Review Engagement • PR Merge Times • Meeting Quality	• Code Review Stale Time • Handoffs
System	• Satisfaction with Engineering System	• Velocity • Lead Time • Customer Satisfaction • MTTR	• Deployment Frequency	• Knowledge Sharing • X-Team Reviews	• Lead Time • Velocity

Figure 1.5 – Examples for SPACE metrics

It is important to not only look at the dimension but also at the scope. Some metrics are valid in multiple dimensions.

It is also very important to select carefully which metrics are being measured. Metrics shape behavior and certain metrics can have side effects you did not consider in the first place. The goal is to use only a few metrics but with the maximum positive impact.

You should select at least three metrics from three dimensions. You can mix the metrics for individual, team, and system scope. Be cautious with the individual metrics—they can have the most side effects that are hard to foresee.

To respect the privacy of the developers, the data should be anonymized, and you should only report aggregated results at a team or group level.

Objectives and key results

Many companies that are practicing DevOps are using objectives and key results (OKRs)—among them Google, Microsoft, Twitter, and Uber.

OKR is a flexible framework for companies to define and track objectives and their outcomes.

The OKR method dates back to the 1970s when Andrew Grove, the *father of OKRs*, introduced the method to Intel. The method was called **iMBO,** which stands for **Intel Management by Objectives**. He described the method in his book *High Output Management* (*Grove, A. S. (1983)*).

In 1999, John Doerr introduced OKR to Google. He had worked for Intel when Andrew Grove introduced iMBO there. OKR quickly became a central part of Google's culture. John Doerr published his book *Measure What Matters* (*Doerr, J. (2018)*), which made OKR famous. If you want to learn more about OKR, I highly recommend reading this book.

What are OKRs?

OKR is a framework that helps organizations to achieve a high alignment on strategic goals while keeping a maximum level of autonomy for teams and individuals. Objectives are qualitative goals that give direction and inspire and motivate people. Each objective is associated with unambiguously measurable quantitative metrics—the key results. The key results should focus on outcomes and not on activities, as illustrated in the following table:

Objectives	Key Results
Qualitative	Quantitative
Describe the WHAT and WHY	Describe the HOW
Inspire and motivate people. Guide the way.	The drivers for the success of the objective that can be influenced. Determine if the objective is achieved.
Simple and clear	Unambiguously measurable
Good objectives are: • Significant • Concrete • Action-oriented • Inspirational	Good key results are: • Specific and time-bound • Aggressive yet realistic • Measurable and verifiable

Table 1.2 – Characteristics of OKRs

OKRs should in no way be associated with the performance management system of the company or bonuses for its employees! The goal is not to achieve a 100% success rate for OKRs—this would mean the OKRs are not aggressive enough.

OKRs are written in the following format:

```
We will [objective]
As measured by [set of key results]
```

It is important that OKRs focus on outcomes and not on activities. A good example is an objective that was set by Google's **chief executive officer (CEO)** Sundar Pichai in 2008 when Google launched their Chrome browser. This was the OKR:

```
We will build the best browser
As measured by 20 million users by the end of 2008
```

The goal was bold for a new browser and Google failed to achieve this in 2008, getting fewer than 10 million users. In 2009, the key result was increased to 50 million users, and again, Google failed to achieve this, with about 37 million users. But instead of giving up, the key result was again increased in 2010—this time, to 100 million users! And this time, Google overachieved their goal, with 111 million users!

How do OKRs work?

For OKRs to work, a company needs a good vision and mission that defines the *WHY*: *Why are we working for this company?* The vision is then broken down into **mid-term goals** (called **MOALS**). The MOALS themselves are also OKRs. They are broken down into OKRs for an OKR cycle, typically between 3 to 4 months. In OKR planning and alignment, OKRs are broken down in the organization so that every individual and every team has its own OKRs that contribute to the bigger goal. The OKRs are then continuously monitored, normally on a weekly basis. At the end of the OKR cycle, the OKRs are reviewed, and the achievements (hopefully) celebrated. With the learning from the cycle, the MOALS get updated and a new cycle begins, (see *Figure 1.6*).

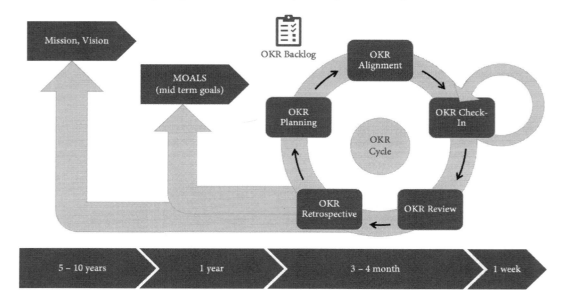

Figure 1.6 – The OKR cycle

OKR in theory is simple, but implementing it is not. Writing good OKRs is especially hard and needs a lot of practice. There are also strong dependencies on the corporate culture and existing metrics and **key performance indicators** (**KPIs**) that are measured.

OKRs and DevOps

Once implemented correctly, OKRs can give you the ability to have a strong alignment between your teams by preserving their autonomy to decide on their own *what* they are building, and not only on *how* they build it, (see *Figure 1.7*). This is important when we talk about experimentation in *Chapter 19, Experimentation and A/B Testing with GitHub*. Your teams can define their own experiments and measure the output. Based on this, they decide which code stays in the projects and which doesn't.

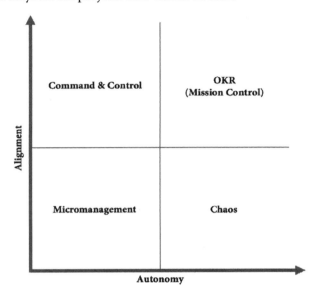

Figure 1.7 – OKRs help to achieve autonomy and alignment

Let's now look at an example.

Your company's vision is to be the market leader in online visual project management tools. Your product has a current market share of 12%. The company MOAL is the following:

```
We will build the best visual project management tool
As measured by a 75% market share by the end of 2025
```

Your product is built by two teams: one team focuses on the core of the product and builds the visuals for project management. They focus on the existing customers and building a product that the customers love. They agree on the following OKR:

```
We will build the visual project management tool that is loved
by our customers
As measured by an NPS of higher than 9
```

The NPS is currently at 7.9, so the team must figure out on their own what they can do to delight the customers. After a few interviews with some customers, they formulate the hypothesis that all the project management tools are based on older project management techniques and are too complicated in a more agile-oriented project world. They decide to conduct an experiment with part of the customers, with a completely new concept on how to visualize the project to confirm or diminish the hypothesis.

The second team is the shared services team. They focus on user management, enterprise integration, and billing. The product needs more new users to achieve the MOAL, not only to make the current ones happy. So, the focus in this OKR cycle is on bringing new customers to the product, as illustrated here:

```
We will build a project management tool that is easy to use for
new customers
As measured by a 20% increased monthly new registered users
```

Currently, newly registered users have flattened, so the intent is to start growing again. The team looks at the numbers and finds that a lot of new customers quit the registration process on the details page, where they must enter their address and banking details. They have the hypothesis that more customers would try the product and hopefully stay on the platform if the registration process were easier. They decide to conduct an experiment and reduce registration to the minimum that is required for authentication. They grant new users a 30-day free trial and request payment details after that period.

I will explain in *Chapter 18, Lean Product Development and Lean Startup*, and *Chapter 19, Experimentation and A/B Testing with GitHub,* how hypothesis-driven development and experimentation work. This is independent of OKR, but both work very well together.

If you are interested in real-world OKRs, GitLab share their OKRs publicly (`https://about.gitlab.com/company/okrs/`). They also share their entire process and how they link OKRs to epics and issues.

OKRs are not a prerequisite for DevOps. But as with agile practices, they are just a natural match. If you are not working in an agile way and start with DevOps, your way of working will become agile anyway, and you can benefit from frameworks such as Scrum to not invent the wheel again. And the same is true for OKRs: they come naturally when you scale DevOps in big organizations and you want to provide teams with great autonomy by maintaining an alignment to global goals.

Summary

In this chapter, I explained how software is taking over the world, its impact on the lifespan of companies, and a need to accelerate software delivery if your company wants to stay in business. This helps you to change your conversation with your management team by making your engineering velocity visible.

Measure metrics that matter for your company and focus on capabilities. Start with the four key metrics from DORA and add more metrics to the mix from different dimensions of the SPACE framework. But remember that metrics shape behavior, so be careful which metrics you choose.

By picking the right metrics, you make your DevOps transformation and acceleration measurable and transparent.

Most of this chapter focuses on efficiency: doing things right. Only OKR also addresses effectiveness: doing the right things. OKR is also relevant for lean product development and is touched on in *Chapter 18, Lean Product Development and Lean Startup*.

In the next chapter, you'll learn how to plan, track, and visualize your work.

Case study

Tailwind Gears is a manufacturing company that produces many different parts that are integrated into other products. They have five different product-centric divisions with a total of more than 600 developers. Each division has its own development process. Some use Scrum, some SAFe, and others use classical waterfall methodologies (**validation model**, or **V-Model**). Two of the five divisions build components that include software used in critical systems and are therefore highly regulated (**International Organization for Standardization (ISO)** *26262* and **generic good practice (GxP)**). The programming languages the software is built with range from embedded C and C++ code on hardware and chips, to mobile apps (Java; Swift) to web applications (JavaScript; .NET).

As with development processes, the tools landscape is very heterogeneous. There are some old **Team Foundation Server** (**TFS**) installations on premises; some teams use Jira, Confluence, and Bitbucket, and some use GitHub and Jenkins. Some teams already have some **continuous integration/continuous deployment** (**CI/CD**) practices in place, while other teams still build, package, and deploy manually. Some teams already work in a DevOps way and operate their own products, while other teams still hand over the production releases to a separate operations team.

Tailwind Gears faces the following problems:

- **No visibility** for top management on how development is doing. Since all teams work differently, there is no common way to measure velocity.

- The divisions report **slow release cycles** (between months and years) and **high failure rates**.

- Every division has its own team to support its toolchain, so there is a lot of **redundancy**. Things such as templates and pipelines are not shared.

- It's difficult to allocate developers and teams to the products with the most business value. Toolchain and development practices are too different and the **onboarding time** is too long.

- Developers feel **unsatisfied** with their work and **not productive**. Some already left the company and it's hard to recruit new talent in the market.

To address these issues, the company decides to implement one common engineering platform. This also intends to unify the development processes. These are the goals of the initiative:

- **Accelerate** software delivery in all divisions.

- **Increase the quality** of the software and reduce failure rates.

- **Save time and money** by raising synergies and only have one platform team that is responsible for the one engineering system.

- **Increase the value** of the software being built by allocating developers and teams to the products with a higher value proposition.

- **Increase developer satisfaction** to retain existing talent and to make it easier to hire new developers.

To make the transformation visible, the company decides to measure the following four key metrics of DORA:

- DLT
- DF
- MTTR
- CFR

Since there is no unified platform yet, the metrics will be collected using surveys. The plan is to move one team after another to the new unified platform and use system metrics there.

Developer satisfaction is an important part of the transformation. Therefore, two more metrics are added, as follows:

- Developer satisfaction
- Satisfaction with the engineering system

This is a mix of six metrics from at least three SPACE dimensions. There is no metric for communication and collaboration yet. This will be added to the system as the transformation evolves.

Further reading

Here are the references from this chapter that you can also use to get more information on the topics:

- *Srivastava S., Trehan K., Wagle D. & Wang J. (April 2020). Developer Velocity: How software excellence fuels business performance:* `https://www.mckinsey.com/industries/technology-media-and-telecommunications/our-insights/developer-velocity-how-software-excellence-fuels-business-performance`

- *Forsgren N., Smith D., Humble J. & Frazelle J. (2019). DORA State of DevOps Report:* `https://www.devops-research.com/research.html#reports`

- *Brown A., Stahnke M. & Kersten N. (2020). 2020 State of DevOps Report:* `https://puppet.com/resources/report/2020-state-of-devops-report/`

- *Forsgren N., Humble, J. & Kim, G. (2018). Accelerate: The Science of Lean Software and DevOps: Building and Scaling High Performing Technology Organizations* (1st ed.) [E-book]. IT Revolution Press.

- To read more on the four key projects, see *Are you an Elite DevOps performer? Find out with the Four Keys Project* (*Dina Graves Portman, 2020*): `https://cloud.google.com/blog/products/devops-sre/using-the-four-keys-to-measure-your-devops-performance`

- *Forsgren N., Storey M.A., Maddila C., Zimmermann T., Houck B. & Butler J. (2021). The SPACE of Developer Productivity:* `https://queue.acm.org/detail.cfm?id=3454124`

- *Grove, A. S. (1983). High Output Management* (1st ed.). Random House Inc.

- *Grove, A. S. (1995). High Output Management* (2nd ed.). Vintage.

- *Doerr, J. (2018). Measure What Matters: OKRs: The Simple Idea that Drives 10x Growth.* Portfolio Penguin

2
Plan, Track, and Visualize Your Work

In the previous chapter, you learned how to measure engineering velocity and performance to make your acceleration visible and change the conversation with management.

In this chapter, we will focus on organizing your work inside your team and applying **Lean principles**. You'll learn how GitHub issues and projects can help you simplify the flow of your work.

In this chapter, we will cover the following topics:

- Work is work
- Unplanned work and rework
- Visualizing your work
- Limiting WIP
- GitHub issues, labels, and milestones
- GitHub projects

Work is work

Work is an activity done in order to achieve a purpose or result. This not only includes the product or project you are working on but also all activities you have to perform for your company. In some teams I work with, there are people that spend up to 50% of their work time on tasks outside their project/product team. Some are team leads and have meetings and responsibilities with their organizational team members. Some are part of the working council. Some have training for personal development paths. Some just have to fix bugs and live-site issues for projects they had worked on in the past.

Many of these tasks cannot be taken away from the team members. The team member may like them or not – but often they are an important part of their personal development.

The problem with this kind of work is that the prioritization and coordination of these tasks are done by the individuals and outside their team context. Who decides whether working on a bug of a previous system the developer worked on should be prioritized over a bug in the current project? Normally, the individuals plan and prioritize the work on their own. This often leads to more planning upfront. When team members report their available times at the beginning of a sprint, the team starts to plan their current tasks *around* these events. This can prevent the entire team from establishing **pull** and forces them to plan the dependent tasks and assign them to individual team members (**push**).

To address this, you should make all work visible to the team and add it to the team backlog. Are you in a working council? Add it to the backlog. Do you have training? Add it to the backlog.

So, the first step is to figure out *what kind of work is performed by your team* and gather everything in **one backlog**.

The second step is to **simplify**. Everyone can make things more complicated – but it takes a touch of genius to make things simpler. That's why in most companies, processes and forms get more complicated over the years. I've seen forms with 300 fields on them and complicated routing rules based on these fields – just to handle live-site incidents. Don't transfer this to your backlog. Independent of the process in the background – the work has a clear trigger for your team, is processed by your team, and then leaves your responsibility – so from your perspective it is done. One process or ticket could lead to multiple small work items in your backlog. Every work item should be simplified to **To Do**, **Doing**, and **Done**.

> **Note**
>
> In *Chapter 18, Lean Product Development and Lean Startup*, we'll focus more on value streams, the theory of constraints, and how to optimize the flow of work. In this chapter, we'll focus on the team level and how you get started to optimize later across team boundaries.

Unplanned work and rework

All developers know that frequent **context switching** leads to less productivity. If we are disturbed while coding, it takes us some time to get back into the code and continue with the same productivity we had when the disturbance occurred. So, working on multiple projects or tasks also reduces productivity. In his book *Quality Software Management: Systems Thinking*, Gerald M. Weinberg presents the result of a study that concludes that when only working on two projects simultaneously, the performance drops by about 20% (Weinberg G.M. 1991). For each project you add, the performance drops 20% further (see *Figure 2.1*):

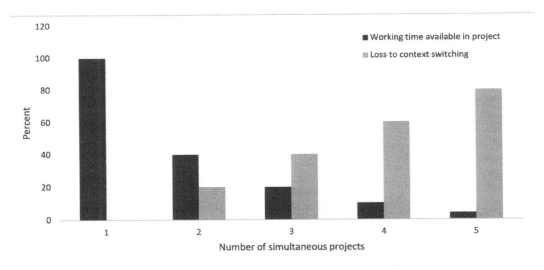

Figure 2.1 – Loss of productivity when context switching

Another study from 2017 shows that developers who work on two or three projects spend on average 17% of their effort on context switching (Tregubov A., Rodchenko N., Boehm B., & Lane J.A., 2017). I think the actual percentage may vary a lot from product to product and from team to team. Developers who work in small batch sizes can switch context easier than others that work in bigger batch sizes. The more complex the matter is, the more effort it requires to pick up work where you left it. Practices such as **Test-Driven Development (TDD)** help you to pick up work easier after context switching.

But independent of the actual percentage: context switching kills productivity and the more focus time developers spend on one task, the more efficient they are. This means you should reduce the **Work in Progress (WIP)** for the team – especially unplanned work and rework.

To help you optimize later, you should label your work items correctly from the beginning. Unplanned work can originate from within your project or outside. Rework can occur if there is a bug, technical debt, or a misunderstood requirement. Make sure you can analyze your work later by applying the correct labels from the beginning. This should not be a complicated governance framework – just pick some labels that will help you later to optimize your work. *Table 2.1* is just an example of how you could classify your work items:

Types of work	Planning	Origin	Priority
Requirement	Planned	Business	Low
Bug	Unplanned	IT	Medium
Documentation	Recovery	Users	High
Infrastructure			Critical
Architecture			
Test			

Table 2.1 – Example taxonomy for your work items

Keep it simple and select a taxonomy with simple wording that is clear to your team.

Visualizing your work

To focus on the important work and reduce multitasking and task switching, you should visualize your work – typically in the form of a **Kanban** board. Kanban has its roots in **Lean manufacturing** but is now considered an important part of **Lean software development**. Kanban can help you improve the efficiency of the flow of work through your system.

The visualization will help you to do the following:

- Identify bottlenecks, wait times, and hand-offs.
- Prioritize work and work on the most important tasks first.
- Break down work into small batch sizes.
- Get things done.

Establish pull

No plan is perfect. If you have ever planned a project, you know the project plan only works with a lot of buffer time – and yet you must always adjust the plan. So, even if you only plan your work for the upcoming 2 or 3 weeks, planning will lead to wait time and context switching. The solution is to stop planning and establish a pull system; team members pull the work with the highest priority from the queue and work on it. Ideally, the task is finished and moved to Done (see *Figure 2.2*):

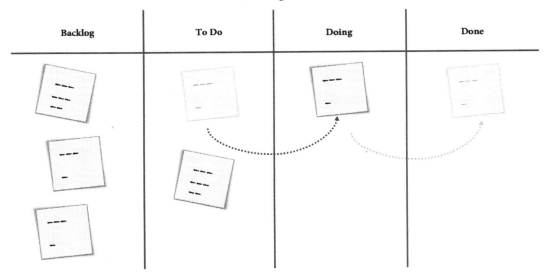

Figure 2.2 – Pulling work from the backlog to indicate a status change

If your task cannot be finished with just you working on it, this might be an indicator that the task is too big and needs to be split into smaller tasks. If you must work on many tasks simultaneously to get anything done, the tasks might be too small. This will adjust over time as the visual representation helps you to spot bottlenecks and wait time.

Prioritize

The benefit of working with visual boards is that it is easy to prioritize your work. Just move work items with the highest priority to the top. If you have different kinds of work on the board, you might want an additional visual separation. This can be done with **swimlanes**. A swimlane is a horizontal grouping of work on the Kanban board (see *Figure 2.3*):

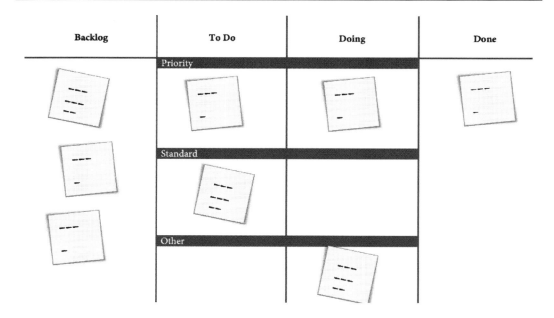

Figure 2.3 – Using swimlanes to organize your work on the board

If your team has to work on live site issues, you might want a priority swimlane that signals to all team members that a current issue has priority over normal work. Or if your team members have responsibilities outside the team, you also want to separate this from your normal work.

Many Kanban boards also allow you to set a different color for each card – normally by applying a label or tag to the card. This can also help you to visually distinguish different kinds of work on the board. Especially when combined with swimlanes, colored cards can help you to see at a first glance how the team is doing and what the most important tasks are that need attention.

Keep it simple!

Start small with three columns (To Do, Doing, and Done) and add more columns and swimlanes if needed to optimize the flow for your team. But be careful to keep it simple! Ask yourself before every customization: is this necessary? Does this bring value? Is there a simpler way?

Complicated things have the tendency to stick – when moving to Kanban boards, I've seen teams grow their board to a monster with 10 columns, 8 swimlanes (most of them collapsed all the time), and many fields and information on the cards.

Kanban is about simplification – try to keep it as simple as possible!

Limiting WIP

One of the goals of Kanban is to limit WIP. With less WIP, you have less context switching and more focus. This helps you to get things done! Stop starting and start finishing!

Even when coaching Scrum teams, I've seen teams that start to work on all the user stories they had planned during the first days of the sprint. Every time a developer was blocked, they just started to work on another story. At the end of the sprint, all stories had been worked on, but none was finished.

In Kanban, you work on a small number of items – and in a constant pace.

Set WIP limits

Most Kanban boards support WIP limits. A WIP limit is an indicator of the maximum number of items you want to have in one column at the same time. Let's say the WIP limit for Doing is five, and you have three items you are working on. The column would display 3/5 – normally in green as the limit is not yet reached. If you start to work on three more items, it will display 6/5 in red as the limit has been reached.

WIP limits can help you to focus on a small number of items and not start too much work. Start with small ones and only increase if absolutely necessary. A good default to start with is five.

Reduce batch size

Limiting your WIP will give you a good indication of whether your work items are the right size. If it's hard to stay within the WIP limit, your work items are probably still too big. Try to split them into smaller tasks before increasing the limit.

Reduce hand-offs

The same is true for hand-offs. If your work items need input from many team members – or worse, input from outside the team – it generates wait times and reduces your **flow efficiency**. Flow efficiency is the time you work on a work item divided by the total time you need to get it done – including the wait time:

$$f = \frac{work}{work + wait\ time}$$

Flow efficiency is a very theoretical metric in software engineering as you normally don't measure exact work and wait times. But if you experience many hand-offs and blocked items, the metric might help to see how your work is flowing through the system. You can start the timer for work if you move your item to Doing and start the timer for wait time if you move it back.

GitHub issues, labels, and milestones

GitHub issues let you keep track of tasks, enhancements, and bugs. They are highly cooperative and have a timeline that shows their history. Issues can be linked to commits, pull requests, and other issues. GitHub issues are part of the experience that developers love on GitHub. That's why they are a good solution to manage your work for your engineering teams.

Creating a new issue

You can create a new issue in your repository under **Issues | New Issue**. The issue has a title and a body that supports Markdown (see *Figure 2.4*):

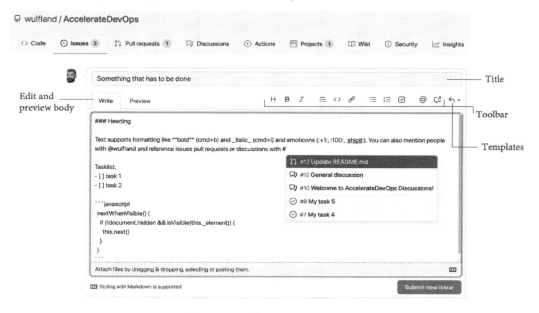

Figure 2.4 – Creating a new issue

A toolbar helps you format the text. Besides normal formatting – such as headings, bold and italic text, lists, links, and images – it has some features that are worth highlighting:

- **Emoticons**: You can add all sorts of emoticons in Markdown. Some of my favorites are `:+1:` (👍) and `:100:` (💯) and the `:shipit:` squirrel, which is typical for GitHub. You can find a complete list here: `https://gist.github.com/rxaviers/7360908#file-gistfile1-md`.

- **Mentions**: You can mention individual members by their GitHub handle or mention entire teams. Just press @ and start typing. Pick the person or team from the list. They'll get notified and the mention is displayed as a link to the profile of the person or team that was mentioned.

- **References**: Reference other issues, pull requests, or discussions by pressing the # key and selecting the item from the list.

- **Task list**: A task list is a list of subtasks that is later used to show the progress of the issues. Tasks in the list can be converted into issues and therefore be used to created nested hierarchies of work items. An incomplete task is prefixed with `- [ ]`. If it is completed, you add x in the center: `- [x]`.

- **Source code**: You can add source code with syntax highlighting to your Markdown. Just use ``` ``` ``` to open and close the code block. The syntax highlighting is done by linguist (`https://github.com/github/linguist`) and most languages are supported.

Markdown

Markdown is a very popular, lightweight markup language. Unlike JSON or HTML, it formats text on a single-line basis and does not have opening and closing tags or brackets. That's why it is very good for versioning with Git and collaborating on changes with pull requests. That's the same reason why YAML is the de facto standard for machine-readable files. Markdown is the equivalent of human-readable files. In DevOps teams, everything is code: diagrams, architecture, design and concept documents, config files, and infrastructure. This means YAML, Markdown, or a mix of both is used.

If you have not learned Markdown yet, it's time to start now. Many teams use Markdown extensively with pull requests to collaborate on human-readable content. Since most work management solutions also support Markdown, it's basically everywhere.

Markdown has a very simple syntax and is easy to learn. After a few uses, it should not be a burden to use it.

You can switch to preview at any time to see the output of your Markdown (see *Figure 2.5*):

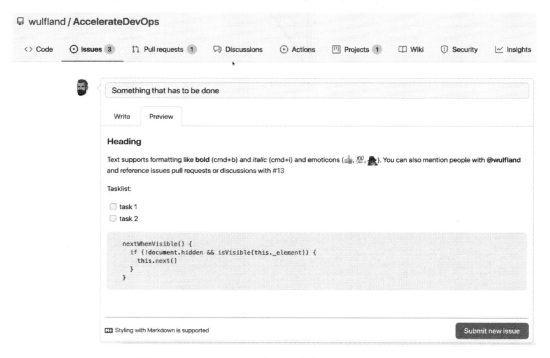

Figure 2.5 – Previewing the Markdown in a new issue

A good introduction to Markdown on GitHub can be found here: `https://guides.github.com/features/mastering-markdown/`.

> **Tip:**
> You can also save replies if you often use similar text blocks. Hit *Ctrl +.* (Windows/Linux) or *Cmd +.* (Mac) and select the reply from the list or create a new saved reply. To learn more, see `https://docs.github.com/en/github/writing-on-github/working-with-saved-replies`.

Collaborating on issues

Once the issue is created, you can add comments at any time. You can assign up to 10 people to the issue and apply labels to it to categorize it. All changes are displayed as events in the history of the issue (see *Figure 2.6*):

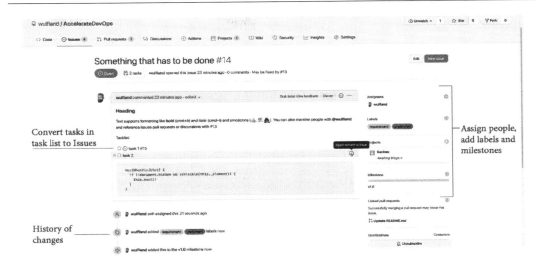

Figure 2.6 – Editing issues

If your issue contains a task list, it is used to display the progress of the issue. You can convert every task into an issue itself that then gets linked to the current issue. If you click the **Open convert to issue** button (note the mouseover visible in *Figure 2.6*), the task gets converted into a new issue and is displayed as a link. If you click the link and open the issue, you can see that the issue is tracked in another issue (see *Figure 2.7*):

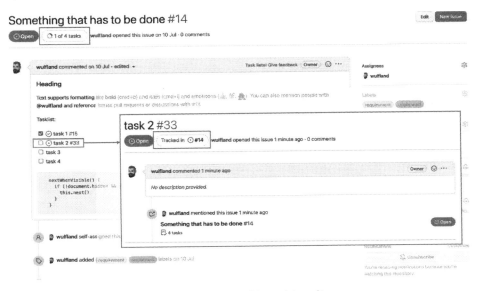

Figure 2.7 – Creating hierarchies of issues

This way, you can create flexible hierarchies of work and split your work into smaller tasks.

The issue backlog

The issues overview is not a real backlog as it cannot be sorted easily by drag and drop. But it has a very advanced syntax for filtering and sorting. Every filter you apply gets added as text to the search field (see *Figure 2.8*):

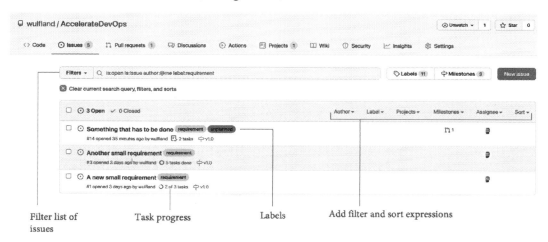

Figure 2.8 – Filtering and sorting the list of issues

In the overview, you see the progress of the tasks and the labels. You also can see pull requests that are linked to the issues.

Milestones

Milestones are a way to group your issues. An issue can only be assigned to exactly one milestone. Milestones measure their progress by the number of closed issues relative to the total issue count. Milestones have a title, an optional due date, and an optional description (see *Figure 2.9*):

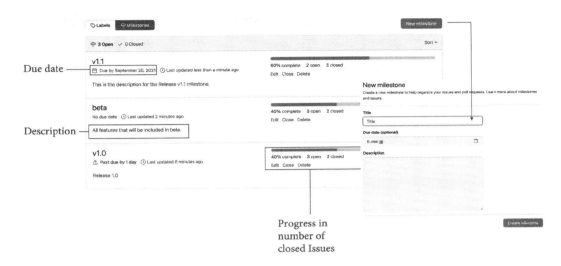

Figure 2.9 – Planning your issues with milestones

Milestones are a good way to group issues to release versions with a specific target date. They can also be used to group issues that do not belong to a release version together.

Pinning issues

You can pin up to three issues to your repository. These issues are displayed at the top of the issues overview (see *Figure 2.10*):

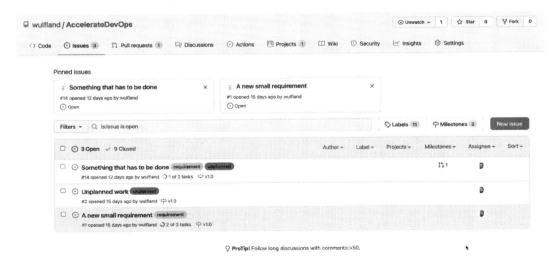

Figure 2.10 – Pinned issues

Pinned issues are a good way to communicate important things to other contributors or new team members.

Issue templates

You can configure different templates for issues that give predefined content. If a user creates a new issue, they can pick the template from a list (see *Figure 2.11*):

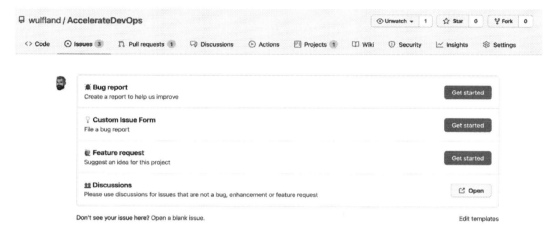

Figure 2.11 – Issue templates

You can activate **issue templates** in your repository under **Settings | Options | Issues | Set up templates**. You can select a basic template for bugs, features, or a custom template. The templates are files that are stored in your repository under `.github/ISSUE_TEMPLATE`. Click **Propose changes** and commit the files to your repository. Once the template files are in your repository, you can edit or delete them directly there. Or you can also add new template files. There is no need to do this (adding new template files) from the settings.

Templates can be a Markdown (`.md`) or a YAML file (`.yml`). Markdown contains a header that specifies the name and a description. It also can set defaults for the title, labels, and assignees. Here is an example of a Markdown template:

```
---
name: 🐛 Bug report
about: Create a report to help us improve
title: '[Bug]:'
labels: [bug, unplanned]
```

```
assignees:
  - wulfland
---


**Describe the bug**
A clear and concise description of what the bug is.


**To Reproduce**
...
```

If you click on **Issues | New Issue**, you can select the template and click **Get started**. A new issue will be filled with the template values. The result looks as in *Figure 2.12*:

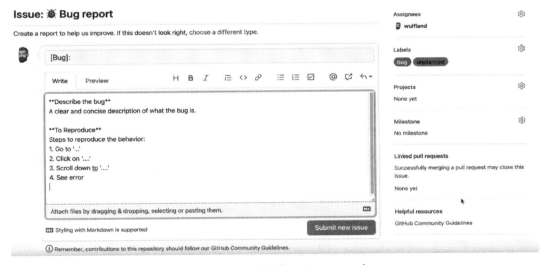

Figure 2.12 – A Markdown issue template

With YAML templates, you can define complete forms with text boxes, dropdowns, and checkboxes. You can configure the controls and mark fields as required. A sample form could be defined like this:

```
name: 💡 Custom Issue Form
description: A custom form with different fields
body:
  - type: input
    id: contact
    attributes:
```

```
      label: Contact Details
      description: How can we get in touch with you if we need
more info?
      placeholder: ex. email@example.com
    validations:
      required: false
  - type: textarea
    id: what-happened
    attributes:
      label: What happened?
      description: Also tell us, what did you expect to happen?
      placeholder: Tell us what you see!
      value: "Tell us what you think"
    validations:
      required: true
  - type: dropdown
    id: version
    attributes:
      label: Version
      description: What version of our software are you
running?
      options:
        - 1.0.2 (Default)
        - 1.0.3 (Edge)
    validations:
      required: true
  - type: dropdown
    id: browsers
    attributes:
      label: What browsers are you seeing the problem on?
      multiple: true
      options:
        - Firefox
        - Chrome
        - Safari
        - Microsoft Edge
```

```
- type: checkboxes
  id: terms
  attributes:
    label: Code of Conduct
    description: By submitting this issue, you agree to
follow our [Code of Conduct](https://example.com)
    options:
      - label: I agree to follow this project's Code of
Conduct
        required: true
```

The result looks as in *Figure 2.13*:

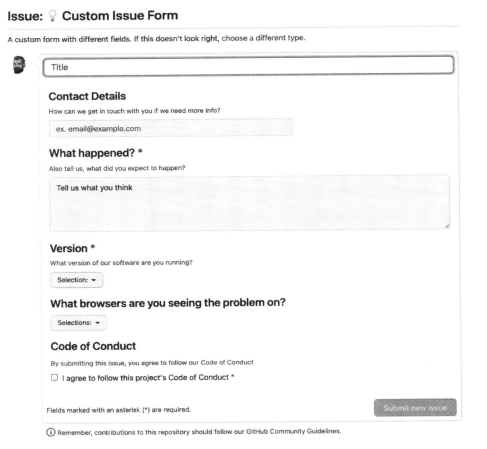

Figure 2.13 – A YAML issue template

You can find more information on **YAML issue templates** here: `https://docs.github.com/en/communities/using-templates-to-encourage-useful-issues-and-pull-requests/syntax-for-issue-forms`.

You can customize the dialog to choose the issue template by adding a `config.yml` file to `.github/ISSUE_TEMPLATE`. You can choose to set whether blank issues should be supported and add additional lines:

```
blank_issues_enabled: true
contact_links:
  - name: 👥 Discussions
    url: https://github.com/wulfland/AccelerateDevOps/discussions/new
    about: Please use discussions for issues that are not a bug, enhancement or feature request
```

The result looks as in *Figure 2.11* – the additional link is displayed as an **Open** button.

> **Note**
> At the time of writing this book, YAML issue templates are still in beta and therefore subject to change.

GitHub Projects

GitHub issues are a great way to collaborate – but with the repository scope and the lack of a drag-and-drop backlog and a visual Kanban board, they are not the perfect place to visualize and track your work.

The central hub in GitHub to manage your work across different repositories is **GitHub Projects**. It is built on top of GitHub issues and supports issues from up to 50 repositories.

GitHub projects is a flexible collaboration platform. You can customize the backlog and boards and share them with other teams or the community.

> **Note: The New GitHub Issues or GitHub Projects (Beta)**
>
> At the time of writing, Git Projects is being completely reworked. The new part is currently called **GitHub Projects (beta)** or the **New GitHub Issues** and will replace GitHub Projects when it is ready. It is not yet 100% clear what the final name will be. Since the new experience is the future, I'll only focus on that one in this book.
>
> Right now, the new experience is not as mature as Jira or Azure Boards. But there is a great team working on it, and I'm convinced it will be one of the best solutions on the market if it is ready!
>
> Note that there are so many new features coming out every month that all screenshots will probably be outdated in no time. Keep an eye on the *changelog* (https://github.blog/changelog/) to stay up to date on all the things that are released multiple times a month.

Get started

GitHub projects can contain issues and pull requests from multiple repos. Therefore, they have to be created at an organization level or in your profile for your personal repos.

To create a new project, navigate to **Projects** on the main page of your organization or on your GitHub profile and click **New Project** (see *Figure 2.14*):

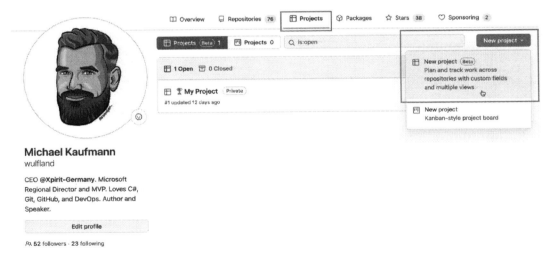

Figure 2.14 – Creating a new project in your profile or organization

Adding work items to projects

The default view in projects is the table view. It is optimized for entering data. Press *Ctrl + space* or click in the last row of the table. You can enter the name of a new work item directly and later convert the item into an issue. Or you can type # and select a repository. You can then select available issues and pull requests (see *Figure 2.15*):

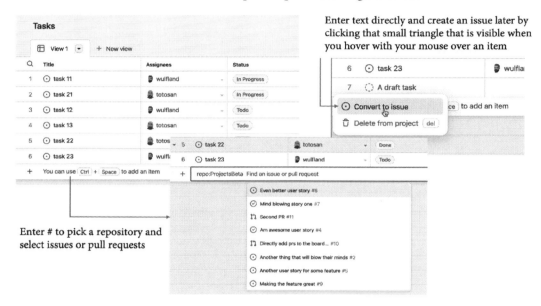

Figure 2.15 – Adding issues, pull requests, or draft work items to the backlog

Adding metadata to your work

You can easily add different metadata fields to your project. Right now, these types are supported:

- **Date fields**: The value must be a valid date.

- **Number fields**: The value must be a number.

- **Single select**: The value must be selected from a list of values.

- **Text field**: The value can be any text.

- **Iteration**: The value must be selected from a set of date ranges. Date ranges in the past are automatically marked as completed. A date range including the current date is marked as current.

To add a new field, press *Cmd + K* (Mac) or *Ctrl + K* (Windows/Linux) to open the command palette and start typing `Create new field`. You can also click the plus sign in the top-right corner and select + **New field**. Enter a name for the field and select the field type.

Working with table views

The default view for the project is the highly flexible **table view**, which you can use to enter data and prioritize it by using drag and drop to order the rows. You can sort, filter, and group the data in your rows by opening the menu in the header of the columns or by opening the command palette (*Cmd + K* or *Ctrl + K*) and selecting one of the commands. If you group the table view, you can directly add items to a group or change the value of an item by dragging it to another group (see *Figure 2.16*):

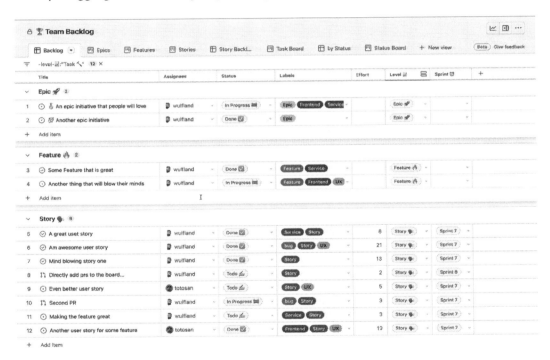

Figure 2.16 – The table view supports grouping, filtering, and sorting

Working with the board view

You can switch your view to a **board view** that displays your work as a configurable Kanban board. The board can display one column for each value in any field! You can set this using the **column field** property of the view. You can drag an item to another column to change the status. You cannot group boards yet or have swimlanes, but you can filter the board to have individual boards for different kinds of work items (see *Figure 2.17*):

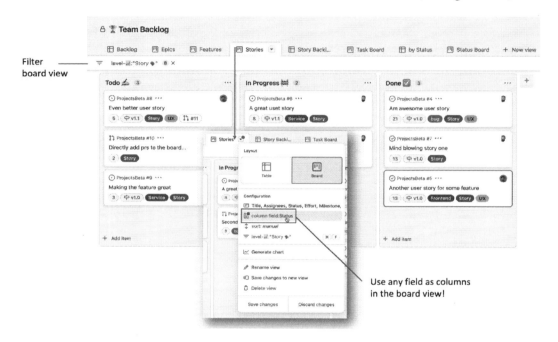

Figure 2.17 – The board view

You can add a new column by clicking the plus sign to the right of the board for any field you choose as the column field. This gives you a very flexible way to visualize your work (see *Figure 2.18*):

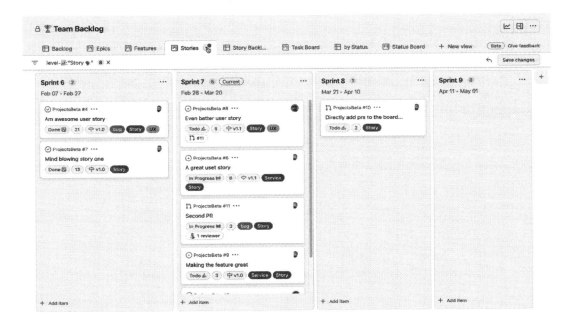

Figure 2.18 – Choose any field as the column field for your boards

The board view is optimized to visualize your work, optimize the flow, and limit WIP.

Working with views

Every time you sort, filter, or group the data in a view, or switch between table and board view, a blue icon in the tab header indicates that the view has unsaved changes. You can see the changes in the menu and save or discard them. You can also save them as a new view (see *Figure 2.19*):

Figure 2.19 – Working with view modifications

It is simple to create new customized views, rename them, and arrange them using drag and drop.

Workflows

You can use **workflows** to define what happens when issues or pull requests transition to another status. Currently, you can only enable or disable default workflows – but in the future, you will be able to write your own workflows (see *Figure 2.20*):

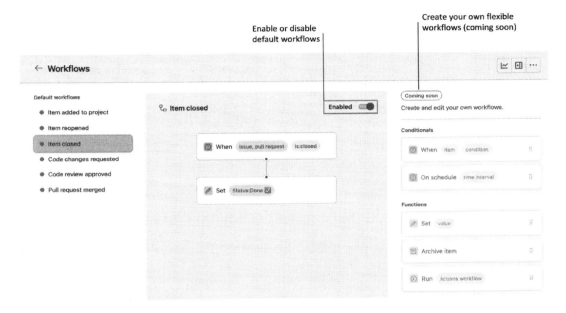

Figure 2.20 – Workflows define what happens when items change

Insights

You can gain **insights** into your progress using the very flexible charts that report on real-time data. You can access insights through the menu in the top-right corner or create a chart from a view. You can use a predefined time frame for the chart or select a custom range. You can filter the chart using macros such as @current or @next for an iteration field or @me for the assignee field. You can disable states in the chart by clicking on them and you can hover with the mouse over dates to see details (see *Figure 2.21*):

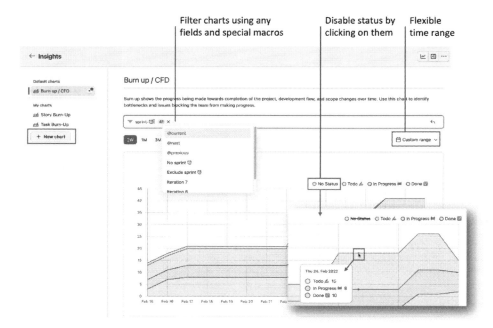

Figure 2.21 – Getting insights with flexible charts on real-time data

At the time of writing, insights only support one type of chart – the burn-up chart – and only by a number of items and statuses. But this will change soon, and you will be able to create a variety of flexible charts that you can change to all kinds of columns.

Managing access

Since projects can be shared across multiple repositories, you can configure the visibility and access permissions in the settings. Projects can have a visibility of public or private. This allows you to create roadmaps that you can share with the public. In organizations, you can set the base permissions for organization members to **No Access**, **Read**, **Write**, or **Admin**. This is not possible in personal projects. But you can invite explicit collaborators and grant them **Read**, **Write**, or **Admin** permissions.

For better discoverability, you can add projects to repositories (see *Figure 2.22*):

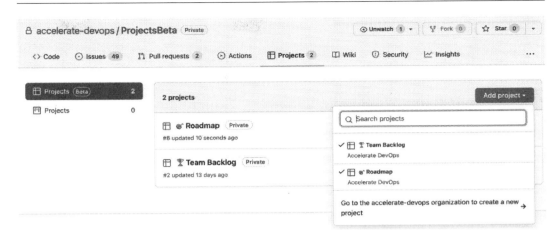

Figure 2.22 – Adding projects to repositories

GitHub projects are a very flexible solution to manage your work and adjust it to your needs. To learn more about GitHub projects, see `https://docs.github.com/en/issues/trying-out-the-new-projects-experience/about-projects`.

Projects are still in beta. But the features that have come out are impressive and in the near future, this will be the most flexible solution that allows the easy sharing of your configuration with the community. Follow the updates in the changelog at `https://github.blog/changelog/label/issues/`.

Third-party integration

If you are already comfortable with a mature solution such as **Jira** or **Azure Boards,** you can also keep using this solution. GitHub has great integration for nearly all available products. I will show you here how to integrate with Jira and Azure Boards – but there are many more solutions in the GitHub marketplace.

> **Is It Simple?**
>
> Jira and Azure Boards are great products that can be highly customized. If you want to stick with your current tool, make sure that everything applies that I described in this chapter. Is it simple? Can you put all your work into it? Do you pull work from a queue? Do you have WIP limits in place? How is the flow efficiency?
>
> You might want to consider adjusting your process and item templates to a leaner way of working. Moving to a new platform is always a good opportunity to reduce ballast. If you integrate, make sure you don't inherit debts that slow you down.

Jira

GitHub and Jira both have an application in their marketplace to connect both applications. If you create a new Jira project, you can directly add GitHub in the process (see *Figure 2.23*). You can also add it later under **Apps | Find new Apps** in Jira.

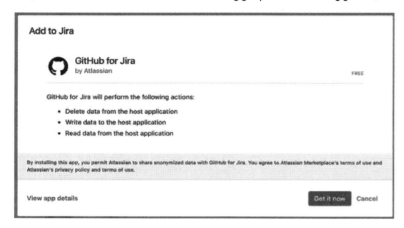

Figure 2.23 – Adding GitHub for Jira to your Jira project

The installation is straightforward and is explained here: `https://github.com/marketplace/jira-software-github`.

You install both apps and connect to the GitHub organization in Jira. In GitHub, you can specify to select all repositories in your organization or just specific ones. If your organization has many repos, the sync can take some time!

You can check your configuration and sync status in Jira under **Apps | Manage your apps | GitHub | Get started** (see *Figure 2.24*):

Figure 2.24 – GitHub configuration and sync status in Jira

Once the synchronization is active, you link issues, pull requests, and commits to Jira issues by mentioning the ID of the Jira issue. The ID always consists of the project key and an integer representing the item (for example, `GI-666`).

If you specify a Jira issue `[GI-1]` and `[GI-2]` in a GitHub issue, the text is automatically linked to the corresponding Jira issue (see *Figure 2.25*):

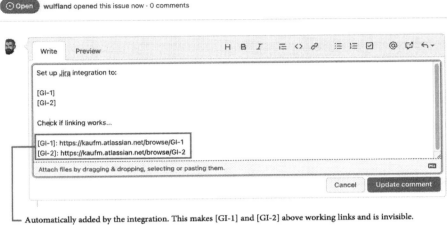

Figure 2.25 – Linking GitHub issues to Jira issues

If you mention Jira issues in your commit messages, they are automatically linked to your Jira issues under **Development** (see *Figure 2.26*). You can also drill into the commits and see the files with the number of changes that are part of the commit.

Figure 2.26 – Linking GitHub artifacts in Jira

You can also use **smart commits** to perform actions with the Jira issues from within your commit message. Smart commits have the following syntax:

```
<ignored text> <ISSUE_KEY> <ignored text> #<COMMAND> <optional
COMMAND_ARGUMENTS>
```

Currently, there are three commands supported:

- `comment`: Add a comment to the Jira issue.
- `time`: Add the time to the Jira issue you worked on it.
- `transition`: Change the state of the Jira issue.

Here are a few examples of how smart commits work:

- The following commit message adds the comment `corrected indent issue` to issue `GI-34`:

  ```
  GI-34 #comment corrected indent issue
  ```

- This commit message adds time to `GI.34`:

  ```
  GI-34 #time 1w 2d 4h 30m Total work logged
  ```

- This commit message adds a comment to `GI-66` and closes the issue:

  ```
  GI-66 #close #comment Fixed this today
  ```

For more information on smart commits, see `https://support.atlassian.com/jira-software-cloud/docs/process-issues-with-smart-commits`.

> **Caution!**
>
> Smart commits only work if your email address used in the commit message has sufficient rights in Jira!

Jira and GitHub have a tight integration. If your teams are already comfortable with Jira, it's best to stay with it and use the integration into GitHub.

Azure Boards

Azure Boards also has very tight integration with GitHub. It's very easy to set it up. You just have to install the Azure Boards app from the GitHub marketplace (see `https://github.com/marketplace/azure-boards`) and follow the instructions.

You can link GitHub commits and GitHub pull requests directly from the Azure Boards issue (or any other work item type you have) in the **Development** section of the work item. Or, you can reference the work item with the following syntax: AB#<id of Azure Board Issue> (for example, AB#26).

The GitHub links get displayed on the cards with the GitHub icon (see *Figure 2.27*):

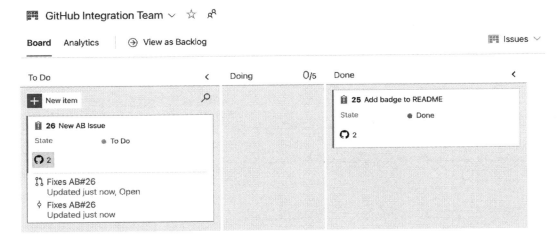

Figure 2.27 – Linking GitHub artifacts in Azure Boards

If you add one of the fix, fixes, or fixed keywords before the AB reference, the Azure Boards issue will automatically transition to the Done state. See the following example:

- The following commit message will link to issue 666 and transition the issue to done if the commit is merged:

```
Fixes AB#666
Update documentation and fixed AB#666
```

- The following commit message will link issues 42 and 666 but only transition 666 to done:

```
Implemented AB#42 and fixed AB#666
```

- The keyword only works with one reference. The following commit message will link all three issues – but only 666 will be moved to done:

```
Fixes AB#666 AB#42 AB#123
```

- If the keyword is not directly before the reference, no issue will be transitioned!

```
Fixed multiple bugs: AB#666 AB#42 AB#123
```

You can add a badge to the README file in GitHub that shows the number of Azure Boards issues. You can get the badge URL from the settings of your Azure Boards (the small gear icon on the right above the board) in the **Status badge** section. You can only show the number of icons that are in progress or the number of all items (see *Figure 2.28*):

Figure 2.28 – Adding a badge to your GitHub README file

The Azure Boards integration is simple to set up and feels very natural. If your teams are already comfortable with Azure Boards, it's a good option to stay in Azure Boards and use the tight integration with GitHub.

Case study

To start with their DevOps transformation, **Tailwind Gears** has selected two teams that will be moved to GitHub as the new DevOps platform.

The strategic decision is to move everything to GitHub and use **GitHub projects** and **GitHub issues** to manage the work. This also enables the end-to-end traceability that is needed for some teams that work in a regulated environment. Also, the development processes should be aligned during the move to the new platform.

One of the pilot teams has already worked with **Scrum** for over a year. They use **Jira** to manage their backlog and work in 3-week sprints. A closer look at the sprints shows that in every sprint, there are a lot of issues that could not be closed. Also, most of the issues are worked on simultaneously from the beginning of the sprint. When asked, the team reports that they plan all the work at the beginning of the sprint. But some of the work is blocked due to dependencies on the company ERP system. When blocked, the developers start to work on another task. In addition, some of the developers still have duties for some of their old projects. They receive tickets from the ticketing system of the help desk and must provide third-level support. These tickets are hard to plan and lead to a wait time for other developers in the team that depend on work from these developers.

To start on the new platform, we import all open requirements from Jira and label them as `requirement`, `planned`, and `business`. If a ticket comes in, we agree to manually add a new issue and label it as `bug`, `unplanned`, and `IT`. We create a separate **swimlane** to track these issues as they are normally live-side issues with a high priority. To automate the integration, we create our first team issue and label it as `infrastructure`, `planned`, and `team` and move it high on the backlog.

To reduce planning and wait times and establish a more pull-based flow of work, we agree to not plan the entire sprint, but to focus on the top three requirements in the backlog. The team breaks down the work for these three items and we establish a **WIP limit** of 5 for tasks that are ongoing.

The second team still works in classical waterfall; their requirements are in IBM Rational DOORS and they are used to working based on the specification documents. To move to a more agile way, the team gets some new team members:

- An **Agile Coach** that acts as a **Scrum Master**
- A **Requirements Engineer** that acts as the **Product Owner**
- An **architect** from the architecture team that is responsible for updating the software architecture before development starts
- A **quality engineer** that is responsible for testing the application before it is released

To start work, we export the requirements from DOORS and import them into GitHub projects. We keep the DOORS ID to be able to track back our backlog to the original requirements.

When breaking down the work for the first requirement, we find that the work is too much for the sprint. The product owner splits the requirement into multiple small items to reduce the **batch size**. The breakdown for the most important two items shows that the items can each be done in about 1 week. There will still be some wait time for the architect and the quality engineer – but the team is confident that they have tasks that these two can help get done. For the team, it is still faster than the wait time if the work is handed over to another team.

Summary

Context switching and unplanned work kill productivity. In this chapter, you learned how to increase your productivity by moving to a lean way of working. You achieve this by establishing pull instead of push on a Kanban board, limiting your WIP and focusing on getting things done, and reducing your batch size and hand-offs.

You learned how to use GitHub issues and GitHub projects to achieve this and how you can integrate Jira and Azure Boards if you prefer to stay in your existing work management system.

In the next chapter, we will have a closer look at teamwork and collaborative development.

Further readings and references

- Tregubov A., Rodchenko N., Boehm B., & Lane J.A. (2017). *Impact of Task Switching and Work Interruptions on Software Development Processes*: https://www.researchgate.net/publication/317989659_Impact_of_task_switching_and_work_interruptions_on_software_development_processes

- Weinberg G.M. (1991), *Quality Software Management: Systems Thinking* (1st ed.). Dorset House

- GitHub issues: https://guides.github.com/features/issues/ and https://docs.github.com/en/issues/tracking-your-work-with-issues/about-issues

- Markdown: https://guides.github.com/features/mastering-markdown/

- Issue templates: `https://docs.github.com/en/communities/using-templates-to-encourage-useful-issues-and-pull-requests/about-issue-and-pull-request-templates`
- GitHub projects: `https://docs.github.com/en/issues/trying-out-the-new-projects-experience/about-projects`
- GitHub Jira integration: `https://github.com/atlassian/github-for-jira`
- GitHub Azure Boards integration: `https://docs.microsoft.com/en-us/azure/devops/boards/github`

3

Teamwork and Collaborative Development

A high-performing team is more than the sum of its members, and it takes a high-performing team to build products that people love.

In this chapter, you'll learn how to set up your team for high collaborative development using pull requests. You'll learn what a pull request is and which features can help you to get a good code review workflow for your team.

In this chapter, we will cover the following core topics:

- Software development is a team sport
- The heart of collaboration: the pull request
- Hands-on: Creating a pull request
- Proposing changes
- Pull request reviews
- Hands-on: Making suggestions
- Best practices for code reviews

Software development is a team sport

The designer and engineer Peter Skillman created an experiment: he challenged teams of four persons to compete against each other in the marshmallow challenge. The rules are simple—build the highest possible structure that can support a marshmallow using the following material:

- 20 pieces of uncooked spaghetti
- 1 yard of transparent tape
- 1 yard of string
- 1 marshmallow

The experiment was not about the problem itself—it was about how the teams would work together to solve the problem. In the experiment, teams of business students from Stanford and the University of Tokyo competed against kindergartners. And guess who was the winner?

The business students examined the materials, discussed the best strategy, and carefully picked the most promising ideas. They acted professionally and in a rational and intelligent way, and yet the kindergartners always won. They did not decide on the best strategy—they just got to work and started experimenting. They stood close together and communicated in short bursts: *Here, no, here!*

The kindergartners did not win because they were more intelligent or skilled. They won because they worked better together as a team (*Coyle D.(2018)*).

And you can observe the same in sports: you can put the best players in one team, and yet if they don't form a good team, they will lose to a team with less skilled individuals who work perfectly together.

In software engineering, we want teams with high cohesion, not just individual experts that work together but team members that experiment together like the kindergartners in the marshmallow experiment. We do this by looking for so-called **E-shaped** team members as the evolution of **T-shaped** team members. **I-shaped** specialists have deep experience in one area but very little skills or experience in other areas. T-shaped people are generalists with deep experience in one area but also a broad set of skills across many areas. The evolution is E-shaped people—**E** for **experience, expertise, exploration**, and **execution**. They have deep experience in multiple areas with proven execution skills. They are always innovating and eager to learn new skills. E-shaped people are the best way to combine different areas of expertise into one high-collaborative team (*Kim G., Humble J., Debois P. and Willis J.*).

You can see very quickly how your team is collaborating by looking at some of the **pull requests**. Who does the code reviews, and on which topics? What are the issues people are discussing about? How is the tone? If you have ever seen pull requests of high-performing teams, you'll know that you can easily spot things that are not going well. Here are some pull request anti-patterns that you can easily spot:

- Pull requests are too big and contain many changes (**batch size**).
- Pull requests are only created when a feature is already finished or on the last day of the sprint (**last-minute approvals**).
- Pull requests are approved without any comments. This is normally because people just approve to not mess with the other team members (**auto-approvals**).
- Comments rarely contain questions. This normally means the discussions are about **irrelevant details**—such as formatting and style—and not about architectural design issues.

I'll show you later *the best practices for code reviews* and how you can avoid these anti-patterns. Let's first have a closer look at what a pull request is.

The heart of collaboration – the pull request

A **pull request** is more than just a classical code review. It's a way to do the following:

- Collaborate on code
- Share knowledge
- Create shared ownership of the code
- Collaborate across team boundaries

But what exactly is a pull request? A **pull request**—also known as a **merge request**—is a process of integrating changes from other branches into a target branch in your **Git** repository. The changes can come from a branch within your repository or from a **fork**—a copy of your repository. Pull request is often abbreviated to **PR**. People without write permissions can fork your repository and create pull requests. This allows owners of open source repositories to allow contributions without giving everyone write access to the repository. That's why in the open source world, pull requests are the default for integrating changes into the repository.

Pull requests can also be used to collaborate cross-team in an open source style called inner source (see *Chapter 5, Influence of Open and Inner Source on Software Delivery Performance*).

About Git

Git is a distributed **revision control system** (**RCS**). In contrast to central RCS, every developer stores the entire repository on their machine and syncs changes with other repositories. Git is based on a few simple architectural decisions. Every version is stored as the entire file—not just the changes. Changes are tracked using a hash algorithm. The revisions and the filesystems are stored as a **directed acyclic graph** (**DAG**) that is linked using the hash of the parent object. This makes it very easy to branch and merge changes. That's why Git states the following about itself: `git - the stupid content tracker` (see Git man page in *Figure 3.1*).

Git was created in 2005 by Linus Torvalds as the RCS for the Linux kernel. Until 2005, BitKeeper was used for that purpose, but due to a license change, BitKeeper could not be used any longer without costs for open source.

Git is the most popular RCS today and there are many books on Git alone (see Chacon S. and Straub B., 2014; Kaufmann M., 2021; and many more). Git is at the heart of GitHub, but in this book, I focus on GitHub as a **DevOps** platform and not as an RCS.

In *Chapter 11, Trunk-Based Development*, I'll talk about branching workflows as this is related to engineering velocity, but I'll not dive deeper into branching and merging. Please refer to the *Further readings and references* section for that.

Figure 3.1 shows the man page for Git:

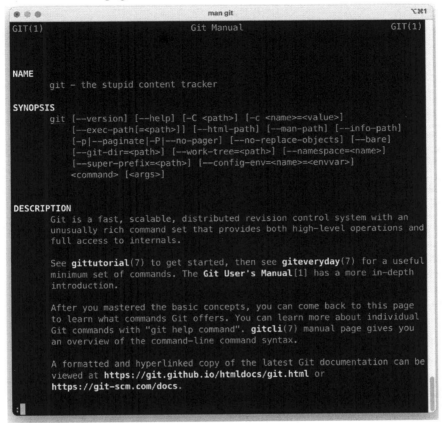

Figure 3.1 – The man page for Git – the stupid content tracker

Git versions text files on a per-line basis. This means the pull request focuses on lines changed: a line can be added, removed, or both—in this case, you can see the differences between the old and the new line. Before merging, the pull request allows you to do the following:

- Review changes and comment on them

- Build and test the changes together with new code in the source repository without merging it first

Only if the changes pass all checks do they get merged back automatically by the pull request.

Since everything is code in modern software engineering, it is not only about source code. You can collaborate on the following:

- Architecture, design, and concept documents
- Source code
- Tests
- Infrastructure (as code)
- Configuration (as code)
- Documentation

Everything can be done in a text file. In the previous chapter, I already talked about **markdown** as the standard for human-readable files. It is perfect for collaborating on concept documents and documentation. You can also render markdown to **Portable Document Format (PDF)** documents if you require physical documents that can be archived or sent to customers. You can extend markdown with diagrams—for example, with *Mermaid* (see `https://mermaid-js.github.io/mermaid/`). While **markdown** is for human-readable files, **YAML Ain't Markup Language (YAML)** is for machine-readable files. So, with a combination of source code, markdown, and YAML, you can automate the creation of all artifacts of your development life cycle and collaborate on changes just as you collaborate on the source code!

> **Example**
>
> At GitHub, everything is basically handled as markdown. Even the legal team and **human resources (HR)** use markdown, issues, and pull requests to collaborate on contracts. One example is the hiring process: job descriptions are stored as markdown and the complete hiring process is tracked using issues. Other examples are the GitHub site policies (such as *Terms of Service* or *Community Guidelines*). They are all in markdown and are open source (`https://github.com/github/site-policy`).
>
> If you want to learn more about GitHub team collaboration, see `https://youtu.be/HyvZO5vvOas?t=3189`.

Hands-on – Creating a pull request

If you are new to pull requests, it's best to create one to experience what it is about. If you are already familiar with pull requests, you can skip this part and continue reading about the *pull request features*. Proceed as follows:

1. Open the following repository and create a fork by clicking **Fork** in the top-right corner of the repository: `https://github.com/wulfland/AccelerateDevOps`.

    In the fork, navigate to `Chapter 3` | **Create a pull request** (`ch3_pull-request/Create-PullRequest.md`). The file also contains instructions so that you don't have to switch between your browser and the book all the time.

    Edit the file by clicking the **Edit** pencil icon above the file content.

2. Delete the row that is marked in the file.

3. Add a few rows of random text.

4. Modify one line by removing letters that exceed the permitted length.

5. Commit your changes, but not directly to the `main` branch. Commit them to a new **branch** like in Figure 3.2:

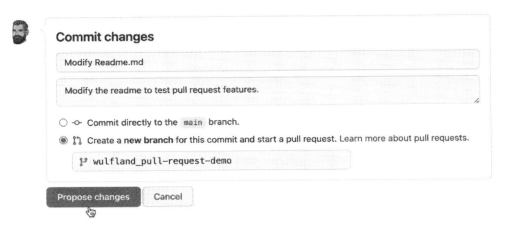

Figure 3.2 – Committing the changes to a new branch

6. You automatically get redirected to a page where you can create a pull request. Enter a title and a description. Note that you have full markdown support with all the features you know from the issues in *Chapter 2, Planning, Tracking, and Visualizing your Work*: emoticons (:+1:), mentions (@), references (#), task lists (– [ ]), and source code with syntax highlighting (```). You also can assign assignees, labels, projects, and milestones.

    At the top of the page, you see that the target branch (base) is main and that the source branch to integrate is the one you just created. The **Create pull request** button is a dropdown. You could also choose to create a draft pull request. For now, we skip this and create a pull request by clicking the **Create pull request** button, (see *Figure 3.3*).

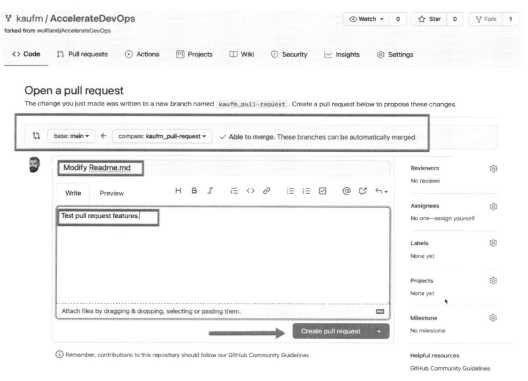

Figure 3.3 – Creating a pull request for the changes you made to the file

7. In the pull request, navigate to **Files changed** and note the changes you made to the file: deleted lines are red, added lines are green, and modified lines are a deleted line followed by an added line. If you hover with your mouse over the lines, you get a plus + icon on the left side. If you click the icon, you can add a single-line comment. If you hold the icon and pull it, you can add a comment for multiple lines. The comment has, again, the same markup support as issues with all the rich features! Add a comment and click **Add single comment** (see *Figure 3.4*):

Figure 3.4 – Adding a comment to a changed line

The important difference between a classical code review and a pull request is that you can update a pull request. This allows you to address comments and work together on issues until they are closed. To show this, you'll edit the file and commit to the new branch to see that the pull request will reflect the changes.

8. You can edit the file directly from the pull request by opening the menu in the top-right corner and selecting **Edit file** (see *Figure 3.5*):

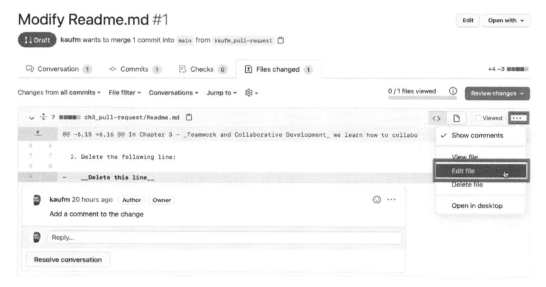

Figure 3.5 – Editing file from within the pull request

9. Modify the file by adding a new line of text to it. Commit the changes to the branch you created before creating the pull request (see *Figure 3.6*):

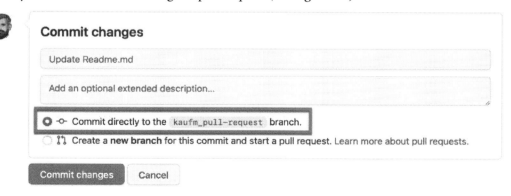

Figure 3.6 – Committing the changes to your branch

10. Navigate back to the pull request and note that your changes are automatically displayed. You can see all changes in a file under **Files changed** or you can see changes in individual commits under **Commits** (see *Figure 3.7*):

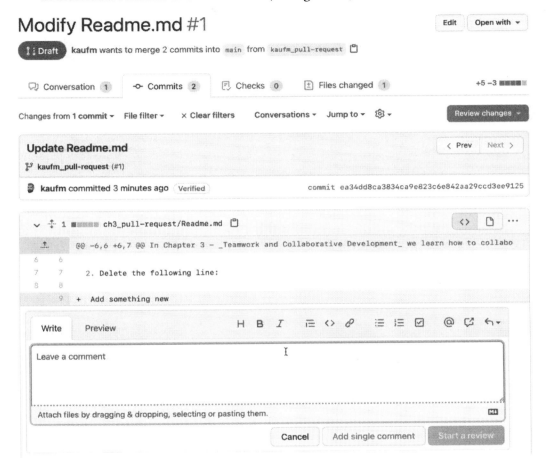

Figure 3.7 – Commenting on changes in individual commits

11. If you are new to pull requests on GitHub, the important takeaways are these:

- A pull request is about the **changes** in a branch to a base branch. If you update the branch, the pull request gets automatically updated.

- You can **collaborate** on all changes using the rich features you already know from GitHub issues: task lists, mentions, references, source code, and so on.

- You can look at changes on a **per-file** base or a **per-commit** base. This helps separate important changes from unimportant ones (for example, refactoring).

Proposing changes

GitHub pull requests have a rich feature set that helps you to improve your collaboration flow.

Draft pull requests

When is the best time to create a pull request? You can argue about this, but I'd say: the earlier the better! Ideally, you create a pull request the moment you start working on something. This way, your team always knows what everybody is working on by just looking at the open pull requests. But if you open a pull request too early, the reviewers don't know when to give feedback. That's where **draft pull requests** come in handy. You can create your pull request early, but everyone knows that the work is still in progress and reviewers do not get notified yet, but you still can mention people in comments to get early feedback on code.

When creating a pull request, you can directly create it in a draft state (see *Figure 3.8*):

Figure 3.8 – Creating a pull request as a draft

Draft pull requests are clearly marked as **Draft** and have their own icon (see *Figure 3.9*). You can also filter your pull requests in a search by using draft:true or draft:false as a search parameter:

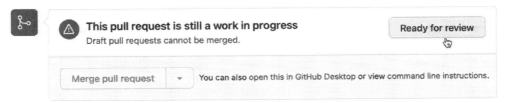

Figure 3.9 – Draft pull requests are marked with their own symbol

If your pull request is already in a review state, you can still change the state back at any time by clicking the link under **Reviewers | Still in progress? | Convert to draft**.

If your pull request is ready to be reviewed, just click on **Ready for review** (see *Figure 3.10*):

Figure 3.10 – Removing the draft state of a pull request

Draft pull requests are a great feature to collaborate early on changes using pull requests in a way that is transparent for the team.

Code owners

Code owners are a good way to automatically add reviewers to a pull request if certain files in your repository are changed. This feature can also be used to collaborate across team boundaries or add approvals in early development stages instead of requiring them in the release pipeline. Let's say you have infrastructure defined as code in your repository. You can use code owners to require a review from a person in the shared operations team, or you have files that define the look and feel of your application. Every time you change them, you might want to have approval from the design team. Code owners are not just about the approval; they can also be used to spread knowledge in communities of practice across team boundaries.

Code owners can be teams or individuals. They need write permissions in order to become a code owner. Code owners get added as a reviewer if a pull request moves out of the draft state.

To define code owners, you create a file with the name CODEOWNERS either in the root of the repository, a docs/ folder, or a .github/ folder. The syntax of the file is simple, as outlined here:

- Use @username or @org/team-name to define the code owners. You can also use the email addresses of users.

- Use patterns to match files to assign code owners. The order is important: the last matching pattern takes precedence.

- Use # for comments, ! to negate a pattern, and [ ] to define character ranges.

Here is an example of a code owner file:

```
# The global owner is the default for the entire repository
*           @org/team1


# The design team is owner of all .css files
*.css       @org/design-team


# The admin is owner of all files in all subfolders of the
# folder IaC in the root of the repository
/IaC/       @admin


# User1 is the owner of all files in the folder docs or
# Docs - but not of files in subfolders of docs!
/[Dd]ocs/*  @user1
```

See the following page, *About code owners*, for more details: `https://docs.github.com/en/github/creating-cloning-and-archiving-repositories/creating-a-repository-on-github/about-code-owners`.

Code owners are a great way to get shared knowledge across team boundaries and to shift approvals from change boards in release pipelines to early approvals when changes happen.

Required reviews

You can require a given number of approvals before merging a pull request. This is set on a **branch protection rule** that can apply to one of many branches. You create branch protection rules under **Settings | Branches | Add rule**. In the rule, you can set the number of **required reviews** before merging, choose whether you want to dismiss approvals when changes are made to the code, and enforce approvals from code owners (see *Figure 3.11*):

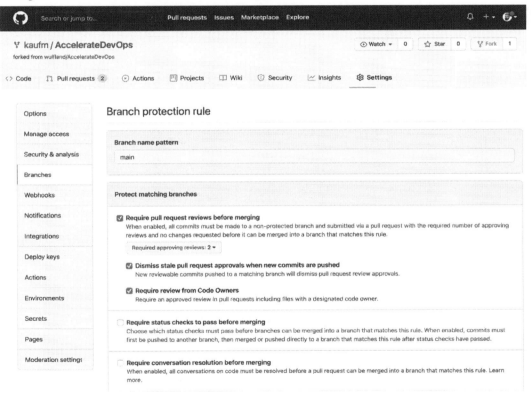

Figure 3.11 – Required reviews for a specific branch

For more information on branch protection, see `https://docs.github.com/en/` `github/administering-a-repository/defining-the-mergeability-of-` `pull-requests/about-protected-branches#about-branch-protection-` `rules`. I will cover this topic in more detail in *Chapter 7, Trunk-Based Development*.

Requesting a pull request review

If your code is ready to be reviewed, you can manually add the required number of reviewers. GitHub provides you with **reviewers' suggestions** based on the author of the code that you have changed (see *Figure 3.12*). You can just click on **Request** or you can manually search for people to perform the review:

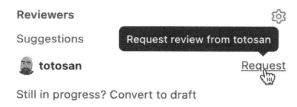

Figure 3.12 – Suggested reviewers

You can also have GitHub automatically assign reviewers to your team. You configure this per team under **Settings | Code review assignment**. You can select the number of reviewers that automatically get assigned and select one of the following two algorithms:

- **Round robin**: Chooses reviewers based on who received the least recent requests so far

- **Load balance**: Chooses reviewers based upon each member's total number of review requests considering outstanding reviews

You can exclude certain members from reviews, and you can select to not notify the entire team when reviewers are assigned. See Figure 3.13 for how to configure code review assignments for your team:

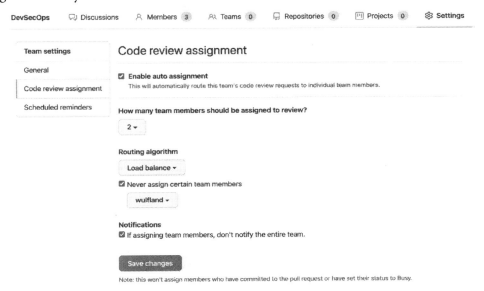

Figure 3.13 – Managing code review assignments for your team

Auto-merge

One of my favorite features from pull requests is **auto-merge**. This allows you to increase your velocity when working on small changes, especially if you have **continuous deployment (CD)** enabled. Auto-merge automatically merges your changes if all policies are met. If you have done your changes, you enable auto-merge and can work on other changes. If your pull request has the required number of approvals and all automatic checks pass, the pull request gets automatically merged and deployed to production.

Pull request reviews

If you have been selected for a review, you can comment on many changes, make suggestions, and in the end submit your review with one of the following notations:

- **Comment**
- **Approve**
- **Request changes**

In the previous section, I focused on pull request features relevant to the author of a pull request. In this section, I describe a feature that helps reviewers to perform a review and give proper feedback to the author.

Reviewing proposed changes in a pull request

You can start your review by looking at the changes one file at a time. If you hover over lines, you see the + icon on the left. It can be used to add a single-line comment, or by dragging it over multiple lines, you can create a multiline comment. If you have a comment, you select **Start review** to start the review process without submitting the comment yet. If you add more comments, the button changes to **Add review comment**; you can add as many comments to a review as you want. Comments are only visible to you until you submit the review! You can cancel a review at any time.

Marking files as viewed

When reviewing, you see a progress bar at the top of the file. When you're done with one file, you can select the **Viewed** checkbox. The file will be collapsed and the progress bar will show the progress (see *Figure 3.14*):

Figure 3.14 – Marking files as viewed

Hands-on – Making suggestions

The best way to give feedback is by making **suggestions** that the author of the pull request can easily integrate into their branch. This feature is so important that it is worth trying it out if you've never tried it. Here's how you'd go about this:

1. Open the fork from the repository you created in the previous hands-on exercise: `https://github.com/<your user name>/AccelerateDevOps`.

   In the fork, navigate to `Chapter 3` | **Review Changes** (`ch3_pull-request/Review-Changes.md`). The file also contains instructions so that you don't have to switch between your browser and the book all the time.

   Copy the sample source code by clicking the **Copy** icon in the top-right corner of the source code block.

2. Navigate to `src/app.js` (use the link in markdown). Select the branch you created in the previous hands-on exercise and edit the file by clicking the **Edit** icon (pencil) in the top-right corner (see *Figure 3.15*):

Figure 3.15 – Editing code file to add sample code

3. Delete *line 2* and insert the code by pressing *Ctrl + V*.

4. Commit directly to the source branch of your pull request.

5. Navigate back to the pull request and look for `src/app.js` under **Files changed**. Note that the nested loop in *lines 6* to *9* is not correctly indented. Mark *lines 6* to *9* and create a multiline comment. Click the **Suggestion** button and you'll see that the code is in the suggestion block, including whitespaces (see *Figure 3.16*):

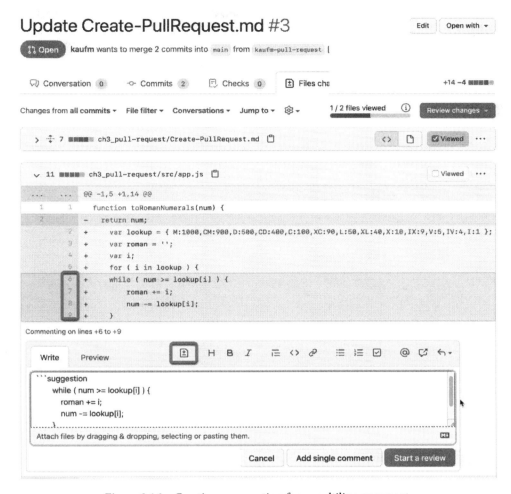

Figure 3.16 – Creating a suggestion for a multiline comment

6. Note that the `suggestion` code block contains the complete code, including whitespaces. Add four blanks at the beginning of each line to fix the indentation.

You can make the suggestion part of a review (**Start a review**) or submit the suggestion directly to the author (**Add single comment**). For this hands-on exercise, we add the suggestion as a single comment.

Incorporating feedback into your pull request

Since you are the reviewer and author, you can directly switch roles. As the author, you see all suggestions for your pull request.

You can commit a suggestion directly to your branch, or you can batch multiple suggestions to one commit and then commit all the changes at once. Add the change to the batch and apply the batch at the top of the file (see *Figure 3.17*):

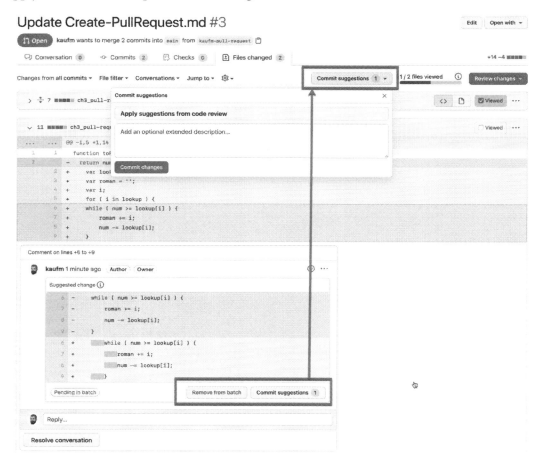

Figure 3.17 – Incorporating suggestions into your code

Suggestions are a great way to provide feedback and suggest code changes. They are really easy for an author to incorporate into their code.

Submitting a review

If you have finished your review and added all your comments and suggestions, you can submit it. The author will be informed about the outcome and can answer your comments. You can leave a final comment and select one of these three options:

- **Approve**: Approves the changes. This is the only option that counts to the required reviewer count!

- **Comment**: Submit feedback without approval or denial.

- **Request changes**: Indicate that changes are needed for approval from your side.

Finish the review by clicking **Submit review** (see *Figure 3.18*):

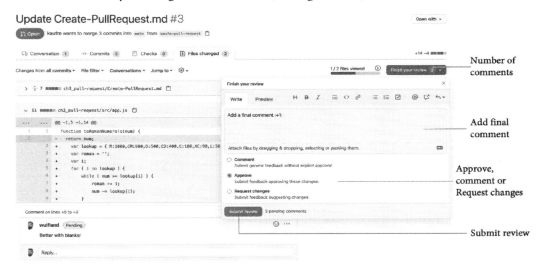

Figure 3.18 – Finishing your review

Finishing your pull request

If you want to abandon the changes in your branch, you can close a pull request without merging. To incorporate your changes into the base branch you have three **merge** options, outlined as follows:

- **Create a merge commit**: This is the default option. It creates a merge commit and displays all commits from your branch as a separate branch in the history. If you have many long-running branches, this can clutter the history. You can see a representation of this merge option here:

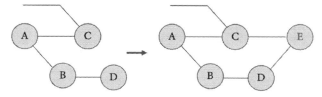

Figure 3.19 – Git history if you do a merge commit

- **Squash and merge**: All the commits from the branch will be combined into a single commit. This creates a clean, linear history and is a good merge method if you delete the branch after merging. It is not recommended if you keep working on the branch. You can see a representation of this merge option here:

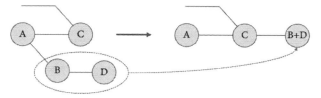

Figure 3.20 – Git history if you do a squash and merge

- **Rebase and merge**: Applies all the commits of the branch to the head of the base branch. This also creates a linear history but keeps the individual commits. It's also not recommended if you keep working on the branch. You can see a representation of this merge option here:

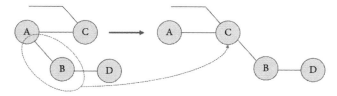

Figure 3.21 – Git history seems linear if you do a rebase and merge

Select the merge method you want and click **Merge pull request** (see *Figure 3.22*):

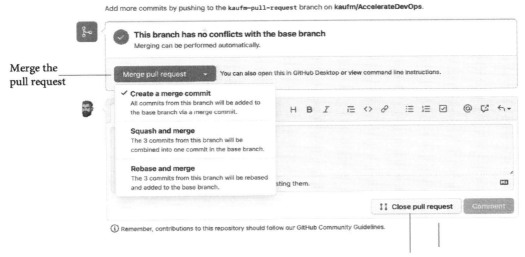

Figure 3.22 – Finishing a pull request

Modify the merge message and click **Confirm merge**. After the merge, you can delete the branch if you want.

Best practices for code reviews

Pull requests are a great way to collaborate on any kind of code. This chapter only scratches the surface of the possibilities you have for your collaboration workflow, but to get your teams to effectively collaborate, you should consider some best practices for effective code reviews.

Teach Git

This one might look obvious, but make sure your teams are well trained in Git. Well-crafted commits with a **good commit message** that only serve **one purpose** are much easier to review than many changes spread randomly across multiple commits. In particular, mixing refactoring and business logic makes reviews a nightmare. If team members know how to fix up commits, patch changes they made in different commits, and how to craft good commit messages, the resulting pull request will be much easier to review.

Link pull request to issue

Link the pull request to the corresponding issue that initiated the work. This helps to give context to the pull request. If you use third-party integration, link the pull request to the Jira ticket, Azure Boards work item, or any other source you have connected to GitHub.

Use draft pull requests

Have the team members create a **draft pull request** right when they **start working** on something. This way, the team knows who is working on what. This also encourages people to use comments with mentions to ask people for feedback before the review starts. Early feedback on changes helps to get faster reviews at the end.

Have a minimum number of two approvers

You should have a **minimum number** of two **required approvers**. The more the better, depending on team size. But one is not enough. Having multiple reviewers gives reviews some kind of dynamic. I noticed big changes in the review practice of some teams by just changing this from one to two!

Do peer reviews

Consider reviews to be **peer reviews**. Do not have senior architects review the code of others! Younger colleagues should also do reviews of peers to learn. A good practice is to add the entire team as reviewers and require a certain percentage of approvals (for example, 50%), and then people pick the pull requests they want. Or, you could use **automatic review assignments** to distribute reviews randomly in your team.

Automate review steps

Many review steps can be automated, especially formatting. Have a good linter **check the formatting** of code (for example, `https://github.com/github/super-linter`), or write some tests to check if the documentation is complete. Use static and dynamic code analysis to find issues automatically. The more you automate banal checks, the more the reviews can concentrate on important things.

Deploy and test changes

Build and test your changes automatically before merging. Install the code to test if necessary. The more confident people are that the changes will not break anything, the more they will trust in the process. Use **auto-merge** to automatically merge and release your changes if all approvals and validation pass. The high automation makes people work in smaller batch sizes, which makes reviews much easier.

Review guidelines/code of conduct

Some engineers have a strong opinion on what is the right way to do something, and debates can run out of hand quickly. You want to have intense discussions to get the best solutions, but you want these to happen in an inclusive way so that everyone in the team can participate equally. Having **review guidelines** and a **code of conduct** in place helps as a gatekeeper. If people do not behave appropriately, you can point to the rules.

Summary

Software development is a team sport, and it is important to have a team with shared ownership for the code that collaborates tightly on new changes. A GitHub pull request can help to achieve this if it is used in the right way.

In the next chapter, you will about asynchronous and synchronous work, and how asynchronous workflows can help you to collaborate from anywhere at any time.

Further readings and references

Here are the references from this chapter that you can also use to get more information on the topics:

- *Coyle D. (2018). The Culture Code: The Secrets of Highly Successful Groups* (1st ed.). *Cornerstone Digital.*

- *Kim G., Humble J., Debois P. and Willis J. (2016). The DevOps Handbook: How to Create World-Class Agility, Reliability, and Security in Technology Organizations* (1st ed.). *IT Revolution Press.*

- Scott Prugh (2014). *Continuous Delivery.* https://www.scaledagileframework.com/guidance-continuous-delivery/

- *Chacon S.* and *Straub B.* (2014). *Pro Git* (2nd ed.). *Apress.* https://git-scm.com/book/de/v2

- *Kaufmann M. (2021). Git für Dummies (1st ed., German). Wiley-VCH.*

- Git: `https://en.wikipedia.org/wiki/Git`

- Pull requests: `https://docs.github.com/en/github/collaborating-with-pull-requests/proposing-changes-to-your-work-with-pull-requests/about-pull-requests`

- Code owners: `https://docs.github.com/en/github/creating-cloning-and-archiving-repositories/creating-a-repository-on-github/about-code-owners`

- Branch protection: `https://docs.github.com/en/github/administering-a-repository/defining-the-mergeability-of-pull-requests/about-protected-branches#about-branch-protection-rules`

- Code review assignments: `https://docs.github.com/en/organizations/ organizing-members-into-teams/managing-code-review-assignment-for-your-team`

- Auto-merge: `https://docs.github.com/en/github/collaborating-with-pull-requests/incorporating-changes-from-a-pull-request/automatically-merging-a-pull-request`

- Pull request reviews: `https://docs.github.com/en/github/collaborating-with-pull-requests/reviewing-changes-in-pull-requests/about-pull-request-reviews`

4

Asynchronous Work: Collaborate from Anywhere

In the previous chapter, you learned about collaborative development with pull requests and how you can leverage them to create shared ownership for the code and the product you built. In this chapter, we'll focus on synchronous and asynchronous work and how you can use the benefits of asynchronous workflows for better collaboration in distributed, remote, and hybrid teams and better cross-team collaboration.

The following topics will be covered in the chapter:

- Comparing synchronous and asynchronous work
- Distributed teams
- Cross-team collaboration
- Shift to asynchronous workflows
- Teams and Slack integration

- GitHub Discussions
- Pages and wikis
- Working from everywhere with GitHub Mobile
- Case study

Comparing synchronous and asynchronous work

Every bit of work we information workers carry out is basically communication. Even everything about programming: you have to communicate what you are coding, you have to communicate the architecture, and even the code itself is communication to people in the future—including yourself—on how to change your program. So, the way we communicate directly influences how we get things done.

The history of communication

How we humans interact and communicate has often changed throughout our history. Communication was mostly pure verbal with some limited written communication until the invention of the print press by Johannes Gutenberg in 1450, which caused a printing revolution with a big impact on religion and education by providing access to information to a broader audience. In the 17th century, the invention of the newspaper again revolutionized communication by reducing the time from sender to recipient tremendously. In the 18th century, the public post system became so efficient that more and more communication took place using letters. This allowed private communication to happen as quickly as in newspapers. In the 19th century, the invention of the telegraph allowed for the first time communication in real time over a great distance. The first telephone was invented in 1861 by Philipp Reis in Frankfurt. The transmission still had fluctuations, and most people thus underestimated the invention. It was 15 years later in 1876 when Alexander Graham Bell finally patented the telephone that revolutionized communication by allowing real-time verbal communication.

Until then, changes in communications were more associated with centuries than with decades. People had time to adapt, and it was always pretty clear and intuitive as to which communication form was the best. This has changed rapidly over the last 30 years. In the late 1990s, cellular phones became pocket-sized and affordable. Anybody could talk to anybody at any time. This, interestingly, led to a new phenomenon: people started to write short messages to each other and often preferred asynchronous communication over synchronous communication. With the rise of the internet, email replaced letters rapidly. But in the beginning, the internet was not mobile, so the expected response for an email was still a few days. This changed in the middle of the first decade of this century. The internet became mobile, and smartphones allowed access to emails everywhere at any time. At the same time, new forms of communication became popular: Facebook, Twitter, Instagram, and Snapchat. They allow different kinds of communication in the forms of text, voice, and video with different groups of audiences (reach and privacy) and different durability (**time to live**, or **TTL**) of the messages.

Figure 4.1 illustrates the relation between the exponential growth of our world population and changes in our communication behavior:

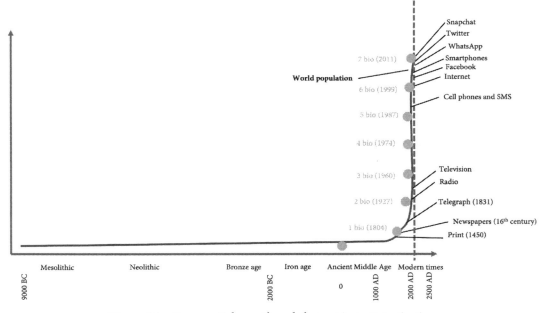

Figure 4.1 – Exponential growth and changes in communication

The rapid development in the last 30 years led to very different communication patterns. Whether you write a text message, make a video call, or send a story to a group depends more on personal preferences than on the content of the message. There is no social consensus anymore as to what is the correct communication form for a particular kind of message.

Work and communication

Work is more than just communication. Information work adds the desired output to a conversation. You can divide work into synchronous and asynchronous work. Synchronous work refers to when two or more people interact in real time to achieve the desired output. Asynchronous work happens when two or more people exchange messages to achieve the desired output.

If you work in a traditional enterprise, the mix of asynchronous and synchronous work might still look like in Figure 4.2. At least it looked like this a few years ago. Most of the work is done by email or in meetings, and meetings normally take place in the same room:

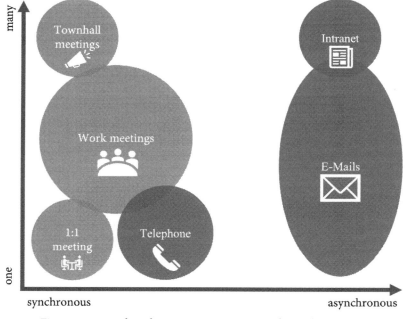

Figure 4.2 – Work and communication in a traditional enterprise

Most asynchronous work is done by email and remotely, while most synchronous work is done in in-person meetings. What is dominant depends strongly on the culture of the company. In companies with a strong email culture, people usually respond to emails within minutes. In these companies, many people have their laptops open during meetings and people normally complain about too many emails. In companies with a strong meeting culture, people often do not respond to emails in a timely fashion because they are attending meetings. This leads to fewer emails but more meetings.

In the last couple of years, this has changed tremendously. Small companies and start-ups, in particular, have abandoned email for work in favor of other asynchronous mediums such as chat. Many companies have also discovered the benefits of remote working, some only after they were forced to do so by the pandemic.

I already showed you in *Chapter 2, Planning, Tracking, and Visualizing Your Work,* how context switching kills productivity. So, for development teams, asynchronous work is desirable as it allows you to establish pull for work items and reduce context switching. A more modern work mix that is optimized for developers could look like this:

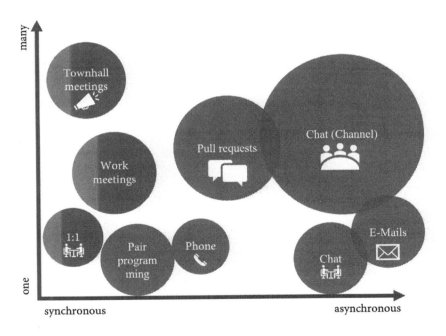

Figure 4.3 – Work and communication optimized for development

The less synchronous work people have, the more focus they can put into their work without context switching and planning. It is important to be intentional: what kind of work do we perform in a synchronous way and what can we do asynchronously? What kind of work do we perform in-person and what can we do remotely?

In-person and remote work

Synchronous work can happen in-person or remotely. Both have their advantages and disadvantages.

In-person meetings are desirable if you must convince someone. A salesperson always prefers an in-person meeting over a phone call or remote meeting as they are also better for socializing and relationship/team building. Critical feedback and sensitive issues are also better discussed in-person than remotely. Complex discussions or problems for which you need creativity can also benefit from physical proximity.

The advantage of remote meetings is that they are more productive due to less travel time. People can participate independently from the physical location, which allows you to have a team that spans multiple time zones. Remote meetings can be recorded, which allows people to watch the meeting even if they could not participate.

Remote meetings should be planned differently than in-person meetings. An 8-hour workshop (2x4) works well in-person but not remotely. Remote meetings should be shorter and more focused. People tend to get distracted rapidly if they are in front of their computers.

In the coming years, we will see more and more **hybrid work**. Hybrid work enables employees to work autonomously from different locations: home, on the go, or in an office. 66% of companies are considering redesigning office spaces for hybrid work, and 73% of employees want more flexible remote-work options (see `https://www.microsoft.com/en-us/worklab/work-trend-index/hybrid-work`). Hybrid work will be a big challenge when organizing your meetings. Remote meetings are optimized for individuals and in-person meetings are optimized for groups. Bringing both together will be a challenge, not only for the technical equipment in the meeting rooms but also for the persons responsible for organizing the meetings.

Distributed teams

Tech companies that are nearly 100% remote and have their teams distributed across the globe have existed for quite some time. I know a company that has a completely remote hiring process. Every employee gets a budget to invest in their home office or to rent something in a co-working space. The company is distributed across the globe and only comes together once a year to meet in person.

With the pandemic and the rise of remote and hybrid working, more and more companies are starting to see the benefits of having distributed teams, which include the following:

- You are not restricted to hiring in a certain metropole region and therefore have more talent and more specialists available to hire (*war of talents*).

- Hiring in other regions often comes with a *cost reduction*.

- If you target multiple markets with your products, it's always beneficial to have team members from these different backgrounds to help understand the customers (*diversity*).

- By providing support, you automatically have more hours covered, which means *less pager duty* outside normal work hours for engineers.

Distributed teams also have their challenges, the biggest one being the language. Non-native speakers have more problems communicating and you need a good base language—most likely English if you want to span many countries. Also, cultural aspects may make communication harder. Team building and a cultural fit for the team must play a much greater role in a remote hiring process.

If you want to increase your team with additional remote engineers, make sure to plan for the time zones accordingly. You should at least have 1 or 2 hours overlap of the normal working hours in the time zones, depending on the number of meetings you have. This means you normally can go a maximum of approximately 8 hours in one direction to have a 1-hour overlap. If you already have a 4-hour shift in one direction, you can only add another with a maximum of 4 hours in the other direction (see *Figure 4.4*).

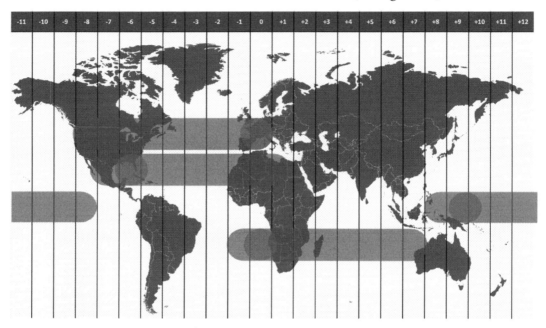

Figure 4.4 – Planning time zones with overlap for meetings

Take into account that daylight-saving times and different working hours make planning for overlap across time zones a quite complex task!

Distributed teams have advantages, and we will see this a lot more in the coming years. It's good to already start with working practices that allow you to later hire experts from other countries in other time zones. This means that it's important to have all communication in English or another common language in your region and have as many asynchronous workflows as possible.

Cross-team collaboration

To accelerate software delivery, you want your teams to be as autonomous as possible. The ability to deliver value to your end users at any time without dependencies on other teams is one of the biggest influences on velocity, and yet you need some alignment across teams: design, security, and architecture are some shared concerns that must be addressed across team boundaries. Good **cross-team collaboration** is a sign of healthy alignment across the teams.

Good cross-team collaboration should not need the involvement of management, usually going up and down the command chain to the first shared manager. Good cross-team collaboration is based on asynchronous workflows that directly get the right people together to solve issues. The fewer meetings that are needed for daily work, the better.

Shift to asynchronous workflows

To shift to a more asynchronous way of working and allow remote and hybrid work, there are some best practices that you can easily adopt, such as the following:

- **Prefer chat over email**: Workflows that rely on emails have many disadvantages: you don't have a common history; if a team member gets sick or leaves, you get blocked; and so on. Try to move all your work-related conversations to a chat platform such as Microsoft Teams or Slack.

- **Make (most) meetings optional**: Make all meetings that are work-related optional. If you don't see value in the meeting, leave. This helps to make meetings more focused and better prepared as nobody wants to be the only participant in their own meeting. Of course, there are some meetings for team building or town hall meetings that should not be optional.

- **Record all meetings**: Recording all meetings gives people the chance to catch up, even if they could not participate. Recorded meetings can be viewed at a faster speed, which helps to digest meetings in a shorter time.

- **Be intentional**: Be intentional about what meetings are and what an asynchronous workflow is (chat, issues, pull requests, and wikis).

- **Review your setting**: Be sure to know your metrics and regularly check your setup. Are meetings successful or can they be moved to discussions in issues or pull requests? Do discussions in issues and pull requests take forever and might some things be resolved faster in a meeting? Don't change the setup too often as it takes some time for people to adopt, but be sure to review and adapt your setup at least every 2 or 3 months.

- **Use mentions and code owners**: Use mentions and code owners (see *Chapter 3, Teamwork and Collaborative Development*) to dynamically get together the right people to finish a task. Both features are also great for cross-team collaboration.

- **Treat everything as code**: Try to treat everything as code and collaborate on it like you do on code: infrastructure, configuration, software architecture, design documents, and concepts.

Teams and Slack integration

If you prefer chat over email, you can use the integration features in GitHub for **Microsoft Teams** (`https://teams.github.com`) or **Slack** (`https://slack.github.com`). These allow you to receive notifications directly in your chat channel and interact with issues, pull requests, or deployments. The features in Slack and Teams are very similar, as outlined here:

- **Notifications**: Subscribe to events in a repository. You can filter notifications with branch or label filters.

- **Details for GitHub links**: GitHub links automatically get unfurled and show details of the item to link points to.

- **Open new issues**: Create new issues directly from your conversations.

- **Interact**: Work directly with issues, pull requests, or deployment approvals from your channels.

- **Schedule reminders**: Receive reminders for code reviews in your channel.

The installation is straightforward. You must install the GitHub app in Microsoft Teams or Slack and the corresponding Teams or Slack app in your organization in GitHub.

Once installed, you can interact with the GitHub bot and send messages. In Teams, you mention the bot with @GitHub, while in Slack, you do this with /GitHub. If you mention the bot, you receive a list of commands that you can use (see *Figure 4.5*):

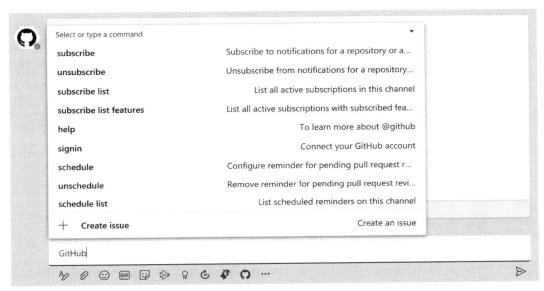

Figure 4.5 – Sending commands to the GitHub bot

The first command you must use is signin. This will link your GitHub account to your Teams/Slack account:

```
@GitHub signin
```

After that, you can subscribe to notifications or schedule reminders. The unfurling of links and the interaction with issues work without needing to configure anything. Figure 4.6 shows an issue in Teams that was created from a conversation. You can directly comment on the issue or close it:

Figure 4.6 – Integration of issues in Microsoft Teams

Chat integration is a powerful feature that will come in handy when more and more of your workflows are initiated and managed through chat instead of through meetings or emails.

GitHub Discussions

In *Chapter 2, Planning, Tracking, and Visualizing Your Work*, you learned how to use GitHub issues and GitHub projects to manage your work. GitHub Discussions is a community forum that allows members to ask questions, share updates, and have open-ended conversations. Discussions are a great way to reduce a load of issues and pull requests by providing a different place for long discussions and **questions and answers (Q&A)**.

Getting started with Discussions

To get started with GitHub Discussions, you must enable it in your repository under **Settings | Options | Features** by checking **Discussions**. Once you have checked this option, you have a new main menu item, **Discussions**, in your repository.

> **Note**
> **GitHub Discussions** is a feature that was still in Beta at the time this book was written. Some features might since have changed. You can give feedback and participate in discussions under `https://github.com/github/feedback/discussions`, which, of course, is itself a GitHub discussion.

Discussions are organized into categories. You can search and filter in discussions the same way you can search and filter issues. Discussions themselves can be upvoted and indicate the number of comments and labeled if they are considered answered. You can pin up to four discussions to the top of the page to make some important announcements. A leader board shows the most helpful users that have answered the most questions in the last 30 days. Figure 4.7 shows how discussions look:

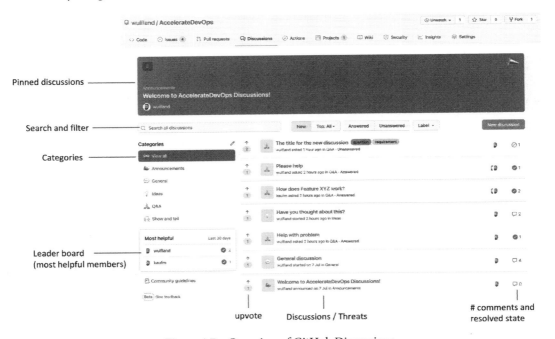

Figure 4.7 – Overview of GitHub Discussions

Discussion categories

You can manage categories by pressing the edit pencil next to **Categories**. You can edit, delete, or add new categories. A category consists of the following:

- Icon
- Title
- An optional description

There are three kinds of categories, as outlined here:

1. **Question/Answer**:

   Discussion category to ask questions, suggest answers, and vote on the best suggested answer. *This category type is the only type that allows the marking of comments as answered*!

2. **Open-ended discussion**:

   A category to have conversations that don't require a definitive answer to a question. Great for sharing tips and tricks or just chatting.

3. **Announcement**:

   Share updates and news with your community. Only maintainers and admins can post new discussions in these categories, but anyone can comment and reply.

Starting a discussion

You can start a discussion by clicking **Discussion | New discussion**. To start a new discussion, you must select a category, and enter a title and a description. Optionally, you can add labels to the discussion. The description has full Markdown support. This includes references (#) to issues, pull requests, and other discussions, as well as mentions (@) of other persons, code with syntax-highlighting, and attachments (see *Figure 4.8*):

Figure 4.8 – Starting a new discussion

Participating in a discussion

You can comment on or directly answer the original discussion description, or you can answer existing comments. In each case, you have full Markdown support! You can add reactions in the form of emoticons to all comments and the original description. You can also upvote the discussion or comments/answers. In the menu on the right, you can convert a discussion into an issue. As an admin or maintainer, you can also lock the conversation, transfer it to another repository, pin the discussion to the top of the forum, or delete it. Figure 4.9 gives an overview of an ongoing discussion:

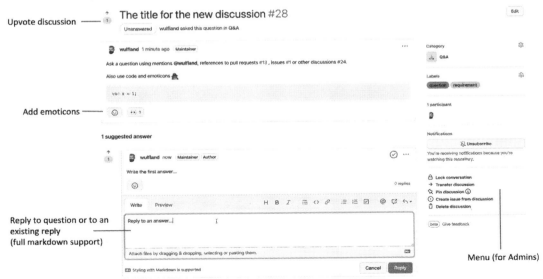

Figure 4.9 – Participating in a discussion

Discussions is a great place to collaborate asynchronously with your peers and across team boundaries. For more information on Discussions, see `https://docs.github.com/en/discussions`.

Pages and wikis

You have many options to share content in a collaborative way. In addition to issues and discussions, you can use **GitHub Pages** and **wikis**.

GitHub Pages

GitHub Pages is a static website-hosting service that serves your files straight from a repository in GitHub. You could host normal **HyperText Markup Language** (**HTML**), **Cascading Style Sheets** (**CSS**), and JavaScript files and build a site yourself. But you can also leverage the built-in preprocessor **Jekyll** (see `https://jekyllrb.com/`), which allows you to build good-looking websites in Markdown.

GitHub Pages sites are hosted by default under the `github.io` domain (such as `https://wulfland.github.io/AccelerateDevOps/`), but you can also use a custom domain name.

GitHub Pages is a free offering for public repositories. For internal use (private repositories), you need GitHub Enterprise.

> **Note**
>
> GitHub Pages is a free service, but it is not intended for running commercial websites! It is forbidden to run webshops or any other commercial websites. It has a quota of 1 **gigabyte** (**GB**) and a bandwidth limit of 100 GB per month. See `https://docs.github.com/en/pages/getting-started-with-github-pages/about-github-pages` for more information.

The best way to learn about GitHub Pages is to see it in action. Here's how:

1. If you have already forked the `https://github.com/wulfland/AccelerateDevOps` repository in the hands-on exercises in previous chapters, you can directly go to your fork. If not, create a fork by clicking the **Fork** button in the top-right corner of the repository. This will create a fork under `https://github.com/<USER>/AccelerateDevOps`.

2. In the forked repository, navigate to **Settings | Pages**. Select the branch you want to run the website from—in this case, `main`—and select the `/docs` folder as the root for the website. You can only choose the root of the repository or `/docs`! No other folders can be used. Click **Save** to initialize the website (see *Figure 4.10*):

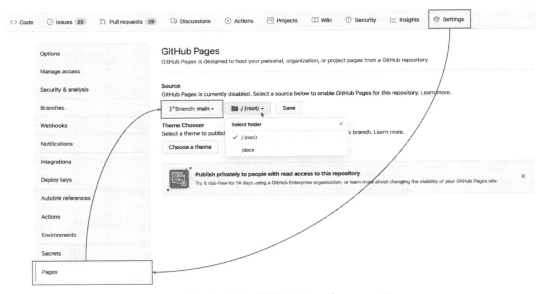

Figure 4.10 – Enabling GitHub Pages for a repository

3. It may take a few minutes until the site creation has finished. Click the link, as highlighted in Figure 4.11 and refresh the page if it is not yet available:

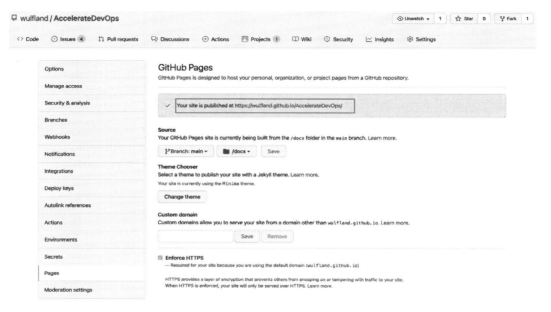

Figure 4.11 – Navigating to the web page

4. Inspect the site and note that it has a menu with static pages and a menu that shows posts with an excerpt (see *Figure 4.12*):

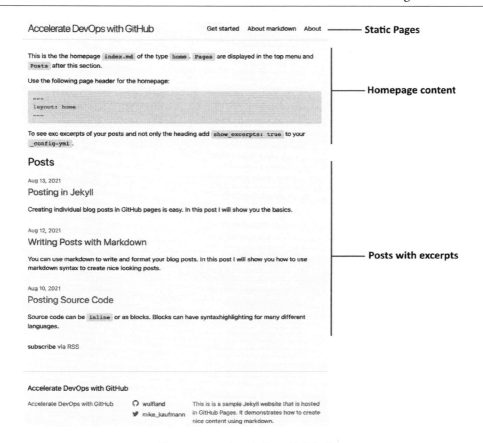

Figure 4.12 – A website with Jekyll

5. Head back to your code. First, inspect the /docs/_config.yaml configuration file. Here, you can place the global configuration for your website, such as the title and description, as illustrated in the following code snippet:

```
title: Accelerate DevOps with GitHub
description: >-
  This is a sample Jekyll website that is hosted in
  GitHub Pages.
  ...
```

There are many themes that you can use to render your site. Each theme has its own features, so be sure to check the documentation. I have the default Jekyll theme **minima**. To render Markdown, you can use **Kramdown** or **GitHub Flavored Markdown (GFM)**. Jekyll also supports different plugins. The **minima** theme supports `jekyll-feed` and, with the `show_excerpts` option, you can set whether excerpts for the posts are displayed on the home page, as illustrated in the following code snippet:

```
theme: minima
Markdown: kramdown
plugins:
  - jekyll-feed
show_excerpts: true
```

Many themes support additional values. For example, you can set social media accounts that get displayed on your site, as follows:

```
twitter_username: mike_kaufmann
github_username: wulfland
```

Normally, static pages are displayed in the top navigation bar in alphabetical order. To filter and sort pages, you can add a section to the config. As we want to add a new page, add a `my-page.md` entry right before `About.md`, like this:

```
header_pages:
- get-started.md
- about-Markdown.md
- my-page.md
- About.md
```

Commit the change directly to the `main` branch.

6. In the `/docs` folder, select **Add file | Create new file** in the top-right corner. Enter `my-page.md` as the filename and add the following header to the file:

```
---
layout: page
title: "My Page"
permalink: /my-page/
---
```

Add some more Markdown if you wish. Commit directly to the `main` branch.

7. Now, head over to the `/docs/_posts/` folder. Select **Add file | Create new file** again in the top-right corner. Enter `YYY-MM-DD-my-post.md` as the filename, where `YYYY` is the current year, `MM` the two-letter month, and `DD` the two-letter day of the month. Add the following header and replace the date with the current date:

```
---

layout: post
title:  "My Post"
permalink: /2021-08-14_writing-with-Markdown/
---
```

Add some more Markdown content to the page and commit it directly to the `main` branch.

8. Give the processor in the background some time and then refresh your page. You should see the page and the post on the start page, and you can navigate to them (see *Figure 4.13*):

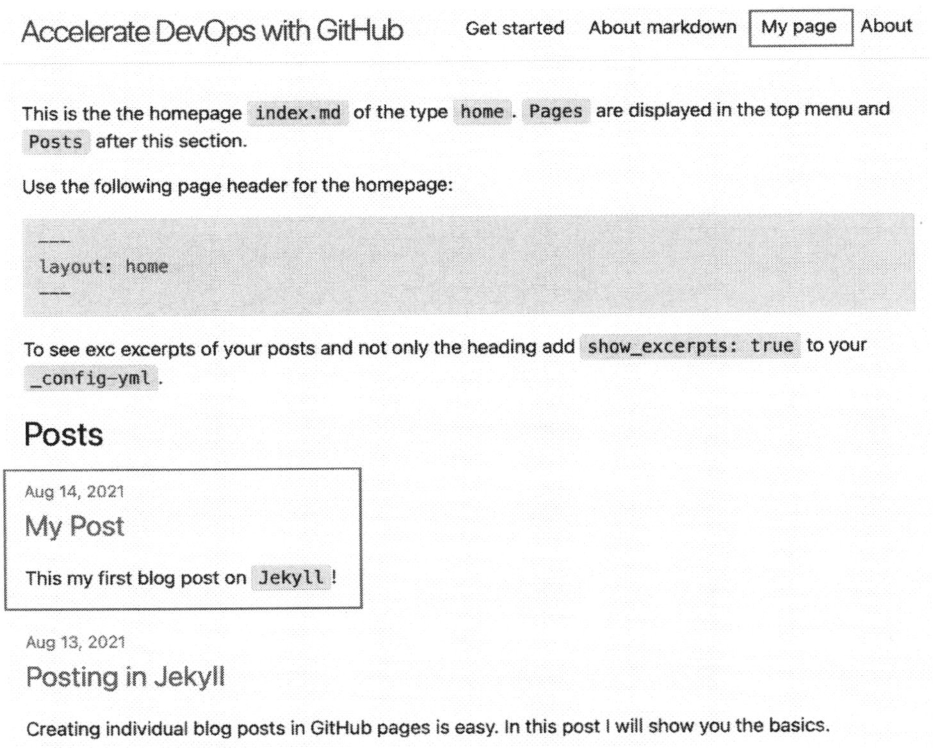

Accelerate DevOps with GitHub   Get started   About markdown | My page | About

This is the the homepage `index.md` of the type `home` . `Pages` are displayed in the top menu and `Posts` after this section.

Use the following page header for the homepage:

```
---
layout: home
---
```

To see exc excerpts of your posts and not only the heading add `show_excerpts: true` to your `_config-yml` .

Posts

Aug 14, 2021
My Post
This my first blog post on `Jekyll` !

Aug 13, 2021
Posting in Jekyll
Creating individual blog posts in GitHub pages is easy. In this post I will show you the basics.

Figure 4.13 – Examining the new page and post in Jekyll

You have seen how easy it is to publish content in GitHub Pages. Jekyll is a very powerful tool, and you can customize nearly everything, including the themes. You can also run your site offline to test it when you install Ruby and Jekyll (see `https://docs.github.com/en/pages/setting-up-a-github-pages-site-with-jekyll/testing-your-github-pages-site-locally-with-jekyll` for more details). However, this is a very complex topic and outside the scope of this book.

GitHub Pages with Jekyll is a great way to present content in a nice way and to *collaborate on the content* as you do on code, with pull requests. You can use it as a technical blog or for user documentation. In a distributed team, you can use it to publish the results of each sprint in a small post, maybe with small videos. This helps to communicate your success, even when people cannot attend the sprint review meeting.

Wikis

GitHub has a simple wiki included in every repository, but you also can choose to create your own Markdown-based wiki alongside your code.

The GitHub wiki

There is a very simple **wiki** available in every repository. You can choose to edit the pages in different formats: **Markdown, AsciiDoc, Creole, MediaWiki, Org-mode, Prod, RDoc, Textile**, or **reStructuredText**. Since everything else in GitHub is Markdown, I think this is the best choice, but if you already have wiki content in one of the other formats, it can help you to move the content over.

> **Note**
>
> Other editing formats, such as **AsciiDoc** or **MediaWiki**, have more advanced features such as an autogenerated **table of contents** (ToC). If your team is already familiar with the syntax, it might make sense to you, but learning Markdown itself and another Markdown language at the same time probably does more harm than good.

Wikis are very simple. There is a home page that you can edit, and you can add a custom sidebar and footer. Links to other pages are specified in double braces as [[Page Name]]. If you want a separate link text, you can use the [[Link Text|Page Name]] format. If you create a link to a page that does not exist yet, it gets displayed in red, and you can create a page by clicking the link.

A wiki is a Git repository with the same name as the repository and the .wiki extension (<name_of_repository>.wiki). You can clone a repository and work locally in branches with a wiki. But unfortunately, up to now there is no way to use pull requests to collaborate on the changes! This is the biggest downside of GitHub wikis!

Also, wikis do not support nested pages. All pages are in the root of the repository. You can use the sidebar to create a menu with a hierarchy using Markdown nested lists, as follows:

```
[[Home]]
* [[Page 1]]
  * [[Page 1.1]]
  * [[Page 1.2]]
```

If you want parts of the menu to be collapsible, you can use the <details></details> GitHub Markdown feature. This creates a collapsible part in Markdown, and with <summary></summary> you can customize the heading, as follows:

```
* [[Page 2]]
  * <details>
    <summary>[[Page 2.1]] (Click to open)</summary>

      * [[Page 2.1.1]]
      * [[Page 2.1.2]]

    </details>
```

Note that the blank lines are necessary for this to work! The result looks like in Figure 4.14:

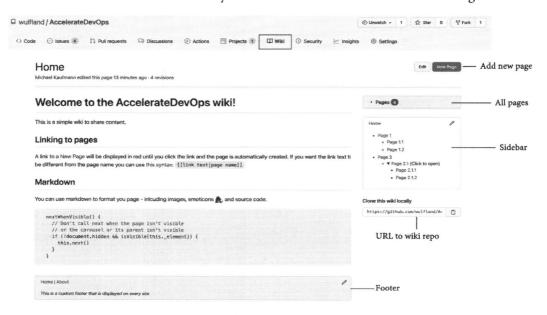

Figure 4.14 – The structure of a GitHub wiki

The GitHub wiki is a very simple wiki solution and lacks many features that other wiki solutions have, especially as you cannot use pull requests, which limits its benefits for asynchronous workflows. But luckily, you can host the Markdown in your own repository and build a custom wiki yourself.

A custom wiki

If you don't want the complexity of GitHub Pages but you still want to work with pull requests on your wiki, you can just put Markdown files into your repository. GitHub will automatically render a ToC for all your Markdown files (see *Figure 4.15*). You may have already noticed this in README files in GitHub repositories:

Auto-generated ToC for all
markdown files in GitHub

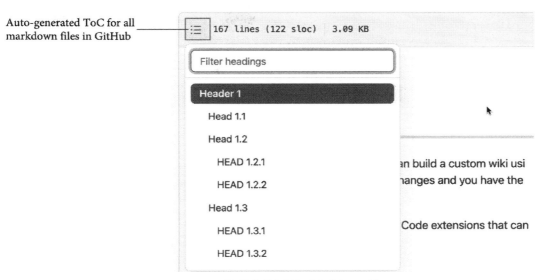

Figure 4.15 – GitHub TOC for Markdown files

The problem with a custom wiki is the navigation. It is easy to build a navigation system using Markdown nested lists and relative links. You can also make it collapsible with `details`, as illustrated in the following code snippet:

```
<details>
    <summary>Menu</summary>

* [Home](#Header-1)
* [Page1](Page1.md)
  * [Page 1.1](Page1-1.md)
  * [Page 1.2](Page1-2.md)
* [Page2](Page2.md)

</details>
```

But if you need it to be on every page, you must copy-paste it to all pages when you change it. You could automate this, but it would still clutter your history. It's better to have breadcrumb-like navigation on every page that people can use to navigate back to the home page and use the menu from there. You can see an example of a custom navigation in Markdown here: `https://github.com/wulfland/AccelerateDevOps/blob/main/ch4_customWiki/Home.md`.

From a community forum, to simple Markdown wikis to a fully customizable web page with Jekyll, there are many options to host additional content for your work on GitHub. Choosing the right one for the task at hand is not easy. Sometimes, you'll just have to try to figure out what works for your team.

Working from everywhere with GitHub Mobile

Most of the time, you will collaborate on GitHub issues, pull requests, and discussions from your browser. But there are also other options that help you to bring GitHub to where you are.

GitHub Mobile is a mobile app that is available for Android and Apple through their marketplaces (see `https://github.com/mobile`). The app gives you access to all your issues, pull requests, and discussions in all your repositories. It has a dark mode and a light mode, and you can pin your favorite repositories to the start screen (see *Figure 4.16*):

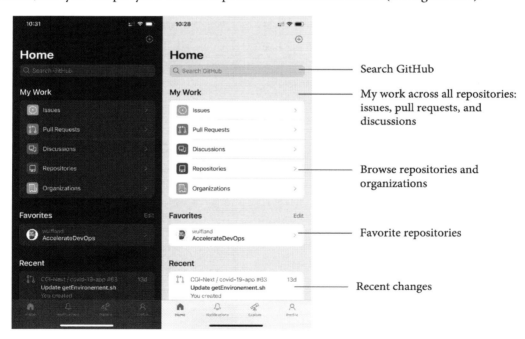

Figure 4.16 – GitHub Mobile home page in dark and light mode

I personally love the GitHub Mobile app—it is very well crafted and helps you in your everyday work to be independent of your workstation or laptop and collaborate on issues and discussions. You can configure notifications so that you get notified when you are mentioned and assigned, or when a review had been requested. The notifications appear in your inbox and you can use configurable swipe actions to mark the notification as **Done**, **Read**, or **Unread**; to save the notification; or to unsubscribe from the notification source. The default mark options are Done and Save. The inbox looks like in Figure 4.17:

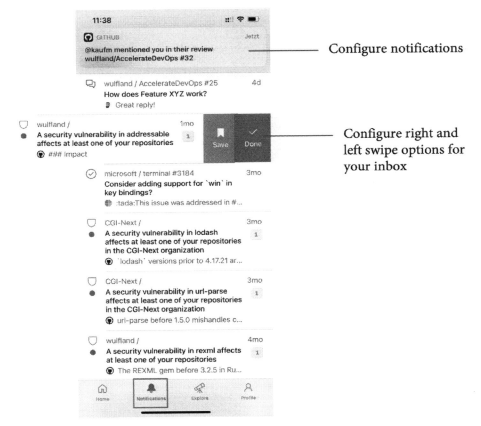

Figure 4.17 – Notifications in GitHub Mobile

What impressed me the most when I used the app for the first time is how well the code review experience works on mobile devices. You can turn line wrapping on, which makes it easy to read the code, see changes, and comment on them (see *Figure 4.18*):

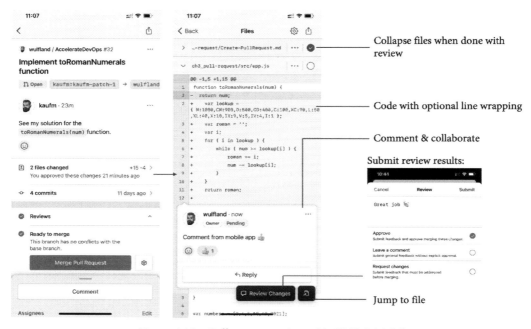

Figure 4.18 – Pull request review with GitHub Mobile

GitHub Mobile is a great way to unblock your teammates, even if you are not in the office. It allows you to participate in discussions and comment on code changes and issues. The possibility to review small changes on the go can help your team to move to smaller batch sizes of work because you have smaller wait times for approvals.

Case study

The first thing our two pilot teams at **Tailwind Gears** do is move their code over to a GitHub repository. One team is already using **Git** on a Bitbucket server. For that team, the migration is as easy as pushing the repository to a new remote. The other team is using **Team Foundation Server** (**TFS**) version control and must migrate the code to Git first on the server before pushing it to GitHub.

Both teams decide to participate in 2-day **Git training** to be able to leverage the full power of Git and craft good commits that are easy to review. They use **draft pull requests** so that everyone in the team always knows what the others are working on, and they set a minimum of two **required reviewers** for the time being.

Many of the work is still outside the repositories and happens in Word, Excel, and Visio documents that are stored on the company SharePoint server. Some of the documents are converted to **Portable Document Format** (**PDF**) and are signed off by management before releasing the product that is compliant with certain regulations. There are too many documents to convert all at once to Markdown. The teams create a **custom Markdown-based wiki** in their code repository to have everything close to the code. They add links to the current documents in SharePoint. Every time a change to a document is necessary, the content will be moved to the Markdown file and the link will be removed. Instead of signing PDF documents, management gets added as **code owners** to the corresponding files and approves the changes directly in the pull request. Together with the audit log, this is valid for all necessary compliance audits.

When moving to the new platform, many aspects are relevant for both teams, and later will be for other teams as they also move over to the new platform. That's why they create a shared platform repository. The repository contains **GitHub Discussions** to collaborate with all engineers, even those who are not yet in one of the two teams. A technical blog is set up using **GitHub Pages** to share tips and tricks. The Jekyll site is also used to collaborate on common review guidelines and a code of conduct.

Summary

In this chapter, you've learned the advantages and disadvantages of synchronous and asynchronous work. You can use this to create effective, asynchronous workflows that allow for better cross-team collaboration and enable you to have remote and hybrid teams that can span multiple areas and time zones. You've learned how GitHub Discussions, Pages, and wikis can help you to have asynchronous workflows for topics other than code and requirements.

In the next chapter, I will explain the influence of open and inner sources on your software delivery performance.

Further readings and references

Here are the references from this chapter that you can also use to get more information on the topics:

- History of communication: `https://en.wikipedia.org/wiki/History_of_communication`, `https://www.g2.com/articles/history-of-communication`, and `https://www.elon.edu/u/imagining/time-capsule/150-years/`

- History in general: `https://www.dhm.de/lemo/kapitel` (German)

- World population growth: `https://ourworldindata.org/world-population-growth`

- Hybrid work: `https://www.microsoft.com/en-us/worklab/work-trend-index/hybrid-work`

- Work trend index: `https://www.microsoft.com/en-us/worklab/work-trend-index`

- GitHub Discussions: `https://docs.github.com/en/discussions`

- GitHub Pages: `https://docs.github.com/en/pages`

- GitHub Mobile: `https://github.com/mobile`

5

The Influence of Open and Inner Source on Software Delivery Performance

20 years ago, on June 1, 2001, former Microsoft CEO Steve Ballmer said the following in an interview with the Chicago Sunday Times:

"Linux is a cancer that attaches itself in an intellectual property sense to everything it touches."

(Greene T. C. (2001))

His concern was not only **Linux** but **open source** licenses in general. Now, 20 years later, Microsoft is the single largest contributor to open source in the world, beating Facebook, Google, Red Hat, and SUSE. Not only do they have many open source products, such as PowerShell, Visual Studio Code, and .NET, they also ship a complete Linux kernel with

Windows 10 so that you can run any distribution on it. Microsoft president Brad Smith admits that "*Microsoft was on the wrong side of history when open source exploded at the beginning of the century*" (*Warren T. (2020)*).

If you look at the top 10 companies that contribute to open source, you will find all the big tech companies that make commercial software:

	Company	Active Contributors	Total Community
1	Microsoft	5,368	10,924
2	Google	4,907	9,635
3	Red Hat	3,211	4,738
4	IBM	2,125	5,062
5	Intel	1,901	3,982
6	Amazon	1,742	4,415
7	Facebook	1,350	4,017
8	GitHub	1,122	2,871
9	SAP	811	1,606
10	VMware	786	1,604

Table 5.1 – Open Source Contributor Index, August 2, 2021 (https://opensourceindex.io/)

What has changed in the last two decades, such that important tech companies now embrace open source?

In this chapter, I will explain the history of free and open source software and why it has become so important over the last few years. I will explain the impact it can have on your engineering velocity and how you can use the principles of open source for better cross-team collaboration in your company (inner source).

The chapter will cover the following topics:

- History of free and open source software
- The difference between open source and open development
- Benefits of embracing open source for companies
- Implementing an open source strategy
- Open and inner source
- The importance of insourcing
- GitHub Sponsors

History of free and open source software

To understand open source, we must go back to the early days of computer science.

Public domain software

During the 1950s and 1960s, the price of software was low compared to the necessary hardware. Any software that was produced was mainly produced by academics and corporate research teams. It was normal for the source code to be distributed with the software – normally as **public domain software**. This means that the software is freely available without ownership, copyright, trademark, or patent. These principles of openness and cooperation had a great influence on the **hacker culture** at that time.

In the late 1960s, the rise of operating systems and compilers increased the costs of software. This was driven by a growing software industry that competed with hardware vendors that bundled their software together with their hardware.

During the 1970s and 1980s, it became common to sell licenses for the use of software and in 1983, IBM stopped distributing their source code together with purchased software. Other software vendors followed their example.

Free software

Richard Stallman was convinced that this is ethically wrong, and he founded the **GNU Project** in 1983 and, shortly later, the **free software movement**. The free software movement believes that software is considered free if the receiver of the software is allowed to do the following:

- Run the program for any purpose.
- Study the software and change it in any way.
- Redistribute the program and make copies of it.
- Improve the software and release the improvements.

Richard founded the **Free Software Foundation (FSF)** in 1985. The FSF is famous for the following saying:

> *"Free as in free speech – not free as in free beer."*

This means that the word *free* means freedom to distribute and not freedom from cost (*Gratis versus libre*). Since much of the free software already was free of charge, such gratis software (Freeware) became associated with free software and zero cost.

The free software movement created a concept called **copyleft**. This grants users the right to use and modify the software, but it preserves the free status of the software. Examples of these licenses include the GNU **General Public License (GPL)**, the Apache License, and the **Mozilla Public License (MPL)**.

Most of the great software that still runs today on millions of devices has been distributed with those copyleft licenses; for example, the **Linux kernel** (published 1992 by *Linus Torvalds*), BSD, MySQL, and Apache.

Open source software

In May 1997, at the Linux congress in Würzburg, Germany, *Eric Raymond* introduced his paper *The Cathedral and the Bazaar* (*Raymond, E. S. 1999*). He reflected on free software principles and the hacker culture and the benefits for software development. The paper received a lot of attention and motivated Netscape to release its browser, **Netscape Communicator**, as free software.

Raymond and others wanted to bring free software principles to more commercial software vendors, but the term *free software* had a negative connotation for commercial software companies.

On February 3, 1998, in Palo Alto, many important people from the free software movement met for a strategy session to discuss the future of free software. Among the participants were *Eric Raymond*, *Michael Tiemann*, and *Christine Peterson*, who are credited with proposing the term **open source** in favor of free software.

The **Open Source Initiative (OSI)** was founded by *Eric Raymond* and *Bruce Perens* in late February 1998, with Raymond as the first president (*OSI 2018*).

In 1998, at publisher *Tim O'Reilly's* historical *Freeware Summit* – later named *Open Source Summit* – the term was swiftly adopted by early supports such as *Linus Torvalds*, *Larry Wall* (creator of Perl), *Brian Behlendorf* (Apache), *Eric Allman* (Sendmail), *Guido van Rossum* (Python), and *Phil Zimmerman* (PGP) (*O'Reilly 1998*).

But *Richard Stallman* and the FSF rejected the new term *open source* (*Richard S. 2021*). That's why the **Free Open Source Software** (**FOSS**) movement is divided and still uses different terminology today.

In the late 1990s and early 2000s, in the dotcom bubble, the terms **open source** and **open source software** (**OSS**) were widely adopted by the public media and ended up as the more popular terms.

The rise of open source software

In the last two decades, open source has continuously increased in popularity. Software such as Linux and Apache drives most of the internet. In the beginning, it was hard to commercialize OSS. The first idea was to provide enterprise-scale support services around the open source products. The companies that had success with this were Red Hat and MySQL. But it was much harder and didn't have the scale that commercial licensing provided. So, the open source companies that invested heavily in building OSS started to create **open core** products: a free, open source core product, as well as commercial add-ons, that could be bought by their customers.

The transition of the software business model from classical licenses to **Software as a Service** (**SaaS**) subscriptions helped the open source companies commercialize their OSS. This motivated traditional software vendors to release their software – at least the core – as open source to engage with the community.

Not only did the big software companies such as Microsoft, Google, IBM, and Amazon become big open source companies. Pure open source companies such as Red Hat and MuleSoft have also gained a lot of worth and market recognition. Red Hat, for example, was acquired by IBM in 2018 for 32 billion US dollars. MuleSoft was acquired in the same year by Salesforce for $6.5 billion.

So, open source today is not from the revolutionary minds that create alternative, free software. Most of the top-notch software that fuels the software and platform services of the cloud providers is open source software (*Volpi M. 2019*).

The difference between open source and open development

So, OSS refers to computer programs is released under a license that grants users the rights to use, study, modify, and share the software and its source code.

But putting your source code in the public under a copyleft license is just the first step. If a company wants to have all the benefits of open source, it must adopt the open source values, which leads to something that is called **open development** or **development in the open**. This means that you do not just give access to the source code. Instead, you must make the entire development and product management transparent. This includes the following:

- Requirements
- Architecture and research
- Meetings
- Standards

The .NET team is a good example of a team that hosts their community standup on Twitch and YouTube (see `https://dotnet.microsoft.com/live/community-standup`).

Open development also means creating an open and inclusive environment in which everyone feels safe to propose changes. This includes a strong code of ethics and a clean code base with a high degree of automation that allows everyone to quickly and easily contribute.

Benefits of embracing open source for companies

So, how is open source connected to better development performance and how can your company benefit from a good open source strategy?

Deliver faster with open source software

Depending on the sources, new products already consist of 70% to 90% open source code. This means that you will write 70% to 90% less code yourself, which can increase your time to market significantly.

Besides reusing open source code in your product, a lot of platform tooling is available as open source. Reusable GitHub Actions, test tooling, or container orchestration… the most efficient and robust tooling you can use to deliver software faster is, in most cases, open source software.

Build better products by engaging the community

If you develop some parts of your products in the open, you can leverage the hive mind of the community to build better and more secure software. It also helps you get early feedback on what you are doing from great engineers around the world.

Especially for complicated, critical, and security-relevant software, engaging with the community often results in better solutions:

> *"The bigger the problem, the more open source developers are drawn, like magnets, to work on it."*

> *(Ahlawat P., Boyne J., Herz D., Schmieg F., & Stephan M. (2021))*

Use tools with a lower risk of obsolescence

Using open source can reduce the risk that a tool becomes obsolete. If you build tools yourself, you must maintain them yourself – which is not your priority. Using tools from small vendors or having them built by partners introduces the risk that the tools do not get maintained or the partner goes out of the market. Investing in open source tools instead can significantly reduce these risks.

Attract talent

Giving your engineers the ability to leverage open source in their work and contribute to open source projects during their work hours can have a significant impact on your hiring abilities. Being engaged in the community and playing a part in open source will help you attract talent.

Influence emerging technologies and standards

Many emerging technologies and standards are developed in the open. Contributing to these initiatives gives your company the ability to influence these technologies and be a part of bleeding-edge development.

Improve your process by learning from open source projects

And, of course, if you embrace open source, your company can learn about collaborative development and apply these principles to improve the cross-team collaboration inside your company (called **inner source**).

Implementing an open source strategy

But with all the benefits of embracing open source, there also are some risks you must address. You must be careful and be license-compliant when you use open source software in your products and toolchains. You must also take on the liability yourself if the open source component causes damage as you don't have a vendor you can sue. Also, there are risks involved if you take on too many dependencies – direct or indirect – and one of them breaks.

> **Note**
> In *Chapter 14, Securing Your Code*, you'll learn how 11 lines of code in a package and a conflict about a name caused severe damage and took off big parts of the internet.

That's why your company should set up an **open source strategy**. This strategy should define what types of open source software developers can use for what purpose. There might be different rules for different purposes. If you want to include open source in your products, you will need some kind of governance to manage the associated risks.

The strategy should also define whether developers are allowed to contribute to open source during work time and what the conditions are for that.

I will not dig deeper into the details of the strategy. It depends a lot on how you plan to use open source and how you develop and release your products. Just make sure your company has a document for your open source strategy – even if it is small. It will evolve as the maturity and experience of open source will grow.

One recommendation is to implement a center or a community of excellence that helps you develop a strategy that developers can turn to if they have questions or are unsure of whether an open source component is compliant (*Ahlawat P., Boyne J., Herz D., Schmieg F., & Stephan M. 2021*).

Open and inner source

The success of open source lies in its open and collaborative culture. Getting the right people to voluntarily collaborate over a big distance asynchronously can help solve a problem in the best way possible. The principles are as follows:

- Open collaboration
- Open communication
- Code reviews

Applying these principles to proprietary software within an organization is called **inner source**. This term is credited to Tim O'Reilly from 2000. Inner source can be a great way to break down silos and foster strong collaboration across teams and products.

But like **open source** and **open development**, just making your code available is not sufficient to create an inner source culture. Many success factors influence whether the inner source approach can succeed:

- **Modular product architecture**: If you have a big, monolithic architecture, this will keep people from contributing. Also, the quality of the code, the documentation, and how fast you can understand the code and contribute have a big influence on how inner source is adopted.

- **Standardized tools and processes**: If every team has a toolchain and workflows, it will also exclude other engineers from contributing. Having a common engineering system and similar approaches for branching and CI/CD will help others focus on the problems and not be hindered by having to learn other tools and workflows first.

- **Autonomy and self-organization**: So long as your organization pushes requirements to your teams and the engineers are busy keeping to their deadlines, contributions to other teams will not happen. Only if the teams can prioritize autonomously and work in a self-organized fashion will they have the freedom to participate in other communities – both open and inner source.

Inner source can help break down silos and increase your engineering velocity. But it is also related to a high level of DevOps maturity. Inner source is something that evolves together with your increased DevOps capabilities and open source maturity. So, treat it as an output rather than an input to your acceleration.

> **Note**
> Technically, inner source is normally done by activating forking in your enterprise. This goes hand in hand with your branching workflows, which we'll cover in *Chapter 11, Trunk-Based Development*.

The importance of insourcing

Many companies do not see software development as their core business, so they tend to outsource it. **Outsourcing** means one company hiring another company or freelancer to perform a specific function. Outsourcing is usually not a bad idea: you have another company that is specialized in one thing do the work for you so that you can put your people and investments in your core products. The specialized company normally does things cheaper and better – and building up these skills yourself can take a lot of time and money.

But now, software is the key differentiator for basically all products. Not only the digital customer experience but also smart manufacturing or supply chain management can give you a competitive advantage. Custom software is becoming part of your core business. Due to this, many companies already have an **insourcing** strategy for software development – that is, recruiting and employing software developers and DevOps engineers in-house.

The problem is that the market for software developers and DevOps engineers is highly competitive (the so-called **war for talent**). This often leads to a scattered landscape where partners work on core products and the developers maintain tooling.

A good insourcing strategy is to ask yourself whether the software is core to your business – that is, whether it gives you a competitive advantage:

- **Core software** should be developed by internal developers. If you can't hire enough skilled developers, you can **co-source** and augment your staff with the engineers of one of your trusted partners. But the goal should always be to replace these developers with your engineers later.

- **Supplementary software** can be outsourced. In the best case, you can use an already existing product for it. If there is no such product, you can have a partner build it. And here is where **open source** comes into play: you can leverage existing open source solutions or have your partner build the solution in the open. This reduces the risk of you being the only customer and the solution becoming obsolete. Since the software is only supplementary to your business, you don't care if other companies also use it. The contrary is that the more your software is used, the smaller the risk of the software becoming obsolete. Also, the quality is reliable if the software is developed in the open.

Paying other companies or individuals to develop special open source software for you or adding features to existing open source solutions is not very common. But with more and more companies having an insourcing strategy and the continuing war for talent, this will significantly increase over the next few years.

GitHub Sponsors

An **open source strategy** seems to conflict with an **insourcing strategy** at first. But the matter is more complex. It might be more useful to the core software to contribute a small feature to an open source project than to implement a workaround yourself. But in many companies, the **make-or-buy decision** at a team level is always decided in favor of making because the process of buying or funding something with money is too complex. A good insourcing strategy should always include a lightweight and fast process with some budget to invest in tools and the software supply chain. If your company is low on in-house developers, buying software or sponsoring open source contributors should be no problem.

A good way to give your teams the ability to invest in open source projects is by utilizing a feature called **GitHub Sponsors**. It allows you to invest in the projects your product depends on (your **software supply chain**) and keeps those projects alive. It can also give the maintainers freedom to write **newly requested features** instead of you having to implement them yourself.

A positive side effect is the sponsorship becoming **visible** to the open source community. This is good marketing and gives your company credibility and can help you **attract new talent**.

You can sponsor individual developers or organizations when they are part of the *GitHub Sponsors* program. You can also sponsor them on behalf of your organization. This sponsorship can be a one-time or monthly payment and is visible in your profile or the profile of your organization (see *Figure 5.1*):

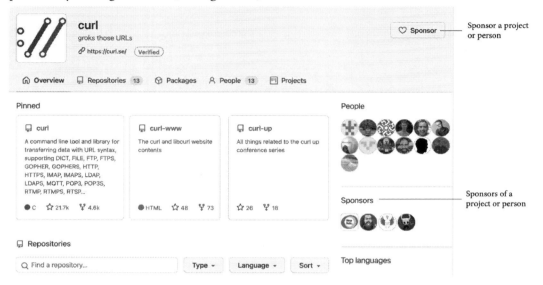

Figure 5.1 – Enabled organization profile in GitHub Sponsors

GitHub Sponsors does not charge any fees for sponsorships from user accounts, so 100% of these sponsorships go to the sponsored developer or organization.

Sponsor tiers

Sponsors can set up different tiers for sponsoring. This can be done for one-time sponsorships as well as for recurring monthly payments (see *Figure 5.2*):

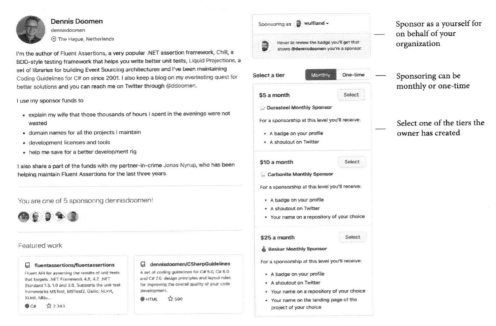

Figure 5.2 – Monthly or One-time tier options

The owner can set up to 10 tiers monthly and up to 10 tiers for one-time payments. This lets them link customized rewards to the different tiers. For example, the rewards could be as follows:

- **Visibility**: Sponsors can be mentioned on the website or social media. There may also be badges (such as Silver, Gold, and Platinum Sponsors) that are used to distinguish different levels of sponsorship.

- **Access**: Sponsors can get access to private repositories or early versions.

- **Prioritization**: Bugs or feature requests from sponsors can be prioritized.

- **Support**: Some sponsors also offer support (to a certain degree) for the solution.

Let's look at sponsorship goals next.

Sponsorship goals

Sponsored accounts can set a funding goal. The goal can be based on the number of sponsors or the sponsorship in dollars per month and is displayed on the sponsorship page (see *Figure 5.3*):

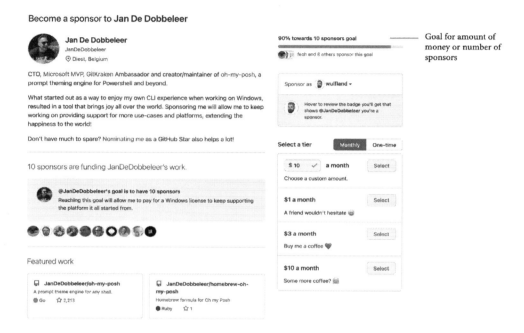

Figure 5.3 – Python's sponsorship goal of getting $12,000 per month

Sponsorship goals can be linked to certain milestones. For example, the maintainer can set a certain amount when they quit their day job and start working full-time on the project. The org can also set the amount required to hire a new developer to help maintain the project.

Summary

In this chapter, you learned about the **history**, **values**, and **principles** of **free and open source software** and the impact it can have on your software delivery performance. A good **open source strategy**, combined with a good **insourcing strategy** and the ability for your teams to sponsor and fund open source projects, can help you shorten your time to market significantly and have your engineers work on the features that matter for your company. Applying the principles to your company as **inner source** can help you build a collaborative culture and achieve better cross-team collaboration.

In the next chapter, we will learn about automation with GitHub Actions.

Further reading and references

Please refer to the following materials for more information about what was covered in this chapter:

- Greene T. C. (2001). *Ballmer: Linux is a cancer*: `https://www.theregister.com/2001/06/02/ballmer_linux_is_a_cancer/`.

- Warren T. (2020). *Microsoft: we were wrong about open source*: `https://www.theverge.com/2020/5/18/21262103/microsoft-open-source-linux-history-wrong-statement`.

- Raymond, E. S. (1999). *The Cathedral and the Bazaar: Musings on Linux and Open Source by an Accidental Revolutionary*. O'Reilly Media.

- O'Reilly (1998). *FREEWARE LEADERS MEET IN FIRST-EVER SUMMIT O'Reilly Brings Together Creators of Perl, Apache, Linux, and Netscape's Mozilla* (Press Release): `https://www.oreilly.com/pub/pr/636`.

- OSI (2018). *Open Source Initiative - History of the OSI*: `https://opensource.org/history`.

- Richard S. (2021). *Why Open Source Misses the Point of Free Software*: `https://www.gnu.org/philosophy/open-source-misses-the-point.en.html`.

- Volpi M. (2019). *How open-source software took over the world*: `https://techcrunch.com/2019/01/12/how-open-source-software-took-over-the-world/`.

- Ahlawat P., Boyne J., Herz D., Schmieg F., & Stephan M. (2021). *Why You Need an Open Source Software Strategy*: `https://www.bcg.com/publications/2021/open-source-software-strategy-benefits`.

- *Inner Source*: `https://en.wikipedia.org/wiki/Inner_source`.

- *GitHub Sponsors*: `https://github.com/sponsors`.

Part 2: Engineering DevOps Practices

Part 2 explains the most important engineering practices for effective DevOps. You'll learn how to use GitHub Actions to automate your release pipelines and other engineering tasks, how to work with trunks and feature flags, and how to shift left security and quality assurance.

This part of the book comprises the following chapters:

- *Chapter 6, Automation with GitHub Actions*
- *Chapter 7, Running Your Workflows*
- *Chapter 8, Managing Dependencies Using GitHub Packages*
- *Chapter 9, Deploy to Any Platform*
- *Chapter 10, Feature Flags and the Feature Lifecycle*
- *Chapter 11, Trunk-Based Development*

6
Automation with GitHub Actions

Many agile adoptions treat engineering practices as less important than management and team practices. But engineering capabilities such as **continuous integration (CI)**, **continuous delivery (CD)**, and **Infrastructure as Code (IaC)** are enablers for more frequent, more stable, and lower-risk releases (*Humble, J., & Farley, D. 2010*). These practices lead to less deployment pain and therefore less overtime and burnout.

Essentially, all these practices are about automation: computers performing repetitive tasks so that people can focus on important problems and creative work.

"*Computers perform repetitive tasks, people solve problems.*"

Forsgren, N., Humble, J., & Kim, G. 2018

Automation has a big influence on corporate culture and the way people work because many habits are created to avoid manual, repetitive tasks – especially if they are error-prone. In this chapter, I will introduce you to GitHub Actions – the automation engine from GitHub that you can use for so much more than just CI/CD.

This chapter will cover the following topics:

- Overview of GitHub Actions
- Workflows, pipelines, and actions
- YAML basics
- The workflow syntax
- Working with secrets
- Hands-on – your first workflow
- Hands-on – your first action
- The GitHub marketplace

Overview of GitHub Actions

GitHub Actions is the native automation engine on GitHub. It allows you to run workflows on any event in GitHub – not only commits to source control! GitHub can trigger your workflows when an issue changes its state or is added to a milestone, when a card is moved in GitHub Projects, when someone clicks *Star* on your repository, or when a comment is added to a discussion. There are triggers for nearly everything. The workflows themselves are built for reuse. You can build reusable actions by just putting code in a repository. Alternatively, you can share actions through the **GitHub Marketplace** (`https://github.com/marketplace`), which currently contains about 10,000 actions.

These workflows can be executed in the cloud on every major platform: Linux, macOS, Windows, ARM, and containers. You can even configure and host runners – in the cloud or your data center – without the need to open incoming ports.

> **GitHub Learning Lab**
>
> A good place to learn about GitHub is **GitHub Learning Lab** (`https://lab.github.com`). It's completely hands-on and is automated with issues and pull requests. There is a complete learning path for **DevOps with GitHub Actions** (`https://lab.github.com/githubtraining/devops-with-github-actions`). Alternatively, you can take individual courses such as **GitHub Actions: Hello World** (`https://lab.github.com/githubtraining/github-actions:-hello-world`). All the courses are free. Give it a try – especially if you are a hands-on learner and you don't have experience with GitHub.

Workflows, pipelines, and actions

A **workflow** in GitHub is a configurable, automated process that consists of different **jobs**. It can be configured in a **YAML** file and is stored in the `.github/workflows` directory of a repository. A workflow can be used to build and deploy software to different environments or stages and is often called a **pipeline** in other CI/CD systems.

A **job** is a part of the workflow that is executed on a configured runner. The runner environment is configured using the `runs-on` attribute. Jobs run in parallel by default. They can be executed sequentially by chaining them together using dependencies (using the `needs` keyword). A job can run in a specific environment. An **environment** is a logical grouping of resources. Environments can be shared in multiple workflows and can be protected using **protection rules**.

A job consists of a sequence of tasks called **steps**. A **step** can run a command, script, or **GitHub Action**. An **action** is a reusable part of the workflow. Not all steps are actions – but all actions are executed as steps inside a job.

The following table shows the most important terms for understanding workflows:

Noun	Description
Workflow	Automated process. Often referred to as a pipeline.
Job	A part of the workflow that consists of a sequence of tasks that are executed on a runner.
Runner	A virtual or physical machine or container that executes a job of a workflow. Can be cloud-hosted or self-hosted. Also referred to an agent.
Step	A single task that is executed as part of a job.
Action	A reusable step that can be used in different jobs and workflows. This can be a Docker container, JavaScript, or a composite action that consists of other steps. It can also be shared via the GitHub marketplace.
Environment	A logical group of resources that can share the same protection rules and secrets. Environments can be used in multiple workflows.

Table 6.1 – Important terms for GitHub Actions

YAML basics

Workflows are written in YAML files that have either a `.yml` or `.yaml` extension. **YAML** (which stands for *YAML Ain't Markup Language*) is a data serialization language that's optimized to be directly writable and readable by humans. It is a strict superset of **JSON** but contains syntactically relevant newlines and indentation instead of braces. Like markdown, it also works very well with pull requests as changes are always per line. Let's look at some YAML basics that should help you get started.

Comments

A comment in YAML starts with a hash, #:

```
# A comment in YAML
```

Scalar types

Single values can be defined using the following syntax:

```
key: value
```

Many data types are supported:

```
integer: 42
float: 42.0
string: a text value
boolean: true
null value: null
datetime: 1999-12-31T23:59:43.1Z
```

Note that keys and values can contain spaces and do not need quotation. But you can quote both keys and values with single or double quotes:

```
'single quotes': 'have ''one quote'' as the escape pattern'
"double quotes": "have the \"backslash \" escape pattern"
```

Strings that span multiple lines – such as script blocks – use the pipe symbol, |, and indentation:

```
literal_block: |
    Text blocks use 4 spaces as indentation. The entire
    block is assigned to the key 'literal_block' and keeps
    line breaks and empty lines.

    The block continuous until the next element.
```

Collection types

Nested array types – also known as **maps** – are often used in workflows. They use two spaces of indentation:

```
nested_type:
  key1: value1
  key2: value2
  another_nested_type:
    key1: value1
```

A sequence uses a dash, –, before each item:

```
sequence:
  - item1
  - item2
```

Since YAML is a superset of JSON, you can also use the JSON syntax to put sequences and maps in one line:

```
map: {key: value}
sequence: [item1, item2, item3]
```

This should be enough to get you started with workflow editing on GitHub. If you want to learn more about YAML, you can have a look at the specification at https://yaml.org/. Now, let's have a look at the workflow syntax.

The workflow syntax

The first thing you will see in your workflow file is its name, which is displayed under **Actions** in your repository:

```
name: My first workflow
```

This name is followed by triggers.

Workflow triggers

Triggers are the values for the on key:

```
on: push
```

Triggers can contain multiple values:

```
on: [push, pull_request]
```

Many triggers contain other values that can be configured:

```
on:
  push:
    branches:
      - main
      - release/**
  pull_request:
    types: [opened, assigned]
```

There are three types of triggers:

- Webhook events
- Scheduled events
- Manual events

Webhooks events are what you have seen so far. There are webhook events for nearly everything: if you push code to GitHub (push), if you create or update a pull request (pull_request), or if you create or modify an issue (issues). For a complete list, go to https://docs.github.com/en/actions/reference/events-that-trigger-workflows.

Scheduled events use the same syntax as cron jobs. The syntax consists of five fields that represent the minute (0 – 59), the hour (0 – 23), the day of the month (1 – 31), month (1 – 12 or JAN – DEC), and the day of the week (0 – 6 or SUN-SAT). You can use the operators shown in the following table:

Operator	Description
*	Any value
,	List separator
-	Range of values
/	Step values

Table 6.2 – Operators for scheduled events

Here are some examples:

```
on:
  schedule:
    # Runs at every 15th minute of every day
    - cron: '*/15 * * * *'
    # Runs every hour from 9am to 5pm
    - cron: '0 9-17 * * *'
    # Runs every Friday at midnight
    - cron: '0 0 * * FRI'
    # Runs every quarter (00:00 on day 1 every 3rd month)
    - cron: '0 0 1 */3 *'
```

Manual events allow you to trigger the workflow manually:

```
on: workflow_dispatch
```

You can configure **inputs** that the users can (or must) specify when they start the workflow. The following example defines a variable named homedrive that you can use in the workflow using the ${{ github.event.inputs.homedrive }} expression:

```
on:
  workflow_dispatch:
    inputs:
      homedrive:
        description: 'The home drive on the machine'
        required: true
        default: '/home'
```

You can also trigger the workflow using the GitHub API. For this, you must define a repository_dispatch trigger and specify one or more names for the events you want to use:

```
on:
  repository_dispatch:
    types: [event1, event2]
```

The workflow then gets triggered when an *HTTP POST* request is sent. Here is an example using `curl` to send the HTTP POST:

```
curl \
  -X POST \
  -H "Accept: application/vnd.github.v3+json" \
  https://api.github.com/repos/<owner>/<repo>/dispatches \
  -d '{"event_type":"event1"}'
```

Here is an example using JavaScript (see `https://github.com/octokit/octokit.js` for more details about **Octokit** API clients for JavaScript):

```
await octokit.request('POST /repos/{owner}/{repo}/dispatches',
{
  owner: '<owner>',
  repo: '<repo>',
  event_type: 'event1'
})
```

Using the `repository_dispatch` trigger, you can use any webhook in any system to trigger your workflows. This helps you automate workflows and integrate other systems.

Workflow jobs

The workflow itself is configured in the `jobs` section. Jobs are maps, not a list, and they run in parallel by default. If you want to chain them in a sequence, you can have a job depend on other jobs with the `needs` keyword:

```
jobs:
  job_1:
    name: My first job
  job_2:
    name: My second job
    needs: job_1
  job_3:
    name: My third job
    needs: [job_1, job_2]
```

Every job is executed on a runner. The runner can be self-hosted, or you can pick one from the cloud. There are different versions available in the cloud for all platforms. If you always want to use the latest version, you can use `ubuntu-latest`, `windows-latest`, or `macos-latest`. You'll learn more about runners in *Chapter 7, Running Your Workflows*:

```
jobs:
  job_1:
    name: My first job
    runs-on: ubuntu-latest
```

If you want to run a workflow with different configurations, you can use a **matrix strategy**. The workflow will execute all the combinations of all the configured matrix values. The keys in the matrix can be anything and you can refer to them using the `${{ matrix.key }}` expression:

```
strategy:
  matrix:
    os_version: [macos-latest, ubuntu-latest]
    node_version: [10, 12, 14]

jobs:
  job_1:
    name: My first job
    runs-on: ${{ matrix.os_version }}
    steps:
      - uses: actions/setup-node@v2
        with:
          node-version: ${{ matrix.node_version }}
```

Workflow steps

A job contains a sequence of steps, and each step can run a command:

```
steps:
  - name: Install Dependencies
    run: npm install
```

Literal blocks allow you to run multi-line scripts. If you want the workflow to run in a different shell than the default shell, you can configure it together with other values, such as `working-directory`:

```
- name: Clean install dependencies and build
  run: |
    npm ci
    npm run build
  working-directory: ./temp
  shell: bash
```

The following shells are available:

Parameter	Description
bash	Bash shell. This is the default shell on all non-Windows platforms with a fallback to `sh`. When specified on Windows, the Bash shell that's included with Git is used.
pwsh	PowerShell Core. Default on the Windows platform.
python	The Python shell. Allows you to run Python scripts.
cmd	Windows only! The Windows Command Prompt.
powershell	Windows only! The classic Windows PowerShell.

Table 6.3 – Available shells in workflows

The default shell on non-Windows systems is `bash` with a fallback to `sh`. The default on Windows is `cmd`. You can also configure a custom shell with the `command [options] {0}` syntax:

```
run: print %ENV
shell: perl {0}
```

Most of the time, you will reuse steps. A reusable step is called a **GitHub Action**. You can reference an action using the `uses` keyword and the following syntax:

```
{owner}/{repo}@{ref}
```

{owner}/{repo} is the path to the action on GitHub. The {ref} reference is the version: it can be a label, a branch, or an individual commit referenced by its **Hash** value. The most common application is using labels for explicit versioning with major and minor versions:

```
# Reference a version using a label
- uses: actions/checkout@v2
- uses: actions/checkout@v2.2.0
# Reference the current head of a branch
- uses: actions/checkout@main
# Reference a specific commit
- uses: actions/checkout@a81bbbf8298c0fa03ea29cdc473d45769f953
675
```

If your action is in the same repository as the workflow, you can use a relative path to the action:

```
uses: ./.github/actions/my-action
```

You can use actions that are stored in a container registry – for example, Docker Hub or GitHub Packages – using the docker//{image}:{tag} syntax:

```
uses: docker://alpine:3.8
```

Context and expression syntax

You saw some expressions when we looked at the matrix strategy. An **expression** has the following syntax:

```
${{ <expression> }}
```

An expression can access context information and combine it with operators. There are different objects available that provide context, such as matrix, github, env, and runner. With github.sha, for example, you can access the commit SHA that triggered the workflow. With runner.os, you can get the operating system of the runner, while with env, you can access environment variables. For a complete list, go to https://docs.github.com/en/actions/reference/context-and-expression-syntax-for-github-actions#contexts.

There are two possible syntaxes you can use to access context properties – the letter, or the property syntax, is the more common:

```
context['key']
context.key
```

Depending on the format of the key, you might have to use the first option. This might be the case if the key starts with a number or contains special characters.

Expressions are often used in the if object to run jobs on different conditions:

```
jobs:
  deploy:
    if: ${{ github.ref == 'refs/heads/main' }}
    runs-on: ubuntu-latest
    steps:
      - run: echo "Deploying branch $GITHUB_REF"
```

There are many predefined functions you can use, such as contains(search, item):

```
contains('Hello world!', 'world')
# returns true
```

Other examples of functions are startsWith() or endsWith(). There are also some special functions that you can use to check the status of the current job:

```
steps:
  ...
  - name: The job has succeeded
    if: ${{ success() }}
```

This step will only be executed if all other steps have been successful. The following table shows all the functions that can be used to respond to the current job status:

Function	Description
success()	Returns true if none of the previous steps have failed or been canceled.
always()	Returns true even if a previous step was canceled and causes the step to always be executed.
cancelled()	Returns true if the workflow was canceled.
failure()	Returns true if a previous step of the job had failed.

Table 6.4 – Special functions to check the status of the job

Besides functions, you can use operators with context and functions. The following table shows a list of the most important operators:

Operator	Description
( )	Logical group
!	Not
< , <=	Less than, less than, or equal to
> , >=	Greater than, greater than, or equal to
==	Equal
!=	Not equal
&&	And
||	Or

Table 6.5 – Operators for expressions

To learn more about context objects and the expression syntax, go to `https://docs.github.com/en/actions/reference/context-and-expression-syntax-for-github-actions`.

Workflow commands

To interact with the workflow from within your steps, you can use **workflow commands**. Workflow commands are normally passed to the process using the `echo` command and by sending a string such as `::set-output name={name}::{value}` to the process. The following example sets the output of one step and accesses it in another step. Note how the ID of the step is used to access the output variable:

```
- name: Set time
  run: |
    time=$(date)
    echo '::set-output name=MY_TIME::$time'
  id: time-gen
- name: Output time
  run: echo "It is ${{ steps.time-gen.outputs.MY_TIME }}"
```

Another example is the `::error` command. It allows you to write an error message to the log. Optionally, you can set a filename, line number, and column number:

```
::error file={name},line={line},col={col}::{message}
```

You can also write warning and debug messages, group log lines, or set environment variables. For more details on workflow commands, go to `https://docs.github.com/en/actions/reference/workflow-commands-for-github-actions`.

Working with secrets

A very important part of all automation workflows is handling secrets. It doesn't matter if you deploy an application or access an API – you always need credentials or keys that you have to handle carefully.

In GitHub, you can store secrets securely at the repository level, organization level, or for an environment. Secrets are stored and transported encrypted, and they do not show up in logs.

For secrets at the organization level, you can define which repositories have access to the secret. For secrets at an environment level, you can define required reviewers: only if they approve the workflow can they access the secrets.

> **Tip**
>
> Secret names are not case-sensitive, and they can only contain normal characters (`[a-z]` and `[A-Z]`), numbers (`[0-9]`), and the underscore character (`_`). They must not start with `GITHUB_` or a number.
>
> A best practice is to name the secrets with uppercase words that are separated by the underscore (`_`) character.

Storing your secrets

To store encrypted secrets, you must be part of the repository's Admin role. Secrets can be created through the web or via the GitHub CLI.

To create a new secret, navigate to **Settings | Secrets**. Secrets are separated into the **Actions** (default), **Codespaces**, and **Dependabot** categories. To create a new secret, press **New repository secret** and enter the name and the secret (see *Figure 6.1*):

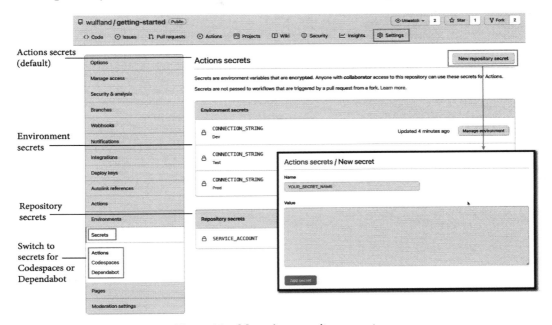

Figure 6.1 – Managing repository secrets

Secrets for organizations work more or less the same. Create the secret under **Settings | Secrets | New organization secret** and set the access policy to either of the following:

- **All repositories**

- **Private repositories**

- **Selected repositories**

When you choose **Selected repositories**, you can grant access to individual repositories.

If you prefer the GitHub CLI, you can use gh secret set to create a new secret:

```
$ gh secret set secret-name
```

You will be prompted for the secret. You can also read the secret from a file, pipe it to the command, or specify it as the body (-b or --body):

```
$ gh secret set secret-name < secret.txt
$ gh secret set secret-name --body secret
```

If the secret is for an environment, you can specify it using the --env (-e) argument. For organization secrets, you can set their visibility (--visibility or -v) to all, private, or selected. For selected, you must specify one or more repositories using --repos (-r):

```
$ gh secret set secret-name --env environment-name
$ gh secret set secret-name --org org -v private
$ gh secret set secret-name --org org -v selected -r repo
```

Accessing your secrets

You can access the secrets in your workflows through the secrets context. Add it to the steps either as an **input** (with:) or **environment** (env:) variable in the workflow file. Organization and repository secrets are read when the workflow run is queued, while environment secrets are read when a job referencing the environment starts.

> **Note**
>
> GitHub automatically removes secrets from the log. But be careful what you do with the secrets inside your steps!

Depending on your shell and environment, the syntax for accessing environment variables is different. In Bash, it is $SECRET-NAME, in PowerShell, it is $env:SECRET-NAME, and in cmd.exe, it is %SECRET-NAME%.

The following is an example of how to access secrets as an input or an environment in different shells:

```
steps:
  - name: Set secret as input
    shell: bash
    with:
      MY_SECRET: ${{ secrets.secret-name }}
    run: |
      dosomething "$MY_SECRET "
```

```
- name: Set secret as environment variable
  shell: cmd
  env:
    MY_SECRET: ${{ secrets.secret-name }}
  run: |
    dosomething.exe "%MY_SECRET%"
```

> **Note**
> These are just examples to show you how to pass secrets to actions. If
> your workflow step is a `run:` step, you can also access the secret context,
> `${{secrets.secret-name}}`, directly. This is not recommended if you
> wish to avoid script injection. But since only administrators can add secrets,
> this is something you might consider for the readability of the workflow.

The GITHUB_TOKEN secret

A special secret is the `GITHUB_TOKEN` secret. The `GITHUB_TOKEN` secret is
automatically created and can be accessed through the `github.token` or `secrets.`
`GITHUB_TOKEN` context. The token can be accessed by a GitHub action, even if the
workflow does not provide it as an input or environment variable. The token can be
used to authenticate when accessing GitHub resources. The default permissions can be
set to `permissive` or `restricted`, though these permissions can be adjusted in the
workflow:

```
on: pull_request_target

permissions:
  contents: read
  pull-requests: write

jobs:
  triage:
    runs-on: ubuntu-latest
    steps:
      - uses: actions/labeler@v2
        with:
          repo-token: ${{ secrets.GITHUB_TOKEN }}
```

You can find more information on the GITHUB_TOKEN secret here: `https://docs.github.com/en/actions/reference/authentication-in-a-workflow`.

Hands-on – your first workflow

That should have been enough theory to get started. We'll dig deeper into runners, environments, and security in the following chapters. If you are new to GitHub Actions, now is the time to create your first workflow and your first action.

> **Tip**
>
> You can find existing GitHub Actions Workflows as templates by using GitHub's code search and filtering by the programming language's YAML (`language:yml`) and the workflow path (`path:.github/workflows`). The following search will return all the workflows for the German Corona-Warn-App:
>
> `language:yml path:.github/workflows @corona-warn-app`

The steps are as follows:

1. Navigate to the repository by going to `https://github.com/wulfland/getting-started` and fork it by using the **Fork** button in the top-right corner.

2. In the fork, click on **Actions**. You should see templates for workflows that you can use. These templates are optimized for the code in the repository – in this case, .NET. Select **Set up this workflow**:

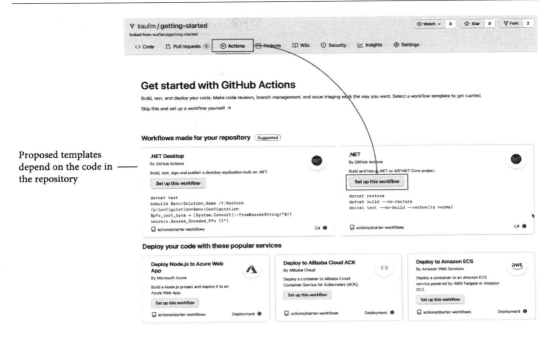

Proposed templates depend on the code in the repository

Figure 6.2 – Setting up a GitHub action for .NET

3. GitHub creates a workflow file and opens the editor. The editor supports syntax-highlighting and auto-complete (press *Ctrl + Space*). You can search the marketplace for actions. Set `dotnet-version` to 3.1.x and commit the workflow file:

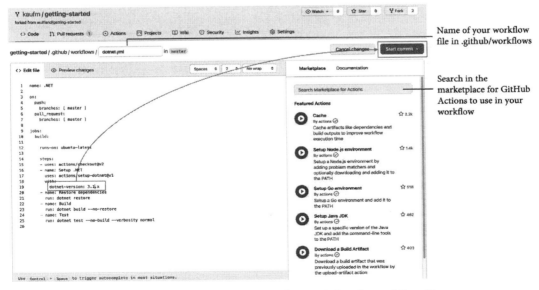

Name of your workflow file in .github/workflows

Search in the marketplace for GitHub Actions to use in your workflow

Figure 6.3 – Setting the version and committing the workflow file

4. The workflow will be automatically triggered and you can find the workflow run under **Actions**. If you open it, you can find the jobs in the workflow, as well as additional header information:

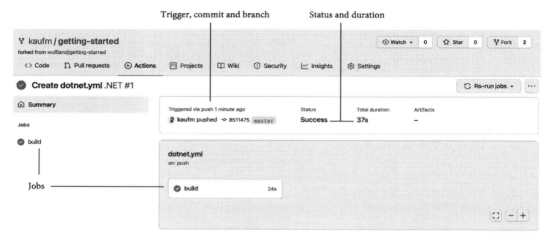

Figure 6.4 – The workflow summary page

5. Click on the job to see details of all the steps:

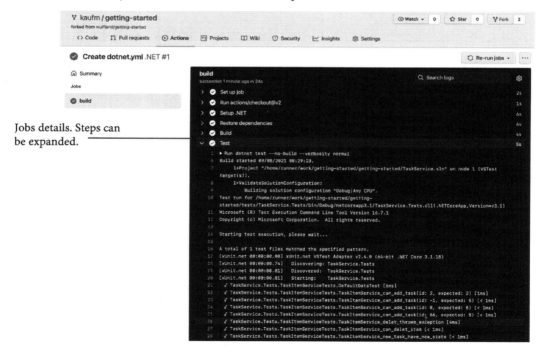

Figure 6.5 – Job and step details

If you prefer other languages, you can use, for example, the following repository, which uses **Java with Maven**: `https://github.com/MicrosoftDocs/pipelines-java`.

When selecting the workflow template, scroll down to **Continuous integration workflows** and click **More continuous integration workflows…**.

Select **Java with Maven** and the workflow should work:

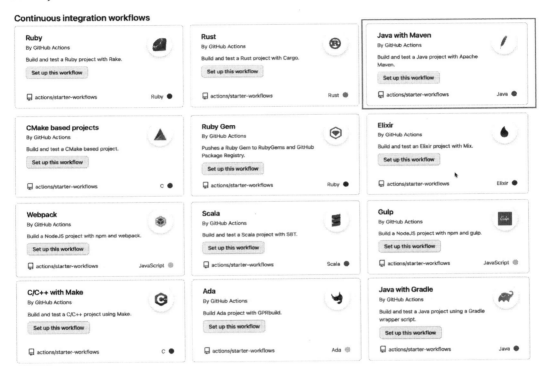

Figure 6.6 – Other CI templates, such as "Java with Maven"

There are templates for everything. It should be easy to set up a basic workflow to build your code.

Hands-on – your first action

The power of GitHub Actions lies in its reusability, so understanding how to create and use Actions is important. In this hands-on exercise, you will create a container action that runs inside a Docker container.

> **Tip**
>
> You can find this example at `https://docs.github.com/en/actions/creating-actions/creating-a-docker-container-action` and you can copy and paste the content of the text files from there. If you want, you can also use the template repository at `https://github.com/actions/container-action` and click **Use this template**. It will create a repository with all files in it for you.

The steps are as follows:

1. Create a new repository called `hello-world-docker-action` and clone it to your workstation.

2. Open a Terminal and navigate to the repository:

    ```
    $ cd hello-world-docker-action
    ```

3. Create a file called `Dockerfile` without an extension. Add the following content to it:

    ```
    # Container image that runs your code
    FROM alpine:3.10

    # Copies your code file from your action repository to
    the filesystem path '/' of the container
    COPY entrypoint.sh /entrypoint.sh

    # Code file to execute when the docker container starts
    up ('entrypoint.sh')
    ENTRYPOINT ["/entrypoint.sh"]
    ```

    This **Dockerfile** defines your container – in this case, it is based on an Alpine Linux 3.1 image. Then, it copies the `entrypoint.sh` file into your container. If the container gets executed, it will run `entrypoint.sh`.

4. Create a new file called `action.yml` that contains the following content:

    ```
    # action.yml
    name: 'Hello World'
    description: 'Greet someone and record the time'
    inputs:
      who-to-greet:  # id of input
        description: 'Who to greet'
    ```

```
    required: true
    default: 'World'
outputs:
  time: # id of output
    description: 'The time we greeted you'
runs:
  using: 'docker'
  image: 'Dockerfile'
  args:
    - ${{ inputs.who-to-greet }}
```

The `action.yml` file defines the action, along with its input and output parameters.

5. Now, create the `entrypoint.sh` script. This script will run in your container and call other binaries. Add the following content to it:

```
#!/bin/sh -l

echo "Hello $1"
time=$(date)
echo "::set-output name=time::$time"
```

The input parameter is passed to the script as an argument and is accessed via `$1`. The script uses the `set-output` workflow command to set the `time` parameter to the current time.

6. You must make `entrypoint.sh` executable. On non-Windows systems, you can just run the following command in your terminal and then add and commit your changes:

```
$ chmod +x entrypoint.sh
$ git add .
$ git commit -m "My first action is ready"
```

On Windows, this will not work. But you can mark the file as executable when it is added to the index:

```
$ git add .
$ git update-index --chmod=+x .\entrypoint.sh
$ git commit -m "My first action is ready"
```

7. The versioning for Actions is done using Git tags. Add a `v1` tag and push all your changes to the remote repository:

```
$ git tag -a -m "My first action release" v1
$ git push --follow-tags
```

8. Your action is now ready to be used. Go back to your workflow in the `getting-started` repository (`.github/workflows/dotnet.yaml`) and edit the file. Delete everything under `jobs` (line 9) and replace it with the following code:

```
hello_world_job:
  runs-on: ubuntu-latest
  name: A job to say hello
  steps:
  - name: Hello world action step
    id: hello
    uses: your-username/hello-world-action@v1
    with:
      who-to-greet: 'your-name'
  - name: Get the output time
    run: echo "The time was ${{ steps.hello.outputs.time }}"
```

The workflow now calls your action (`uses`) and points to the repository you created (`your-username/hello-world-action`), followed by the tag (`@v1`). It passes your name as an input parameter to the action and receives the current time as output, which is then written to the console.

9. Save the file and the workflow will run automatically. Check the details to see the greeting and the time in the log.

> **Tip**
>
> If you want to try other types of actions, you can use existing templates.
> If you want to try a **JavaScript** action, use `https://github.com/actions/javascript-action`. If you want to try a **TypeScript** action, use `https://github.com/actions/typescript-action`.
> A **composite action** is even easier as you only need an `action.yml` file (see `https://docs.github.com/en/actions/creating-actions/creating-a-composite-action`).
>
> Handling the actions is the same – only the way they are created is different.

The GitHub marketplace

You can use the GitHub marketplace (`https://github.com/marketplace`) to search for **Actions** to use in your workflows. It's easy to publish an action to the marketplace, which is why there are already nearly 10,000 actions available. You can filter the actions by categories or use the search bar to limit the number of actions you see (see *Figure 6.7*):

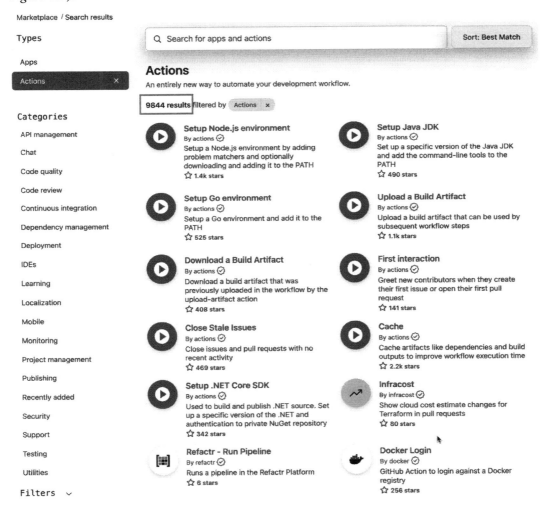

Figure 6.7 – The marketplace contains nearly 10,000 actions

The action shows the readme from the repository and additional information. You can see the full list of versions and get information on how to use the current version:

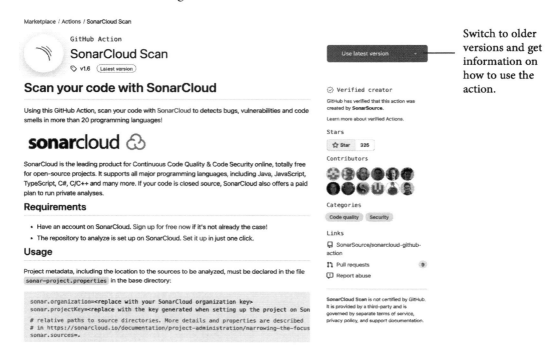

Figure 6.8 – An action in the marketplace

It's easy to publish an action to the marketplace. Make sure that the Action is in a public repository, that the name of the action is unique, and that the action contains a good readme. Pick an icon and color and add it to `action.yml`:

```
branding:
  icon: 'award'
  color: 'green'
```

GitHub automatically detects the `action.yml` file and provides a button called **Draft a release**. If you select **Publish this Action to the GitHub Marketplace**, you have to agree to the terms of service, and your action will be checked for all the required artifacts. Here, you can pick a tag or create a new one and add a title and description for the release:

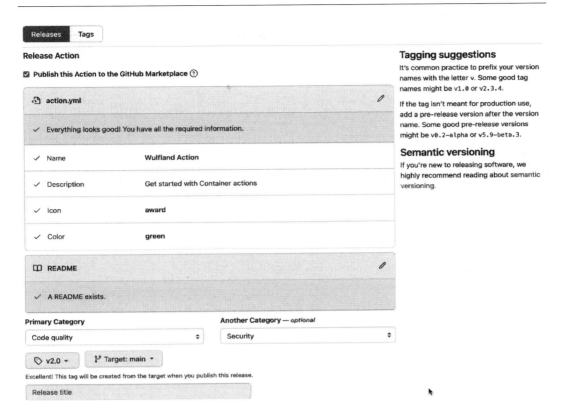

Figure 6.9 – Publishing an action to the marketplace

Publish the release or save it as a draft.

The marketplace is growing fast, and it makes automation simple as there is almost an action for everything.

Summary

In this chapter, I explained the importance of automation and introduced you to GitHub Actions as a flexible and extendible engine for any kind of automation.

In the next chapter, you'll learn about the different hosting options and how you can host workflow runners.

Further reading

For more information about the topics that were covered in this chapter, please take a look at the following references:

- Humble J., & Farley, D. (2010). *Continuous Delivery: Reliable Software Releases through Build, Test, and Deployment Automation.* Addison-Wesley Professional.

- Forsgren, N., Humble, J., & Kim, G. (2018). *Accelerate: The Science of Lean Software and DevOps: Building and Scaling High Performing Technology Organizations* (1st ed.) [E-book]. IT Revolution Press.

- *YAML*: https://yaml.org/

- *GitHub Actions*: https://github.com/features/actions and https://docs.github.com/en/actions

- *GitHub Learning Lab*: https://lab.github.com

- *Workflow Syntax*: https://docs.github.com/en/actions/reference/workflow-syntax-for-github-actions

- *GitHub Marketplace*: https://github.com/marketplace

7

Running Your Workflows

In this chapter, I'll show you the different options for running your **workflows**. We'll investigate hosted and self-hosted runners, and I'll explain how you can tackle hybrid-cloud scenarios or hardware-in-the-loop tests using the different hosting options. I'll also show you how to set up, manage, and scale self-hosted runners, and I'll show you how you can approach monitoring and troubleshooting.

The following are the core topics that we will cover in this chapter:

- Hosted runners
- Self-hosted runners
- Managing access with runner groups
- Using labels
- Scaling your self-hosted runners
- Monitoring and troubleshooting

Hosted runners

We already used **hosted runners** in the previous chapter. Hosted runners are GitHub-hosted virtual machines that can be used to run your workflows. The runners are available for **Linux**, **Windows**, and **macOS** operating systems.

Isolation and privileges

Each job in a workflow executes in a fresh instance of the virtual machine and is completely isolated. You have *full admin access* (**passwordless sudo** on Linux), and the **user account control** (**UAC**) is disabled on Windows machines. That means you can install any tools you might need in your workflow (this just comes with the price of build time).

The runner can also access **user interface** (**UI**) elements. This enables you to execute **UI tests** such as **Selenium** inside the runner without the need to do this through another virtual machine.

Hardware

GitHub hosts Linux and Windows runners on **Standard_DS2_v2** virtual machines in **Microsoft Azure**. The hardware specifications for Windows and Linux virtual machines are as follows:

- 2-core CPU
- 7 GB of RAM
- 14 GB of SSD disk space

MacOS runners are hosted on GitHub's macOS cloud and have the following hardware specifications:

- 3-core CPU
- 14 GB of RAM
- 14 GB of SSD disk space

Software

In *Table 7.1*, you can see a list of the currently available images:

Virtual environment	YAML workflow label	Notes
Windows Server 2022	`windows-2022`	Currently in beta. The `windows-latest` label currently uses the Windows Server 2019 runner image and will switch to 2022 when it is out of beta.
Windows Server 2019	`windows-latest` or `windows-2019`	The `windows-latest` label currently points to this image.
Windows Server 2016	`windows-2016`	
Ubuntu 20.04	`ubuntu-latest` or `ubuntu-20.04`	The `ubuntu-latest` label currently points to this image.
Ubuntu 18.04	`ubuntu-18.04`	
Ubuntu 16.04	`ubuntu-16.04`	Deprecated and limited to existing customers only. Customers should migrate to Ubuntu 20.04.
macOS Big Sur 11	`macos-11`	
macOS Catalina 10.15	`macos-latest` or `macos-10.15`	The `macos-latest` label currently uses the macOS 10.15 runner image.

Table 7.1 – The currently available images for hosted runners

You can find the current list and all included software at `https://github.com/actions/virtual-environments`.

This is also the repository you can raise an issue in if you would like to request a new tool to be installed as a default tool. This repository also contains announcements about all major software updates on the runners, and you can use the *watch* feature of GitHub repositories to get notified if new releases are created.

Networks

The IP addresses that are used by the hosted runners change from time to time. You can get the current list using the GitHub API:

```
curl \
  -H "Accept: application/vnd.github.v3+json" \
  https://api.github.com/meta
```

More information on this can be found at `https://docs.github.com/en/rest/reference/meta#get-github-meta-information`.

You can use this information if you require an allow-list to prevent access to your internal resources from the internet. But remember that everyone can use the hosted runners and execute code! Blocking other IP addresses does not make your resources safe. Do not oppose internal systems to these IP addresses that are not secured in a way that you would trust them to be accessed from the public internet! This means the systems must be patched and have secure authentication in place. If this is not the case, you have to use self-hosted runners.

> **Note**
>
> If you use an *IP address allow list* for your GitHub organization or enterprise account, you cannot use GitHub-hosted runners and must instead use self-hosted runners.

Pricing

The usage of hosted runners is free for public repositories. Depending on your GitHub edition, you will have an allotted storage amount and monthly free build minutes (see *Table 7.2*):

GitHub edition	Storage	Minutes	Max concurrent jobs
GitHub Free	500 MB	2,000	20 (5 for macOS)
GitHub Pro	1 GB	3,000	40 (5 for macOS)
GitHub Free for organizations	500 MB	2,000	20 (5 for macOS)
GitHub Team	2 GB	3,000	60 (5 for macOS)
GitHub Enterprise Cloud	50 GB	50,000	180 (50 for macOS)

Table 7.2 – The included storage and build minutes for different GitHub editions

If you have purchased **GitHub Enterprise** through your **Microsoft Enterprise Agreement**, you can connect your **Azure Subscription ID** to your GitHub Enterprise account. This enables you to pay for extra **GitHub Actions** usage, in addition to what is included with your GitHub edition.

Jobs that run on Windows and macOS runners consume more build minutes than Linux! Windows consumes minutes with *factor 2* and macOS with *factor 10*. That means using 1,000 Windows minutes would consume 2,000 of the minutes included in your account, whereas using 1,000 macOS minutes would consume 10,000 minutes included in your account.

That's because the build minutes are more expensive. You can pay for additional minutes on top of those included in your GitHub edition. These are the build minute costs for each operating system:

- On Linux: $0.008

- On macOS: $0.08

- On Windows: $0.016

> **Tip**
>
> You should use as much Linux for your workflows as possible and reduce macOS and Windows to a minimum to reduce your build costs. Linux also has the best starting performance.

The costs for additional storage are the same for all runners, which is $0.25 per GB.

If you are a monthly-billed customer, your account will have a default spending limit of $0 (USD). This prevents additional build minutes or storage from being used. If you pay by invoice, your account will have an unlimited spending limit by default.

If you configure a spending limit higher than $0, you will be billed for any additional minutes or storage beyond the included amounts in your account until the spending limit is reached.

Self-hosted runners

If you need more control than GitHub-hosted runners allow for hardware, operating systems, software, and network access, you can host the runners yourself. **Self-hosted runners** can be installed on physical machines, virtual machines, or in a container. They can run on-premises or in any public cloud environment.

Self-hosted runners allow for easy migration from other build environments. If you already have automated builds, you just install the runner on the machines and your code should build. But if your build machines are still the ped-like machines that are manually maintained – sometimes positioned physically beyond the desk of a developer – then this is not a permanent solution. Keep in mind that building and hosting a dynamically scaling environment needs expertise and costs money, whether it is hosted in the cloud or on-premises. So, if you can use hosted runners, it is always the easier option. However, if you need a self-hosted solution, make sure to make it an elastically scalable solution.

> **Note**
>
> Hosting your own runners enables you to build and deploy safely in your on-premises environment from within **GitHub Enterprise Cloud**. This allows you to run GitHub in a *hybrid mode* – that is, you can use GitHub Enterprise in the cloud together with hosted runners for basic automation and deployments to cloud environments, but use self-hosted runners to build or deploy applications that are hosted on-premises. This can be a cheaper and simpler solution than running **GitHub Enterprise Server** and the build environments *for all of your builds and deployments yourself.*

If you are depending on hardware to test your software (for example, when using hardware-in-the-loop tests), there is no way around using self-hosted runners. This is because there is no way to attach hardware to the GitHub-hosted runners.

The runner software

The runner is open source and can be found at `https://github.com/actions/runner`. It supports x64 processor architecture on Linux, macOS, and Windows. It also supports ARM64 and ARM32 architecture, but only on Linux. The runner supports many operating systems, including **Ubuntu**, **Red Hat Enterprise Linux 7** or later, **Debian 9** or later, **Windows 7/8/10** and **Windows Server**, **macOS 10.13** or later, and many more. For a complete list, see the documentation at `https://docs.github.com/en/actions/hosting-your-own-runners/about-self-hosted-runners#supported-architectures-and-operating-systems-for-self-hosted-runners`.

The runner auto-updates itself, so you don't have to take care of this.

Communication between the runner and GitHub

The runner software polls GitHub using **HTTPS long polling** over port 443, using an outbound connection. It opens a connection for 50 seconds and times out if no response is received.

You must ensure that the machine has appropriate network access to the following URLs:

```
github.com
api.github.com
*.actions.githubusercontent.com
github-releases.githubusercontent.com
github-registry-files.githubusercontent.com
codeload.github.com
```

```
*.pkg.github.com
pkg-cache.githubusercontent.com
pkg-containers.githubusercontent.com
pkg-containers-az.githubusercontent.com
*.blob.core.windows.net
```

You don't have to open any inbound ports on your firewall. All communication runs through the client. If you use an IP address allow list for your GitHub organization or enterprise, you must add the IP address range of your self-hosted runners to that allow list.

Using self-hosted runners behind a proxy server

If you need to run the self-hosted runner behind a proxy server, you can do so. But be aware that this can cause a lot of problems. The runner itself can communicate fine – however, package management, container registries, and everything that is executed by the runner and needs to access resources creates an overhead. If you can avoid this, I advise you to do so. But if you must run the workflows behind a proxy server, you can configure the runner with the following environment variables:

- `https_proxy`: This includes the proxy URL for HTTPS (port 443) traffic. You can also include basic authentication (such as `https://user:password@proxy.local`).

- `http_proxy`: This includes the proxy URL for HTTP (port 80) traffic. You can also include basic authentication (such as `http://user:password@proxy.local`).

- `no_proxy`: This includes a comma-separated list of hosts that should bypass the proxy server.

If you change the environment variables, you have to restart the runner for the changes to take effect.

An alternative to using environment variables is to use a `.env` file. Save a file with the name `.env` in the application folder of the runner. After that, the syntax is the same as the environment variables:

```
https_proxy=http://proxy.local:8081
no_proxy=example.com,myserver.local:443
```

Next, let's have a look at how to add self-hosted runners to GitHub.

Adding self-hosted runners to GitHub

You can add runners at different levels in GitHub: repository, organization and enterprise. If you add runners at the repository level, they are dedicated to that single repository. Organization-level runners can process jobs for multiple repositories in an organization and enterprise-level runners can be assigned to multiple organizations in your enterprise.

Installing the runner and registering it on your GitHub instance is easy. Just go to **Settings | Actions | Runners** at the level you want to add them. Then, select the operating system and processor architecture (see *Figure 7.1*):

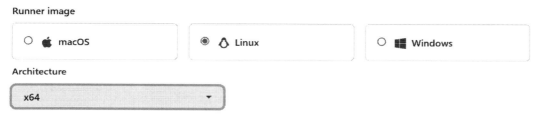

Figure 7.1 – Installing a self-hosted runner

This generates a script for you that does the following:

1. Downloads and unpacks the runner
2. Configures the runner with the corresponding values
3. Starts the runner

The first part of the script always creates a folder called `actions-runner` and then changes the working directory to that folder:

```
$ mkdir actions-runner && cd actions-runner
```

Downloading the latest runner package is done on Linux and macOS with the `curl` command and on Windows with `Invoke-WebRequest`:

```
# Linux and macOS:
$ curl -o actions-runner-<ver>.tar.gz -L https://github.com/
actions/runner/releases/download/<ver>/actions-runner-<ver>.
tar.gz
# Windows:
$ Invoke-WebRequest -Uri https://github.com/actions/runner/
releases/download/<ver>/actions-runner-<ver>.zip -OutFile
actions-runner-<ver>.zip
```

For security reasons, the hash of the downloaded package is validated to ensure the package has not been compromised:

```
# Linux and macOS:
$ echo "<hash> actions-runner-<ver>.tar.gz" | shasum -a 256 -c
# Windows:
$ if((Get-FileHash -Path actions-runner-<ver>.zip -Algorithm
SHA256).Hash.ToUpper() -ne '<hash>'.ToUpper()){ throw 'Computed
checksum did not match' }
```

Then, the runner gets extracted from the ZIP/TAR file:

```
# Linux and macOS:
$ tar xzf ./actions-runner-<ver>.tar.gz
# Windows:
$ Add-Type -AssemblyName System.IO.Compression.FileSystem ;
[System.IO.Compression.ZipFile]::ExtractToDirectory("$PWD/
actions-runner-<ver>.zip", "$PWD")
```

The configuration is done using the `config.sh` / `config.cmd` script and the URL and token are automatically created by GitHub for you:

```
# Linux and macOS:
$ ./config.sh --url https://github.com/org --token token
# Widows:
$ ./config.cmd --url https://github.com/org --token token
```

The configuration asks for the runner group (where the default is the `Default` group), the name of the runner (where the default is the machine name), and additional labels. Default labels are applied to describe the self-hosted status, the operating system, and the processor architecture (for example, `self-hosted`, `Linux`, and `X64`, respectively). The default working folder is `_work` and should not be changed. On Windows, you can also choose to run the action runner as a service. On Linux and macOS, you have to install the service using another script after the configuration:

```
$ sudo ./svc.sh install
$ sudo ./svc.sh start
```

If you don't want to run the runner as a service, you can run it interactively using the `run` script:

```
$ ./run.sh
$ ./run.cmd
```

If the runner is up and running, you can see it listed under **Settings | Actions | Runners** with its status and tags (see *Figure 7.2*):

Figure 7.2 – Self-hosted runners with their tags and status

Let's now learn how to remove these self-hosted runners from GitHub.

Removing self-hosted runners

If you want to reconfigure or remove a runner from GitHub, you have to use the `config` script with the `remove` option. If you open the details of the runner by clicking its name, you see a **Remove** button (see *Figure 7.2*). If you click this button, it generates the script and token for you.

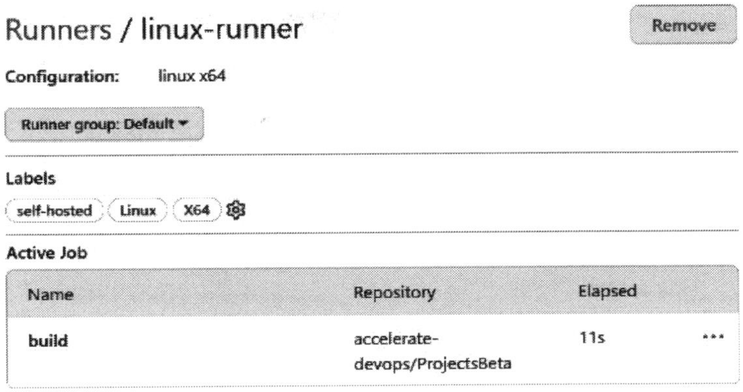

Figure 7.3 – The runner details

The script looks like this for the different operating systems:

```
# Linux and macOS
./config.sh remove --token <token>
# Windows
./config.cmd remove --token <token>
```

Always remove the runners before destroying your machines! If you forget to do this, you can still use the **Force remove this runner** button in the **Remove** dialog. But this should only be used as a last resort.

Managing access with runner groups

If you register your runners at the organization or enterprise level, **runner groups** are used to control access to the self-hosted runners. Enterprise administrators can configure access policies that control which organizations in an enterprise have access to runner groups, and organization administrators can configure access policies that control which repositories in the organization have access to runner groups. Every enterprise and every organization has a default runner group named Default that cannot be deleted.

> **Note**
> A runner can only be in one runner group at a time.

To manage access, open **Policies** at the enterprise level or **Settings** at the organization level and locate **Actions | Runner Groups** in the menu. Here, you can create a new runner group or click on an existing one to adjust its access settings. Depending on whether your level is enterprise or organization, you can either allow access to specific organizations or repositories (see *Figure 7.3*):

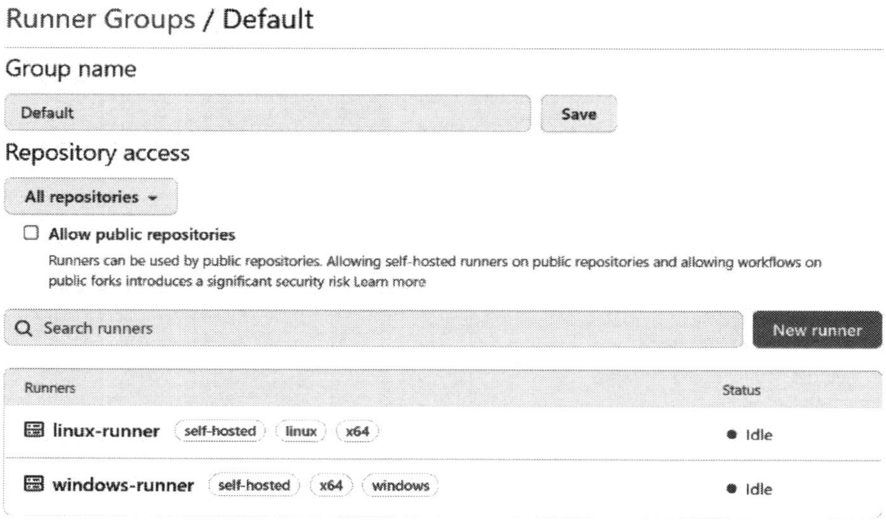

Figure 7.4 – Options for runner groups

> **Warning**
>
> Access for public repositories is disabled by default. Leave this! You should not use self-hosted runners with public repositories! Forks may execute malicious code on your runners, so this is a risk. If you need self-hosted runners for a public repository, make sure to use *ephemeral* and *hardened* runners that don't have access to your internal resources. This might be the case if you need a special tooling for an open source project that takes too long to install on the hosted runners. But these are rare cases and you should try to avoid them.

When you register a new runner, you are asked for the name of the runner group. You can also pass this as an argument to the `config` script:

```
$ ./config.sh --runnergroup <group>
```

Now that we've learned to manage access with runner groups, we will learn to use labels.

Using labels

GitHub Actions matches your workflow with your runners by searching for the correct labels. The labels are applied when you register a runner. You can also pass them to the `config` script as an argument:

```
$ ./config.sh --labels self-hosted,x64,linux
```

You can later modify the labels and create new labels in the details of the runner by pressing the gear icon next to **Labels** (see *Figure 7.4*):

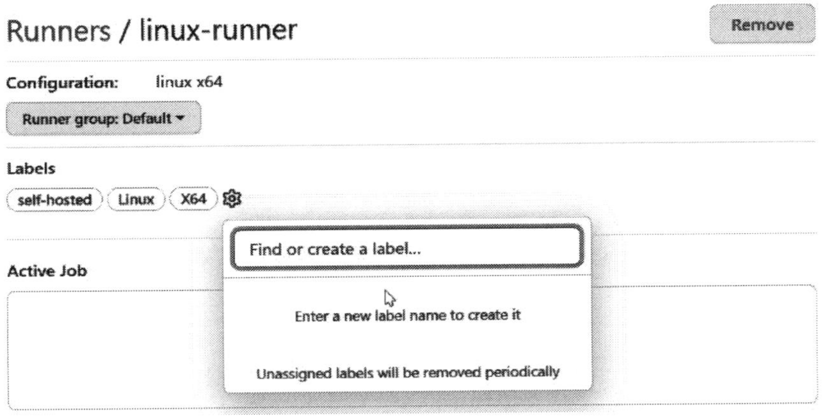

Figure 7.5 – Creating new labels for a runner

If your workflows have specific demands, you can create custom labels for them. An example of a custom label could be adding a tag for a tool such as `matLab` or necessary `gpu` access.

All self-hosted runners have the `self-hosted` tag by default.

To use the runners in your workflows, you specify the demands in the form of tags:

```
runs-on: [self-hosted, linux, X64, matlab, gpu]
```

This way, your workflow finds the corresponding runner that fulfills the necessary demands.

Scaling your self-hosted runners

Installing the action runner on existing build machines allows for easy migration to GitHub. But this is not a long-term solution! If you can't use the hosted runners, you should build an elastically scaling build environment yourself.

Ephemeral runners

If you build an elastic scaling solution for your build machines or container, you should use ephemeral runners. This means you use a virtual machine or **Docker** image from a blank image and install a temporary runner. Then, everything gets erased after the run. An elastic scaling solution with persistent runners is not recommended!

To configure your runner to be *ephemeral*, you pass the following argument to the `config` script:

```
$ ./config.sh --ephemeral
```

Scaling up and down with GitHub webhooks

To scale your virtual environments up and down, you can use **GitHub webhooks**. The `workflow_job` webhook gets called with the `queued` action key if a new workflow is queued. You can use this event to spin up a new build machine and add it to the pool of machines. The `workflow_job` webhook is called with the `completed` action if the workflow run has finished. You can use this event to clean up and destroy the machine.

For more information, see the documentation at `https://docs.github.com/en/developers/webhooks-and-events/webhooks/webhook-events-and-payloads#workflow_job`.

Existing solutions

Building an elastic virtual build environment in **Kubernetes**, **AWS EC2**, or **OpenShift** is beyond the scope of this book. GitHub does not provide a solution for this itself, but there are many open source solutions on GitHub that can save you a lot of time and effort if you want to utilize them. Johannes Nicolai (`@jonico`) has curated a matrix with all of the solutions out there. You can find the repository at `https://github.com/jonico/awesome-runners`. The matrix is more readable in the form of GitHub pages, so you might prefer to visit `https://jonico.github.io/awesome-runners`. The matrix compares the solutions based on their target platform, whether they have GitHub Enterprise support, their automatic scaling capabilities, their cleanup factors, and other criteria.

> **Tip**
> Keep in mind that building and running a scalable build environment with your custom images takes a lot of time and effort that can also be spent on other things. Using hosted runners is the cheaper and more sustainable solution. Make sure if you really need to make this investment in your own platform before doing so. Often, there are other options to hosting your own runners – such as bringing your own Docker images into GitHub Actions or using a bot to automate deployments to your on-premises resources.

Monitoring and troubleshooting

If you have problems with your self-hosted runners, there are several things that can help you when troubleshooting.

Checking the status of the runners

You can check the status of your runners under **Settings | Actions | Runners**. The status of a runner can be Idle, Active, or Offline. If the runner status is Offline, the machine could be down or not connected to the network, or the self-hosted runner application might not be running on the machine.

Reviewing the application log files

Log files are kept on the runner in the _diag folder in the runner's root directory. You can review the runner **application log files** in _diag. The application log filenames begin with Runner_ and have a UTC timestamp appended to them:

```
Runner_20210927-065249-utc.log
```

Reviewing the job log files

The **job log files** are also located in _diag. Each job has its own log. The application log filenames begin with Worker_ and also have a UTC timestamp appended:

```
Worker_20210927-101349-utc.log
```

Checking the service status

If your runner runs as a service, you can check the service status, depending on your operating system.

Linux

On Linux, you can get the name of your service from the `.service` file in your runner's folder. Use the `journalctl` tool to monitor the real-time activity of your runner service:

```
$ sudo journalctl -u $(cat ~/actions-runner/.service) -f
```

The configuration for your service can be checked and customized under `/etc/systemd/systemd/`:

```
$ cat /etc/systemd/system/$(cat ~/actions-runner/.service)
```

macOS

On macOS, you can use the `svc.sh` script to check the status of the service:

```
$ ./svc.sh status
```

The output of the preceding script contains the *service name* and the *process ID*.

To check the service configuration, locate the file in the following location:

```
$ cat /Users/<user_name>/Library/LaunchAgents/<service_name>
```

Windows

On Windows, you can use **PowerShell** to retrieve information about your service:

```
$ Get-Service "action*"
```

Use `EventLog` to monitor the recent activities of your service:

```
Get-EventLog -LogName Application -Source ActionsRunnerService
```

Monitoring the runner update process

The runner should update itself automatically. If this fails, the runner will not be able to run workflows. You can check its update activity in the `Runner_*` log files in the `_diag` directory.

Case study

The two pilot teams at *Tailwind Gears* start their first sprints on the new platform. The first thing they automate is the build process so that all of their pull requests can be built before merging. Tailwind Gears tries to use the GitHub-hosted runners as much as possible. Most of the software builds just fine. However, some of the code written in **C** uses an older compiler version and has some other dependencies installed on the current build machines. The code is currently built on two local **Jenkins** servers that are maintained by the developers themselves. These servers are also attached to hardware that is used for hardware-in-the-loop testing. For an easy transition, self-hosted runners are installed on these machines and the build runs fine. The IT department wants to get rid of the local servers anyway, so they work together with their GitHub partner to build an elastic, scalable, container-based solution that can run custom images that have access to the attached hardware.

Summary

In this chapter, you learned about two hosting options for running your workflows:

- GitHub-hosted runners
- Self-hosted runners

We explained how self-hosted runners allow you to run GitHub in a hybrid-cloud scenario. You learned how to set up self-hosted runners and where you can find information to help you build your own elastic scalable build environment.

In the next chapter, you will learn how you can manage your code dependencies using **GitHub Packages**.

Further reading

For more information about the topics in this chapter, you can refer to the following resources:

- *Using GitHub-hosted runners*: `https://docs.github.com/en/actions/using-github-hosted-runners`
- *Hosting your own runners*: `https://docs.github.com/en/actions/hosting-your-own-runners`
- *awesome-runners – A curated list of awesome self-hosted GitHub Action runner solutions in a large comparison matrix*: `https://jonico.github.io/awesome-runners`

8
Managing Dependencies Using GitHub Packages

Using a package registry to manage your dependencies should be an absolute no-brainer. If you are writing .NET, you use NuGet, if you are writing JavaScript, it's probably npm, and if you are using Java, it's Maven or Gradle. And yet, I meet many teams that still use their filesystem or Git submodules to reuse code files in multiple code bases. Or they build assemblies and store them in source control. Moving to packages with **semantic versioning** is easy and cheap, and it boosts the quality and discoverability of your shared code.

In this chapter, I show you how you can use GitHub Packages to manage your internal dependencies like you manage your software supply chain. The main topics are as follows:

- GitHub Packages
- Using npm packages with Actions
- Using Docker with Packages
- Apache Maven, Gradle, NuGet, and RubyGems packages

Semantic Versioning

Semantic versioning is a formal convention for specifying version numbers for software. It consists of different parts with different meanings. Examples of semantic version numbers are `1.0.0` or `1.5.99-beta`. The format is as follows:

`<major>.<minor>.<patch>-<pre>`

Major version: A numeric identifier that gets increased if the version is not backward compatible and has breaking changes. An update to a new major version must be handled with caution! A major version of zero is for the initial development.

Minor version: A numeric identifier that gets increased if new features are added but the version is backward compatible with the previous version and can be updated without breaking anything if you need the new functionality.

Patch: A numeric identifier that gets increased if you release bug fixes that are backward compatible. New patches should always be installed.

Pre-version: A text identifier that is appended using a hyphen. The identifier must only use ASCII alphanumeric characters and hyphens (`[0-9A-Za-z-]`). The longer the text, the smaller the pre-version (meaning `-alpha` < `-beta` < `-rc`). A pre-release version is always smaller than a normal version (`1.0.0-alpha` < `1.0.0`).

See `https://semver.org/` for the complete specification.

Using packages does not automatically mean you are using a loosely coupled architecture. Packages are, in most cases, still hard dependencies. It depends on how you use the packages to really decouple your release cadence.

GitHub Packages

GitHub Packages is a platform for hosting and managing your packages, containers, and other dependencies.

You can integrate GitHub Packages with GitHub Actions, the GitHub APIs, and webhooks. This allows you to create an end-to-end workflow to release and consume your code.

GitHub Packages currently supports the following registries:

- **Container** registry supporting **Docker** and **OCI** images
- **npm** registry for JavaScript using npm (`package.json`)
- **NuGet** registry for .NET (`nupkg`)
- **Apache Maven** registry for Java (`pom.xml`)
- **Gradle** registry for Java (`build.gradle`)
- **RubyGems** registry for Ruby (`Gemfile`)

Pricing

Packages are free for public packages. For private packages, each GitHub version includes a certain amount of storage and data transfer. Any usage beyond that amount is charged separately and can be controlled using spending limits.

Monthly billed customers have a default spending limit of $0 US dollars, which prevents additional usage of storage or data transfer. Invoiced customers have an unlimited default spending limit.

The amount of included storage and data transferred for each product is listed in *Table 8.1*:

Product	Storage	Data transfer (per month)
GitHub Free	500 MB	1 GB
GitHub Pro	2 GB	10 GB
GitHub Free for organizations	500 MB	1 GB
GitHub Team	2 GB	10 GB
GitHub Enterprise Cloud	50 GB	100 GB

Table 8.1 – Included storage and data transfer for Packages in GitHub products

All outbound data transfer is free when triggered by GitHub Actions. All inbound data transfer from any source is also free.

When the included limits are reached, the following costs are charged:

- **Storage**: $0.25 USD per GB

- **Data Transfer**: $0.50 USD per GB

For more details on pricing, see `https://docs.github.com/en/billing/managing-billing-for-github-packages/about-billing-for-github-packages`.

Permissions and visibility

A package that is published to a repository inherits the permissions and visibility of the repository that owns the package. Currently, only container packages offer granular permissions and access control (see *Figure 8.1*).

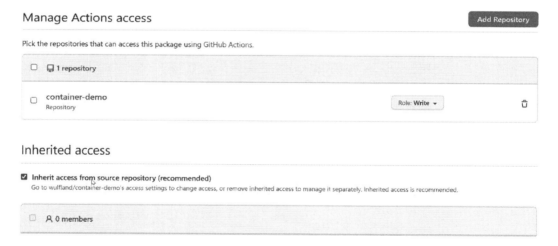

Figure 8.1 – Managing access to container packages

All other package types follow the repository access for repository-scoped packages. At the organization level, packages are private with write permissions for owners and read permissions for members.

If you have admin permissions to a container image, you can set the access permissions for the container image to `private` or `public`. Public images allow anonymous access without authentication. You can also grant access permissions for a container image that are separate from the permissions you've set at the organization and repository levels.

At the organization level, you can set the kind of container packages members can publish. You can also see and restore deleted packages (see *Figure 8.2*).

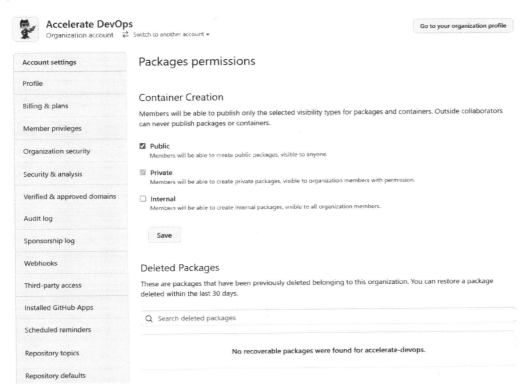

Figure 8.2 – Package permissions on organization level

For container images owned by a user account, you can give any person an access role. For container images published and owned by an organization, you can only grant access roles to persons or teams in your organization.

For more details on permissions and visibility, see `https://docs.github.com/en/packages/learn-github-packages/configuring-a-packages-access-control-and-visibility`.

Using npm packages with Actions

It is very easy to set up a release workflow for packages with GitHub Actions. You can use `GITHUB_TOKEN` to authenticate and the native clients of your package managers. To try it out with npm, you can follow the step-by-step instructions here: `https://github.com/wulfland/package-demo`.

You can create the package using npm init if you have installed npm on your machine. Otherwise, just copy the contents of package.json and package-lock.json from the aforementioned repository.

The workflow to publish the package is simple. It gets triggered every time a new release is created:

```
on:
  release:
    types: [created]
```

The workflow consists of two jobs. The first one only builds and tests the package using npm:

```
build:
  runs-on: ubuntu-latest
  steps:
    - uses: actions/checkout@v2
    - uses: actions/setup-node@v2
      with:
        node-version: 12
    - run: npm ci
    - run: npm test
```

The second one published the image to the registry. This one requires permission to write packages and to read content. It uses ${{ secrets.GITHUB_TOKEN }} to authenticate to the registry:

```
publish-gpr:
  needs: build
  runs-on: ubuntu-latest
  permissions:
    packages: write
    contents: read
  steps:
    - uses: actions/checkout@v2
    - uses: actions/setup-node@v2
      with:
        node-version: 12
        registry-url: https://npm.pkg.github.com/
```

```
- run: npm ci
- run: npm publish
  env:
    NODE_AUTH_TOKEN: ${{secrets.GITHUB_TOKEN}}
```

The workflow is simple and will publish a new package to your npm registry every time you create a new release in GitHub. You can find the details and settings for the package under **Code | Packages** (see *Figure 8.3*).

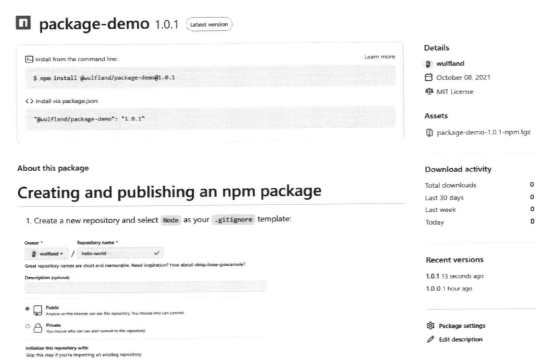

Figure 8.3 – Details and settings of the package

You can then consume the package in other projects using npm install @<owner-name>/<package-name>.

> **Note**
> Note that the version of the package is not the tag or release. It is the version that is in the package.json file. If you don't update the version before creating a second release, the workflow will fail.

If you want to automate this, there are a few actions that can help. You can use **NPM-Version** (see `https://github.com/marketplace/actions/npm-version`) to automatically set the version of npm before publishing. You could use the name of the release (`github.event.release.name`) or tag (`github.event.release.tag_name`) and set the package version to it:

```
- name: 'Change NPM version'
  uses: reedyuk/npm-version@1.1.1
  with:
    version: ${{github.event.release.tag_name}}
```

If you want a more flexible approach that calculates your semantic version number based upon tags and branches, you can use **GitVersion** (see `https://gitversion.net/`). **GitVersion** is part of the **GitTools** action (see `https://github.com/marketplace/actions/gittools`).

For **GitVersion** to function properly, you have to perform a so-called **shallow clone**. You do this by adding the `fetch-depth` parameter to the checkout action and setting it to `0`:

```
steps:
  - uses: actions/checkout@v2
    with:
      fetch-depth: 0
```

Next, install **GitVersion** and run the `execute` action. Set an `id` if you want to get details of the semantic version:

```
- name: Install GitVersion
  uses: gittools/actions/gitversion/setup@v0.9.7
  with:
    versionSpec: '5.x'

- name: Determine Version
  id:   gitversion
  uses: gittools/actions/gitversion/execute@v0.9.7
```

The calculated final semantic version number is stored as the environment variable $GITVERSION_SEMVER. You can use this, for example, as the input for **npm-version**.

> **Note**
>
> Note that **GitVersion** supports configuration files to learn how it should calculate the version! See https://gitversion.net/ for more information.

If you need to access details from **GitVersion** (such as major, minor, or patch), you can access them as output parameters of the gitversion task:

```
- name: Display GitVersion outputs
  run: |
      echo "Major: ${{ steps.gitversion.outputs.major }}"
```

With **GitVersion**, you can extend your workflow to create packages from branches or tags – not only releases:

```
on:
  push:
    tags:
      - 'v*'
    branches:
      - 'release/*'
```

Building a release workflow with automated semantic versioning is complex and depends a lot on the workflow and package manager you use. This chapter should get you started. The techniques can also be applied to **NuGet**, **Maven**, or any other package manager.

Using Docker with Packages

The container registry of GitHub is ghcr.io. Container images can be owned by an organization or personal account, but you can customize the access to each of them. By default, the images inherit the visibility and permission model of the repository where the workflow is run.

If you want to try it out yourself, you can find the step-by-step guide here: `https://github.com/wulfland/container-demo`. Follow these steps to understand what the build does:

1. Create a new repository called `container-demo` and add a very simple `Dockerfile` (without extension):

    ```
    FROM alpine
    CMD ["echo", "Hello World!"]
    ```

    The Docker image inherits from the alpine distribution and outputs `Hello World!` to your console. If you are new to Docker and want to try it out, clone the repository and change your directory in the root of the local repository. Build the image for the container:

    ```
    $ docker build -t container-demo
    ```

    And then run the container:

    ```
    $ docker run --rm container-demo
    ```

    The `--rm` argument automatically removes the container when it is done. This should write `Hello World!` to your console.

2. Now create a workflow file called `release-container.yml` in `.github/workflows/`. The workflow will be triggered every time a new release is created:

    ```
    name: Publish Docker image

    on:
      release:
        types: [published]
    ```

    The registry and the name of the image are set as environment variables. I use the repository name as the name for the image. You can also set a fix name here:

    ```
    env:
      REGISTRY: ghcr.io
      IMAGE_NAME: ${{ github.repository }}
    ```

    The job needs write permission to `packages` and it will need to clone the repository:

    ```
    jobs:
      build-and-push-image:
    ```

```
runs-on: ubuntu-latest
permissions:
  contents: read
  packages: write
steps:
  - name: Checkout repository
    uses: actions/checkout@v2
```

`docker/login-action` authenticates the workflow using `GITHUB_TOKEN`. This is the recommended way to do it:

```
- name: Log in to the Container registry
  uses: docker/login-action@v1.10.0
  with:
    registry: ${{ env.REGISTRY }}
    username: ${{ github.actor }}
    password: ${{ secrets.GITHUB_TOKEN }}
```

`metadata-action` extracts metadata from the Git context and applies tags to the Docker image. When we create a release, we push a tag (`refs/tags/<tag-name>`). The action will create a Docker tag with the same name as the Git tag and also create the latest tag for the image. Note that the metadata is passed as output variables to the next step! That's why I set an `id` for this step:

```
- name: Extract metadata (tags, labels)
  id: meta
  uses: docker/metadata-action@v3.5.0
  with:
    images: ${{ env.REGISTRY }}/${{ env.IMAGE_NAME }}
```

`build-push-action` builds the image and pushes it to the container registry. The tags and labels are pulled from the outputs of the `meta` step:

```
- name: Build and push Docker image
  uses: docker/build-push-action@v2.7.0
  with:
    context: .
    push: true
    tags: ${{ steps.meta.outputs.tags }}
    labels: ${{ steps.meta.outputs.labels }}
```

3. Create a new release and tag to trigger the workflow. Once the workflow is complete, you can find the details and settings for the package under **Code | Packages** (see *Figure 8.4*).

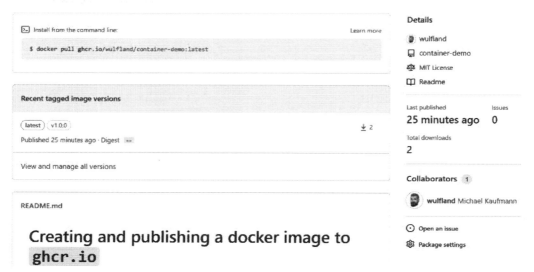

Figure 8.4 – Details and settings of the container package

GitHub will now create a new Docker image and add it to the registry if you create a new release.

4. You can pull you container locally from the registry and run it:

```
$ docker pull ghcr.io/<user>/container-demo:latest
$ docker run --rm ghcr.io/<user>/container-demo:latest
> Hello World!
```

Note that you have to authenticate using `docker login ghcr.io` before pulling the image if your package is not public.

The container registry is a great way to release software. From command-line tools to complete microservices, you can ship your software with all its dependencies for others to consume it.

Apache Maven, Gradle, NuGet, and RubyGems packages

The other package types are basically the same as npm and Docker: if you know the native package manager, they are really easy to use. I will only give a very brief introduction to each one.

Java with Apache Maven

For **Java** packages with **Maven**, you just have to add your package registry to the pom.xml file:

```
<distributionManagement>
  <repository>
    <id>github</id>
    <name>GitHub Packages</name>
    <url>https://maven.pkg.github.com/user/repo</url>
  </repository>
</distributionManagement>
```

You can then publish your package in a workflow using GITHUB_TOKEN:

```
- name: Publish package
  run: mvn --batch-mode deploy
  env:
    GITHUB_TOKEN: ${{ secrets.GITHUB_TOKEN }}
```

To retrieve packages from your development machine, you have to authenticate using a **Personal Access Token (PAT)** with read:packages scope. You can generate a new token in GitHub under **Settings | Developer Settings | Personal access tokens**. Add your user and the PAT to the ~/.m2/settings.xml file.

For more information, see https://docs.github.com/en/packages/working-with-a-github-packages-registry/working-with-the-apache-maven-registry.

Gradle

In **Gradle**, you have to add the registry to the build.gradle file. You can read the username and access token from the environment variables:

```
repositories {
  maven {
    name = "GitHubPackages"
    url = "https://maven.pkg.github.com/user/repo"
    credentials {
      username = System.getenv("GITHUB_ACTOR")
      password = System.getenv("GITHUB_TOKEN")
    }
  }
}
```

In the workflow, you can publish using gradle publish:

```
- name: Publish package
  run: gradle publish
  env:
    GITHUB_TOKEN: ${{ secrets.GITHUB_TOKEN }}
```

For more details, see https://docs.github.com/en/packages/working-with-a-github-packages-registry/working-with-the-gradle-registry.

RubyGems

If you want to build and publish all **gems** for your .gemspec files in your repository, you can use an action from the marketplace:

```
- name: Build and publish gems got .gemspec files
  uses: jstastny/publish-gem-to-github@master
  with:
    token: ${{ secrets.GITHUB_TOKEN }}
    owner: OWNER
```

To work with packages, you need at least RubyGems 2.4.1 and bundler 1.6.4. Modify the `~/.gemrc` file and add the registry as the source by providing your username and personal access token to install packages:

```
---
:backtrace: false
:bulk_threshold: 1000
:sources:
- https://rubygems.org/
- https://USERNAME:TOKEN@rubygems.pkg.github.com/OWNER/
:update_sources: true
:verbose: true
```

To install packages using **bundler**, you also must configure it with your user and token:

```
$ bundle config \
https://rubygems.pkg.github.com/OWNER \
USERNAME:TOKEN
```

For more details, see `https://docs.github.com/en/packages/working-with-a-github-packages-registry/working-with-the-rubygems-registry`.

NuGet

To publish **NuGet** packages, you can use the `setup-dotnet` action. It has additional parameters for `source-url`. The token is set using an environment variable:

```
- uses: actions/setup-dotnet@v1
  with:
    dotnet-version: '5.0.x'
    source-url: https://nuget.pkg.github.com/OWNER/index.json
  env:
    NUGET_AUTH_TOKEN: ${{secrets.GITHUB_TOKEN}}
```

You can then build and test your project. After that, just pack and push the package to the registry:

```
- run: |
  dotnet pack --configuration Release
  dotnet nuget push "bin/Release/*.nupkg"
```

To install packages, you have to add the registry as a source to the nuget.config file, including your user and token:

```xml
<?xml version="1.0" encoding="utf-8"?>
<configuration>
    <packageSources>
        <add key="github" value="https://nuget.pkg.github.com/
OWNER/index.json" />
    </packageSources>
    <packageSourceCredentials>
        <github>
            <add key="Username" value="USERNAME" />
            <add key="ClearTextPassword" value="TOKEN" />
        </github>
    </packageSourceCredentials>
</configuration>
```

For more information, see https://docs.github.com/en/packages/working-with-a-github-packages-registry/working-with-the-nuget-registry.

Summary

Working with packages is straightforward. The biggest challenge is authentication. But with GITHUB_TOKEN in GitHub Actions, it is easy to set up a completely automated release workflow. That's why it is important for your teams to have it in your toolbox. A lot of problems in releasing code can be reduced if you share code as containers or packages using semantic versioning and a separate release flow.

In this chapter, you have learned how you can use semantic versioning and packages to better manage your internal dependencies and to share code. You have learned what packages are and how you can set up release workflows for each package type.

In the next chapter, we'll have a closer look at environments and how you can deploy with GitHub actions to any platform.

Further reading

For more information about the topics in this chapter, refer to the following:

- *Semantic versioning*: https://semver.org/
- *Billing and pricing*: https://docs.github.com/en/billing/managing-billing-for-github-packages/about-billing-for-github-packages
- *Access control and visibility*: https://docs.github.com/en/packages/learn-github-packages/configuring-a-packages-access-control-and-visibility
- *Working with the registry* (Container, Apache Maven, Gradle. NuGet, npm, RubyGems): https://docs.github.com/en/packages/working-with-a-github-packages-registry

9
Deploying to Any Platform

Now that you have learned how to use GitHub Actions as an automation engine and GitHub Packages to easily share code and containers, we can complete our **Continuous Integration/Continuous Delivery (CI/CD)** capabilities by automating deployments.

In this chapter, I'll show you how to easily deploy to any cloud or platform in a secure and compliant way.

In this chapter, we will cover the following main topics:

- Staged deployments
- Automating your deployments
- Infrastructure as Code
- How to deploy to Azure App Service
- How to deploy to AWS **Elastic Container Service (ECS)**
- How to deploy to **Google Kubernetes Engine (GKE)**
- Measuring success

> **CI/CD**
>
> CI means that every time you push code changes to your repository, the code is built and tested, and the output is packaged as a build artifact. In CD, you automatically deploy your build artifacts to your environments whenever a new build artifact is created.
>
> When practicing CI/CD, the development and delivery phases are completely automated. The code is ready to be deployed to production at any time.
>
> There are various definitions that distinguish between **continuous delivery** and **continuous deployment** (both **CD**) – but these definitions are not consistent in the literature and only add little to no value to the topic.

Staged deployments

A **stage** or **tier** is an environment in which a piece of software is deployed and executed. Typical stages include `Development`, `Test`, `Staging` (or `Pre-Production`), and `Production`. Typically, the `Staging`, or `Pre-Production`, stage is a complete mirror of the production environment, and sometimes, it is used for zero-downtime deployments by switching the two environments using load balancing. Typically, stages that are closer to production require manual approval before deployment.

If a company works with feature flags (please refer to *Chapter 10, Feature Flags and the Feature Lifecycle*) and CD, normally, the number of stages decreases. Instead of stages, we can talk about **ring-based deployments** or **scaling units**. The idea of ring-based deployments is that you have customers in different productions rings. You deploy your update to one ring and automatically monitor the system for unexpected exceptions or unusual metrics such as CPU or memory usage. Additionally, you can run automated tests in the production environment. If there are no errors, the release process is continuous and deploys to the next ring. When discussing ring-based deployments, often, we imply that no manual approval is involved. However, there can also be manual approval between the rings.

In GitHub, you can perform staged and ring-based deployments using **Environments**. You can view, configure, or create new ones in your repository under **Settings | Environments**.

For each environment, you can define the following:

- **Required reviewers**: These include up to five users or teams as manual approvers. One of these approvers must approve the deployment before it is executed.

- **Wait timer**: This refers to a grace period that the deployment will wait before executing. The maximum time is 43,200 minutes or 30 days. Additionally, you can use an API to cancel the deployment if you find any errors at a previous stage.

- **Deployment branches**: Here, you can restrict what branches are deployed to an environment. You can select all `Protected branches` or define your own pattern. The pattern can include wildcards (such as `release/*`).

- **Environment secrets**: Secrets in an environment override secrets from the repository or organization scope. The secrets are only loaded after the required reviewers have approved the deployment.

The configuration looks similar to *Figure 9.1*:

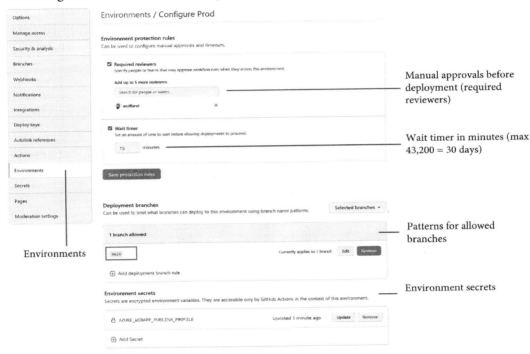

Figure 9.1 – Configuring an environment in GitHub

In the workflow file, you specify the environment at the job level:

```
jobs:
  deployment:
    runs-on: ubuntu-latest
    environment: prod
```

Additionally, you can specify a URL that is then displayed on the overview page:

```
jobs:
  deployment:
    runs-on: ubuntu-latest
    environment:
      name: production
      url: https://writeabout.net
```

With the `needs` keyword, you can define dependencies between jobs and, therefore, environments (see *Figure 9.2*):

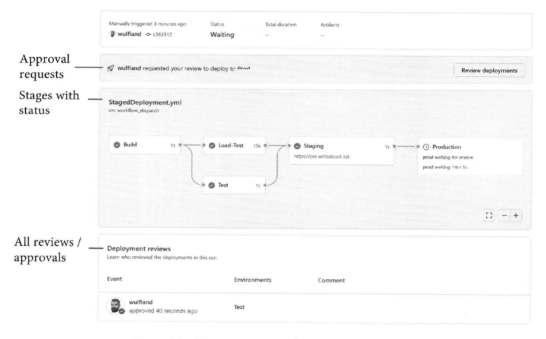

Figure 9.2 – The overview page for staged deployments

The status of the environments is also displayed on the home page of the repository (see *Figure 9.3*):

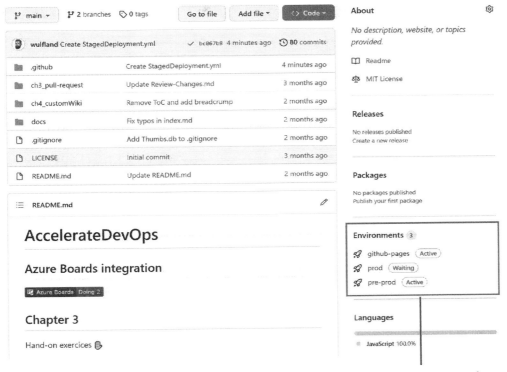

Environments and status on the home page of the repository

Figure 9.3 – Environments on the home page

If you want to play around with the environments, you can run the **Staged Deployment** workflow in the fork of `https://github.com/wulfland/AccelerateDevOps/` and add yourself as a required reviewer for some stages.

Automating your deployments

If I ask my customers whether they have automated their deployments, normally, the answer is *yes*. However, on closer look, automation means *we have a script*, or *we have an answer file for an installer*. That is only partial automation. As long as someone has to log in to a server, create accounts or DNS records, or manually configure a firewall, your deployment is not automated!

Humans make mistakes – machines do not! Make sure you automate all the steps of your deployment and not just the last steps. Since GitHub Actions is the perfect automation engine, it is a good practice to have a workflow execute all of your automated deployments.

How to deploy to Azure App Service

To get you started with automated deployments with GitHub Actions, I created three hands-on labs:

- Deploying to Azure App Service
- Deploying to AWS ECS
- Deploying to GKE

All hands-on labs assume that you have an account set up in the specified cloud. If you have a single-cloud strategy, you can simply jump to the hands-on step that's relevant for you and skip the others.

The step-by-step instructions for the hands-on lab are located in GitHub at `https://github.com/wulfland/AccelerateDevOps/blob/main/ch9_release/Deploy_to_Azure_App_Service.md`. It is recommended that you follow the steps there, as it provides links that are easy to copy and paste. Here, I will explain the background as a step-by-step guide with a focus on how to deploy the application.

Deployment of Azure resources

The deployment of the Azure resources takes place in the `setup-azure.sh` script. It creates a resource group, an app service plan, and an app service. You could easily execute the script in a workflow. After the deployment, we get the `publish` profile from the web app and store it inside a secret in GitHub. You can either get the publish profile in the Azure portal or from the Azure CLI:

```
$ az webapp deployment list-publishing-profiles \
    --resource-group $rgname \
    --name $appName \
    --xml
```

Deploying the application with GitHub Actions

The workflow consists of two jobs: `Build` and `Deploy`. The build job configures the runner for the correct **NodeJS** and **.NET** versions and builds the application. The following task uses `dotnet publish` to publish the website to a folder named `publish`:

```
- name: Build and publish with dotnet
  working-directory: ch9_release/src/Tailwind.Traders.Web
  run: |
    dotnet build --configuration Release
    dotnet publish -c Release -o publish
```

The next step uploads the artifact to GitHub so that it can be used in subsequent jobs. This allows you to publish the same package to multiple environments:

```
- name: Upload Artifact
  uses: actions/upload-artifact@v2
  with:
    name: website
    path: ch9_release/src/Tailwind.Traders.Web/publish
```

Additionally, you can see and inspect the artifact after the workflow has been completed (see *Figure 9.4*):

Figure 9.4 – Workflow artifacts

The `Deploy` job depends on `Build` and deploys to the `prod` environment. Within the environment, you set the secret and add a required reviewer:

```
Deploy:
    runs-on: ubuntu-latest
    environment: prod
    needs: Build
```

The workflow downloads the artifact, named `website`, into a folder called `website`:

```
- uses: actions/download-artifact@v2
  with:
    name: website
    path: website
```

Then, it uses the `azure/webapps-deploy` action to deploy the website using the publish profile:

```
- name: Run Azure webapp deploy action using publish profile
  credentials
  uses: azure/webapps-deploy@v2
  with:
    app-name: ${{ env.appName }}
    slot-name: Production
    publish-profile: ${{ secrets.AZUREAPPSERVICE_PUBLISHPROFILE
}}
    package: website
```

The last step is just an example of how you could validate a deployment. Of course, you would have to `curl` a URL to a site that also targets the database:

```
u=https://${{ env.appName }}.azurewebsites.net/
status=`curl --silent --head $u | head -1 | cut -f 2 -d' '`
if [ "$status" != "200" ]
then
  echo "Wrong HTTP Status. Actual: '$status'"
  exit 1
fi
```

If you complete the step-by-step guide in the hands-on lab, you will have a playground where you can add additional environments and deploy to different App Service deployment slots (for more information, please visit `https://docs.microsoft.com/en-us/azure/app-service/deploy-staging-slots`).

How to deploy to AWS ECS

We will deploy the same code to **AWS** – but this time, we will do so from a **Docker** container to **ECS**. ECS is a highly scalable container management service that allows you to run, stop, and manage containers on a cluster. You can find the step-by-step guide at `https://github.com/wulfland/AccelerateDevOps/blob/main/ch9_release/Deploy_to_AWS_ECS.md`.

Here are some additional notes and background information.

Deployment of AWS resources

I could not find an easy script in which I could deploy everything to AWS that did not also include some complex JSON. That's why I'm using the manual steps in the hands-on lab. First, you create an **Elastic Container Registry (ECR)** repository to which you can deploy the container. The secrets we use to deploy are called **Access keys,** and they consist of two values: `Access Key ID` and `Secret Access Key`.

After the first deployment, the container is in the registry, and you can use it together with the wizard to set up your ECS resources.

You have to extract your task definition and save it to the `aws-task-definition.json` file. The second time the workflow runs, it successfully deploys the container to ECS.

Deploying the container with GitHub Actions

I also split up the workflow into a `Build` stage and a `Deploy` stage. This enables you to easily add environments and more stages later. For this to work, you must pass the image name from the `Build` job to the `Deploy` job. To do this, you can use `job outputs`:

```
jobs:
  Build:
    runs-on: ubuntu-latest
    outputs:
      image: ${{ steps.build-image.outputs.image }}
```

To configure the authentication, we use the `configure-aws-credentials` action with the `Access Key ID` and `Secret Access Key` values.

Note that GitHub masks part of the image name and does not pass it to the next job. To avoid this, you must prevent the `configure-aws-credentials` action from masking your account ID:

```
- name: Configure AWS credentials
  uses: aws-actions/configure-aws-credentials@v1
  with:
    aws-access-key-id: ${{ secrets.AWS_ACCESS_KEY_ID }}
    aws-secret-access-key: ${{ secrets.AWS_SECRET_ACCESS_KEY }}
    aws-region: ${{ env.AWS_REGION }}
    mask-aws-account-id: no
```

The login to ECR returns the name of the registry that you use in the subsequent action:

```
- name: Login to Amazon ECR
  id: login-ecr
  uses: aws-actions/amazon-ecr-login@v1
```

In the next step, you build the image and push it to ECR. Additionally, you set the output for the next job:

```
- name: Build, tag, and push image to Amazon ECR
  id: build-image
  env:
    ECR_REGISTRY: ${{ steps.login-ecr.outputs.registry }}
    IMAGE_TAG: ${{ github.sha }}
  working-directory: ch9_release/src/Tailwind.Traders.Web
  run: |
    imagename=$ECR_REGISTRY/$ECR_REPOSITORY:$IMAGE_TAG
    echo "Build and push $imagename"
    docker build -t $imagename .
    docker push $imagename
    echo "::set-output name=image::$imagename"
```

The next job depends on `Build` and runs on the `prod` environment:

```
Deploy:
  runs-on: ubuntu-latest
  environment: prod
  needs: Build
```

Additionally, it has to configure the AWS credentials and then configure the `aws-task-definition.json` file using the image name that has been passed to the job access through the `needs` context:

```
- name: Fill in the new image ID in the ECS task definition
  id: task-def
  uses: aws-actions/amazon-ecs-render-task-definition@v1
  with:
    task-definition: ${{ env.ECS_TASK_DEFINITION }}
    container-name: ${{ env.CONTAINER_NAME }}
    image: ${{ needs.Build.outputs.image }}
```

The last step is to deploy the container with the output of the previous task:

```
- name: Deploy Amazon ECS task definition
  uses: aws-actions/amazon-ecs-deploy-task-definition@v1
  with:
    task-definition: ${{ steps.task-def.outputs.task-definition }}
    service: ${{ env.ECS_SERVICE }}
    cluster: ${{ env.ECS_CLUSTER }}
    wait-for-service-stability: true
```

If you perform the step-by-step guide, you have a staged working workflow that deploys to ECS. You can add more stages and run different versions of the container in different services.

How to deploy to GKE

We also deploy the same code to GKE. You can find the hands-on steps at `https://github.com/wulfland/AccelerateDevOps/blob/main/ch9_release/Deploy_to_GKE.md`.

Before you perform these hands-on steps, here are some details regarding what is happening.

Deployment of Google resources

The complete deployment happens in the `setup-gke.sh` script that you execute in Cloud Shell. The script creates a GKE cluster with one node. For testing purposes, this is enough:

```
gcloud container clusters create $GKE_CLUSTER --num-nodes=1
```

Additionally, the script creates an artifact repository for Docker containers and a service account to perform the deployments.

In Kubernetes, there is the concept of **pods**. These contain the containers and are deployed using deployments in a YAML file, which, in this case, is `Deployment.yaml`. The deployment defines the container and binds it to an image:

```
spec:
  containers:
```

```
- name: $GKE_APP_NAME
  image: $GKE_REGION-docker.pkg.dev/$GKE_PROJECT/$GKE_
PROJECT/$GKE_APP_NAME:$GITHUB_SHA
  ports:
  - containerPort: 80
  env:
    - name: PORT
      value: "80"
```

I use environment variables in the file and replace them with `envsubst` before passing them to the `kubectl apply` command:

```
envsubst < Deployment.yml | kubectl apply -f -
```

A service exposes the pods – in this case, to the internet. The service is deployed, in the same way, using the `Service.yml` file:

```
spec:
  type: LoadBalancer
  selector:
    app: $GKE_APP_NAME
  ports:
  - port: 80
    targetPort: 80
```

The deployment of the service takes some time. You might have to execute the following command multiple times:

```
$ kubectl get service
```

If you get an external IP address, you can use it to test your deployment (see *Figure 9.5*):

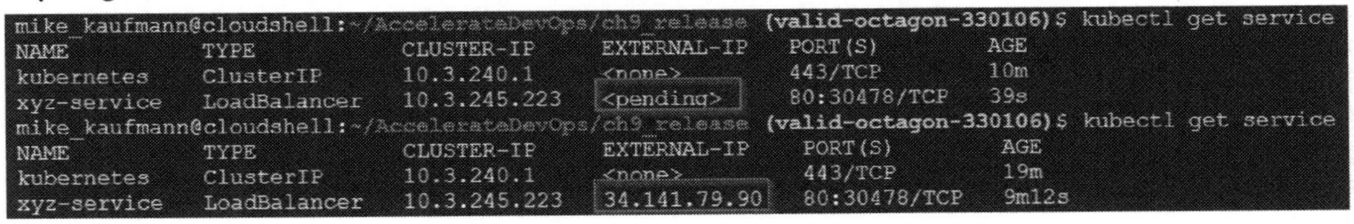

```
mike_kaufmann@cloudshell:~/AccelerateDevOps/ch9_release (valid-octagon-330106)$ kubectl get service
NAME           TYPE           CLUSTER-IP     EXTERNAL-IP    PORT(S)        AGE
kubernetes     ClusterIP      10.3.240.1     <none>         443/TCP        10m
xyz-service    LoadBalancer   10.3.245.223   <pending>      80:30478/TCP   39s
mike_kaufmann@cloudshell:~/AccelerateDevOps/ch9_release (valid-octagon-330106)$ kubectl get service
NAME           TYPE           CLUSTER-IP     EXTERNAL-IP    PORT(S)        AGE
kubernetes     ClusterIP      10.3.240.1     <none>         443/TCP        19m
xyz-service    LoadBalancer   10.3.245.223   34.141.79.90   80:30478/TCP   9m12s
```

Figure 9.5 – Getting the external IP of the GKE LoadBalancer

The credentials of the service account are in the key.json file. You have to encode them and save them inside an encrypted secret in GitHub, named GKE_SA_KEY:

```
$ cat key.json | base64
```

The script has already done this. So, you can just copy the output and paste it to the secret.

Deploying the container with GitHub Actions

The deployment in the GitHub Actions workflow is straightforward. The authentication and setup of the gcloud CLI take place in the setup-gcloud action:

```
- uses: google-github-actions/setup-gcloud@v0.2.0
  with:
    service_account_key: ${{ secrets.GKE_SA_KEY }}
    project_id: ${{ secrets.GKE_PROJECT }}
    export_default_credentials: true
```

The workflow then builds and pushes the container to the registry. It uses gcloud to authenticate to the Docker registry:

```
gcloud auth configure-docker \
    $GKE_REGION-docker.pkg.dev \
    --quiet
```

To deploy the new image to GKE, we authenticate using the get-gke-credentials action:

```
- uses: google-github-actions/get-gke-credentials@v0.2.1
  with:
    cluster_name: ${{ env.GKE_CLUSTER }}
    location: ${{ env.GKE_ZONE }}
    credentials: ${{ secrets.GKE_SA_KEY }}
```

Following this, we just replace the variables in the deployment files and pass them to kubectl apply:

```
envsubst < Service.yml | kubectl apply -f -
envsubst < Deployment.yml | kubectl apply -f -
```

That's it. Following the hands-on steps, you should have a working copy of a deployment to GKE!

Deployments to Kubernetes

Deployments to Kubernetes can be very complex; however, this is beyond the scope of this book. There are different strategies that you can use: **recreate**, **rolling updates** (also known as **ramped updates**), **blue/green deployments**, **canary deployments**, and **A/B testing**. A good starting point is the official documentation, which can be found at `https://kubernetes.io/docs/concepts/workloads/controllers/`. Additionally, a useful visualization of the strategies along with practical examples of how to perform the deployments can be found at `https://github.com/ContainerSolutions/k8s-deployment-strategies`.

There are also many other tools that you can leverage when working with Kubernetes. For instance, **Helm** (`https://helm.sh/`) is a package manager for Kubernetes, and **Kustomize** (`https://kustomize.io/`) is a tool that can help you manage multiple configurations.

Infrastructure as code

Infrastructure as code (**IaC**) is the process of managing and provisioning all your infrastructure resources through machine-readable files. Often, these files are versioned and managed in Git-like code. In this case, it is often referred to as **GitOps**.

IaC can be imperative, declarative, or a mix of both. Imperative means the files are procedural, such as scripts, whereas declarative refers to a functional approach that describes the desired state in a markup language such as YAML or JSON. To get the full power of *IaC*, you should manage it in a way where you can also apply changes, not just complete provisioning and deprovisioning. This is often referred to as **Continuous Configuration Automation** (**CCA**).

Tools

There are many tools that you can use for *IaC* and *CCA*. For instance, there are cloud-specific tools such as **Azure ARM**, **Bicep**, or **AWS CloudFormation**. However, there are also many independent tools that you can use for on-premises infrastructure. Some of the most popular are listed as follows:

- **Puppet**: This was released by Puppet in 2005 (`https://puppet.com`).
- **Chef**: This was released by Chef in 2009 (`https://www.chef.io`).

- **Ansible**: This was released by RedHat in 2021 (`https://www.ansible.com`).

- **Terraform**: This was released by HashiCorp in 2014 (`https://www.terraform.io`).

- **Pulumi**: This was released 2017 by Pulumi (`https://www.pulumi.com`).

> **IaC and Multi-Cloud Deployments**
>
> Note that an *IaC* tool supporting multiple cloud providers does not mean it can deploy the same resources to multiple clouds! This is a common misconception. You still have to write cloud-specific automations. But you can use the same syntax and tooling.

This is just the tip of the iceberg. There are many tools on the market. The process of finding the best combination can be very complex and is beyond the scope of this book. If you have a single-cloud strategy, it's probably best if you just start with the cloud-native tools. If you have a complex environment with multiple clouds and on-premises resources and you want to manage them all with the same tooling, you must invest in doing a detailed analysis.

Best practices

Independent of the tool you are using, there are some things you should consider when implementing *IaC*:

- Store the configuration in Git and treat it like code using protected branches, pull requests, and code owners. Code owners are a great way to ensure compliance, particularly if you store it close to the application code.

- Execute the deployment using GitHub Actions. It's okay to publish the resources interactively while *writing* and debugging your IaC. However, once you are finished, you should have complete automated publishing that is done via a workflow. IaC is code, and, as with application code, deploying it from a developer machine comes with the risk of not being reproducible.

- Secrets and key management are the most critical parts of IaC. Make sure that you do not save them in the code but keep them in a secure place (such as GitHub Secrets). A vault such as **Hashicorp Vault** or **Azure KeyVault** allows for easy key rotation if one of your secrets is compromised. Additionally, it decouples your secure management from the provisioning of resources.

- When possible, use **OpenID Connect (OIDC)**. This is to avoid using credentials to access cloud resources but short-lived tokens instead, which can also be rotated (for more information, please refer to `https://docs.github.com/en/actions/deployment/security-hardening-your-deployments`).

I use the cloud-native tools in this book. It is easier to transition from them to an *IaC* or *CCA* tool than vice versa.

Strategies

There are different strategies regarding how to organize your infrastructure code in a manageable, scalable, and compliant way. Essentially, it depends on your organizational structure and which one is the best for you. They are as follows:

- **Central**: The infrastructure resources live in central repositories, and feature teams can provision from there using a self-service (that is, triggering a workflow). This approach has the benefit of having all resources in one place, and the responsible unit will have strong control over it. The disadvantage is that it is not very flexible for developers and that the *distance* from the code to the infrastructure will impact the way the engineers treat the infrastructure.

- **Decentral**: The infrastructure resources live alongside the code. You can use templates (please refer to the *Workflow templates* section) to help engineering teams set up the infrastructure. Additionally, you can use **CODEOWNERS** and protected branches to require approval from a shared, responsible team. This approach is very flexible, but the control of costs and governance are more difficult.

  You could deploy – or ensure the correct state of – the infrastructure with every build. But this would slow down build times and cost valuable build minutes. In most cases, it is preferable to deploy the resources in a separate workflow on demand.

- **Templated**: The team that is responsible for the shared infrastructure provides fixed templates that can be used by the feature teams. The templates could be **Actions**, that is, composite actions with preconfigured native actions or completely customized ones in Docker or JavaScript. Alternatively, you can use a reusable workflow (refer to the *Reusable workflows* section). In any case, the ownership of the reused workflow or action stays with the central team. This approach works well if you limit the number of allowed actions within your enterprise.

- **Mixed**: This is a mix of the preceding three strategies. For example, the test and development infrastructures could be decentralized, and production environments could be templated.

No matter which strategy you use, be intentional about it. The solution will greatly impact how your teams work together and how infrastructure is used in value delivery!

Workflow templates

Workflow templates are workflow files stored in a `workflow-templates` folder in the `.github` repository of an organization alongside a metadata file and an icon file (see *Figure 9.6*):

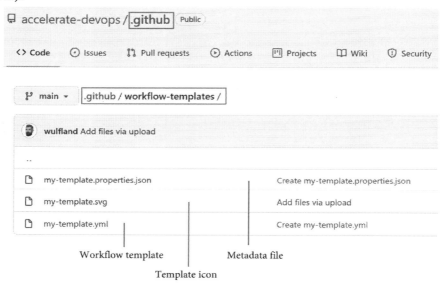

Figure 9.6 – Workflow templates for an organization

The template itself is a normal workflow file. You can use the `$default-branch` variable for triggers to filter by the default branch.

Along with the template, you need to save an icon in `.svg` format and a properties file. The properties file looks like this:

```
{
    "name": "My Workflow Template",
    "description": "Description of template workflow",
```

```
    "iconName": "my-template",
    "categories": [
        "javascript"
    ],
    "filePatterns": [
        "package.json$",
        "^Dockerfile",
        ".*\\.md$"
    ]
}
```

Here, the `name`, `description`, and `iconName` values are required. Note that the `iconName` value is without the extension. In the `categories` array, you can specify the coding languages that this workflow template is relevant for. The same is true for file patterns: you can specify patterns for certain files in the user's repository. The template will be displayed more prominently if the repository contains files that match a pattern.

Now if a user of the organization creates a new workflow, they are presented with the templates of the organization (see *Figure 9.7*):

Figure 9.7 – Creating a workflow from a template

The template has been copied and *can be modified*! That's why workflow templates are not suitable for the templated strategy.

To learn more about workflow templates, please visit `https://docs.github.com/en/actions/learn-github-actions/creating-workflow-templates`.

Reusable workflows

A **reusable workflow** is a workflow that can be called by another workflow. A workflow must have the `workflow_call` trigger to be reusable:

```
on:
  workflow_call:
```

You can define inputs that can be passed to the workflow. Inputs can be `boolean`, `number`, `string`, or a **secret**:

```
on:
  workflow_call:
    inputs:
      my_environment:
        description: 'The environment to deploy to.'
        default: 'Prod'
        required: true
        type: string
    secrets:
      my_token:
        description: 'The token to access the environment'
        required: true
```

You can access the inputs in the reusable workflow using the `inputs` context (`${{ inputs.my_environment }}`) and the secrets using the `secrets` context (`${{ secrets.my_token }}`).

To use a reusable workflow, you have to reference the file in the following format:

```
{owner}/{repo}/{path}/{filename}@{ref}
```

The workflow is called in a job, and you specify the inputs and secrets as follows:

```
jobs:
  call-workflow-1:
    uses: org/repo/.github/workflows/reusable.yml@v1
    with:
```

```
    my_environment: development
  secrets:
    my_token: ${{ secrets.TOKEN }}
```

Reusable workflows are perfect to avoid duplication. Together with semantic versioning and tags, this is a great way to release reusable workflows to the teams in your organization.

To learn more about reusable workflows, please visit `https://docs.github.com/en/actions/learn-github-actions/reusing-workflows`.

Measuring success

In *Chapter 1*, *Metrics that Matter*, I introduced you to the **Four Keys dashboard**. This is a dashboard that displays the DORA metrics. If you deploy automatically to production, it's time to shift from surveys to real metrics. The dashboard is one way to do this.

To install the dashboard, follow the instructions at `https://github.com/GoogleCloudPlatform/fourkeys/blob/main/setup/README.md`.

First, create a project in Google Cloud with billing enabled and note the project ID (not the name!). Then, open **Google Cloud Shell** (located at `https://cloud.google.com/shell`), clone the repository, and execute the deployment script:

```
$ git clone \
    https://github.com/GoogleCloudPlatform/fourkeys.git
$ cd fourkeys
$ gcloud config set project <project-id>
$ script setup.log -c ./setup.sh
```

The script asks you some questions that you can use to tailor your deployment. If everything went well, you should see a nice dashboard in Grafana. To configure GitHub to send data to the event handlers in Google, you have to get the event handler endpoint and secret. Just execute the following two commands in Cloud Shell and copy the output:

```
$ echo $(terraform output -raw event_handler_endpoint)
> https://event-handler-dup4ubihba-uc.a.run.app
$ echo $(terraform output -raw event_handler_secret)
> 241d0765b5a6cb80208e66a2d3e39d254051377f
```

Now, head over to the repository in GitHub where you want to send data to the dashboard and create a webhook under **Setting | Webhooks | Add webhook**. Paste the URL of the event handler and the secret into the fields and select **Send me everything**. Click on **Add webhook** to start sending all the events to the event handler (see *Figure 9.8*):

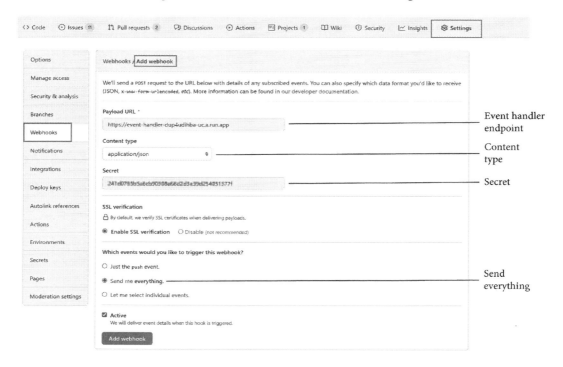

Figure 9.8 – Adding a webhook to send data to the four keys dashboard

Unfortunately, you can currently only send the deployment data to the dashboard. In previous versions, you were able to send individual events to the workflows.

To indicate a live-site issue, you must add a tag named `Incident` to an open issue. In the body, you add `root cause:` followed by `SHA` of the commit that caused the event.

The **Four Keys** dashboard is a nice way to view your DevOps metrics (see *Figure 9.9*):

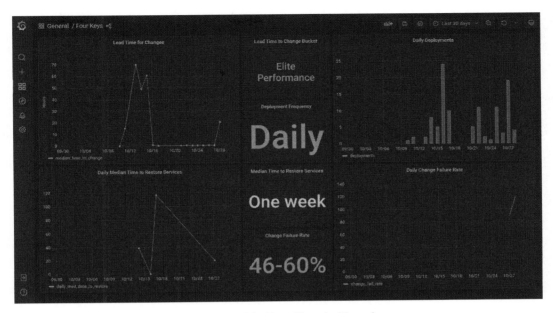

Figure 9.9 – The Four Keys dashboard

However, don't forget that these are not metrics to compare teams with each other. Don't let the metrics be the goal!

Case study

With CI set up, the next thing our two pilot teams at **Tailwind Gears** need to do is automate the deployment and release processes of the software.

The first team runs some web applications that are still hosted on-premises. Instead of automating the on-premises deployment, the team moves the applications to a hosted **Kubernetes** service in the **cloud**. The cluster instances, network, and other cloud resources have already been set up by the IT department during the last sprints. Therefore, the team can easily transition the deployment to a staged deployment process. They deploy to a test instance and run all of the automated tests they have. They also add a test using **curl**, which calls a website that checks the database and backend accessibility to ensure everything is working as expected. If all tests pass, the deployment automatically deploys to production using a rolling update to ensure zero downtime for users.

Some of the code of the web applications, which contains shared concerns, needs to be adjusted to work in the cloud. This code is also contained in web applications from other teams. The team decides to move the code to **GitHub Packages** (**NPM** for the JavaScript and **NuGet** for .NET) with its own release cycle and **semantic versioning** to allow other teams, in the future, to reuse the code easily when they move to the cloud.

The second team produces software for hardware products that are used in machines for safety-critical functions. This means the development process is highly regulated. They are required to have end-to-end traceability for all changes they do. Since all the requirements were imported into GitHub issues and are linked using nested issues, this is not an issue. They just have to reference the lowest-level issue in the commit message. In addition to end-to-end traceability, there are some test documentations for different levels of requirements that are not yet automated. Plus there are some documents for risk management. To ensure all these criteria are met before releasing the product, **required reviewers** manually approve a release before deploying to production to ensure that all requirements are in place to be compliant. Together with **protected branches** and **codeowners** (the required documents were already converted into markdown), this reduces the effort of releasing a lot at once.

The installation of the binaries onto the hardware is performed by a custom tool that is owned by the company and runs on a machine in production. This tool is used to pick the binaries up from a file share. This was not optimal for end-to-end traceability and relied on log files. The deployment to test environments was performed manually, which means the way the binaries were distributed was not consistent. To address this, the team puts the binaries together with the tool in a **Docker container** and publishes the image to the **container registry** of GitHub Packages. The Docker image can then be used to transfer versions to test machines and during the assembly process in the same way.

Summary

In this chapter, you learned how to use **GitHub environments** to stage and protect your deployments and how to use GitHub Actions to deploy to any cloud or platform in a secure manner. I demonstrated how to use workflow templates and reusable workflows to help you collaborate on your **IaC**.

In the next chapter, you will learn how to optimize the rolling out of your features and the entire feature life cycle using **FeatureFlags/FeatureToggles**.

Further reading

Here is a list of references from this chapter that you can also use to gain more information about the topics we discussed:

- CI/CD: `https://azure.microsoft.com/en-us/overview/continuous-delivery-vs-continuous-deployment/`

- Deployment rings: `https://docs.microsoft.com/en-us/azure/devops/migrate/phase-rollout-with-rings`

- *Deploying to Azure App Service*: `https://docs.github.com/en/actions/deployment/deploying-to-your-cloud-provider/deploying-to-azure-app-service`

- *Deploying to Google Kubernetes Engine*: `https://docs.github.com/en/actions/deployment/deploying-to-your-cloud-provider/deploying-to-google-kubernetes-engine`

- *Deploy to Amazon Elastic Container Service*: `https://docs.github.com/en/actions/deployment/deploying-to-your-cloud-provider/deploying-to-amazon-elastic-container-service`

- *Security hardening your deployments*: `https://docs.github.com/en/actions/deployment/security-hardening-your-deployments`

- Kubernetes deployments: `https://kubernetes.io/docs/concepts/workloads/controllers/`

- Kubernetes deployment strategies: `https://github.com/ContainerSolutions/k8s-deployment-strategies`

- *Helm*: `https://helm.sh/`

- *Kustomize*: `https://kustomize.io/`

- *Infrastructure as code*: `https://en.wikipedia.org/wiki/Infrastructure_as_code`

- IaC and environment or configuration drift: `https://docs.microsoft.com/en-us/devops/deliver/what-is-infrastructure-as-code`

- *Creating workflow templates*: `https://docs.github.com/en/actions/learn-github-actions/creating-workflow-templates`

- Reusable workflows: `https://docs.github.com/en/actions/learn-github-actions/reusing-workflows`

- The four keys project: `https://github.com/GoogleCloudPlatform/fourkeys/`

10

Feature Flags and the Feature Lifecycle

Feature Flags are one of the most game-changing capabilities I've seen over the years when working with teams. They have many different use cases. They can help you to reduce complexity in your development workflow by merging code early, or they can help you to perform zero-downtime deployments. Feature Flags help you to get more value out of your features by managing the entire feature lifecycle.

In this chapter, I will explain what Feature Flags – also known as **Feature Toggles** – are and what you can do with them. Unfortunately, there is no native solution in GitHub to help with Feature Flags. There are too many frameworks and services available that you could use to introduce them all. But I will give you some guidance on how to pick the best tools for your use case.

The main topics of this chapter are as follows:

- What are Feature Flags?
- The lifecycle of features
- The benefits of Feature Flags

- Getting started with Feature Flags
- Feature Flags and technical debt
- Experimentation with Feature Flags

What are Feature Flags?

Feature Flags are a technique in software development that allows modifying runtime behavior without changing code. It decouples the release of functionality to the end users from the rollout of the binaries.

Feature Flags work like a switch or toggle and are, therefore, often called **Feature Toggles** or **Feature Switches** because of their Boolean nature. But Feature Flags can have many different use cases and can be more complex than a toggle. That's why the term *Feature Flag* is more suitable.

Feature Flags allow you to encapsulate new code behind a Feature Flag and roll it out to the production system. The feature can then be enabled based on the context for a given target audience only (see *Figure 10.1*):

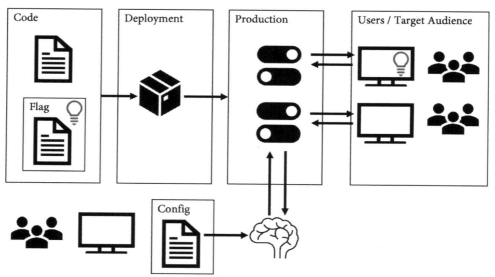

Figure 10.1 – How Feature Flags work

Feature Flags are a very natural technique for developers if you have continuous delivery available and a separate team that is responsible for the infrastructure. It's easier for developers to add a flag to the code than to change infrastructure, so you often end up with flags that allow testers to do different things than normal users or with some that allow some beta users to test some stuff. The problem is that if you are not explicit about Feature Flags, the configuration will normally end up in different places: config files, group memberships, and the application database. Being explicit about flags helps to improve the transparency in the team and ensures a uniform approach, and it enables more advanced use cases and ensures security and scalability.

The lifecycle of features

Until a few years ago, most software was released every 1 or 2 years in major versions that had to be purchased separately or at least were coupled tightly to licensing through subscriptions. All the new features were squeezed into these new release versions. The new releases normally came with pieces of training, books, and online courses to teach the users the new features.

These sales models basically do not exist anymore today. Customers want their software as a service. No matter if we talk about mobile apps such as Facebook or WhatsApp, or desktop software such as Office or Windows, software is updated and optimized continuously, and new features are added constantly. This brings the challenge of educating your end users on how to use the new features properly. An intuitive user experience and easy discoverability of new features are more important than they were with the old sales model. Features must be self-explanatory, and a simple on-screen dialog must be sufficient to educate users on how to use the new feature.

Also, value creation is completely different. Customers do not make their buy decision every few years. They decide every day if they use the software for a task at hand or not. So, instead of putting a ton of new features into a new version to influence buy decisions, the focus is on delivering fewer features with a high value by removing features that are not used or optimizing them until they are of high value.

This means every feature is subject to a lifecycle. The lifecycle of a feature could look like the one in *Figure 10.2*:

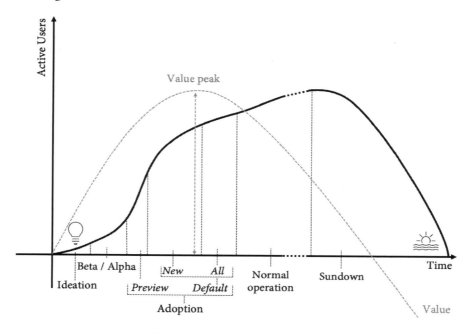

Figure 10.2 – The lifecycle of features

The lifecycle is subject to the following phases:

- **Ideation and development**: After the idea for a new feature, the implementation starts with a few internal users. The feedback of these users is used to improve the feature.

- **Alpha or beta**: In the alpha and/or beta phase, the feature is provisioned to a broader, but still very limited, audience. The audience can be internal or selected external customers. The alpha or beta phase can be closed (private) or open (public), but the feature in this phase is still very dynamic and can change dramatically.

- **Adoption**: If the feature is mature enough for the market, it is gradually exposed to a broader audience. The adoption phase can be divided into the following sub-phases:

  A.   **Preview**: The users can **opt in** and enable the preview feature.

B. **Default for new users**: The feature is the default for new users – but users could still **opt out** if they don't want to use it.

C. **Default for all users**: The feature is enabled for all users, but users can still opt out.

- **Normal operation**: The feature is used by all users and an opt-out is not possible anymore. Previous versions of the feature get removed from the system. The normal operation can go on for many years.

- **Sundown**: The feature is replaced by a newer and hopefully better feature. The number of users that use this feature declines and the cost of maintaining the feature exceeds its value. The feature is removed from the system when all users can be redirected to a new feature.

Note that the value of the feature is the biggest in the early adoption phase as it attracts new users to your application. In the normal operations phase, the hype has probably flattened, and the competition has also learned from your feature and reacted by adjusting their software.

The benefits of Feature Flags

Managing the lifecycle of a feature without using Feature Flags is impossible, but there are many other use cases where Feature Flags can bring value to your DevOps teams:

- **Release flags**: These are used to roll out code behind a flag. Release flags normally stay in the code until the feature is rolled out completely. This can be weeks or months. Release flags change with each deployment or with the system's configuration. This means they can be implemented very easily by just reading a configuration value. But if you want to use release flags for **canary releases** (gradually exposing the feature to more and more users) or **blue-green deployments** (swapping staging and production environments), they are much more dynamic.

- **Experimentation flags**: If you roll out multiple versions of the same feature and expose it to different audiences, it is called **A/B testing** or **experimentation**. It is normally used to confirm or diminish a hypothesis by measuring certain metrics of how users interact with the version of the feature. Experimentation flags are highly dynamic and rely on a lot of contexts to use them to address different target audiences.

- **Permission flags**: A common use case of Feature Flags is to control what users can access. This can be *administration features* or *testing features* that are only exposed to certain audiences, or *premium features* that are only exposed to paying customers. Permission flags are highly dynamic and normally stay in the code for a long time – sometimes until the end of the application lifecycle. They also expose a high risk of fraud and must, therefore, be used carefully.

- **Operation flags**: Some flags are used for operational aspects of the application – for example, *kill switches* used to disable certain functionality that can be a bottleneck for other features (also known as a *circuit breaker*). A flag to control different versions of a backend system is also considered an operation flag. Multi-variant flags are often used to control logging verbosity or other operational aspects.

Figure 10.3 shows an overview of the different types of Feature Flags categorized by dynamic and the time they stay in the system:

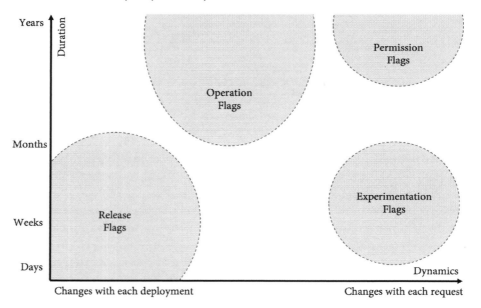

Figure 10.3 – Types of Feature Flags

Now that we have learned what Feature Flags are and what you can do with them, I will show you how you can implement them in code.

Getting started with Feature Flags

In code, a Feature Flag is nothing more than an `if` statement. Let's assume you have a current implementation of the dialog to register new users:

```
function showRegisterDialog(){
    // current implementation
}
```

Now, you want to create a new dialog using a Feature Flag and be able to switch on the new dialog at runtime:

```
function showRegisterDialog(){
    var newRegisterDialog = false;

    if( newRegisterDialog ){
        return showNewRegisterDialog();
    }else{
        return showOldRegisterDialog();
    }
}

function showNewRegisterDialog(){
    // new implementation
}

function showOldRegisterDialog(){
    // old implementation
}
```

To enable or disable the feature dynamically, you have to extract the validation of the Feature Flag into its own function:

```
function showRegisterDialog(){
    if( featureIsEnabled("new-register-user-dialog") ){
        return showNewRegisterDialog();
    }else{
```

```
        return showOldRegisterDialog();
    }
}
```

There are many options where you can store the configuration of the Feature Flag:

- The system configuration
- The user configuration
- The application database
- A separate database
- A separate system (accessed through an API)

It highly depends on your use case what locations work or don't work.

Feature Flags and technical debt

If you start using Feature Flags, you normally end up with a highly configurable system that can change its behavior at runtime – normally by many flags that are scattered across multiple configuration sources. The flags tend to have dependencies between each other, so enabling or disabling flags exposes a great risk to the stability of the system. You managed to escape *merge hell* by avoiding parallel branches, but ended up in *feature flag hell*, with hundreds of flags that nobody knows what they are for.

To avoid this, you should follow these best practices:

- **Metrics**: Even with all the value they provide, Feature Flags in your code are some kind of technical debt. You should measure them as you do code coverage or other code-related metrics. Measure the *number* of Feature Flags, how long they exist (*duration*), how they evaluate in each environment (*value*, 100% true in production probably means the flag can be removed), and how often the flags are used (*calls*).

- **Central management**: Manage your flags in one central place, especially if you use different methods to manage the flags. Each flag should have an *owner* and a *description*. Document the *dependencies* between Feature Flags.

- **Integration into your process**: Integrate the management of Feature Flags into your process. For example, if you use Scrum, you can integrate the review of the Feature Flags in the *review* meeting. Make sure that all the people who work with the flags regularly go through all the flags and check which ones can be removed from the system.

- **Naming conventions**: Use naming conventions for all types of flags that you use. You could use `tmp-` as a prefix for temporary flags and `perm-` for permanent ones. Don't make it too complicated, but the name of the flag should immediately indicate what kind of flag it is and how long it is supposed to stick around in the code base.

A technique that some teams like and others do not is **cleaning up branches**. You can see if this technique works for you. The idea is that the moment you create the flag and write the code, you know best how the code should look if the flag is removed one day. So, you create a cleanup branch and pull request alongside the code and leave the pull request open until the flag is removed. The technique works best with good naming conventions.

Take the preceding example; you have a flag for a new feature dialog. The code with the flag looks like this:

```
function showRegisterDialog(){
    if( featureIsEnabled("tmp-new-register-user-dialog") ){
        return showNewRegisterDialog();
    }else{
        return showOldRegisterDialog();
    }
}
```

The code is developed in a `features/new-register-dialog` branch and you create the pull request to merge the code.

You already know that the final state of the code, when the flag is removed, will only use the new dialog, so you create a new branch (for example, `cleanup/new-register-dialog`) and add the final version of the code:

```
function showRegisterDialog(){
    return showNewRegisterDialog();
}
```

You can then create a pull request and leave it open until the feature is rolled out completely and you want to clean up the code.

As I said, this technique is not well suited for all teams. Maintaining the cleanup branches can be a lot of work in a complex environment, but you can give it a try.

Feature Flags that do not get cleaned up and are not actively maintained are technical debt, but the advantages outweigh the disadvantages. If you are careful from the beginning, you can avoid the feature flag hell and only benefit from the flexible power they provide you when releasing and operating your application.

Frameworks and products

There are many frameworks available that you can leverage when implementing Feature Flags. The framework that is the best for you depends a lot on your programming languages and use cases. Some focus more on UI integration, some more on rollout and operations. When picking your framework, you should consider the following aspects:

- **Performance**: Feature Flags must be fast and must not reduce the performance of your application. Proper caching should be used and also default values that are used if the data store cannot be reached on time.

- **Supported programming languages**: Your solution should work with all your languages, especially when you use client-side flags; you must also evaluate them on the server for security reasons. You don't want to configure the flags in different locations.

- **UI integration**: If you want to provide the users with the ability to opt in or out of features, you want a good integration into your UI. Normally, you need two flags for that: one to control the visibility, and one to enable or disable the feature.

- **Context**: When you want to use Feature Flags for A/B testing and experimentation, you need a lot of context information to evaluate the flags: the user, group memberships, the region, and the server, for example. This is where many frameworks fail.

- **Central management**: Flags that you configure for each environment separately, for example, are impossible to maintain. You need one central management platform where you can control all the flags in one place.

- **Data store**: Some frameworks store the configuration in your application database. This is problematic for many scenarios. Normally, you have a different database in all your environments, so managing the settings across the environments is difficult.

Building a scalable, performant, and mature solution takes a lot of time and effort, even when using frameworks, but there are also products available that you can install or consume as a service. A product that has been around for many years and is established mature is **LaunchDarkly** (https://launchdarkly.com/). There is a lot of competition now, including the following:

- **Switchover** (https://switchover.io/)
- **VWO** (https://vwo.com/)

- **Split** (`https://www.split.io/`)

- **Flagship** (`https://www.flagship.io/`)

- **Azure App configuration** (`https://docs.microsoft.com/en-us/azure/azure-app-configuration/overview`)

Unleash (`https://www.getunleash.io/`) is also worth mentioning. It has an **open core** (`https://github.com/Unleash/unleash`) and can be self-hosted free of charge as a Docker container. Unleash is also the solution that is used by GitLab.

I could not find a good resource that compares the solutions, so I added a page on GitHub (`https://wulfland.github.io/FeatureFlags/`) that provides an independent comparison of the solutions.

When it comes to the make-or-buy decision, most companies are better off using an existing service or product. Building and running a good solution for Feature Flags is difficult and time-consuming, especially if you are new to Feature Flags. Start with a good product. If, after some time, you still find it necessary to build your own solution, at least you have experience knowing what a solution should be able to do.

Experimentation with Feature Flags

Experimentation and A/B testing cannot only be done using Feature Flags. You can also develop containers in different branches and use Kubernetes to run different versions in production; however, this will increase your complexity in Git and does not scale well. You don't have the context for the users either, so gathering the data to prove or diminish your hypothesis is much harder. Most of the solutions for Feature Flags have built-in support for experiments, so this is the fastest way to get started.

To experiment, you define a hypothesis, conduct an experiment, and then learn from the results. An experiment can be defined as follows (see *Figure 10.4*):

- **Hypothesis**: We believe *{customer segment}*, wants *{product/feature}* because *{value prop}*.

- **Experiment**: To prove or disprove the preceding, the team will conduct an experiment.

- **Learning**: The experiment will prove the hypothesis by impacting the following metrics.

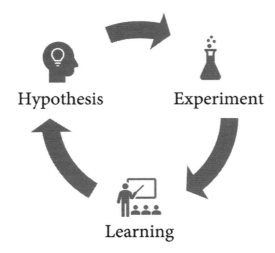

Figure 10.4 – Conducting experiments with Feature Flags

Let's have a look at an example. By looking into the usage data of your application, you realize that the page views for the first page of the registration dialog for new users are much higher than the number of people that finish the registration process. Only about 20% of them finish the registration. The hypothesis is that the register dialog is too complex and that the number of people finishing the registration will increase dramatically when the dialog is simplified.

To conduct the experiment, you add two new metrics to your application: `started-registration`, which increases every time a user clicks on the **Register** link, and `finished-registrations`, which increase after the user successfully registers for your application. The two metrics make it easy to calculate `aborted-registrations`. You gather the data during the next few weeks and confirm that the aborted registration rate has an average of 80% over these weeks. Your team creates a new, simple dialog using a `new-register-dialog` Feature Flag. It removes all required fields that are not necessary for the registration itself, such as address and payment information, and ships the code to production. The data is validated before checkout anyway, so the simplified registration works, even if this might be a usability problem for the checkout.

In production, you turn on the flag for 50% of the new users and compare the `aborted-registrations` rate for the two groups. The users that see the old dialog stay as expected at around 70% to 80% aborted, whereas the users with the new dialog only have an aborted rate of 55%.

The result is still not perfect so you start adding new metrics to find out where in the dialog the people are struggling. This leads to the next hypothesis (see *Figure 10.5*):

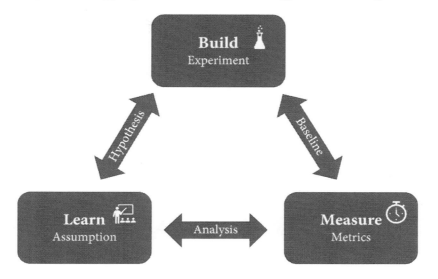

Figure 10.5 – Conducting experiments with Feature Flags

To experiment with Feature Flags, you need data. Only with the right metrics and the ability to map the metrics to audiences that have certain flags on or off are you able to really perform evidence-based development.

In *Chapter 19, Experimentation and A/B Testing with GitHub*, we will, unsurprisingly, have a closer look into experimentation and A/B testing with GitHub.

Summary

Feature Flags are one of the most important capabilities for the acceleration of DevOps teams. Unfortunately, GitHub does not have a built-in solution so far. But there are many products that can help you to get up to speed.

In this chapter, you learned about the feature lifecycle and how you can manage it using Feature Flags. You also learned how you can leverage Feature Flags to reduce complexity by checking code early.

In the next chapter, you'll learn about trunk-based development and the best Git workflow to support fast DevOps teams.

Further reading

You can get more information on the topics here:

- Martin Fowler, *Feature-Toggles (aka Feature Flags)*, 2017: `https://martinfowler.com/articles/feature-toggles.html`

- Comparison of Feature Flag solutions: `https://wulfland.github.io/FeatureFlags/`

- LaunchDarkly: `https://launchdarkly.com/`

- Switchover: `https://switchover.io/`

- VWO: `https://vwo.com/`

- Split: `https://www.split.io/`

- Flagship: `https://www.flagship.io/`

- Unleash: `https://www.getunleash.io/` and `https://github.com/Unleash/unleash`

11
Trunk-Based Development

One of the capabilities that are highly correlated with accelerated engineering velocity is **trunk-based development** (also known as **TBD**). High-performing teams have fewer than three active branches at any time, and their branches have a short lifetime (less than a day) before being merged into the main branch (Forsgren N., Humble, J., and Kim, G. 2018, page 98). Unfortunately, TBD is not a `git` **workflow** but rather a branching model of choice that has been in use since the 80s. It is not well defined and leaves a lot of room for interpretation, especially when it comes to using it with GitHub. Also, I personally find that only moving to a trunk-based workflow does not increase the performance too much. Only large teams with a highly complex workflow that are already stuck in **merge hell** really have this high impact. For most teams, it is more a combination of different capabilities such as feature flags and **continuous integration/continuous deployment (CI/CD)**, together with a trunk-based workflow, that makes a big difference.

In this chapter, I'll explain the benefits of trunk-based workflows. We'll also cover their difference from other branching workflows, and I'll introduce you to what I believe is the best `git` workflow to accelerate your software delivery.

The chapter covers the following topics:

- Trunk-based development
- Why you should avoid complex branching
- Other `git` workflows
- Accelerating with MyFlow
- Case study

Trunk-based development

Trunk-based development is a source-control branching model, where developers merge small and frequent updates to a single branch (often called a **trunk**, but in `git`, this is commonly referred to as the `main` branch) and resist any pressure to create other long-lived development branches (see `https://trunkbaseddevelopment.com`).

The base idea is that the main branch is always in a clean state so that any developer, at any time, can create a new branch based upon the main branch that builds successfully.

To keep the branch in a clean state, developers must take multiple measures to ensure only code that does not break anything is merged back to the main branch, as outlined here:

- Fetch the newest changes from the main branch
- Perform a clean test
- Run all tests
- Have high cohesion with your team (pair programming or code review)

As you can see, this is predestined for a protected main branch and **pull requests (PRs)** with a CI build that has a PR trigger and builds and tests your changes. However, some teams prefer to do these steps manually and directly push to `main` without branch protection. In small, highly cohesive, and co-located teams that practice pair-programming, this can be very effective, but it takes a lot of discipline. In complex environments or in distributed teams that work asynchronously, I would always recommend using branch protection and PRs.

Why you should avoid complex branching

When we talk about branches, we often use the terms long-lived and short-lived, which refer to time. I find this somehow misleading. Branches are about changes, and changes can hardly be measured in time. Developers can write 8 hours of code with a lot of refactoring and try to merge that very complex branch in 1 day. This would still be considered short-lived if they measured it in time only. Conversely, if they have a branch with just one line changed—for example, the update of a package that the code depends on—but the branch stays open for 3 weeks as the team must solve some architectural questions regarding the change, from a time perspective it would be long-lived, even if it would be very simple to rebase the changes on top of `main`.

Time doesn't seem to be the best measure to distinguish good and bad practices for branches; it is a combination of complexity and time.

The more changes that happen in the base branch from which you created your branch until you try to merge your changes back, the harder it is to merge these changes with changes in your branch. The complexity can come from one very complex merge, or from many developers merging many small changes. To avoid merging, many teams try to finish work on a feature before merging back. This, of course, leads to more complex changes that then make it difficult for the other features to merge—so-called **merge hell**— whereby before releasing, all the features have to be integrated into the new release.

To avoid merge hell, you should pull the latest version of the main branch regularly. As long as you can merge or rebase without problems, the integration of your branch is not a problem, but if your changes get too complex, it is a problem for the other developers, as they will probably have a problem if you merge your changes back. That's why you should merge your changes before they exceed a certain amount of complexity. The extent of the complexity depends a lot on the code you modify and you would need to consider the following points:

- Are you working with existing code or new code?

- Is the code complex with a lot of dependencies, or is it simple code?

- Are you working with isolated code or code with high cohesion?

- How many people change the code at the same time?

- Is there refactoring of a lot of code at the same time?

I believe this is why people tend to use time as a measure instead of complexity—there is just no good measure for complexity. So, as a rule of thumb: if you work on a more complex feature, you should at least merge your changes back to the main branch once a day, but if your changes are simple, there is no problem leaving your branch/PR open for a longer time. Remember that it is not about time but complexity!

Other git workflows

Before we have a closer look into what I believe to be the most effective `git` **workflow** for DevOps teams using GitHub, I want to make an introduction to the most popular workflows.

Gitflow

Gitflow is still one of the most popular workflows. It was introduced in 2010 by Vincent Driessen (see `https://nvie.com/posts/a-successful-git-branching-model/`) and became very popular. **Gitflow** has a nice poster, and it is a very descriptive introduction on how to solve problems in `git` such as releasing using tags and working with branches that get deleted after they have been merged (see *Figure 11.1*):

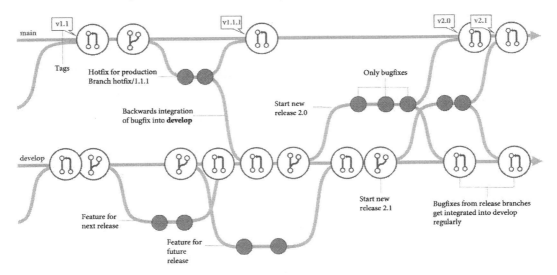

Figure 11.1 – Gitflow overview

Gitflow is great if you ship your software every few months to different customers, want to bundle some features to a new major version that is licensed separately, and have to maintain many versions for many years. In 2010, this was the common release flow for nearly all software, but in complex environments, the workflow raises some problems. The workflow is *not* trunk-based and has multiple long-lived branches. The integration between these branches can lead to merge hell in complex environments. With the rise of DevOps and CI/CD practices, the workflow got a bad reputation.

If you want to accelerate your software delivery with DevOps, Gitflow is not the right branching workflow for you! But many of the concepts can be found in other workflows.

GitHub flow

GitHub flow focuses a lot on collaboration with PRs. You create a branch with a descriptive name and make your first changes. Then, you create a PR and collaborate with your reviewers through comments on the code. Once the PR is ready, it gets shipped to production *before* merging it to the main branch (see *Figure 11.2*)

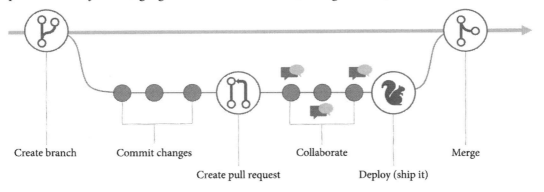

Figure 11.2 – GitHub flow

GitHub flow is trunk-based, and it is very popular. The basic part—without the deployment of PRs—is the base for most other workflows. The problem is the deployment. Deploying each PR to production creates a bottleneck and does not scale very well. GitHub itself uses ChatOps and deploy trains to solve that issue (Aman Gupta, 2015), but this seems a bit of overkill to me. The idea that only changes that have proven to work in production are merged to `main` is compelling, but it is a goal that basically cannot be reached in complex environments. You would need quite some time to see the changes work isolated in production to really be sure that they did not break anything, but with that time, the bottleneck prevents other teams or team members to merge their changes. I think that in a DevOps world with the principles of **fail fast** and **roll forward**, it's best to validate PRs in an isolated environment and deploy them to production *after* you have merged the PR using the `push` trigger of your main branch. If the changes break production, you still can deploy the last version that worked (**roll back**), or you fix the error and deploy the fix right away (**roll forward**). You don't need a clean main branch to perform either of these options.

Another thing I dislike about GitHub flow is that it is not very explicit about the number of users, branches, and PRs. A feature branch might imply that multiple persons commit to the same feature branch. I don't see this happen often, but just from the documentation, it is not unambiguous.

Release flow

Release flow is based upon GitHub flow, but instead of deploying PRs continuously, it adds one-way release branches. The branches do not get merged back, and bug fixes follow the **upstream-first** principle: they get fixed in a branch of `main`, and changes get cherry-picked into a branch of the release branch (Edward Thomson, 2018). This way, it is impossible to forget to apply a bug fix to `main` (see *Figure 11.3*):

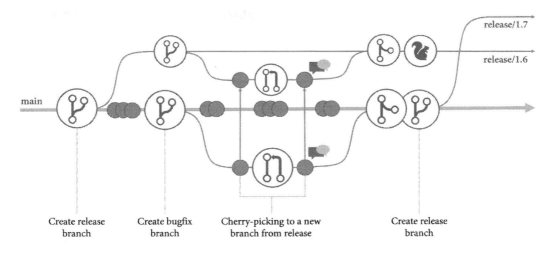

Figure 11.3 – Release flow

Release flow is not CD! Creating releases is still a process that has to be triggered separately. If you have to maintain different versions of your software, release flow is a good way to do it. But if you can, you should try to achieve CD.

GitLab flow

GitLab flow is also based upon GitHub flow. It adds environment branches (such as development, staging, pre-production, and production), and each deployment happens on a merge to these environments (see *Figure 11.4*):

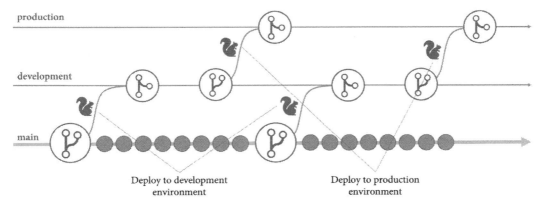

Figure 11.4 – GitLab environment branches

Since the changes only flow downstream, you can be sure that all changes are tested in all environments. GitLab flow also follows the **upstream-first** principle. If you find a bug in one of the environments, you create a feature branch of `main` and cherry-pick changes to all environments. Bug fixing works in GitLab flow the same way it works in release flow.

If you don't have pipelines that support multiple environments—such as GitHub Actions—GitLab flow might provide a nice way to automate your approvals and deployments for your environments. Personally, I don't see the value in having code for environments separated if you perform bug fixes upstream anyway. I prefer to build the code once and then deploy the output to all environments in a sequence. But there might be situations in which this workflow makes sense—for example, for static websites that deploy directly from the repository.

Accelerating with MyFlow

As you can see, `git` workflows are just a collection of solutions for different use cases. The main difference is in whether they are trunk-based or not and if they are explicit about some things or not. As I find all workflows lacking something, I created my own workflow: **MyFlow**.

MyFlow is a lightweight, trunk-based workflow based on PRs. MyFlow is not a new invention! Many teams already work this way. It is a very natural way to branch and merge if you focus on collaboration with PRs. I just gave it a name, and I can see people picking it up easily.

The main branch

Since MyFlow is trunk-based, there is only one main branch called `main`, and it should always be in a clean state. The main branch should always build, and it should be possible to release it to production at any time. That's why you should protect `main` with a branch protection rule. A good branch protection rule would include at least the following criteria:

- Require a minimum of two PR reviews before merging
- Dismiss stale PR approvals when new commits are pushed
- Require reviews from code owners
- Require status checks to pass before merging that includes your CI build, test execution, code analysis, and linters
- Include administrators in restrictions
- Permit force pushes

The more you automate using the CI build, the more likely you can keep your branch in a clean state.

All other branches are always branched off `main`. Since this is the default branch, you never have to specify a source branch when you create a new one. This simplifies things and removes a source of error.

Private topic branches

Figure 11.5 shows the basic concept of MyFlow:

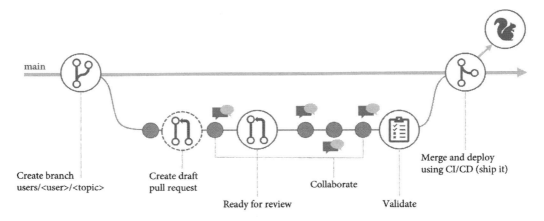

Figure 11.5 – Basics of MyFlow

Private topic branches can be used to work on new features, documentation, bugs, infrastructure, and everything else that is in your repository. They are private, which means they only belong to one specific user. Other team members can check out the branch to test the solution, but they are not allowed to directly push changes to this branch. Instead, they must use `suggestions` in PRs to suggest changes to the author of the PR.

To indicate that branches are private, I recommend a naming convention such as `users/*` or `private/*` that makes this obvious. I also recommend including the **identifier (ID)** of the issue or bug in the name. This makes it easy to reference it later in the commit message. A good convention would look like this:

```
users/<username>/<id>_<topic>
```

To start working on a new topic, you create a new local branch, as follows:

```
$ git switch -c <branch> main
```

You can see an example here:

```
$ git switch -c users/kaufm/42_new-feature main
> Switched to a new branch 'users/kaufm/42_new-feature'
```

Create your first modifications and commit and push them to the server. It does not matter what you modify—you could just add a blank to a file. You can overwrite it later anyway. You can see an example here:

```
$ git add .
$ git commit
$ git push --set-upstream origin <branch>
```

Now, here's the preceding example with further information:

```
$ git add .
$ git commit -m "New feature #42"
$ git push --set-upstream origin users/kaufm/42_new-feature
```

> **Note**
>
> Note that I use GitHub **command-line interface (GitHub CLI)** (https://cli.github.com/) to interact with PRs as I find it easier to read and understand than to use screenshots of the web **user interface (UI)**. You can do the same using the web UI.

Create a PR and mark it as draft, as follows:

```
$ gh pr create --fill --draft
```

This way, the team knows that you are working on that topic. A quick view of a list of open PRs should give you a nice overview of the topics the team currently is working on.

> **Note**
>
> You can omit the -m argument when committing changes and add a multiline commit message in your default editor. The first line will be the title of the PR; the rest of the message will be the body. You could also set title (--title or -t) and body (--body or -b) when creating a PR instead of --fill.

You can now start working on your topic, and you can use the full power of `git`. If you want to add changes to your previous commit, for example, you can do so with the `--amend` option, as follows:

```
$ git commit --amend
```

Or, if you want to combine the last three commits into one single commit, you can run the following command:

```
$ git reset --soft HEAD~3
$ git commit
```

If you want to merge all commits in a branch into one commit, you can run the following command:

```
$ git reset --soft main
$ git commit
```

Or, if you want complete freedom to rearrange and squash all your commits, you can use interactive rebase, like this:

```
$ git rebase -i main
```

To push changes to the server, you use the following command:

```
$ git push origin +<branch>
```

Here's the preceding example with the branch name populated:

```
$ git push origin +users/kaufm/42_new-feature
```

Note the + plus sign before the branch name. This causes a force push, but only to a specific branch. If you are not messing with your branch history, you can perform a normal `git push` operation, and if your branches are well protected and you know what you are doing, a normal force push might be more convenient, as illustrated here:

```
$ git push -f
```

If you already want help or the opinions of teammates on your code, you can mention them in comments in the PR. If they want to propose changes, they use the `suggestions` feature in PR comments. This way, *you* apply the changes, and you can make sure that you have a clean state in your repository before doing so.

Whenever you feel your work is ready, you change the state of your PR from `draft` to `ready` and activate auto-merge, as follows:

```
$ gh pr ready
$ gh pr merge --auto --delete-branch --rebase
```

> **Note**
>
> Note that I specified `--rebase` as the merge method. This is a good merge strategy for small teams that like to craft a good and concise commit history. If you prefer `--squash` or `--merge`, adjust your merge strategy accordingly.

Your reviewers can still create suggestions in their comments, and you can keep collaborating. But once all approvals and all automated checks have completed, the PR will be merged automatically and the branch gets deleted. Automated checks run on the `pull_request` trigger and can include installing the application in an isolated environment and running all sorts of tests.

If your PR has been merged and the branch has been deleted, you clean up your local environment, like this:

```
$ git switch main
$ git pull --prune
```

This will change your current branch to `main`, pull the changed branch from the server, and delete local branches that have been deleted on the server.

Releasing

Once your changes are merged to `main`, the `push` trigger on `main` will start the deployment to production, independent of whether you use environments or a ring-based approach.

If you have to maintain multiple versions, you can use tags together with **GitHub releases** (as I showed you in *Chapter 8, Managing Dependencies Using GitHub Packages*). Use the `release` trigger in a workflow and deploy the application, and use `GitVersion` to automatically generate your version numbers, as illustrated here:

```
$ gh release create <tag> --notes "<release notes>"
```

Here's an example of this:

```
$ gh release create v1.1 --notes "Added new feature"
```

You can also take advantage of the autogeneration of release notes. Unfortunately, this feature is not yet available through the CLI. You must create your release using the UI for that to work.

As we fix bugs following the **upstream-first** principle anyway, there is no real benefit in creating a release branch for every release if we don't have to perform a hotfix. The tag that is generated when you create your release works just fine.

Hotfix

If you have to provide a hotfix for older releases, you can check out the tag and create a new hotfix branch, like this:

```
$ git switch -c <hotfix-branch> <tag>
$ git push --set-upstream origin <branch>
```

Here's an example of this:

```
$ git switch -c hotfix/v1.1.1 v1.1
$ git push --set-upstream origin hotfix/1.1.1
```

Now, switch back to main and fix the bug in a **normal topic branch** (for example, users/kaufm/666_fix-bug). Now, **cherry-pick** the commit with the fix to the hotfix branch, as follows:

```
$ git switch <hotfix-branch>
$ git cherry-pick <commit SHA>
$ git push
```

You can use the **secure hash algorithm (SHA)** of the commit you want to cherry-pick. Or you can use the name of the branch if the commit is the tip of the branch, as follows:

```
$ git switch hotfix/v1.1.1
$ git cherry-pick users/kaufm/42_fix-bug
$ git push
```

This will cherry-pick the tip of the topic branch. *Figure 11.6* shows how a hotfix for an older release works:

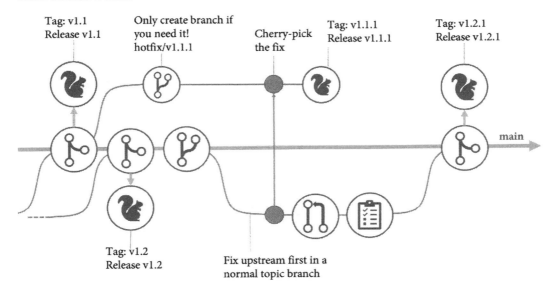

Figure 11.6 – Performing hotfixes on older releases

You could also merge the fix to `main` first and then cherry-pick the commit from there. This ensures that the code adheres to all your branch policies.

You could also cherry-pick into a temporary branch based on the hotfix branch and merge the cherry-picked fix using another PR. This depends on how complex your environment is and how big the differences between the main and hotfix branches are.

Automation

If you have a workflow with naming conventions, there are certain sequences of commands that you use very often. To reduce typos and simplify your workflow, you can automate these using `git` **aliases**. The best way to do this is to edit your `.gitconfig` file in the editor of your choice, like this:

```
$ git config --global --edit
```

Add a section, `[alias]`, if it does not exist yet and add an alias, like this:

```
[alias]
    mfstart = "!f() { \
        git switch -c users/$1/$2_$3 && \
```

```
        git commit && \
        git push --set-upstream origin users/$1/$2_$3 && \
        gh pr create --fill --draft; \
    };f"
```

This alias is called `mfstart` and would be called specifying the username, issue ID, and topic, as illustrated here:

```
$ git mfstart kaufm 42 new-feature
```

It switches to a new branch and commits the current changes in the index, pushes them to the server, and creates a PR.

You can reference individual arguments ($1, $2, ...) or all arguments using $@. If you want to chain commands independent of the exit code, you must terminate a command using `;`. If you want the next command only to execute if the first one was successful, you can use `&&`. Note that you have to end each line with a backslash (\). This is also the character you use to escape quotation marks.

You can add `if` statements to branch your logic, like so:

```
mfrelease = "!f() { \
    if [[ -z \"$1\" ]]; then \
        echo Please specify a name for the tag; \
    else \
        gh release create $1 --notes $2; \
    fi; \
};f"
```

Or, you can store values in variables to use them later, as in this example—the current name of the branch your head (HEAD) points to:

```
mfhotfix = "!f() { \
    head=$(git symbolic-ref HEAD --short); \
    echo Cherry-pick $head onto hotfix/$1 && \
    git switch -c hotfix/$1 && \
    git push --set-upstream origin hotfix/$1 && \
    git cherry-pick $head && \
    git push; \
};f"
```

These are just examples and the automation depends a lot on the details of the way you work, but it is a very powerful tool and can help you to become more productive.

Case study

With the automation of the release process in place, the two pilot teams have already noted a great boost in productivity. Metrics for **lead time** and **deployment frequency** have increased significantly.

The team that used `git` before they moved from Bitbucket to GitHub followed **Gitflow** as their branching workflow. Since their web application can be released continuously using their staged deployment workflow, they move to a **trunk-based** workflow with PR and private branches and deploy after the merge to the main branch using their CI/CD workflow (**MyFlow**). To integrate often, they decide to use **feature flags**. As the company needs feature management in the cloud and on-premises, they decide to go with **Unleash**. The team can use the **software-as-a-service** (**SaaS**) service and can start using it right away without having to wait for an on-premises solution.

The second team that migrated from **Team Foundation Server** (**TFS**) had been used to a complex branching workflow with a long-living release, service pack, hotfix branches, and a development branch where all features were integrated. As the software is installed on hardware products, multiple releases are stabilized in parallel, and also multiple versions that have to be maintained for years. This means the software cannot be continuously released. The team chooses **release flow** to manage releases and hotfixes. For development, they also use private branches with PRs and a trunk-based approach. As the products are not connected to the internet, the team relies on their configuration system for feature flags. This technique had been used before to enable the testing of new features on hardware. The team now extends it to integrate changes more frequently.

Summary

`git` workflows are not so different from each other, and most are built on top of others. It is more important to follow the principles of **fail fast** and **roll forward** instead of treating a certain workflow like a dogma. All workflows are just a collection of best practices, and you should only take what you need.

What is important is the size of your changes and the frequency in which you merge them back.

Always follow these rules:

- Always branch your topic branches of the main branch (**trunk-based**).
- If you're working on complex features, make sure to commit at least **once per day** (using feature flags).
- If your changes are simple and you only need to change a few lines of code, you can leave your PR open for a longer time. But check that you don't have too many **open PRs**.

With these rules, the workflow you are actually using is not so important. Pick the things that work for you.

In this chapter, you learned about the benefits of TBD and how you can use it together with `git` workflows to increase your engineering velocity.

In the next chapter, I will explain how you can use shift-left testing for increased quality and to release with more confidence.

Further reading

You can use the following references from this chapter to get more information on the topics covered:

- *Forsgren N., Humble, J.*, and *Kim, G.* (2018). *Accelerate: The Science of Lean Software and DevOps: Building and Scaling High Performing Technology Organizations* (1st ed.) [E-book]. IT Revolution Press.
- Trunk-based development: `https://trunkbaseddevelopment.com`
- Gitflow: *Vincent Driessen* (2010), *A successful Git branching model*: `https://nvie.com/posts/a-successful-git-branching-model/`
- *GitLab flow*: `https://docs.gitlab.com/ee/topics/gitlab_flow.html`
- *Edward Thomson* (2018). *Release Flow: How We Do Branching on the VSTS Team*: `https://devblogs.microsoft.com/devops/release-flow-how-we-do-branching-on-the-vsts-team/`
- *Aman Gupta* (2015). *Deploying branches to GitHub.com*: `https://github.blog/2015-06-02-deploying-branches-to-github-com/`
- *GitHub flow*: `https://docs.github.com/en/get-started/quickstart/github-flow`
- GitHub CLI: `https://cli.github.com/`

Part 3: Release with Confidence

Part 3 explains how you can accelerate even further and release frequently with confidence by baking quality assurance and security into your release pipelines. This includes concepts such as shifting left testing and security, testing in production, chaos engineering, DevSecOps, securing your software supply chain, and ring-based deployments.

This part of the book comprises the following chapters:

- *Chapter 12, Shift Left Testing for Increased Quality*
- *Chapter 13, Shift Left Security and DevSecOps*
- *Chapter 14, Securing Your Code*
- *Chapter 15, Securing Your Deployments*

12

Shift Left Testing for Increased Quality

Testing and **quality assurance (QA)** is still one of the practices that holds back most companies. In this chapter, we'll take a closer look at the role that QA and testing play in terms of developer velocity and how to shift left test.

In this chapter, we will cover the following topics:

- Shift left testing with test automation
- Eradicating flaky tests
- Code coverage
- Shift right – testing in production
- Fault injection and chaos engineering
- Testing and compliance
- Test management in GitHub

Shift left testing with test automation

If you practice agile development and try to ship frequently, then manual testing isn't a scalable option. Even if you don't practice CI/CD and only ship on a sprint cadence, running all the necessary regression tests would take enormous manpower and a lot of time and money. But getting test automation right is not an easy task. Automated tests that have been created and maintained by a QA department or outsourced entity, for example, are *not* correlated with higher engineering velocity (*Forsgren N., Humble, J., & Kim, G., 2018, Page 95*). To notice an impact on your velocity, you need reliable tests that have been created and maintained by the team. The theory behind this is that if developers maintain tests, they produce more testable code.

Everybody knows what a good test portfolio should look like: you have a big base of automated unit tests (Level 0), fewer integration tests (Level 1), some integration tests that need test data (Level 2), and only a few functional tests (Level 3). This is called the test pyramid (*see Figure 12.1*):

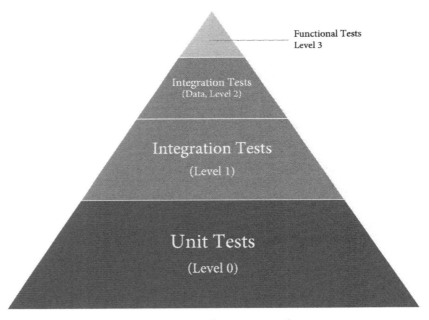

Figure 12.1 – The test pyramid

However, in most companies, the portfolio does not look like this. Sometimes, there are some unit tests, but most of the other tests are still at a very high level (*see Figure 12.2*):

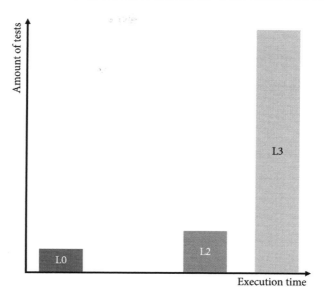

Figure 12.2 – Example test portfolio

These high-level tests might be automated or manual. But still, it is not a test portfolio that will help you to release continuously with high quality. To achieve continuous quality, you must shift left your test portfolio (*see Figure 12.3*):

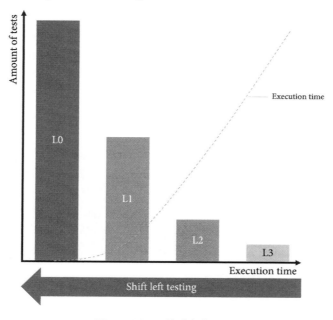

Figure 12.3 – Shift left testing

This is not an easy task. Here are some principles that help with shift left testing:

- **Ownership**: The team is responsible for QA and the tests are developed alongside the code – preferably with the test-first approach. QA engineers should be included in the team.
- **Shift left**: Tests should always be written at the lowest level possible.
- **Write once – execute everywhere**: Tests should be executed in all environments, even in production.
- **Test code is production code**: The same quality standards that apply to normal code apply to test code. No shortcuts should be allowed here.
- **You code it – you test it**: As a developer, you are responsible for the quality of your code, and you must make sure that all the tests are in place to ensure this quality.

In 2013, a testing manifesto was created that describes the transformation of the QA role (*Sam Laing, 2015*):

- Testing throughout *over* testing at the end
- Preventing bugs *over* finding bugs
- Testing understanding *over* checking functionality
- Building the best system *over* breaking the system
- Team responsibility for quality *over* tester responsibility

This sounds easy, but it isn't. Developers have to learn to think like testers and testers have to learn to think like engineers. Selling the vision and establishing the change's sustainability is not an easy task.

Test-driven development

The key to test automation is having a testable software architecture. To get one, you must start as early as possible – that is, in the inner loop, when developers write their code.

Test-driven development (**TDD**) is a software development process where you write your automated test first and then the code that makes the test pass. It has been around for more than 20 years and the quality benefits have been proven in different studies (for example, *Müller, Matthias M.; Padberg, Frank, 2017* and *Erdogmus, Hakan; Morisio, Torchiano, 2014*). TDD not only has a big impact on the time that's spent on debugging and overall code quality; it also has a big influence on solid and testable software design. That's why it is also called **test-driven design**.

TDD is simple. The steps are as follows:

1. **Add or modify a test**: Always start with a test. While writing the test, you **design** what your code will look like. There will be a time when your test will not compile because the classes and functions that you are calling do not exist yet. Most development environments support creating the necessary code right from within your test. This step is completed once your code compiles and the test can be executed. The test is supposed to fail. If the test passes, modify it or write a new test until it fails.

2. **Run all tests**: Run all the tests and verify that only the new test fails.

3. **Write code**: Write some simple code that makes the test pass. Always run all your tests to check if the test passes. The code does not need to be pretty in this stage and shortcuts are allowed. Just make the test pass. Bad code will give you an idea of what test you need next to ensure that the code gets better.

4. **All tests pass**: If all the tests pass, you have two options: write a new test or modify the existing one. Alternatively, you can refactor your code and tests.

5. **Refactor**: Refactor the code and the tests. Since you have a solid test harness, you can do more extreme refactoring than you normally would without TDD. Make sure that you run all the tests after each refactoring. If one test fails, undo the last step and retry until the tests keep passing after the refactoring step. After a successful refactoring, you can start a new iteration with a new failing test.

Figure 12.4 shows an overview of the TDD cycle:

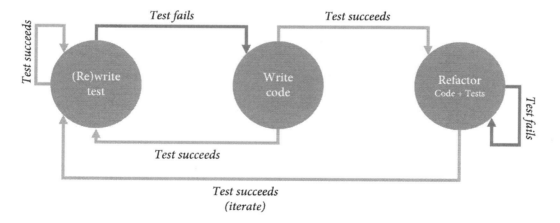

Figure 12.4 – The TDD cycle

A good test follows the following pattern:

- **Arrange**: Set up the necessary objects for the test and the **system under test** (**SUT**) itself – normally, this is a class. You can use **mocks** and **stubs** to simulate system behavior (to learn more about mocks and stubs, see *Martin Fowler, 2007*).

- **Act**: Execute the code that you want to test.

- **Assert**: Verify the results, ensure that the state of the system is in the desired state, and ensure that the method has called the correct methods with the correct parameters.

Each test should be completely autarkic – that is, it shouldn't depend on a system state that's been manipulated by previous tests, and it can be executed in isolation.

TDD can also be used in pair programming. This is called **Ping Pong Pair Programming**. In this form of pair programming, one developer writes the test and the other writes the code that makes the test pass. This is a great pattern for pair programming and a good way to teach younger colleagues the benefits of TDD.

TDD has been around for so long and the teams that practice it gain so much value – and yet I have met many teams that are not using it. Some don't use it because their code runs on embedded systems, while others don't use it because their code depends on SharePoint classes that are hard to mock. But these are just excuses. There might be some plumbing code that cannot be tested, but when you write logic, you can always test it first.

Managing your test portfolio

With TDD, you should get a testable design in no time. And even in a brownfield environment, the number of automated tests will grow rapidly. The problem is that often, the quality of the tests is not optimal and with a growing test portfolio, you often get very long execution times and non-deterministic (flaky) tests. It is better to have fewer tests that are of higher quality. Long execution times hinder you from releasing quickly, and flaky tests produce unreliable quality signals and reduce the trust in your test suite (*see Figure 12.5*). With more QA maturity in the team, the quality of the test suite constantly rises – even if the amount of tests reduces after the first peak:

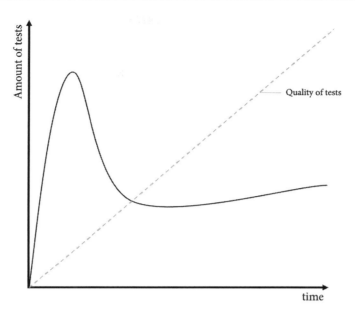

Figure 12.5 – Amount and quality of automated tests

To actively manage your test portfolio, you should define ground rules for your tests and constantly monitor the number of tests and their execution time. As an example, let's look at the **taxonomy** that's used by a team at Microsoft for their test portfolio.

Unit tests (Level 0)

Here, we have in-memory unit tests with no external dependencies and no deployment. They should be fast with an average execution time of fewer than 60 milliseconds. Unit tests are co-located with the code under test.

With unit tests, you can't change to the system's state (such as the filesystem or its registry), queries to external data sources (web services and databases), or the mutexes, semaphores, stopwatches, and `Thread.sleep` operations.

Integration tests (Level 1)

This level involves tests with more complex requirements that may depend on a lightweight deployment and configuration. The tests should still be very fast, and each test must run under 2 seconds.

With integration tests, you can't have dependencies on other tests and store large amounts of data. You also can't have too many tests in one assembly as this prevents the tests from being executed in parallel.

Functional tests with data (Level 2)

Functional tests run against a testable deployment with test data. Dependencies on systems such as the authentication provider can be stubbed out and allow dynamic identities to be used. This means that there's an isolated identity for every test so that the test can be executed in parallel against a deployment without them impacting each other.

Production tests (Level 3)

Production tests run against production and require a full product deployment.

This is just an example, and your taxonomy may look different, depending on your programming language and product.

If you have defined your taxonomy, you can set up reporting and start to transform your test portfolio. Make sure that you make it easy to write and execute high-quality unit and integration tests first. Then, start analyzing your legacy tests – manual or automated – and check which ones you can throw away. Convert the others into good functional tests (*Level 2*). The last step is to write your tests for production.

The team at Microsoft started with 27,000 legacy tests (in orange) and reduced them to zero in 42 sprints (126 weeks). Most of the tests were replaced with unit tests; some were replaced with functional tests. Many were simply deleted, but there was a steady growth in unit tests, with there being over 40,000 in the end (*see Figure 12.6*):

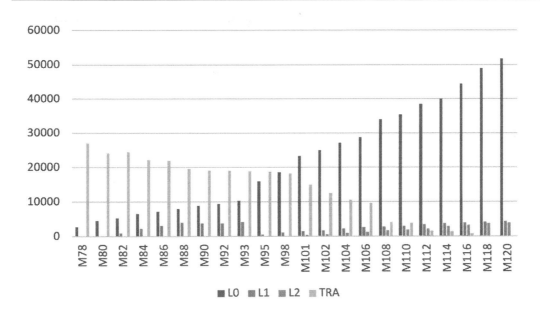

Figure 12.6 – Test portfolio over time

See *Shift left to make testing fast and reliable*, in the *Further reading* section, for more information on how the team at Microsoft shifted their test portfolio left.

Eradicating flaky tests

Non-deterministic or **flaky tests** are tests that sometimes pass and sometimes fail with the same code (*Martin Fowler, 2011*). Flaky tests can destroy the trust in your test suite. This can lead to teams just ignoring red test results, or developers deactivating tests, thereby reducing the test coverage and reliability of the suite.

There are lots of reasons for flaky tests. Often, they are due to a lack of isolation. Many tests run in the same process on a machine – so each test must find and leave a clean state of the system. Another common reason is asynchronous behavior. Testing asynchronous code has its challenges as you never know which order the asynchronous tasks are executed in. Other reasons may include resource leaks or calls to remote resources.

There are different ways to deal with flaky tests:

- **Retry failing tests**: Some frameworks allow you to retry failing tests. Sometimes, you can even configure a higher level of isolation. If a test passes in a rerun, it is considered flaky, and you should file a reliability bug using `git blame`.

- **Reliability runs**: You can execute workflows on code that has green builds. Tests that fail are flaky and you can file a reliability bug using `git blame`.

Some companies quarantine flaky tests, but this also keeps you from collecting additional data as the test can't run. It's best practice to keep executing flaky tests but exclude them from the reporting.

If you want to learn how GitHub or Google are dealing with flaky tests, read *Jordan Raine, 2020* or *John Micco, 2016*.

Code coverage

Code coverage is a metric (in percent) that calculates the number of code elements that get called by tests, divided by the total amount of code elements. Code elements can be anything, but lines of code, code blocks, or functions are common.

Code coverage is an important metric as it shows you what parts of your code are not covered by your test suite. I like to watch the code coverage before I finish a code change as I often forget to write tests for edge cases such as exception handling, or more complex statements such as lambda expressions. It's no problem to add these tests the moment you are coding – it's much harder to add them later.

But you should not focus on the absolute number as code coverage itself says nothing about the quality of the tests. It's better to have 70% code coverage with high-quality tests than 90% percent code coverage with low-quality tests. Depending on the programming language and frameworks you use, there might be some plumbing code that has a high effort in terms of testing but with very low value. Normally, you can exclude that code from code coverage calculations, but this is why the absolute value of code coverage is limited. However, measuring the value in each pipeline and focusing on new code helps improve the quality of your automated tests over time.

Shift right – testing in production

If you start with automated testing, you rapidly see improved quality and a decline in the debugging effort of your engineers. But at some point, you must increase the effort tremendously to see a significant impact on quality. On the other hand, the time your tests need to execute slows down your release pipeline, especially if you add **performance tests** and **load tests** to the mix (*see Figure 12.7*):

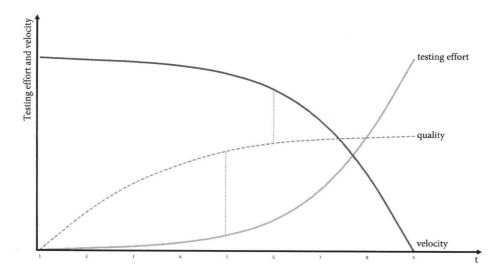

Figure 12.7 – The impact of testing effort on quality and velocity

It's impossible to release multiple times a day if your pipeline runs for more than 24 hours! The increased execution time of your pipeline also reduces your ability to roll forward quickly and deploy a fix if a bug occurs in production.

The solution to this is simple: **shift right** some of the tests to production. All the tests that you run in production do not impact your ability to release fast, and you don't need performance or load tests as your code already has production load.

However, there are some prerequisites to testing in production that increase the performance quality for your users instead of decreasing it. Let's take a look.

Health data and monitoring

For testing in production, you must be constantly aware of the health of your application. This goes beyond normal logging. You need deep insights into how your application is operating. A good practice is to have test code that calls all dependent systems – such as the database, a Redis cache, or dependent REST services – and makes these tests available to your logging solutions. This way, you can have a constant **heartbeat** that indicates that all the systems are up and running and working together. If the test fails, you can have an alert that instantly notifies the team that something is wrong. You can also automate these alerts and have them trigger certain functions, such as activating a **circuit breaker**.

> **Circuit Breaker**
>
> A **circuit breaker** is a pattern that prevents an application from repeatedly trying to execute an operation that is likely to fail, allowing the application to continue with altered functionality without having to wait for the failing operation to succeed (see *Michael Nygard, 2018*).

Feature flags and canary releases

You don't want to test in production and cause a complete outage for all your customers. That's why you need feature flags, canary releases, a ring-based deployment, or a mix of those techniques (see *Chapter 9* and *Chapter 10*). It's important to gradually expose the changes so that if an outage occurs, you don't take down the complete production environment.

Business continuity and disaster recovery

Another form of testing in production is **business continuity and disaster recovery (BCDR)** or failover testing. There should be a BCDR for every service or subsystem of your product, and you should execute a BCDR drill regularly. There is nothing worse than disaster recovery that is not working if your system is down. And you only know that it is working if you regularly test it.

Exploratory testing and usability testing

Test automation does not imply that you should completely abandon manual testing. But the focus of manual tests shifts away from validating functionality and executing regressions tests manually on every release toward usability, fast and high-quality feedback, and bugs that are hard to find with structured test approaches.

Exploratory testing was introduced by Cem Kaner in 1999 (*Kaner C., Falk J., H. Q. Nguyen, 1999*). It is an approach to testing that focuses simultaneously on discovery, learning, test design, and execution. It relies on the individual tester to uncover defects that can't easily be discovered in other tests.

There are many tools available that can facilitate exploratory testing. They help you record your sessions, take annotated screenshots, and often allow you to create a test case from the steps you have performed. Some extensions integrate with Jira, such as Zephyr and Capture, and there are browser extensions such as the Test and Feedback client for Azure Test Plans. The latter is free if you use it in standalone mode. These tools provide the high-quality feedback of stakeholders to developers – not only in terms of the defects that were discovered.

Other ways to gather feedback include using **usability testing** techniques – such as **hallway testing** or **guerrilla usability** – to evaluate your solution by testing it on new, unbiased users. A special form of usability testing is A/B testing, which we'll cover in more detail in *Chapter 19, Experimentation and A/B Testing with GitHub*.

The important part here is that all these tests can be executed in production. You should not have any manual tests in your CI/CD pipeline. Release fast and allow manual testing in production using feature flags and canary releases.

Fault injection and chaos engineering

If you want to level up testing in production, you can practice **fault injection** – also known as **chaos engineering**. This means that you inject faults into your production system to see how it behaves under pressure and if your failover mechanisms and circuit breakers work. Possible faults could include high CPU load, high memory usage, disk I/O pressure, low disk space, or a service or entire machine being shut down or rebooted. Other possibilities include processes being killed, the system's time being changed, network traffic being dropped, latency being injected, and DNS servers being blocked.

Practicing chaos engineering makes your system resilient. You cannot compare this to classical load or performance testing!

Different tools can help you with chaos engineering. **Gremlin** (`https://www.gremlin.com/`), for example, is an agent-based SaaS offering that supports most cloud providers (Azure, AWS, and Google Cloud) and all operating systems. It can also be used with Kubernetes. **Chaos Mesh** (`https://chaos-mesh.org/`) is an open source solution that's specialized for Kubernetes. **Azure Chaos Studio** (`https://azure.microsoft.com/en-us/services/chaos-studio`) is a solution that's specialized for Azure. What tool is best for you depends on the platforms that you support.

Chaos engineering can be very effective and make your systems resilient, but it should be limited to canary environments that have little or no customer impact.

Tests and compliance

Most **compliance** standards, such as **ISO26262** for automotive or **GAMP** for pharma, follow the **V-Model** as a development process. The V-Model requires the user and system requirements to be decomposed and specifications to be created at different levels of detail. This is the left-hand side of the *V*. It also requires all the levels to be validated to ensure that the system fulfills the requirements and specifications. This is the right-hand side of the *V*. Both sides can be seen in *Figure 12.8*:

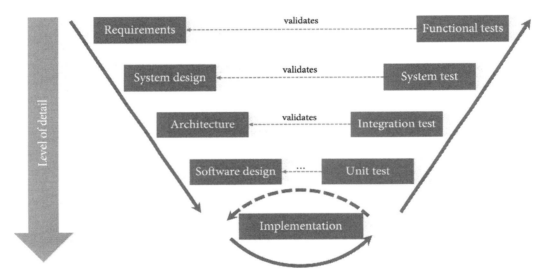

Figure 12.8 – Validation in the V-Model

This model must be combined with risk analysis, which is performed at every level of detail. Many documents must be signed during the release phase. This leads to a slow waterfall process with long specification, development, and release phases.

But the standards are based on good practices – and if your practices are better than the ones in the standard, you can justify that in the audits. The standards don't require you to do validation manually, nor do they say anything about the time of the phases. The solution is to automate all the validation logic and add the approvals as code reviews in the pull requests when you're modifying the tests (shift left). Tests that you cannot automate must be moved to production (shift right). This way, you can automate the entire V and run through it multiple times a day:

1. Add or modify a requirement (for example, an issue).

2. Create a pull request and link it to the issue.

3. Modify your system design and architecture in your repository (for example, in markdown) or state that no modifications are needed in the pull request.

4. Write your unit tests (this is, your software design) and the code to implement.

5. Write or modify your functions, system, and integration tests.

6. Have all the necessary roles approve the pull requests and make sure that the approvals are stale if new changes are pushed.

7. Ship your changes to production and run your final tests there.

You can also manage your risks as code. This way, you can integrate them into your automated process. If not, you can still attach the documents to the issue. This way, you have the end-to-end traceability for all your changes, all your necessary approvals, and all the validation steps completed. And you can still iterate fast and release to production regularly.

Test management in GitHub

Unfortunately, GitHub doesn't have a great way to track your test runs and code coverage over time, nor can it help you detect or quarantine flaky tests. You can execute your tests as part of your workflow and can signal back the result – but for reporting, you have to rely on your test tooling.

A good solution that integrates well with GitHub is **Testspace** (https://www.testspace.com/). It is a SaaS offering and is free for open source projects. It's easy to set up – just install the extension from the marketplace (https://github.com/marketplace/testspace-com), select the plan you want, and grant access to your repositories. Then, add the following step to your workflow:

```
- uses: testspace-com/setup-testspace@v1
  with:
    domain: ${{github.repository_owner}}
```

If your repository is private, then you must create a token in *Testspace* and add it as a secret to that step as well: `token: ${{ secrets.TESTSPACE_TOKEN }}`.

Then, you must add a step to push your test and code coverage results to *Testspace* after the step that executes the tests. You can use glob syntax to specify files in dynamic folders. Make sure that you execute the step, even if an error occurs (`if: '!cancelled()'`):

```
- name: Push test results to Testspace
  run: |
    testspace **/TestResults.xml **/coverage.cobertura.xml
  if: '!cancelled()'
```

Testspace provides reliable detection for flaky tests. It has a *Build Bot* that sends you a notification if new results arrive. You can comment on the results by answering the email (*see Figure 12.9*):

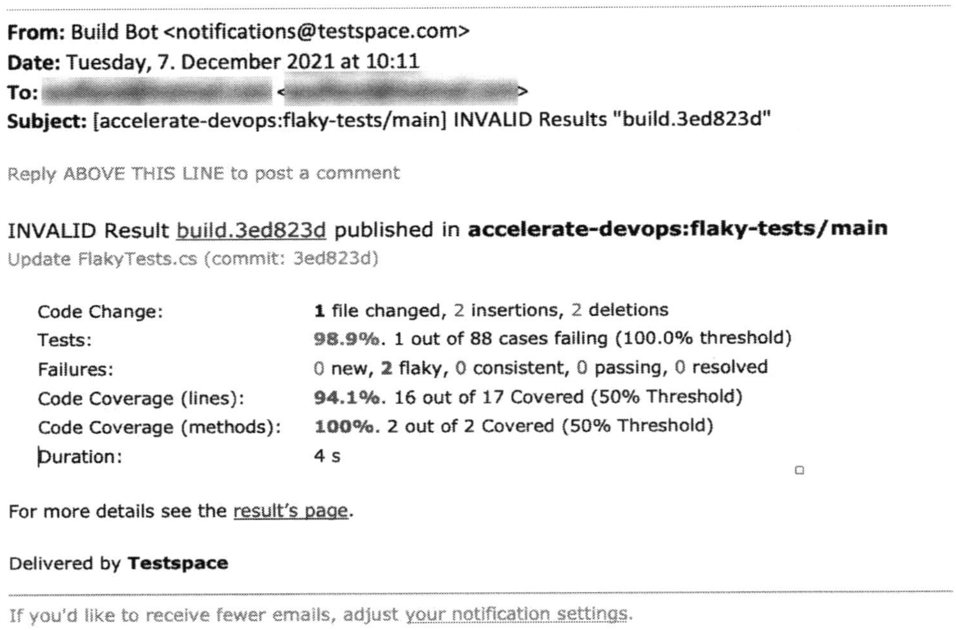

From: Build Bot <notifications@testspace.com>
Date: Tuesday, 7. December 2021 at 10:11
To: <   >
Subject: [accelerate-devops:flaky-tests/main] INVALID Results "build.3ed823d"

Reply ABOVE THIS LINE to post a comment

INVALID Result build.3ed823d published in **accelerate-devops:flaky-tests/main**
Update FlakyTests.cs (commit: 3ed823d)

Code Change:	**1** file changed, 2 insertions, 2 deletions
Tests:	**98.9%**. 1 out of 88 cases failing (100.0% threshold)
Failures:	0 new, **2** flaky, 0 consistent, 0 passing, 0 resolved
Code Coverage (lines):	**94.1%**. 16 out of 17 Covered (50% Threshold)
Code Coverage (methods):	**100%**. 2 out of 2 Covered (50% Threshold)
Duration:	4 s

For more details see the result's page.

Delivered by **Testspace**

If you'd like to receive fewer emails, adjust your notification settings.

Figure 12.9 – Notification from Testspace about your build results

It automatically integrates as a check into your pull request (*see Figure 12.10*):

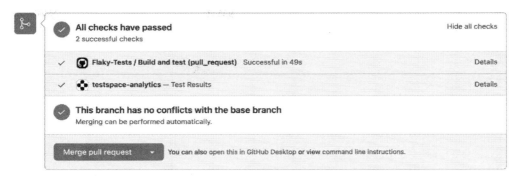

Figure 12.10 – Testspace integrates into your pull request checks

The UI of *Testpace* doesn't look very fancy, but it has really rich reports and a ton of functionality (*see Figure 12.11*):

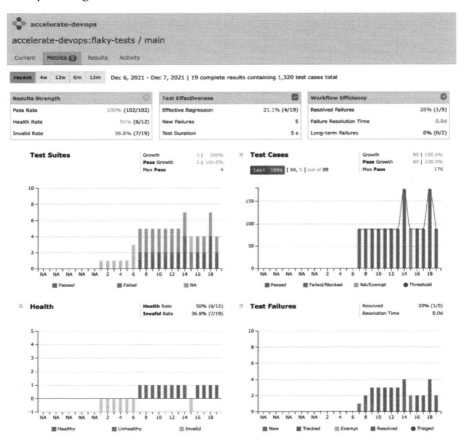

Figure 12.11 – Rich reports of your test metrics

If you don't have a solution for test management yet, you can try *Testspace*. If you already have one, then it should be straightforward to integrate it into your workflow.

Case study

The two pilot teams at **Tailwind Gears** have achieved a much higher **delivery lead time** and **deployment frequency** thanks to the DevOps practices that have been applied. The **mean time to restore** is also much better because the release pipelines help ship fixes faster. However, the **change failure rate** has dropped. Releasing more frequently also means that more deployments fail and finding bugs in the code is hard. The quality signals that come from the automated test suites are just not reliable enough and fixing one bug often introduces another bug in another module. There are still many parts of the application that need manual testing – but with one QA engineer in the team, this was not an option. So, some of these parts have been replaced with UI tests, while others have just been dropped.

To evaluate the test portfolio, the teams must introduce a test taxonomy and include reporting in their pipelines. The QA engineers in the team are responsible for the taxonomy and the reports show that there are way too many functional and UI tests – and not enough unit tests. Many of the engineers are still not convinced that TDD would save them time and that it is possible to develop with TDD in certain cases, especially when the team is developing the embedded software. The teams decide to book a TDD training session together to learn about and practice TDD.

After that, all the new code is written in TDD with a **code coverage** of 90% (at a minimum) for the new code. The teams also spend 30% of their time every sprint eradicating **flaky tests** and rewriting tests at a lower level.

To discover flaky tests, the teams run reliability runs on pipelines with green tests. Flaky tests have the highest priority. After that, the team picks the tests with the longest execution time and decides what to do for each test. Most of the tests get converted into unit tests, though some get converted into integration tests. Some of the tests can be deleted as they bring no additional value.

Structured manual tests get replaced completely by **exploratory testing**. If anything is found in these sessions, a unit test is created before they're fixed.

The team that runs the web application also includes a new test category with tests that get executed in production. They implement **application performance monitoring** and collect many metrics so that they're aware of the health of the application in all environments. They also perform their first BCDR drills once per sprint to get started with **testing in production** and **chaos engineering**.

Summary

In this chapter, you learned how to accelerate your software delivery by shifting testing to the left via test automation and then to the right with testing in production and chaos engineering. This way, you can release at a fast pace without making compromises in terms of quality. Finally, you learned how to manage your test portfolio, eradicate flaky tests, and make your application more resilient by injecting faults and chaos.

In the next chapter, you will learn how to shift left security and implement DevSecOps practices into your development process.

Further reading

The following references were used in this chapter to help you learn more about the topics that were discussed:

- Forsgren N., Humble, J., & Kim, G. (2018). *Accelerate: The Science of Lean Software and DevOps: Building and Scaling High Performing Technology Organizations* (1st ed.) [E-book]. IT Revolution Press.

- Eran Kinsbruner (2018), *Continuous Testing for DevOps Professionals: A Practical Guide From Industry Experts* (Kindle Edition). CreateSpace Independent Publishing Platform.

- Sam Laing (2015), *The Testing Manifesto*, https://www.growingagile. co.za/2015/04/the-testing-manifesto/.

- Wolfgang Platz, Cynthia Dunlop (2019), *Enterprise Continuous Testing: Transforming Testing for Agile and DevOps* (Kindle Edition), Independently published.

- Tilo Linz (2014): *Testing in Scrum* (E-book), Rocky Nook.

- Kaner C., Falk J., H. Q. Nguyen (1999), *Testing Computer Software* (2nd Edition) Wiley.

- Roy Osherove (2009), *The Art of Unit Testing* (1st edition), Manning.

- Martin Fowler (2007), *Mocks Aren't Stubs* https://martinfowler.com/ articles/mocksArentStubs.html.

- Müller, Matthias M.; Padberg, Frank (2017). *About the Return on Investment of Test-Driven Development* (PDF). Universität Karlsruhe, Germany.

- Erdogmus, Hakan; Morisio, Torchiano (2014). *On the Effectiveness of Test-first Approach to Programming.* Proceedings of the IEEE Transactions on Software Engineering, 31(1). January 2005. (NRC 47445).

- *Shift left to make testing fast and reliable*: `https://docs.microsoft.com/en-us/devops/develop/shift-left-make-testing-fast-reliable`.

- Martin Fowler (2011), *Eradicating Non-Determinism in Tests*, `https://martinfowler.com/articles/nonDeterminism.html`.

- Jordan Raine (2020). *Reducing flaky builds by 18x*. `https://github.blog/2020-12-16-reducing-flaky-builds-by-18x/`.

- John Micco (2016). *Flaky Tests at Google and How We Mitigate Them*. `https://testing.googleblog.com/2016/05/flaky-tests-at-google-and-how-we.html`.

- *Shift right to test in production*: `https://docs.microsoft.com/en-us/devops/deliver/shift-right-test-production`.

- Michael Nygard (2018). *Release It! Design and Deploy Production-Ready Software* (2nd Edition). O'Reilly.

13
Shift-Left Security and DevSecOps

The total number of losses caused by cyber-crimes that have been reported to the **Internet Crime Complaint Center** (**IC3**) of the **Federal Bureau of Investigation** (**FBI**) has increased to an all-time high, from 3.5 billion **United States dollars** (**USD**) in 2019 to 4.1 billion USD in 2020 (*IC3*, 2019 and 2020). This continues the trend with a strong increase over the last years (*see Figure 13.1*):

2019	2020
$ 3,500,000,000	$ 4,100,000,000

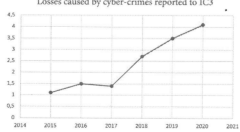

Figure 13.1 – Total losses caused by cyber-crimes reported to IC3

Among the affected companies are start-ups, as well as *Fortune 500* enterprises. Affected are tech giants such as Facebook, Twitter, T-Mobile, and Microsoft, as well as public institutions such as San Francisco International Airport or security companies such as FireEye. No company can claim that cyber-crimes are not a threat to them!

In this chapter, we take a broader look at the role of security in development and how you can bake it into your process and enable a zero-trust culture.

These are the key points that we will cover in this chapter:

- Shift-left security
- Assume-breach, zero-trust, and security-first mindset
- Attack simulations
- Red team-blue team exercises
- Attack scenarios
- GitHub Codespaces

Shift-left security

In classical software development, security was handled downstream: when the software was ready to be released, a security department or external company would perform a security review. The problem with this approach is that it's hard to fix architectural problems at that point. In general, the later you fix a security vulnerability, the more expensive it gets; and if you don't fix vulnerabilities, the costs can be many millions, which can lead to bankruptcy for some companies. The earlier you fix a security vulnerability in the development life cycle, the cheaper it is (*see Figure 13.2*):

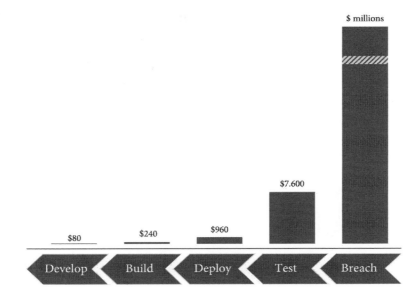

Figure 13.2 – Costs for fixing security vulnerabilities in the development life cycle

That's what we call **shift-left security**: baking security into the development life cycle and making it an essential part of all activities.

The problem is that there are not enough security specialists out there to put them in every engineering team. Shifting security left is about educating engineers and creating a security-first mindset.

Assume-breach, zero-trust, and security-first mindset

The classical approach to security was to **prevent breaches**. The most important measures were these:

- **Layers of trust**: The internal network was considered secure and protected with firewalls. Access to the network was only allowed by company-owned devices and **virtual private network** (**VPN**) tunnels. The public internet was not trusted—and in between were **demilitarized zones** (**DMZs**).

- **Risk analysis**: Risk analysis with threat modeling.

- **Security reviews**: Architecture and code reviews from security experts.

- **Security testing**: External security testing with a specific scope.

But with the prevent-breach approach, the question as to whether a company was already under attack could basically not be answered.

In an interview in 2012, General Michael Hayden, former director of the **National Security Agency (NSA)** and the **Central Intelligence Agency (CIA)**, said the following:

> *"Fundamentally, if somebody wants to get in, they're getting in...*
> *accept that."*

This is the basis of the assume-breach paradigm: you are most probably already under attack, whether you know it or not. Always assume that you already have been breached. This way of thinking identifies gaps in the prevent-breach approach. How do you do the following?

- **Detect** attacks and penetrations?
- **Respond** to attacks?
- **Recover** from data leakage or tampering?

This shifts the measures for security and adds a completely new focus. With the assume-breach paradigm, you need the following:

- A central **security monitoring** or **security information and event management (SIEM)** system to detect anomalies.
- Ongoing live site testing of your **incident response (IR) (fire drills)**.
- War games (**red team-blue team simulations**) to detect vulnerabilities, create awareness, learn to think like attackers, and train your responses.
- **Live site penetration tests**: Sophisticated attack simulations including phishing, social engineering, and physical security.
- Don't trust identities and devices, even when in your network (**zero trust**).

If your security is mainly based upon layers, once a hacker is inside your network—through phishing, social engineering, or a physical attack—it's child's play for them to advance. In a trusted network, you normally find unprotected file shares, unpatched servers without **Secure Sockets Layer (SSL)** protection, weak passwords, and **single-factor authentication (SFA)** in most systems. In a cloud-first world, this makes absolutely no sense.

With zero-trust access to your services, you always verify the identity—for example, with **multi-factor authentication (MFA)**, you verify the device, access, and services involved in transactions. *Figure 13.3* shows an example of how zero-trust access can be implemented for your services:

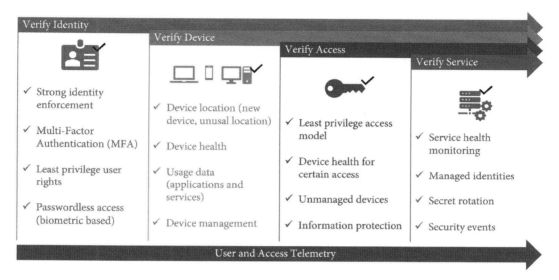

Figure 13.3 – Zero-trust access to your company services

If you are using **software-as-a-service (SaaS)** cloud services in your company, you're probably familiar with zero trust. You must authenticate using MFA but can trust your browser and device for more comfort. If you travel, you get notified or must approve your login attempts from an unusual location. If you install third-party apps, you must grant the apps permissions to access information, and you're probably not allowed to access highly confidential information from a public, not-trusted device.

Zero trust means applying the same principles to all your services, independently of whether you access them from within your internal network or not.

Attack simulations

To know what to do in case of an incident, you should regularly perform drills to practice your **standard operating procedures (SOPs)** for IR and improve your response times. As with fire drills in your offices, if you do not practice these drills, you don't know if your security measures will really work in the event of a real fire.

You should try to improve on the following metrics:

- **Mean Time To Detect (MTTD)**
- **Mean Time To Recover (MTTR)**

In such a drill, you would simulate an attack scenario, practice your IR process, and conduct a **post-mortem** with the learnings of the drill.

Here are some example attack scenarios:

- Service compromise
- Inside attacker
- Remote code execution
- Malware outbreak
- Customer data compromised
- **Denial of service (DoS)** attack

Practicing these drills will give you confidence that your SOPs work and let you react in case of a real incident quickly and efficiently.

Red team-blue team exercises

A special form of these drills is **red team-blue team** exercises, also known as **war games**, whereby two teams with insider know-how play against each other. The red team is the attacker and tries to access a production system or capture user data, and the blue team defends against the attack. If the blue team detects the attack and can prevent it, the blue team wins. If the red team has proof that they could access production or capture data, the red team wins.

Team constellation

The difference from a normal attack simulation is the insights the team has on your systems, so it's easier to find vulnerabilities. Red team-blue team simulations are the most sophisticated attacks with the most insights compared to all other efforts you can do to reduce your security risks (*see Figure 13.4*):

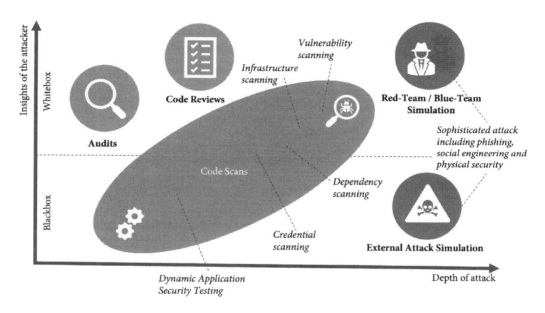

Figure 13.4 – Risk reduction by insights of the attacker and depth of the attack

The teams should be mixed from different organizational units. Do not just pick one team for red and one team for blue. The composition of the team is the key to a successful game.

For the red team, do the following:

- Use creative engineers from different teams that already have an interest in security.
- Add security experts with experience from within your organization, or get external support.

For the blue team, do the following:

- Take ops-minded engineers that are familiar with logging, monitoring, and site reliability.
- Add engineers that have knowledge of your network security and identity.

Both teams should have the possibility to ask experts for help. If, for example, the red team needs to write a **Structured Query Language (SQL)** statement to perform a sophisticated SQL injection attack, they can get help from the **database administrator (DBA)** team; or, when the blue team needs insider information on how an application works or it needs the application to log additional data, it can directly approach the team that builds and maintains the application.

Rules of the game

The main goal of the game is the learning of all participants—learning to think like an attacker, learning to detect and respond to an incident, and learning which vulnerabilities exist in the company that can be exploited. The second goal is fun. As with a hackathon, the exercise should be a team-building event that is fun for all that participate.

But to be successful without harming anyone, you need some ground rules for the game.

Duration

A red team-blue team exercise can last for days, weeks, or even months. Choose a period in which the attack can happen and the duration of the attack itself. A good starting point would be a 3-week period and a 3-day attack. Adjust the time to your needs.

Codex and rules

To make the exercise successful, you must establish some rules and a code of conduct that players must adhere to, as outlined here:

- Both teams may not cause real harm. This also means the red team should not do more than is necessary to achieve their goal, and physical attacks should follow common sense (do not harass or threaten anyone, don't steal keys or badges from your coworkers, and so on).
- Don't expose the names of persons compromised.
- Don't cause downtime for paying customers or breach their data!

- Compromised data must be stored encrypted and protected and not be exposed to real attackers.

- The security of the production system must not be weakened to expose customers to risk. If, for example, the red team could modify the source code to disable authentication for all production systems, then leave a comment in the code and claim victory when the deployment is done. However, you cannot disable authentication for the production system that real customers are using.

This might seem all obvious, but if you have competitive teams, they might get carried away with the game. It's better to state the obvious and lay out some ground rules.

Delivery items

At the end of the game, the teams deliver the following items:

- A backlog with vulnerabilities that must be fixed. Critical vulnerabilities must be fixed right away.

- A backlog with items to improve the forensic and analytic capabilities.

- An open report for the entire organization about the learnings from the exercise.

Remember to make this all blameless, and don't expose the names of people that have been compromised.

Where to start

I know a lot of people think that red team-blue team exercises are only suited to companies with a very high maturity level, but I believe red team-blue team exercises are a great way for each company to create awareness and to learn and grow, especially when they're still preventing breaches and consider their intranet safe. If your maturity level is not so high, attacks are much easier. If the maturity is very high, attacks need to be much more sophisticated, and it is a lot harder to perform successful attacks without causing real harm.

I would prefer red team-blue team exercises over normal attack simulations—they are more fun and a better way to learn. Get external help if you don't know where to start.

If you have many findings in your first game and it was really easy for the red team to win, you might want to consider doing the exercises more often. If not, once a year is a good rhythm I see companies doing successfully, but it depends a lot on your situation.

Just do your first exercise—the rest will follow automatically.

Attack scenarios

The first attack scenarios most people think of in the context of DevOps and DevSecOps are code execution on production systems using vulnerabilities such as **SQL injection**, **cross-site scripting** (**XSS**), or **memory leaks** such as **buffer overflows**. In *Chapter 14, Securing Your Code*,
we'll have a closer look at how you can hunt for these kinds of vulnerabilities and how you can integrate this into your delivery pipeline.

But there are far easier attack scenarios, such as the following:

- **Unprotected file shares** and repositories
- **Secrets in text files**, config files, and source code (such as test accounts, **personal access tokens** (**PATs**), connection strings, and so on)
- **Phishing attacks**

Phishing attacks are an especially easy way to start an attack. According to a study from 2021, 19.8% of recipients of a phishing mail clicked on a link in an email, and 14.4% downloaded the attached document (see *Terranova and Microsoft*, 2021), and in companies that regularly do phishing campaigns, the numbers are more or less the same. At one of my customers, nearly 10% of employees who received an email during a phishing campaign entered their credentials in the login dialog that was displayed after they clicked the link in the phishing mail! And this was a company that had already been practicing phishing campaigns for years.

The problem with phishing is a psychological effect called **priming**. Even if you know in general what phishing attacks look like and the signs to look for to detect them, the moment you are expecting a mail or you think the mail belongs to some context you are in, the more likely you are not to look for those signs. A good example would be a phishing mail at the end of the month that claims to be from your **human resources** (**HR**) department and says there was a problem with the payment of your salary. Since it is the end of the month and you are expecting your salary, the mail does not seem strange. Maybe you had problems before. Maybe you just checked, and the money was not there yet. It also generates some urgency. If you are in a hurry, you may want to quickly solve this so that your salary comes on time. If you send a phishing mail such as this at the end of the month, chances are much higher that people will then click for the rest of the month. Another example is a shared document. If you were just on the phone with a colleague that said they'll share a file with you, you may just wonder why they're choosing this way, but you're not suspicious as you are expecting a file anyway. The more phishing mails you send, the higher the possibility someone has just the right context and that you will fall for it.

Once an attacker has managed to compromise the first victim and has company credentials or access to the victim's machine, the game changes completely. Now, the attack is performed by an **inside attacker**, and they can target specific people in the company from an internal address. This is called **spear phishing** and is extremely hard to detect.

A good target for spear phishing is administrators or engineers. If you don't practice **least-privilege** user rights, the attacker might already have access to a production system or is a domain administrator, and the game is over. But if they compromise a developer, they have also a variety of options, as outlined here:

- **Development environments**: Development environments are the dream of every attacker. Most developers work as local administrators, and you can already find a ton of tools preinstalled that help an attacker to progress. Chances are high they can find secrets in text files to access various systems. Or, as they are administrators, they can use a tool called `mimikatz` (see `https://github.com/gentilkiwi/mimikatz/wiki`) to read credentials from memory.

- **Test environments**: Many developers have access to test environments, often as administrators. Attackers can log in and use mimikatz to steal other credentials.

- **Modify code**: One line of code is usually enough to disable authentication. The attacker can try to modify code or change the version of a dependency to one with a known vulnerability that can be exploited.

- **Execute scripts**: If the developer can modify pipeline code or scripts that get executed during deployment, the attacker can insert code that gets executed during deployment.

That's why it is so important in engineering to be extra cautious when it comes to security. There is much more attack surface than in most other departments in an organization.

To get from one compromised account to the domain administrator or at least an administrator with production access, you can use a tool called **BloodHound** (`https://github.com/BloodHoundAD/BloodHound`). It supports **Active Directory** (**AD**) and **Azure AD** (**AAD**) and reveals all the hidden relationships: Who has a session on which machines? Who is a member of which group? Who is an administrator of a certain machine?

Both blue teams and red teams can use this tool to analyze relationships in an AD environment.

GitHub Codespaces

Since development environments are a big problem when it comes to security, it's a good idea to virtualize them and have a specific machine for each product. This way, you can implement least-privilege user rights and your engineers do not have to work with local administrator rights on their machines. You also can limit the number of tools that are needed for a specific product and minimize the attack surface.

Of course, you can use classical **virtual desktop infrastructure (VDI)** images for that, but you can also use a more lightweight option: **dev containers** (see `https://code.visualstudio.com/docs/remote/containers`, which is an extension for **Visual Studio Code (VS Code)** that is built on top of its client-server architecture). You can connect VS Code to a running container or instantiate a new instance. The complete configuration is stored in the repository (config as code), and you can share the same config for the dev container with your team.

A special form of dev containers is **GitHub Codespaces**, which is a virtual development environment hosted in Azure. You can pick different **virtual machine (VM)** sizes between 2-core/4 **gigabytes (GB) random-access memory (RAM)**/32 GB storage and 32 core/64 GB RAM/128 GB storage. The start time of the VM is blasting fast. The default image is more than 35 GB and starts in less than 10 seconds!

The base image contains everything necessary to develop with Python, Node.js, JavaScript, TypeScript, C, C++, Java, .NET, **PHP: Hypertext Preprocessor (PHP)**, PowerShell, Go, Ruby, Rust, and Jekyll. It also includes a ton of other developer tools and utilities such as `git`, **Oh My Zsh**, **GitHub command-line interface (GitHub CLI)**, `kubectl`, Gradle, Maven, and `vim`. Run `devcontainer-info content-url` inside your codespace and open the **Uniform Resource Locator (URL)** that it returns for a complete list of all preinstalled tools.

But you don't have to use the base image—you can completely customize your codespace using dev containers. You can work with a codespace using either VS Code in the browser, your local VS Code instance, or using **Secure Shell (SSH)** from a terminal. If you run your application inside the codespace, you can forward ports to test it from your local machine. *Figure 13.5* shows the architecture of GitHub Codespaces:

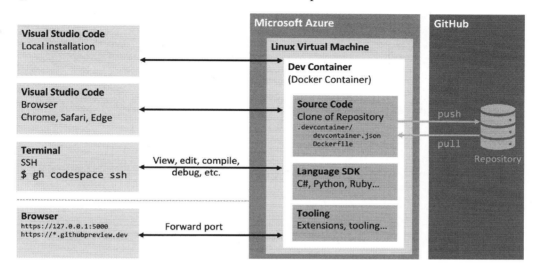

Figure 13.5 – Architecture of GitHub Codespaces

You can open, for example, the `https://github.com/wulfland/`
`AccelerateDevOps` repository in a new codespace under **Code | Codespaces | New codespace** (*see Figure 13.6*), if you have Codespaces enabled for your account. The repository does not have a dev container configuration, so it will load the default image:

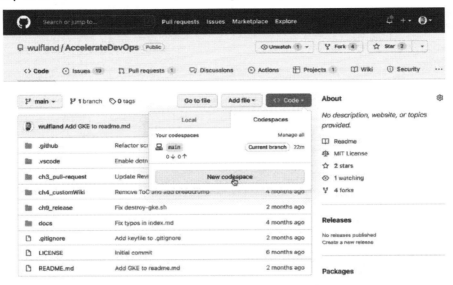

Figure 13.6 – Opening a repository in a codespace

You can see in the preceding screenshot that I already have a codespace running on the `main` branch. Instead of creating a new one, I could also open the existing one. Pick the VM size (*see Figure 13.7*):

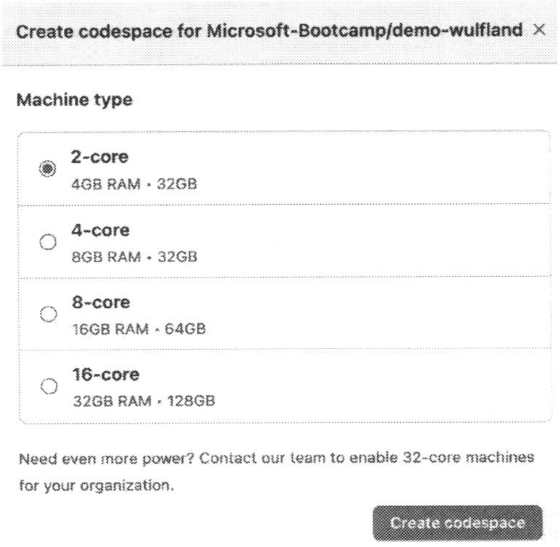

Figure 13.7 – Picking the VM size for your codespace

In the terminal, change the directory to `ch9_release/src/Tailwind.Traders.Web` and build and run the application with the following commands:

```
$ cd ch9_release/src/Tailwind.Traders.Web
$ dotnet build
$ dotnet run
```

This will start a web server listening on ports `5000` and `5001`. Codespaces automatically detects this and forwards port `5000` to a local port. Just click **Open in Browser** to see the application that is running inside your codespace in your local browser (*see Figure 13.8*):

Figure 13.8 – Forwarding a port to your machine

You can also add ports that should be forwarded manually in the **PORTS** tab and change the visibility if you want to share a link with your coworkers—for example, to let them try a new feature (*see Figure 13.9*):

	Port		Local Address	Running Process	Visibility	Origin
●	5000	⊘ ×	https:... 🗐 🌐 🗗	/workspaces/AccelerateDevOps/c...	◎ Public	Auto Forwarded
●	5001		https://wulfla Open in Browser paces/AccelerateDevOps/c...	🔒 Private	Auto Forwarded
	Add Port					

Copy local address, open in browser, or preview in editor

Set the port visibility to public to share the link with your stakeholders

Figure 13.9 – Configuring port forwarding in your codespace

If you want more control over your development environment, you can create a dev container in your codespace. Open the *Command Palette* in VS Code by clicking the green **Codespaces** button in the bottom-left corner or by pressing *Shift + Command + P* on Mac or *Ctrl + Shift + P* on Windows. Select `Codespaces: Add Development Container Configuration Files....` and follow the wizard to select languages and features that get installed. The wizard will create a `.devcontainer` folder in the root of your repository and, in it, two files: a `devcontainer.json` file and a `Dockerfile` file.

The `Dockerfile` file defines the container that is created when your codespace is initialized. The `Dockerfile` file can be really simple—it is enough if it contains a FROM clause that indicates from which base image it inherits.

In the `devcontainer.json` file, you can pass arguments to the image creation, you can define VS Code settings that are shared with all teammates, you can use VS Code extensions that are installed per default, and you can run commands that are run after the container was created (*see Figure 13.10*):

Figure 13.10 – Example Dockerfile file and devcontainer.json file

See `https://code.visualstudio.com/docs/remote/devcontainerjson-reference` for a complete reference on how you can customize your `devcontainer.json` file.

If you change either the `Dockerfile` file or the `devcontainer.json` file, you can rebuild the container by opening the Command Palette and executing `Rebuild Container`.

If you need secrets inside your codespace, you can create them—as with all other secrets—under **Settings | Secrets | Codespaces** (`settings/secrets/codespaces`) in the organization or repository level. Secrets are available as environment variables inside the codespace container. If you add a new secret, you have to stop the current codespace—a rebuild container is not enough.

Of course, GitHub Codespaces is not available for free—you have to pay for the uptime minutes of your instances. The minutes are reported to billing daily and billed monthly. The rate depends on the size of your VM (*see Table 13.1*):

Central processing unit (CPU)	RAM	Disk	Price
2-core	4 GB	32 GB	$0.18/hour
4-core	8 GB	32 GB	$0.36/hour
8-core	16 GB	32 GB	$0.72/hour
16-core	32 GB	64 GB	$1.44/hour
32-core	64 GB	128 GB	$2.88/hour

Table 13.1 – Pricing for GitHub Codespaces

Additionally, you pay $0.07 per GB and month for the storage used.

Codespaces do not get terminated if you close your browser. If they are still running in the background, you can connect much faster, but you must still pay for them. The default idle timeout is 30 minutes, which is equivalent to $0.18 for the 4-core machine. That's really cheap, but it is still money. You should always stop your codespace if you don't need it anymore. You can change the default idle timeout under **Settings | Codespaces**.

GitHub Codespaces is not only great for security—it can also boost your onboarding time and productivity. GitHub itself uses it for its development, and it reduced onboarding time for new engineers from days to under 10 seconds! And that for a repository with almost 13 GB on disk that normally takes 20 minutes to clone (Cory Wilkerson, 2021).

Codespaces might not be suited for all products, but for web applications, it's the future, and it will revolutionize how we think of managing developer machines. It also helps you to close a security gap in your development pipeline—your local developer machines.

Summary

In this chapter, you've learned how important security is for your development process and how you can start to **shift security left** and implement an **assume-breach** and **zero-trust** culture. I introduced you to **attack simulations** and **red team-blue team** exercises to raise awareness for security, find vulnerabilities, and practice your IR.

I've also shown you how **GitHub Codespaces** can help you to reduce the risk of local development environments and make you more productive.

In the next chapter, you'll learn how to secure your code and your software supply chain.

Further reading

You can use the following references from this chapter to get more information on the topics covered:

- *IC3 (2020). Internet Crime Report 2020*: `https://www.ic3.gov/Media/PDF/AnnualReport/2020_IC3Report.pdf`

- *IC3 (2019). Internet Crime Report 2019*: `https://www.ic3.gov/Media/PDF/AnnualReport/2019_IC3Report.pdf`

- Data breaches in 2020: `https://www.identityforce.com/blog/2020-data-breaches`

- Data breaches in 2021: `https://www.identityforce.com/blog/2021-data-breaches`

- *Terranova* and *Microsoft* (2021). *Gone Phishing Tournament – Phishing Benchmark Global Report 2021*: `https://terranovasecurity.com/gone-phishing-tournament/`

- *GitHub Codespaces*: `https://docs.github.com/en/codespaces/`

- `devcontainer.json` *reference*: `https://code.visualstudio.com/docs/remote/devcontainerjson-reference`

- *Introduction to dev containers*: `https://docs.github.com/en/codespaces/setting-up-your-project-for-codespaces/configuring-codespaces-for-your-project`

- *Cory Wilkerson* (2021). *GitHub's Engineering Team has moved to Codespaces*: `https://github.blog/2021-08-11-githubs-engineering-team-moved-codespaces/`

14
Securing Your Code

In 2016, a dispute about the name *Kik* between the messenger service Kik (`https://www.kik.com/`) and open source contributor *Azer Koçulu*, who maintained a project with the same name, led to a complete outage of the internet. At least everybody noticed that day that something was wrong. What happened? Because of the dispute and npm siding with the messenger service, Azer retracted all his packages from the npm registry. Among the packages was a package called `left-pad`. Its purpose was to add characters to the beginning of a string of text. `left-pad` was a simple module with only 11 lines of code:

```
module.exports = leftpad;
function leftpad (str, len, ch) {
  str = String(str);
  var i = -1;
  if (!ch && ch !== 0) ch = ' ';
  len = len - str.length;
  while (++i < len) {
    str = ch + str;
  }
  return str;
}
```

This is a simple, single-purpose function that every developer should be able to write on their own. And yet the package made it into globally used frameworks such as *React*. React didn't require these 11 lines of code directly, of course. But it depended on packages that depend on other packages – and one package in this tree depended on `left-pad`. And that package missing basically broke the internet (see *Keith Collins 2016* and *Tyler Eon 2016*).

Software today depends on a lot of different software – tools, packages, frameworks, compilers, and languages – and each of these has its own dependency tree. It's important to ensure security and license compliance not just for your code but for your entire software supply chain.

In this chapter, you'll learn how GitHub Actions and Advanced Security can help you to eliminate bugs and security issues in your code and successfully manage your software supply chain.

The key topics in this chapter are as follows:

- Dependency management and Dependabot
- Secret scanning
- Code scanning
- Writing your own CodeQL queries

> **GitHub Advanced Security**
>
> Many features discussed in this chapter are only available for GitHub Enterprise if you acquire the **Advanced Security License**. Some of them are free for open source – but if some are not available in your organization, then you probably have not acquired the corresponding license.

Dependency management and Dependabot

To manage your dependencies, you can use **Software Composition Analysis (SCA)** tools. GitHub offers **Dependency graphs**, **Dependabot alerts**, and **Dependabot security updates** to manage your software dependencies.

Dependency graph helps you to understand your dependency tree. **Dependabot alerts** check your dependencies for known vulnerabilities and alert you in case Dependabot finds any. If you enable **Dependabot security updates**, Dependabot will automatically create pull requests that update your dependencies if the author of the dependent package releases a fix for a vulnerability.

The dependency graph is enabled by default for public repositories but not for private ones. Dependabot alerts and updates must be enabled for all repositories. You can do this under **Settings | Security & Analysis** (see *Figure 14.1*):

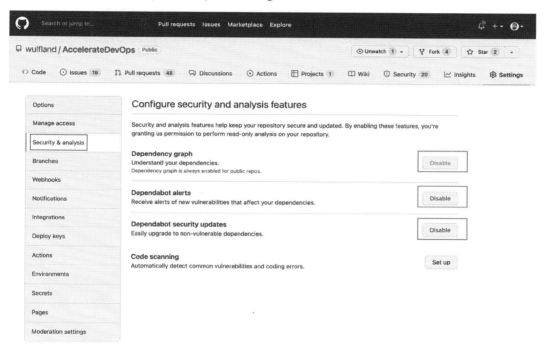

Figure 14.1 – Enable the dependency graph and Dependabot

On the organizational level, you can enable these options for all repositories and make them the default for new repositories.

Exploring your dependencies

If you enable the dependency graph, it will start looking for dependencies. The following package ecosystems are supported (see *Table 14.1*):

Package manager	Languages	Recommended formats	All supported formats
Composer	PHP	composer.lock	composer.json, composer.lock
dotnet CLI	.NET languages (C#, C++, F#, and VB)	.csproj, .vbproj, .nuspec, .vcxproj, .fsproj	.csproj, .vbproj, .nuspec, .vcxproj, .fsproj, packages.config
Go	Go	go.sum	go.mod, go.sum
Maven	Java and Scala	pom.xml	pom.xml
npm	JavaScript	package-lock.json	package-lock.json, package.json
Python pip	Python	requirements.txt, pipfile.lock	requirements.txt, pipfile, pipfile.lock, setup.py
Python Poetry	Python	poetry.lock	poetry.lock, pyproject.toml
RubyGems	Ruby	Gemfile.lock	Gemfile.lock, Gemfile, .gemspec
Yarn	JavaScript	yarn.lock	package.json, yarn.lock

Table 14.1 – Supported formats for the dependency graph and Dependabot

To explore your dependencies, you can navigate to **Insights | Dependency graph**. On the **Dependencies** tab, you can find all the dependencies for the manifest files that were found in your repository. You can open the dependencies for each dependency and navigate the tree. If the dependency has a known vulnerability, you can see it on the right side. The vulnerability has an assigned severity and a **Common Vulnerabilities and Exposures (CVE)** identifier. With this identifier, you can look up the details for the vulnerability in the **National Vulnerability Database** (nvd.nist.gov). Click on the link, and it will direct you to the entry in the database (https://nvd.nist.gov/vuln/detail/CVE-2021-3749) or to the **GitHub Advisory Database** (https://github.com/advisories). If there is a fix for the vulnerability, the dependency graph suggests the version you should upgrade the dependency to (see *Figure 14.2*):

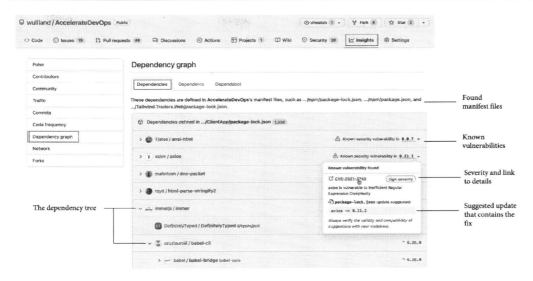

Figure 14.2 – Exploring your dependencies with the dependency graph

On the *organization level*, under **Insights | Dependencies**, you can find all dependencies from all repositories that have turned on the dependency graph. In addition to the repository insights, you can find all the used licenses here. This can help you to check the license compliance of your products (see *Figure 14.3*):

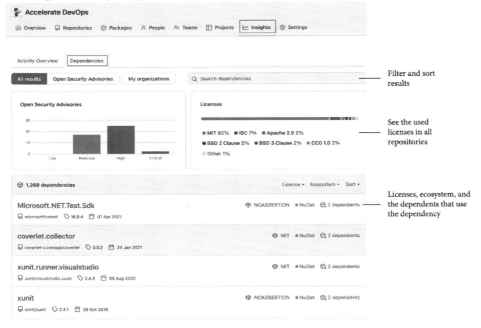

Figure 14.3 – Dependency insights on the organization level

If you want to leverage GitHub to inform others that depend on your packages, you can draft a new **security advisory** under **Security | Security Advisories | New draft security advisory**. The security advisor contains a title, description, the ecosystem, the package name, the affected versions (that is, < 1.2.3), the patched versions (1.2.3), and the severity. You can optionally add multiple **Common Weakness Enumerators (CWEs)** (see `https://cwe.mitre.org/`). If you already have a CVE ID, you can add it here; if not, you can select to add it later.

The draft is only visible to repository owners until it is published. Once published, security advisories on public repositories are visible to everyone and are added to the **GitHub Advisory Database** (`https://github.com/advisories`). For private repositories, they are only visible to everyone that has access to the repository, and they do not get added to the advisory database until you request an official CVE identifier.

Dependabot

Dependabot is a bot in GitHub that can check your dependencies for known vulnerabilities. It can also automatically create pull requests to keep your dependencies up to date.

Dependabot supports npm, GitHub Actions, Docker, git submodules, .NET (NuGet), pip, Terraform, Bundler, Maven, and many other ecosystems. For a complete list, see `https://docs.github.com/en/code-security/supply-chain-security/keeping-your-dependencies-updated-automatically/about-dependabot-version-updates#supported-repositories-and-ecosystems`.

To enable Dependabot, create a `dependabot.yml` file in the `.github` directory. You select the package ecosystem and the directory that contains the package file (that is, the `package.json` file). You have to specify whether Dependabot should check for updates `daily`, `weekly`, or `monthly`:

```
version: 2
updates:
  - package-ecosystem: "npm"
    directory: "/"
    schedule:
      interval: "daily"
```

You can authenticate to private registries using **Dependabot secrets**. Add a new secret under **Settings | Secrets | Dependabot** (see Figure 14.4):

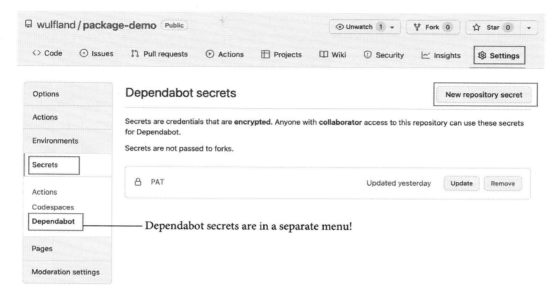

Figure 14.4 – Adding a Dependabot secret

Then, add the registry to the `dependabot.yml` file and access the secret from the `secret` context:

```
version: 2
registries:
  my-npm-pkg:
    type: npm-registry
    url: https://npm.pkg.github.com
    token: ${{secrets.PAT}}

updates:
  - package-ecosystem: "npm"
    directory: "/"
    registries:
      - my-npm-pkg
    schedule:
      interval: "daily"
```

There are many more options to configure Dependabot – you can allow or deny certain packages, apply metadata to pull requests (such as labels, milestones, and reviewers), customize the commit message, or you can change the merge strategy. For a complete list of options, see `https://docs.github.com/en/code-security/supply-chain-security/keeping-your-dependencies-updated-automatically/configuration-options-for-dependency-updates`.

You can check the status of Dependabot updates under **Insights | Dependency graph | Dependabot**. Each update entry has a row with a status and warning icons if something is wrong. Click the status to see the complete log (see *Figure 14.5*):

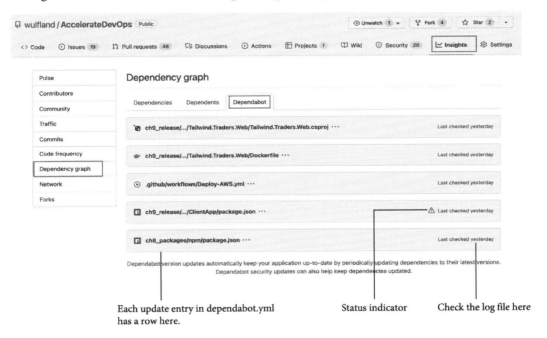

Figure 14.5 – Viewing Dependabot status and log files

You can find all the Dependabot alerts under **Security | Dependabot alerts**. You can click on each item to see details. If Dependabot has already created a pull request to fix the vulnerability, you can see a link with a fly-out menu in the list (see *Figure 14.6*):

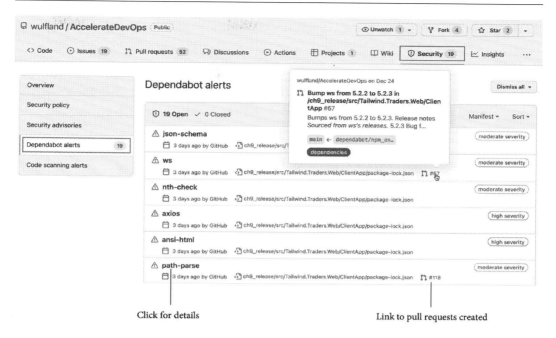

Figure 14.6 – Viewing Dependabot alerts

Note that only the security alerts are in this list – not all the pull requests that get created to update your dependencies. There are also a lot of security alerts here that don't have a fix yet. Sometimes, the only fix is a downgrade, and if one of your dependents states a minimum higher version, there is no automated fix (see *Figure 14.7*):

Figure 14.7 – Details of a vulnerability that has no fix

If you have a closer look at the pull requests of Dependabot, you'll notice a lot of additional information. Of course, the changes themselves are only updated version numbers in a manifest file. But in the description, it adds the release notes from the package – if there are any – and a complete list of the commits that are in the new release. Dependabot also adds a compatibility score that indicates how likely it is that this update will be compatible with your code (see *Figure 14.8*):

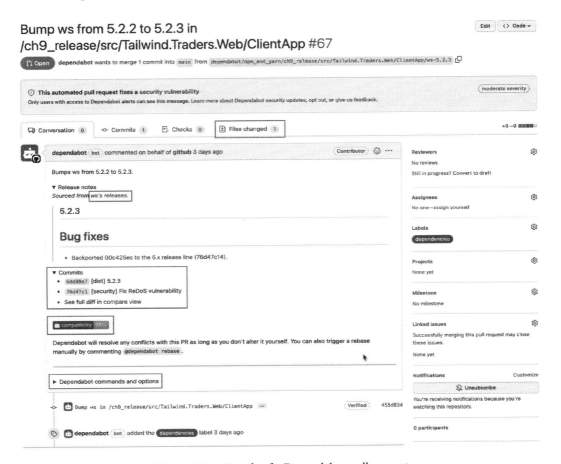

Figure 14.8 – Details of a Dependabot pull request

In the description, you will also find a list of commands that you can send to the bot by commenting on the pull request. You can use any of the following commands:

- `@dependabot cancel merge`: Cancels a previously requested merge.

- `@dependabot close`: Closes the pull request and prevents Dependabot from recreating it. You can achieve the same result by closing the pull request manually.

- `@dependabot ignore this dependency`: Closes the pull request and prevents Dependabot from creating any more pull requests for this dependency (unless you reopen the pull request or upgrade to the suggested version of the dependency yourself).

- `@dependabot ignore this major version`: Closes the pull request and prevents Dependabot from creating any more pull requests for this major version (unless you reopen the pull request or upgrade to this major version yourself).

- `@dependabot ignore this minor version`: Closes the pull request and prevents Dependabot from creating any more pull requests for this minor version (unless you reopen the pull request or upgrade to this minor version yourself).

- `@dependabot merge`: Merges the pull request once your CI tests have passed.

- `@dependabot rebase`: Rebases the pull request.

- `@dependabot recreate`: Recreates the pull request, overwriting any edits that have been made to the pull request.

- `@dependabot reopen`: Reopens the pull request if the pull request is closed.

- `@dependabot squash and merge`: Squashes and merges the pull request once your CI tests have passed.

Just comment on one of the commands in the pull request, and Dependabot will do the rest for you.

Automate Dependabot updates with GitHub Actions

You can use GitHub Actions to add even more automation to Dependabot updates, but there are some things you have to be aware of. If Dependabot triggers a workflow, the GitHub actor is Dependabot (`github.actor == "Dependabot[bot]"`). This means that `GITHUB_TOKEN` has only read-only permissions by default, and you must grant write permissions if necessary. The secrets that are populated in the secret context are the Dependabot secrets! GitHub Actions secrets are not available to the workflow.

The following is an example of a workflow that only gets triggered by Dependabot pull requests and gets granted write permissions to pull requests, issues, and projects:

```
name: Dependabot automation
on: pull_request

permissions:
  pull-requests: write
  issues: write
  repository-projects: write

jobs:
  Dependabot:
    runs-on: ubuntu-latest
    if: ${{ github.actor == 'Dependabot[bot]' }}
```

You can use the `Dependabot/fetch-metadata` action to extract information about the dependencies being updated. Here is an example that uses the information to apply a label to the pull request:

```
steps:
  - name: Dependabot metadata
    id: md
    uses: Dependabot/fetch-metadata@v1.1.1
    with:
      github-token: "${{ secrets.GITHUB_TOKEN }}"
  - name: Add label for production dependencies
    if: ${{ steps.md.outputs.dependency-type ==
'direct:production' }}
    run: gh pr edit "$PR_URL" --add-label "production"
    env:
      PR_URL: ${{ github.event.pull_request.html_url }}
```

Using the GitHub CLI, it's really easy to add automation. You can, for example, auto-approve and auto-merge all new patches:

```
- name: Enable auto-merge for Dependabot PRs
  if: ${{ steps.md.outputs.update-type == 'version-
update:semver-patch' }}
  run: |
    gh pr review --approve "$PR_URL"
    gh pr merge --auto --merge "$PR_URL"
  env:
    PR_URL: ${{github.event.pull_request.html_url}}
    GITHUB_TOKEN: ${{ secrets.GITHUB_TOKEN }}
```

The combination of GitHub Actions and Dependabot is very powerful and can remove nearly all manual tasks to keep your software up to date. In combination with a good CI build and a test suite you trust, you can basically auto-merge all the Dependabot pull requests that pass the tests.

Use Dependabot to keep your GitHub actions up to date

GitHub actions are also dependencies you must manage. Each action is pinned to a version (the part behind @, such as `uses: Dependabot/fetch-metadata@v1.1.1`). The version can also be a branch name – but this would result in flaky workflows, as your actions would change without you knowing. It's better to pin the versions to a tag or an individual commit SHA. You can let Dependabot check for updates and create pull requests for you as with any other ecosystem. Add the following section to your `Dependabot.yml` file:

```
version: 2
updates:
  - package-ecosystem: "github-actions"
    directory: "/"
    schedule:
      interval: "daily"
```

Dependabot will create pull requests if new versions of your actions are available.

Secret scanning

One of the most common attack vectors is secrets in plain text files. Secrets should never be stored unencrypted and unprotected. GitHub helps you with this by constantly scanning all your public repositories for secrets. You can also enable this for private repositories that belong to an organization where **GitHub Advanced Security** is enabled.

Currently, there are nearly 100 secrets in public and 145 in private repositories that get detected – Adobe, Alibaba, Amazon, Atlassian, Azure, and so on. For a complete list, see `https://docs.github.com/en/code-security/secret-scanning/about-secret-scanning`.

As a service provider, you can sign up for the **secret scanning partner program** (see `https://docs.github.com/en/developers/overview/secret-scanning-partner-program`). Your secrets get detected by a regular expression and are then sent to an endpoint, where you can verify whether the secret is real or whether it is a false positive. It is the decision of the partner to revoke the secret or just inform the customer that the secret is compromised.

You can enable secret scanning for private repositories in **Settings | Security & analysis | GitHub Advanced Security**. Here, you can also define custom patterns by clicking **New pattern** (see *Figure 14.9*):

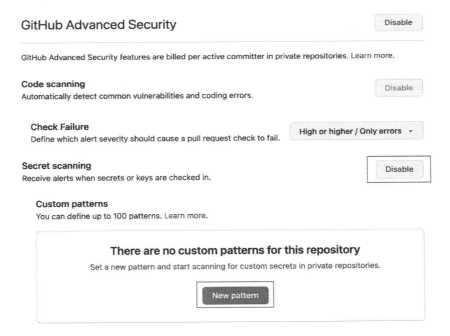

Figure 14.9 – Enabling secret scanning and adding custom patterns

A custom pattern is a regular expression that matches the secrets you want to detect. You have to provide some test strings to see whether your pattern works. GitHub marks the secrets found in the test strings yellow (see *Figure 14.10*):

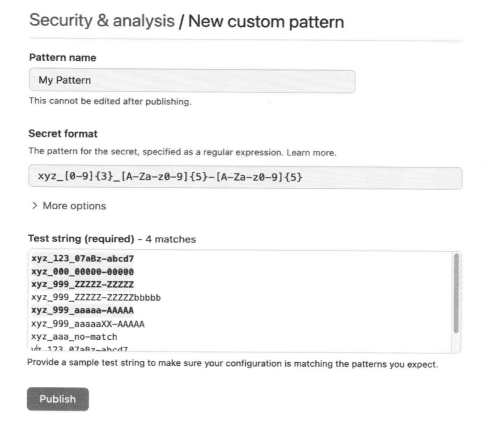

Figure 14.10 – Adding a custom secret pattern

You can also customize the patterns before and after the secret, and you can add patterns that must match or must not patch – for example, you can enforce with the additional pattern ([A-Z]) that the string must at least contain one uppercase letter (see *Figure 14.11*):

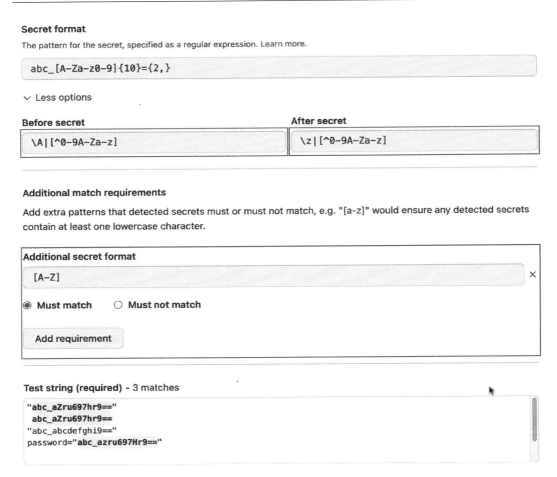

Secret format

The pattern for the secret, specified as a regular expression. Learn more.

```
abc_[A-Za-z0-9]{10}={2,}
```

∨ Less options

Before secret

```
\A|[^0-9A-Za-z]
```

After secret

```
\z|[^0-9A-Za-z]
```

Additional match requirements

Add extra patterns that detected secrets must or must not match, e.g. "[a-z]" would ensure any detected secrets contain at least one lowercase character.

Additional secret format

```
[A-Z]                                                                              ×
```

◉ **Must match**   ○ **Must not match**

Add requirement

Test string (required) - 3 matches

```
"abc_aZru697hr9=="
 abc_aZru697hr9==
"abc_abcdefghi9=="
password="abc_azru697Hr9=="
```

Figure 14.11 – Advanced options for custom patterns

Custom patterns can also be defined on the organization and enterprise level, and GitHub will scan all repositories in the enterprise or organization with GitHub Advanced Security enabled.

When a new secret is detected, GitHub notifies all users with access to security alerts for the repository according to their notification preferences. You will receive alerts if you are watching the repository, have enabled notifications for security alerts or all activity on the repository, are the author of the commit that contains the secret, and are not ignoring the repository.

You can manage the alerts under **Security | Secret scanning alerts** (see *Figure 14.12*):

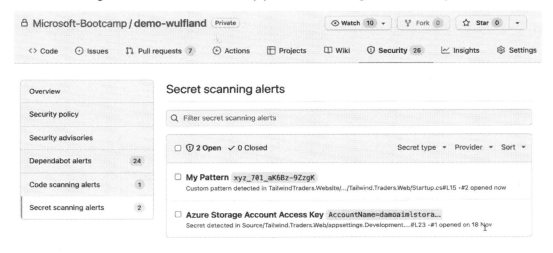

Figure 14.12 – Managing secret scanning alerts

You should consider a secret that has been committed to GitHub compromised – even if it has only been to a private repository. Rotate and revoke the secret. Some service providers will revoke it for you.

You can close an alert with the `Revoked`, `False positive`, `Used in tests`, or `Won't fix` status (see *Figure 14.13*):

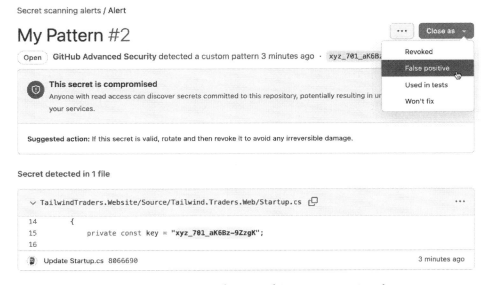

Figure 14.13 – Managing the status for a secret scanning alert

You can also exclude paths in your source code from secret scanning by adding a `secret_scanning.yml` file to the `.github` folder. The file supports multiple path patterns with wildcard support:

```
paths-ignore:
  - "tests/data/**/*.secret"
```

But be careful! This should not be used to store real secrets in source files, even for testing – store secrets as GitHub encrypted secrets or in a secure vault.

Secret scanning is easy – you basically just have to turn it on. But the value of security should not be underestimated.

Code scanning

To find vulnerabilities in your own code, you can use **Static Application Security Testing (SAST)**. SAST is considered white-box testing, as it has full access to the source code. It is not a pure static code analysis, as that normally includes building software. But unlike **Dynamic Application Security Testing (DAST)** – we will learn more about that in *Chapter 15, Securing Your Deployments* – it is not executed at runtime but at compile time.

Code scanning in GitHub

In GitHub, SAST is called **code scanning**, and it is available for all public repositories and for private repositories that have GitHub Advanced Security enabled. You can use code scanning with all tools that support the **Static Analysis Results Interchange Format (SARIF)**. SARIF is an **OASIS Standard** based upon JSON that defines the output format for static analysis tools. GitHub code scanning currently supports **SARIF 2.1.0**, which is the newest version of the standard (see `https://docs.github.com/en/code-security/code-scanning/integrating-with-code-scanning/sarif-support-for-code-scanning`). So, any tool that supports SARIF 2.1.0 can integrate into code scanning.

Running your code scans

Code scanning uses GitHub Actions to execute the analysis. Most code scanning tools automatically upload the results to GitHub – but if your code scanning tool does not, you can upload any SARIF file using the following action:

```
- name: Upload SARIF file
  uses: github/codeql-action/upload-sarif@v1
  with:
    sarif_file: results.sarif
```

The action accepts individual `.sarif` (or `.sarif.json`) files or a folder with multiple files. This is useful if your scanning tool does not support SARIF, but the results can be converted. An example would be `ESLint`. You can use `@microsoft/eslint-formatter-sarif` to convert the output to SARIF and upload the results:

```
jobs:
  build:
    runs-on: ubuntu-latest
    permissions:
      security-events: write
    steps:
      - uses: actions/checkout@v2
      - name: Run npm install
        run: npm install
      - name: Run ESLint
        run: node_modules/.bin/eslint build docs lib script
spec-main -f node_modules/@microsoft/eslint-formatter-sarif/
sarif.js -o results.sarif || true
      - uses: github/codeql-action/upload-sarif@v1
        with:
          sarif_file: results.sarif
```

However, most code scanning tools integrate natively into GitHub.

Getting started

To get started with code scanning, go to **Settings | Security & analysis | Code scanning | Set up** or **Security | Code scanning alerts**. Both take you to /security/code-scanning/setup, which shows you a list of code scanning options. On top, you can see the native GitHub code scanning tool – **CodeQL Analysis**. But GitHub analyses your repository and also shows you all the other tools it can find in the marketplace that fit the languages that were detected in your repository – **42Crunch, Anchore, CxSAST, Veracode**, and many more. In this book, we'll focus on **CodeQL** – but the integration of the other tools works the same way. If you click **Set up this workflow**, GitHub will create a workflow for you (see *Figure 14.14*):

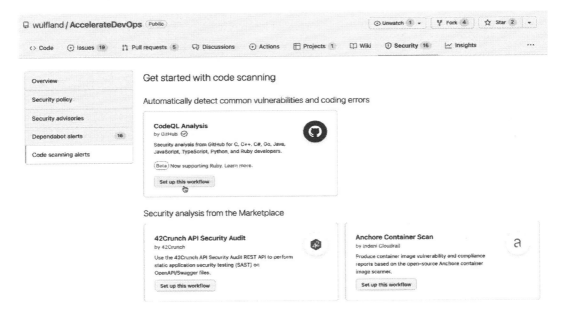

Figure 14.14 – Setting up code scanning

If you have already set up code scanning, you can add additional tools from the results page by clicking **Add more scanning tools** (see *Figure 14.15*):

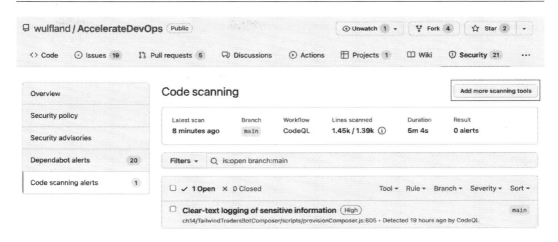

Figure 14.15 – Code scanning alerts in a repository

The workflow template has a trigger for push, pull_request, and schedule. The schedule might surprise you, but it has a simple explanation – there might be new rules that detect vulnerabilities in your codebase that have not been recognized before. So, it is a good idea to run the build also on a scheduled basis. The trigger runs once per week on a random day and to a random time. Of course, GitHub does not want all code scans to run at the same time. Adjust the schedule to your needs:

```
on:
  push:
    branches: [ main ]
  pull_request:
    branches: [ main ]
  schedule:
    - cron: '42 16 * * 2'
```

The workflow needs write permissions for security events:

```
jobs:
  analyze:
    name: Analyze
    runs-on: ubuntu-latest
    permissions:
      actions: read
      contents: read
      security-events: write
```

CodeQL supports C++ (cpp), C# (csharp), Go, Java, JavaScript, Python, and Ruby. GitHub tries to detect the languages used in your repository and sets up the matrix so that each language gets built independently. Add additional languages if necessary:

```
strategy:
  fail-fast: false
  matrix:
    language: [ 'csharp', 'javascript' ]
```

The analysis itself is quite simple – check out the repository, initialize the analysis for the given language, run autobuild, and perform the analysis:

```
steps:
- name: Checkout repository
  uses: actions/checkout@v2
- name: Initialize CodeQL
  uses: github/codeql-action/init@v1
  with:
    languages: ${{ matrix.language }}
- name: Autobuild
  uses: github/codeql-action/autobuild@v1
- name: Perform CodeQL Analysis
  uses: github/codeql-action/analyze@v1
```

The autobuild step tries to build your source code. If it fails, you have to change the workflow and build the code yourself. Sometimes, it is enough to set up the right version in the environment – for example, the version of Node.js or .NET:

```
- name: Setup Node
  uses: actions/setup-node@v2.5.0
  with:
    node-version: 10.16.3
```

Code scanning alerts

You can manage your code scanning alerts in each repository under **Settings | Security & analysis | Code scanning** – as you saw in *Figure 14.15*. On the organization level, you get an overview of all repositories, and you can jump to the individual results page (see *Figure 14.16*):

Figure 14.16 – The security overview for an organization

You can filter, sort, and search alerts the same way you can with issues.

Severity

Every code scanning alert has a severity assigned. The severity is calculated using the **Common Vulnerability Scoring System (CVSS)**. The CVSS is an open framework for communicating the characteristics and severity of software vulnerabilities (see *GitHub Blog 2021* for more information).

The severity helps you to triage your alerts.

Tracking alerts in issues

The best way to track a code scanning alert is in an issue. You can create one by clicking **Create issue** inside the alert (see *Figure 14.17*):

Figure 14.17 – Creating an issue from a code scanning alert

But it is just opening a new issue and adding the link to the alert into a Markdown task list (see *Figure 14.18*):

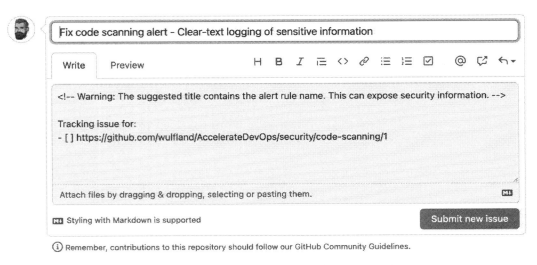

Figure 14.18 – Linking an issue to a code scanning alert

The alert will have an indicator that it is being tracked in an issue – like nested issues do (see *Figure 14.19* in the next).

Data-flow analysis

In the area under the code, you can see the details of the alert in your code. CodeQL supports **data-flow analysis** and can detect issues that arise from the flow of data through your application. Click on **Show paths** to see how the data flows through your application (see *Figure 14.19*):

Figure 14.19 – Details of the code scanning alert

You can follow the data through your entire application. In the example here, you can see 12 steps where the data is assigned and passed along until it is logged (see *Figure 14.20*):

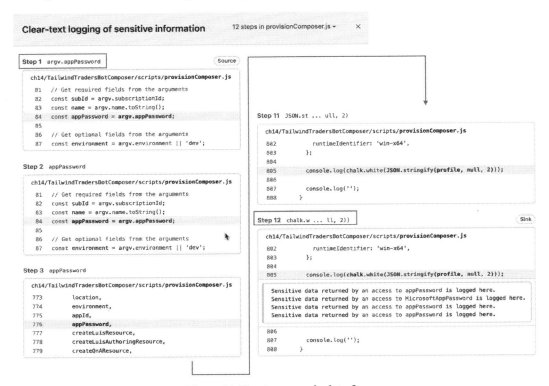

Figure 14.20 – An example data flow

This is the real power of CodeQL. It is not just a semantic analysis of your source code.

CodeQL queries

In the code scanning alert, you can find a reference to the query that detected the issue. Click on **View source** to see the query on GitHub (see *Figure 14.21*):

Figure 14.21 – The CodeQL queries are open source

The queries are open source, and you'll find them under `https://github.com/github/codeql`. Every language has a folder here, and inside the CodeQL folder, you'll find the queries under `ql/src`. The queries have the `.ql` file extension.

Timeline

The code scanning alert also contains a concrete timeline with git blame information – when and in what commit was the issue first detected? When and where was it fixed? Did it reappear? This can help you to triage the alerts (see *Figure 14.22*):

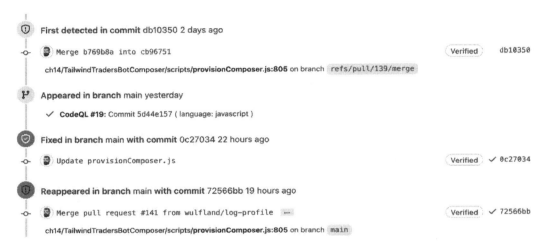

Figure 14.22 – A timeline of a code scanning alert

Pull request integration

Code scanning integrates well with pull requests. Code scanning results are integrated into the pull request checks, and the details page shows you the overview of the results (see *Figure 14.23*):

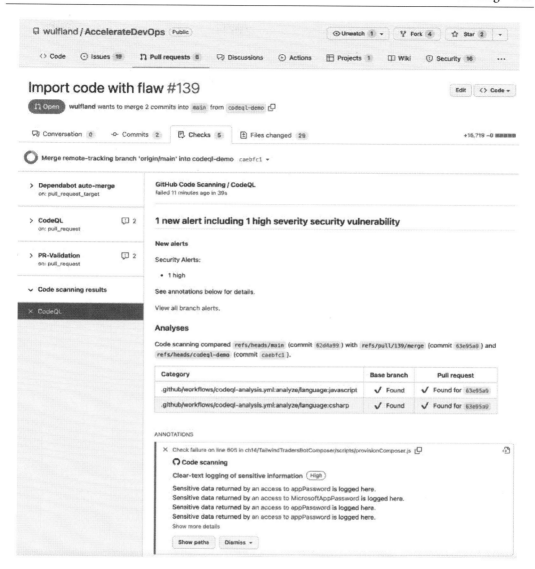

Figure 14.23 – Code scanning results in a pull request

Code scanning also adds comments for the alerts in the code, and you can directly triage the findings there, changing the status to **False positive**, **Used in tests**, or **Won't fix** (see *Figure 14.24*):

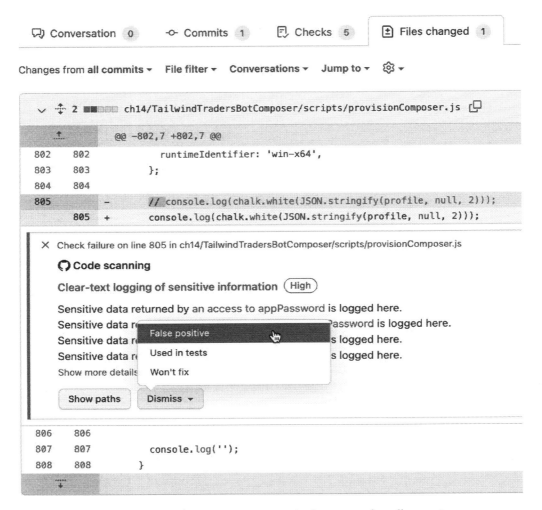

Figure 14.24 – Code scanning comment in the source of a pull request

You can define which alert severity should cause the pull request to fail for security issues and other findings under **Settings | Security & analysis | Code scanning** (see *Figure 14.25*):

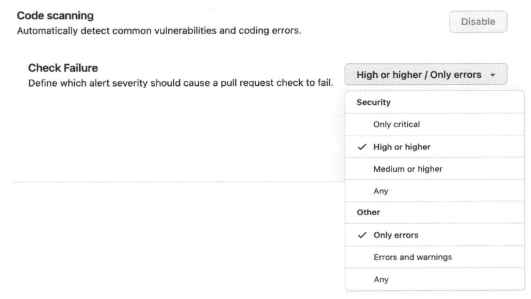

Figure 14.25 – Configure which level of severity causes pull requests to fail

The pull request integration helps you to keep your main branch clean and detect issues before merging and making the code analysis part of the review process.

Code scanning configuration

There are many options to configure code scanning. The `init` CodeQL action in your workflow has a parameter called `queries`. You can use it to pick one of the default query suits:

- `security-extended`: More queries of lower severity than the default
- `security-and-quality`: Queries from `security-extended`, plus maintainability and reliability queries

```
- name: Initialize CodeQL
  uses: github/codeql-action/init@v1
  with:
    languages: ${{ matrix.language }}
    queries:  security-and-quality
```

You can also use the `queries` parameter to add custom queries. The parameter accepts local paths or references to other repositories, including a git reference (`branch`, `tag`, or `SHA`). Add a plus sign to add the queries on top of the default:

```
with:
    queries: +.github/codeql/custom.ql,org/repo/query.ql@v1
```

CodeQL packs are YAML-based query suits that are used to create, share, depend on, and run CodeQL queries. They can be set using the `packs` parameter:

```
with:
    packs: +.github/codeql/pack1.yml,org/repo/pack2.yml@v1
```

> **Important Note**
>
> **CodeQL packs** are still in beta at the time of writing. See `https://codeql.github.com/docs/codeql-cli/about-codeql-packs/` for more information about packs.

You can also use a configuration file – for example, `./.github/codeql/codeql-config.yml`:

```
- uses: github/codeql-action/init@v1
  with:
      config-file: ./.github/codeql/codeql-config.yml
```

If any of the preceding is located in another private repository, then you can add an access token that is used to load queries, packs, or the config file:

```
external-repository-token: ${{ secrets.ACCESS_TOKEN }}
```

In the config file, you normally disable the default queries and specify your own. You can also exclude specific paths. Here is an example – `codeql-config.yml`:

```
name: "Custom CodeQL Configuration"
disable-default-queries: true

queries:
    - uses: ./.github/codeql/custom-javascript.qls

paths-ignore:
    - '**/node_modules'
    - '**/test'
```

Your custom query suit (`custom-javascript.qls`) can then import other query suites (`javascript-security-extended.qls`) from *CodeQL packs* (`codeql-javascript`) and exclude specific rules:

```
- description: "Custom JavaScript Suite"

- import: codeql-suites/javascript-security-extended.qls
  from: codeql-javascript
- exclude:
    id:
      - js/missing-rate-limiting
```

You can also add individual queries (`- query : <path to query>`), multiple queries (`-queries: <path to folder>`), or packs (`- qlpack: <name of pack>`).

CodeQL is very powerful, and you have many options to finetune the configuration. See `https://docs.github.com/en/code-security/code-scanning/automatically-scanning-your-code-for-vulnerabilities-and-errors/configuring-code-scanning` for more details.

Writing your own CodeQL queries

CodeQL comes with a lot of out-of-the-box queries – especially if you use the `security-and-quality` suite. But the full power of CodeQL comes if you start to write your own queries. Of course, this is not trivial. CodeQL is a complex query language, and if you look at some of the queries at `https://github.com/github/codeql`, you'll see that they can get quite complex. But if you know your coding language, it should be quite easy to create some simple queries.

To write CodeQL queries, you need **Visual Studio Code (VS Code)** and the **GitHub CodeQL extension** (`https://marketplace.visualstudio.com/items?itemName=GitHub.vscode-codeql`).

If you have both installed, clone the starter workspace:

```
$ git clone --recursive https://github.com/github/vscode-codeql-starter.git
```

Note the `--recursive` parameter! If you forget it, you have to load the submodules manually:

```
$ git submodule update --remote
```

In VSCode, select **File | Open Workspace from File…** and select the `vscode-codeql-starter.code-workspace` file from the starter workspace.

To create a database from your source code, you need the **CodeQL CLI**. On a Mac, you can install it using Homebrew:

```
$ brew install codeql
```

For other platforms, you can download the binaries here: `https://github.com/github/codeql-cli-binaries/releases/latest`.

Extract them to a folder and add them to the `$PATH` variable (`%PATH%` on windows).

Now, go into the folder where you want to store the database and run the following command:

```
$ codeql database create <database name> \
  --language=<language> \
  --source-root=<path to source code>
```

This will create a database for the language in your repository. Repeat the step for all the languages in your repository.

Now, open the QL extension in VSCode and click **Databases | From a folder**. Select the database that you've created in the previous step. You can attach multiple databases and switch between them (see *Figure 14.26*):

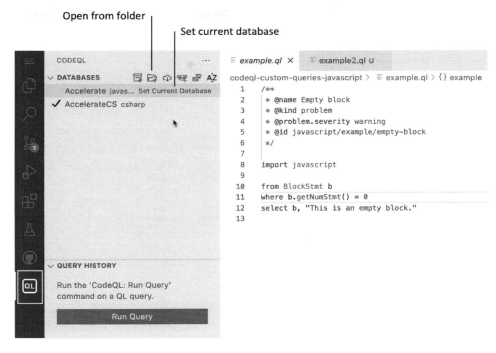

Figure 14.26 – Attaching databases to the VSCode CodeQL extension

You can find sample queries for all supported languages in the starter workspace
(codeql-custom-queries-<language>/example.ql). The queries have a
comment header with metadata:

```
/**
 * @name Empty block
 * @kind problem
 * @problem.severity warning
 * @id javascript/example/empty-block
 */
```

Then, they import the necessary modules. They are normally named after the language
(javascript, csharp, java, and so on), but they could also be something like
DataFlow::PathGraph:

```
import javascript
```

The query itself has a variable declaration, an optional `where` block to limit the results, and the `select` statement:

```
from BlockStmt b
where
  b.getNumStmt() = 0
select b, "This is an empty block."
```

Look at the CodeQL samples on GitHub to get an idea of how to start. The better you know a language, the easier it is to write the queries. The following query would search for empty catch blocks in C#:

```
import csharp

from CatchClause cc
where
  cc.getBlock().isEmpty()
select cc, "Poor error handling: empty catch block."
```

You have full IntelliSense support in VSCode (see *Figure 14.27*), which helps a lot when writing the queries:

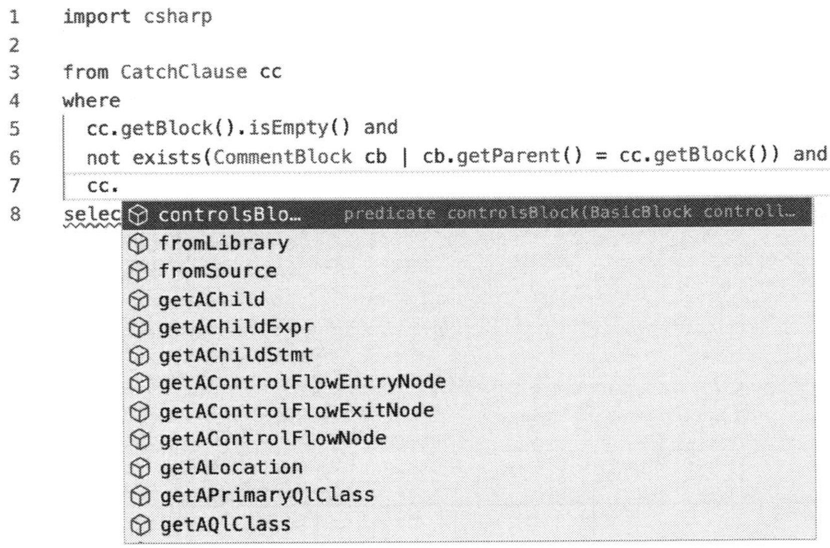

```
1    import csharp
2
3    from CatchClause cc
4    where
5      cc.getBlock().isEmpty() and
6      not exists(CommentBlock cb | cb.getParent() = cc.getBlock()) and
7      cc.
8    selec  ⊙ controlsBlo…      predicate controlsBlock(BasicBlock controll…
           ⊙ fromLibrary
           ⊙ fromSource
           ⊙ getAChild
           ⊙ getAChildExpr
           ⊙ getAChildStmt
           ⊙ getAControlFlowEntryNode
           ⊙ getAControlFlowExitNode
           ⊙ getAControlFlowNode
           ⊙ getALocation
           ⊙ getAPrimaryQlClass
           ⊙ getAQlClass
```

Figure 14.27 – IntelliSense in VSCode

If you run a query from the context menu (**CodeQL: Run query**), it will display the results in the results window (see *Figure 14.28*):

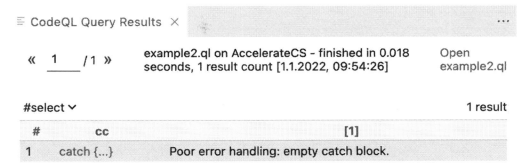

Figure 14.28 – CodeQL query results

Every element in the `select` clause has a column. You can click on code elements and VSCode will open the corresponding source file at the exact location.

You could easily fill an entire book just about CodeQL. This is just a very brief introduction, but I see a lot of value in being able to extend code scanning with your own rules.

See the CodeQL documentation and language reference for further information.

Summary

In this chapter, you've learned how to secure your code and control your dependencies:

- You've learned about SCA, and you know how to use dependency graphs, Dependabot alerts, and Dependabot security updates to manage your software dependencies.

- You've learned about secret scanning, which prevents secrets from being leaked in your source code.

- You've learned about SAST, and you know how to use code scanning with CodeQL or other tools that support SARIF to find problems already during development. You can now write your own queries to enforce quality and coding standards.

In the next chapter, we'll have a look into how we can secure our release pipeline and our deployments.

Further reading

These are the references from this chapter that you can also use to get more information on the topics:

- *How one programmer broke the internet by deleting a tiny piece of code, Keith Collins* (2016): `https://qz.com/646467/how-one-programmer-broke-the-internet-by-deleting-a-tiny-piece-of-code/`

- *Kik, Left-Pad, and NPM – Oh My!, Tyler Eon* (2016): `https://medium.com/@kolorahl/kik-left-pad-and-npm-oh-my-e6f216a22766`

- *Secure at every step: What is software supply chain security and why does it matter?, Maya Kaczorowski* (2020): `https://github.blog/2020-09-02-secure-your-software-supply-chain-and-protect-against-supply-chain-threats-github-blog/`

- *About the dependency graph*: `https://docs.github.com/en/code-security/supply-chain-security/understanding-your-software-supply-chain/about-the-dependency-graph`

- *About Dependabot version updates*: `https://docs.github.com/en/code-security/supply-chain-security/keeping-your-dependencies-updated-automatically/about-Dependabot-version-updates`

- *About secret scanning*: `https://docs.github.com/en/code-security/secret-scanning/about-secret-scanning`

- *About GitHub Advanced Security*: `https://docs.github.com/en/get-started/learning-about-github/about-github-advanced-security`

- *About code scanning*: `https://docs.github.com/en/code-security/code-scanning/automatically-scanning-your-code-for-vulnerabilities-and-errors/about-code-scanning`

- *CodeQL code scanning: new severity levels for security alerts*, GitHub Blog (2021): `https://github.blog/changelog/2021-07-19-codeql-code-scanning-new-severity-levels-for-security-alerts/`

- *Common Vulnerability Scoring System (CVSS)*: `https://www.first.org/cvss/v3.1/specification-document`

- *CodeQL documentation*: `https://codeql.github.com/docs/`

- *QL language reference*: `https://codeql.github.com/docs/ql-language-reference`

15

Securing Your Deployments

In this chapter, we'll talk about securing your complete deployment and release pipeline beyond code and dependencies, to be able to deliver your software in a fast but secure and compliant way to secure environments and meet regulatory requirements.

We will cover the following main topics in this chapter:

- Container and infrastructure security scanning
- Automating the infrastructure change process
- Source code and infrastructure integrity
- Dynamic application security testing
- Security hardening your release pipeline

Container and infrastructure security scanning

One of the most prominent hacks in the last years was **SolarWinds**, a software company that provides system management tools for network and infrastructure monitoring. Attackers managed to introduce a backdoor in the **Orion** software that got rolled out to over 30,000 clients and compromised them using this backdoor. Among the clients were the Department of Homeland Security and the Department of Treasury (*Oladimeji S., Kerner S. M., 2021*).

The SolarWinds attack is considered a software supply chain attack, and this is true for the customers of Orion that installed the compromised version. But the attack on Orion was far more sophisticated than just an update of an infected dependency; the attacker gained access to the SolarWinds network and managed to install a malware called **Sunspot** on the SolarWinds build servers. Sunspot inserted the backdoor **Sunburst** into the software builds of Orion by replacing a source file without tracing any build failures or other suspicious outputs (*Eckels S., Smith J., & Ballenthin W., 2020*).

The attack shows how deadly insider attacks are if your network is breached, and how important it is to secure your complete assembly line – not just the code, dependencies, and development environment. Build servers and all other systems included in the production of software must be kept secure.

Container scanning

Containers play an important part in every infrastructure today. They have a lot of advantages over classical **virtual machines (VMs)**, but they also have their disadvantages. Containers need a new operational culture and existing processes, and practices might not be directly applicable (see *Souppaya M., Morello J., & Scarfone K., 2017*).

Containers consist of many different layers, and like software dependencies, these layers can introduce vulnerabilities. To detect these, you can use so-called **container vulnerability analysis (CVA)**, also known as **container security analysis (CSA)**.

GitHub does not have a built-in CVA tool, but nearly all solutions integrate very well into GitHub.

A very popular open source vulnerability scanner for container images and filesystems is **grype** (https://github.com/anchore/grype/) from Anchore (https://anchore.com/opensource/). It's really easy to integrate it into your GitHub Actions workflow:

```
- name: Anchore Container Scan
  uses: anchore/scan-action@v3.2.0
  with:
    image: ${{ env.REGISTRY }}/${{ env.IMAGE_NAME }}
    debug: true
```

Another example of a CVA scanner is **Clair** (https://github.com/quay/clair), also an open source solution for static analysis of vulnerabilities in Docker and **Open Container Initiative** (**OCI**) containers. Clair can run as a container and store the scanning results in a Postgres database. See https://quay.github.io/clair/ for the complete documentation.

There are commercial container scanners that are normally part of more holistic security platforms. One example is **Container Security** from **Aqua** (https://www.aquasec.com/products/container-security/). The **Aqua Platform** (https://www.aquasec.com/aqua-cloud-native-security-platform/) is a cloud-native security platform for containerized, serverless, and VM-based applications. Aqua runs either as a SaaS or as a self-hosted edition.

Another example is **WhiteSource** (https://www.whitesourcesoftware.com/solution-for-containers/). They have the **GP Security Scan** Action in the GitHub marketplace to scan images before pushing them to GitHub packages (https://github.com/marketplace/actions/gp-security-scan).

Both are great solutions, but as they are not cheap and have a big overlap with GitHub's advanced security, I'll not cover them in more detail here.

Infrastructure policies

Not everything infrastructure-related are containers. There are far more things to consider from a security perspective, especially in the cloud.

If you are using cloud providers, it's worth looking at their security portfolio. Microsoft Azure, for example, contains Microsoft **Defender for Cloud**, a **cloud security posture management** (CSPM) tool to protect workloads across multi-cloud and hybrid environments and to find weak spots across your cloud configuration (`https://azure.microsoft.com/en-us/services/defender-for-cloud`). It supports Microsoft Azure, AWS, Google Cloud Platform, and on-premises workloads (using Azure Arc). Some of the capabilities in Microsoft Defender for Cloud are free for Microsoft Azure – but not all.

Microsoft Azure also contains **Azure Policy** (`https://docs.microsoft.com/en-us/azure/governance/policy/`), a service that helps you to enforce standards and assess compliance. It allows you to define certain rules as policy definitions and evaluate these policies on demand. This example is in a GitHub Action workflow that runs every morning at 8 am:

```
on:
  schedule:
    - cron: '0 8 * * *'
jobs:
  assess-policy-compliance:
    runs-on: ubuntu-latest
    steps:
    - name: Login to Azure
      uses: azure/login@v1
      with:
        creds: ${{secrets.AZURE_CREDENTIALS}}

    - name: Check for resource compliance
      uses: azure/policy-compliance-scan@v0
      with:
        scopes: |
          /subscriptions/<subscription id>
          /subscriptions/<...>
```

Together with the AI-powered **security information and event management (SIEM)** system called **Microsoft Sentinel** (https://azure.microsoft.com/en-us/services/microsoft-sentinel), this is a very powerful security toolchain. But whether it makes sense for you depends a lot on your setup. If your primary cloud provider is not Azure, your decision for CSPM and SIEM might look completely different, and the **AWS Security Hub** would make more sense for you.

A great open source tool to secure **Infrastructure as Code (IaC)** is **Checkov** (https://github.com/bridgecrewio/checkov) – a static code analysis tool that scans cloud infrastructure provisioned using **Terraform, Terraform plan, CloudFormation, AWS Serverless Application Model (SAM), Kubernetes, Dockerfile, Serverless**, or **ARM templates**, and detects security and compliance misconfigurations. It comes with over 1,000 built-in policies for the different platforms. It is really easy to use in GitHub, just use the **Checkov GitHub Action** (https://github.com/marketplace/actions/checkov-github-action) in your workflow and point it to the directory that contains your infrastructure:

```
- name: Checkov GitHub Action
  uses: bridgecrewio/checkov-action@master
  with:
    directory: .
    output_format: sarif
```

The action supports SARIF output and can be integrated into GitHub's advanced security:

```
- name: Upload SARIF file
  uses: github/codeql-action/upload-sarif@v1
  with:
    sarif_file: results.sarif
  if: always()
```

The results show up under **Security | Code scanning** alerts (see *Figure 15.1*):

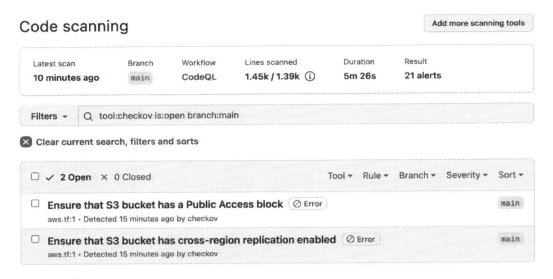

Figure 15.1 – Checkov results in GitHub

Checkov is great to check your IaC, but it does not check your infrastructure for changes. But if you have a solution such as Terraform or ARM, you can regularly run a validation in a workflow to check that nothing has changed.

Automate the infrastructure change process

Most IT organizations have a change management process in place to reduce operations and security risks. Most companies follow the **Information Technology Infrastructure Library (ITIL)**. In ITIL, you have a **Request for Change (RFC)** that has to be approved by a **Change-Advisory Board (CAB)**. The problem is that approvals by a CAB are related to a bad software delivery performance (see *Forsgren N., Humble, J., & Kim, G., 2018*).

From a security standpoint, **change management** and **segregation of duties** are important, and they are often also required for compliance. The key is again to rethink the underlying principles in a DevOps way.

With IaC and fully automated deployment, there is a complete audit trail for all infrastructure changes. If you have full control over the process, the best thing to do is to set up the CAB as CODEOWNERS for IaC files and do the approvals in pull requests. For simple standard changes on the application layer (for example, containers in a Kubernetes cluster), a peer review might be enough. For infrastructure changes on deeper levels with effects on networks, firewalls, or secrets, the number of reviewers will increase, and you can add specialists accordingly. These files normally also reside in other repositories and do not affect the developer velocity and slow down your releases.

If you are bound to a corporate process, this might not be so easy. In this case, you have to try to recategorize your changes to get most of them pre-approved and use peer reviews and automated checks for these changes for security reasons. Then, automate the process for higher-risk changes so that the information for the CAB is as complete and correct as possible to come to a fast approval (see *Kim G., Humble J., Debois P. & Willis J., 2016, Part VI, Chapter 23*).

Source code and infrastructure integrity

In manufacturing, it's a normal practice to provide a **bill of materials (BOM)** for a production order. A BOM is a list of raw materials, subassemblies, intermediate assemblies, subcomponents, and parts that have been used to manufacture the end product.

The same thing exists for software: the **software bill of materials (SBOM)**, but it is still less common.

The SBOM

If you have a close look at software supply chain attacks such as the **event-stream incident** (see *Thomas Claburn, 2018*), you'll find that they inject malicious code in a release, so the source code in GitHub did not match the files that were included in the npm package. An SBOM can help here with the forensic and it can be used to compare the hashes of different versions.

In the **SolarWinds attack** (see the *Crowdstrike blog, 2021*) dependencies were not tempered. Instead, there was an additional process running that manipulated the file system during the execution of MsBuild.exe. To help prevent and investigate these kinds of attacks, you'll have to extend the SBOM to include details for all tools included in the build process and all the running processes on the build machine.

There are different common formats for SBOM:

- **Software Package Data Exchange** (**SPDX**): SPDX is an open standard for SBOM with origins in the Linux Foundation. Its origin was license compliance, but it also contains copyrights, security references, and other metadata. SPDX was recently approved as ISO/IEC standard (*ISO/IEC 5962:2021*), and it fulfills the NTIA's *Minimum Elements For a Software Bill of Materials*.

- **CycloneDX** (**CDX**): CDX is a lightweight open source format with origins in the **OWASP** community. It is optimized for integrating SBOM generation into a release pipeline.

- **Software Identification** (**SWID**) tags: SWID is an ISO/IEC industry standard (*ISO/IEC 19770-2*) used by various commercial software publishers. It supports automation of software inventory, assessment of software vulnerabilities on machines, detection of missing patches, targeting of configuration checklist assessments, software integrity checking, installation and execution whitelists/blacklists, and other security and operational use cases. It is a good format for doing the inventory of the software installed on your build machines.

There are different tools and use cases for each format. **SPDX** is generated by **syft**. You can use the **Anchore SBOM Action** (see `https://github.com/marketplace/actions/anchore-sbom-action`) to generate an SPDX SBOM for a Docker or OCI container:

```
- name: Anchore SBOM Action
  uses: anchore/sbom-action@v0.6.0
  with:
    path: .
    image: ${{ env.REGISTRY }}/${{ env.IMAGE_NAME }}
    registry-username: ${{ github.actor }}
    registry-password: ${{ secrets.GITHUB_TOKEN }}
```

The SBOM is being uploaded as a workflow artifact (see *Figure 15.2*):

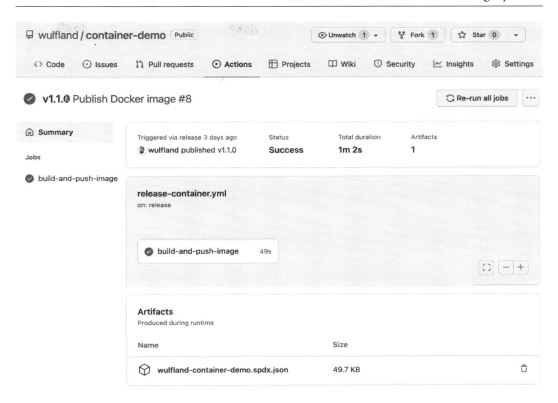

Figure 15.2 – SPDX SBOM uploaded as a build artifact

FOSSology (`https://github.com/fossology/fossology`) is an open source license compliance solution that also uses SPDX.

CDX (`https://cyclonedx.org/`) is more focused on application security. There are versions for **Node.js**, **.NET**, **Python**, **PHP**, and **Go** in the marketplace, but many more languages are supported using CLI or other package managers (such as **Java**, **Maven**, and **Conan**). The usage is simple. Here is an example of the action for `.NET`:

```
- name: CycloneDX .NET Generate SBOM
  uses: CycloneDX/gh-dotnet-generate-sbom@v1.0.1
  with:
    path: ./CycloneDX.sln
    github-bearer-token: ${{ secrets.GITHUB_TOKEN }}
```

The SBOM does not get uploaded automatically, unlike the Anchore action; you would have to do that manually:

```
- name: Upload a Build Artifact
  uses: actions/upload-artifact@v2.3.1
  with:
    path: bom.xml
```

CDX is also used in **OWASP Dependency Track** (see `https://github.com/DependencyTrack/dependency-track`) – a component analysis platform that you can run as a container or in Kubernetes. You can upload the SBOM directly into your `DependencyTrack` instance:

```
uses: DependencyTrack/gh-upload-sbom@v1.0.0
with:
  serverhostname: 'your-instance.org'
  apikey: ${{ secrets.DEPENDENCYTRACK_APIKEY }}
  projectname: 'Your Project Name'
  projectversion: 'main'
```

SWID tags are more used in **Software Asset Management (SAM)** solutions such as snow (`https://www.snowsoftware.com/`), **Microsoft System Center**, or **ServiceNow ITOM**. CDX and SPDX can use SWID tags if they are present.

If you want to learn more about SBOM, see `https://www.ntia.gov/sbom`.

If you are working completely on GitHub Enterprise Cloud and use the hosted runners, SBOM is not so important. All the relevant data is connected on GitHub anyway. But, if you are on GitHub Enterprise Server, have self-hosted runners, and other commercial software in your release pipeline that is not consumed by public package managers, an SBOM for all your releases can help to detect vulnerabilities, license issues, and help with the forensic in case of an incident.

Signing your commits

A discussion I often have is whether you should sign all your commits or not. Git is very powerful and gives you the possibility to alter existing commits. But this also means that the author of a commit is not necessarily the one that is committing the code. A commit has two fields: `author` and `committer`. Both fields get set to the values of `user.name` and `user.email` from `git config` plus a timestamp. If you rebase, for example, the committer changes to the current value, but the author stays the same. Both fields have absolutely nothing to do with the authentication to GitHub.

You can look up the email address of **Linus Torvalds** in the Linux repository, configure your local Git repository to use this email address, and commit it to your repository. The commit will appear as if the author was Linus (see *Figure 15.3*):

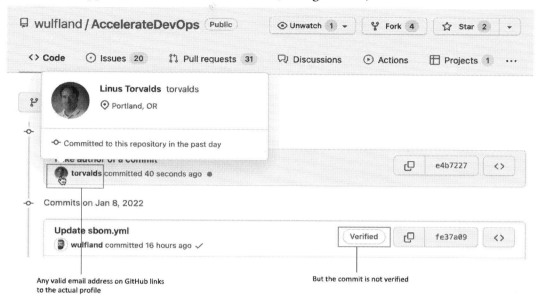

Figure 15.3 – A commit's author information is completely decoupled from the authentication

The link in the profile picture will also work and redirect you to the correct profile page. But the commit does not have a `Verified` badge unlike commits that you perform on the server either by modifying a file in the web UI or by using a pull request to merge your changes on the server. The verified badge shows that the commit was signed with a **GNU Privacy Guard** (**GPG**) key that contains a verified email address of your account (see *Figure 15.4*):

Figure 15.4 – Signed commits have a verified badge on GitHub

You can create a GPG key locally and sign your commits with it (`git commit -S`). You are, of course, completely free to set a name and email address in the key, they just must match the email and user configured in `git config`. The signature is valid as long as you don't modify the commit (see *Figure 15.5*):

```
 ~/source/AccelerateDevOps   main .1 ...........................
> git log -1 --show-signature
commit bb99f47152b2d9ecfdf372cd3da702e7b2b13470 (HEAD -> main)
gpg: Signature made So  9 Jan 11:24:06 2022 CET
gpg:                using RSA key EC1031188BE09A8704EFFAD7A4E11737C8F499ED
gpg:                issuer "                                "
gpg: Good signature from "Linus Torvalds <                        >" [ultimate]
Author: Linus Torvalds <                        >
Date:   Sun Jan 9 11:23:57 2022 +0100

    Signed commit
```

Figure 15.5 – Locally signed commits are valid if email and name match

But even if you upload the **Pretty Good Privacy** (**PGP**) key to your GitHub profile (`https://github.com/settings/gpg/new`), the commit will not be verified, as GitHub looks in the profile with the verified email address for the key (see *Figure 15.6*):

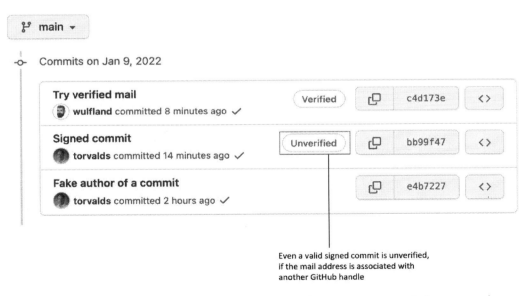

Figure 15.6 – Signed commits from another user are not verified

Does this mean you must sign all your commits locally? I believe not. The problem is that enforcing developers to sign all commits will slow you down. Many IDEs and tools do not support signing. Keeping the keys in sync, dealing with multiple email addresses – everything becomes more painful. It might work very well if all your developers work on corporate devices with the same email address. But this is normally not the case. People work remotely, on different machines, and in different environments, and they work on the same machine on open source software with a different email than on corporate code. The benefit is just not worth it. If an attacker has push permissions to your repository, the last thing you worry about is a faked email address.

What I recommend is the following:

- Pick a workflow that relies on **pull requests** and `merge`, `squash`, or `rebase` the changes on the server so that they get signed by default.

- If you need to ensure integrity for releases, sign your tags (`git tag -S`). Since Git is an SHA-1 or SHA-256-based tree, signing a tag will ensure that all parent commits have not been modified.

Instead of requiring your developers to sign all commits locally and slow your team down, invest in signing your code during the build process to ensure that nobody tampers with your files after the build process.

Signing your code

Signing your binaries is called **code signing**, even if you sign the binaries and not the code. You need a certificate from a trusted authority to do this. How you sign your code during the build process depends a lot on your language and how it gets compiled.

To sign your Apple XCode applications in GitHub Actions, you can use this documentation to install the `base64` encoded certificate and publishing profile during your build: `https://docs.github.com/en/actions/deployment/deploying-xcode-applications/installing-an-apple-certificate-on-macos-runners-for-xcode-development`. Don't forget to clean this up on self-hosted runners that are shared with other teams. On GitHub-hosted runners, every build gets a clean environment anyway.

Depending on your code signing solution, you can find multiple actions in the marketplace for Authenticode and `signtool.exe`. But as all signing solutions are command-line based, you can pass your signing certificate to your workflow using the `secret` context as in the example for Apple.

Dynamic application security testing

To harden your application security, you can integrate **dynamic application security testing (DAST)** into your release workflow. DAST is black-box testing that simulates a real-world attack on the running application.

There are many commercial tools and SaaS solutions (such as **Burp Suit** from **PortSwigger** or **WhiteHat Sentinel**) but it's outside the scope of this book to analyze them.

There are also some open source solutions. One example is the **Zed Attack Proxy** (**ZAP**) (`https://www.zaproxy.org/`) from OWASP. It's a stand-alone application that runs on Windows, macOS, and Linux (see `https://www.zaproxy.org/download/`) and can be used to attack web applications. The application allows you to analyze a web application, intercept and modify traffic, and run an attack using the ZAP Spider against the website or parts of it (see *Figure 15.7*):

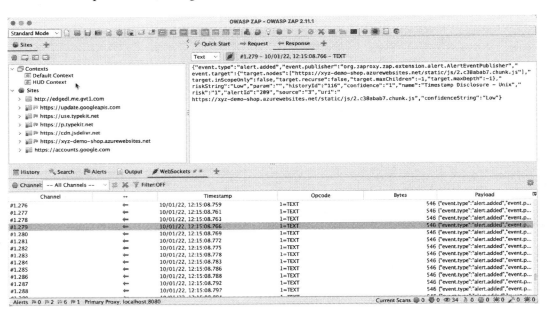

Figure 15.7 – The OWASP ZAP application

OWASP ZAP launches a browser and uses a **heads-up display** (**HUD**) to display controls on top of the website. You can use these controls to analyze the site, run attacks using the spider, or intercept requests without leaving the application (see *Figure 15.8*):

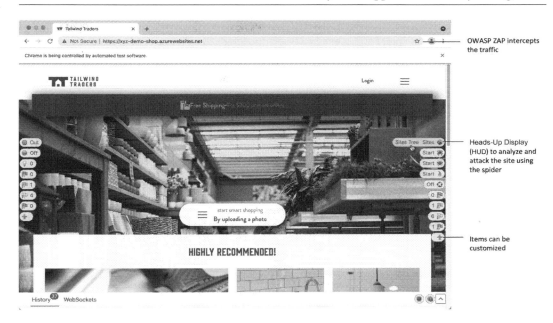

OWASP ZAP intercepts the traffic

Heads-Up Display (HUD) to analyze and attack the site using the spider

Items can be customized

Figure 15.8 – The HUD displays controls on the website being attacked

Even if you are not a pen tester, as a web developer, it should be easy to get started and learn how to attack your site using OWASP ZAP. But to shift left security, you should integrate the scan into your workflow. OWASP ZAP has three Actions in the GitHub marketplace (see *Figure 15.9*):

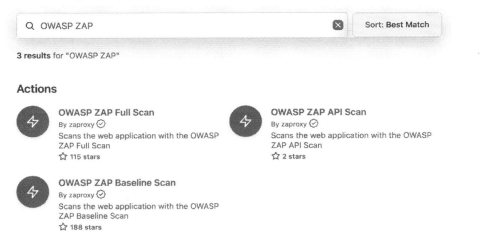

Figure 15.9 – Available OWASP ZAP Actions in the GitHub marketplace

The **Baseline Scan** is faster than the **Full Scan**. The **API Scan** can be used to scan an **OpenAPI**, **SOAP**, or **GraphQL** API. The usage of the Actions is straightforward:

```
- name: OWASP ZAP Full Scan
  uses: zaproxy/action-full-scan@v0.3.0
  with:
    target: ${{ env.TARGET_URL }}
```

The action uses `GITHUB_TOKEN` to write the results to a GitHub Issue. It also adds a report as a build artifact. The report is available as HTML, JSON, or Markdown (see *Figure 15.10*):

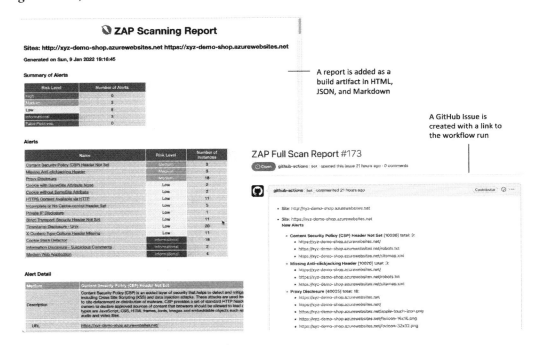

Figure 15.10 – Findings from OWASP ZAP scan

Of course, this is just suitable for web applications. There are other DAST tools used for other scenarios. But the example shows how easy it can be included in your pipeline. Most DAST tools are command-line tools or containers, or they already have integration such as OWASP ZAP.

Security hardening your release pipeline

CI/CD pipelines are complex and have a big surface to attack. Basically, release pipelines are remote code execution environments and should be treated like this with caution (see *Haymore A., Smart I., Gazdag V., Natesan D., & Fernick J., 2022* for some attack examples).

Model your pipelines with caution and follow best practices, especially when you are building highly customized ones. It's better to ask for external help than to be sorry if it is too late.

Secure your runners

If you use GitHub-hosted runners, it's their job to keep them safe. The runners are ephemeral, and every execution starts in a clean state. But you execute code that can access your resources in GitHub, including secrets. Make sure to security-harden your GitHub Actions (see the *Secure your Actions* section) and limit permissions for GitHub_TOKEN (workflows should run with the least-possible privileges).

Self-hosted runners run in your environment, and you are responsible for keeping them safe! Here are some rules you should follow:

- Never use self-hosted runners for **public repositories**.
- Make your runners **ephemeral** (or at least clean up after each run and don't leave artifacts on disk or in memory).
- Keep your images **lean** and **patched** (only install the tools you need and keep everything up to date).
- Don't have **universal runners** for all teams and technologies. Keep the images separated and specialized.
- Keep runners in an **isolated network** (only allow runners to access the resources they need).
- Only run **secure Actions**.
- Include the runners in your **security monitoring** and check for unusual processes or network activity.

The best solution is to have a dynamically scaling environment (for example, a Kubernetes service) and run ephemeral runners with lean and patched images.

See *Chapter 7, Running Your Workflows*, for details on self-hosted and hosted runners.

Secure your Actions

GitHub Actions are very useful, but they are code you execute and grant access to your resources. You should be very careful what actions you use, especially in self-hosted runners. Actions from trusted sources, such as GitHub, Microsoft, AWS, or Google, are not the problems. But even they accept pull requests, so there is still a chance a vulnerability might slip through. Best practices for Actions are as follows:

- Always **review the code** of the Action. Also, look at the **owner**, number of contributors, number and dates of commits, number of stars, and all these kinds of indicators to see that the Action belongs to a healthy community.

- Always reference an Action by the explicit **commit SHA**. The SHA is immutable, whereas tags and branches might be modified and lead to new code getting executed by you without your knowledge.

- If you are working with forks, **require approval** for all outside collaborators and not just first-time contributors.

- Use **Dependabot** to keep your actions up to date.

If you are self-hosting your runners, you should even be more restrictive and limit the actions that can be used. There are two possibilities:

- **Allow local actions only** and create a fork from the action you have analyzed and reference the fork. This is extra work but gives you full control over the actions you use. You can add the actions to a local marketplace for easier discoverability (see *Rob Bos, 2022*).

- **Allow select actions** from GitHub and a list of specific allowed actions (**whitelist**). You can use wildcards to allow all actions from the same owner (for example, `Azure/*`). This option is less secure than option 1, but it is also less effort to maintain.

You can configure these options as enterprise policies or for each organization.

Actions are code from other people that you execute in your environment. They are dependencies that can break your ability to ship and introduce vulnerabilities. Ensure that your policies find the best balance for your needs between velocity and security.

Secure your environments

Use **environment protection rules** with **required reviewers** to approve releases before they get deployed to an environment (see **staged deployments** in *Chapter 9, Deploy to Any Platform*). This ensures that a release was reviewed before accessing the secrets of the environment and executing code.

Combine it with **branch protection** and **code owners** (see *Chapter 3, Teamwork and Collaborative Development*) by only allowing certain branches into your environment. This way, you are sure that necessary automated tests and approvals from code owners are in place when approving the deployment.

Use tokens when possible

Instead of using credentials stored as secrets to connect to a cloud provider – such as Azure, AWS, GCP, or HashiCorp – you can use **OpenID Connect (OIDC)**. OIDC will exchange short-lived tokens to authenticate instead of credentials. Your cloud provider also needs to support OIDC on their end.

Using OIDC, you don't have to store cloud credentials in GitHub, you have more granular control over what resources the workflow can access, and you have rotating, short-lived tokens that will expire after the workflow run.

Figure 15.11 shows an overview of how OIDC works:

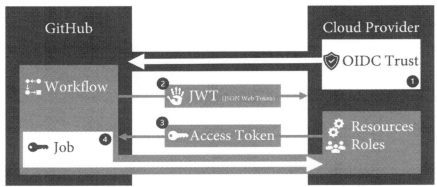

Figure 15.11 – OIDC integration with a cloud provider

The steps are as follows:

1. Create an **OIDC trust** between your cloud provider and GitHub. Limit the trust to an organization and repository and further limit access to an environment, branch, or pull request.

2. The GitHub OIDC provider **auto-generates a JSON Web Token** during a workflow run. The token contains multiple claims to establish a secure and verifiable identity for the specific workflow job.

3. The cloud provider validates the claims and provides a **short-lived access token** that is available only for the lifetime of the job.

4. The access token is used to access resources that the identity has access to.

You can use the identity to directly access resources, or you can use it to get credentials from a secure vault (such as **Azure Key Vault** or **HashiCorp Vault**). This way, you can safely connect to services that do not support OIDC and automated secret rotation using the vault.

In GitHub, you can find instructions on configuring OIDC for AWS, Azure, and GDP (see `https://docs.github.com/en/actions/deployment/security-hardening-your-deployments`). The steps are straightforward. In Azure, for example, you create an app registration in **Azure Active Directory** (**AAD**):

```
$ az ad app create --display-name AccelerateDevOps
```

Then, create a service principal using the app ID from the registration output:

```
$ az ad sp create --id <appId>
```

Then, you can open the app registration in AAD and add the OIDC trust under **Certificates & secrets | Federated credentials | Add a credential**. Fill out the form, as in *Figure 15.12*:

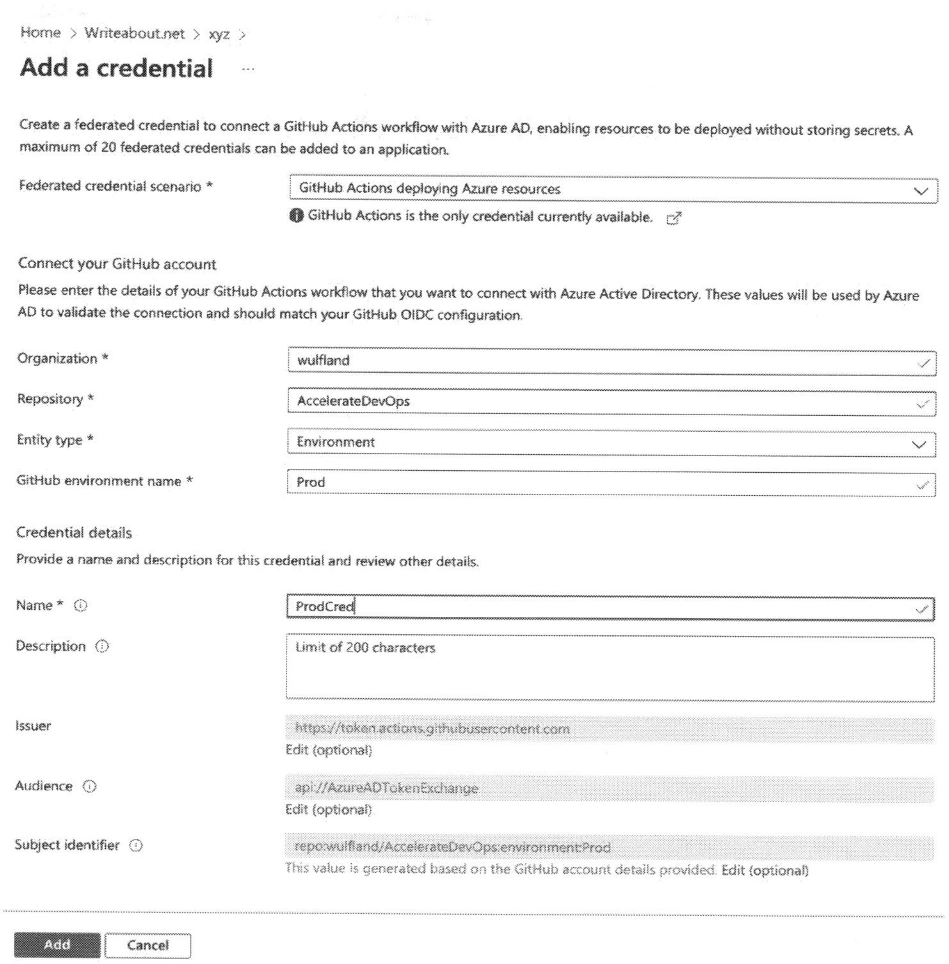

Home > Writeabout.net > xyz >

Add a credential   ...

Create a federated credential to connect a GitHub Actions workflow with Azure AD, enabling resources to be deployed without storing secrets. A maximum of 20 federated credentials can be added to an application.

Federated credential scenario *

| GitHub Actions deploying Azure resources | ⌄ |

ⓘ GitHub Actions is the only credential currently available.   ⌐ᵗ

Connect your GitHub account

Please enter the details of your GitHub Actions workflow that you want to connect with Azure Active Directory. These values will be used by Azure AD to validate the connection and should match your GitHub OIDC configuration.

Organization *

| wulfland | ✓ |

Repository *

| AccelerateDevOps | ✓ |

Entity type *

| Environment | ⌄ |

GitHub environment name *

| Prod | ✓ |

Credential details

Provide a name and description for this credential and review other details.

Name * ⓘ

| ProdCred | ✓ |

Description ⓘ

| Limit of 200 characters |

Issuer

https://token.actions.githubusercontent.com
Edit (optional)

Audience ⓘ

api://AzureADTokenExchange
Edit (optional)

Subject identifier ⓘ

repo:wulfland/AccelerateDevOps:environment:Prod
This value is generated based on the GitHub account details provided. Edit (optional)

[Add]   [Cancel]

Figure 15.12 – Creating the OIDC trust for an app registration

Then, assign the service principal a role on the subscription level. Open the subscription in the portal. Under **Access control (IAM) | Role assignment | Add | Add role assignment**, follow the wizard. Select a role (for example, **Contributor**) and click **Next**. Select **User, group, or service principal** and select the service principal you created earlier.

In GitHub, your workflow needs `write` permissions for `id-token`:

```
permissions:
        id-token: write
        contents: read
```

In the Azure Login Action, use the client ID (`appId`), tenant ID, and subscription ID to retrieve the token from Azure:

```
- name: 'Az CLI login'
  uses: azure/login@v1
  with:
      client-id: ${{ secrets.AZURE_CLIENT_ID }}
      tenant-id: ${{ secrets.AZURE_TENANT_ID }}
      subscription-id: ${{ secrets.AZURE_SUBSCRIPTION_ID }}
```

After that, you can use the **Azure CLI** to access resources:

```
- run: az account show
```

You can also work with other Azure Actions and remove the authentication part, in this example, the publishing profile. They will use the access token form provided by the login action:

```
- name: Run Azure webapp deploy action using OIDC
  uses: azure/webapps-deploy@v2
  with:
    app-name: ${{ env.APPNAME }}
    slot-name: Production
    package: website
```

Every cloud provider is different, but the documentation should get you up and running quickly: https://docs.github.com/en/actions/deployment/security-hardening-your-deployments.

Collect security telemetry

To secure your entire pipeline from code to production, you need real-time insights on all levels. There are different monitoring solutions on different layers (see *Figure 15.13*):

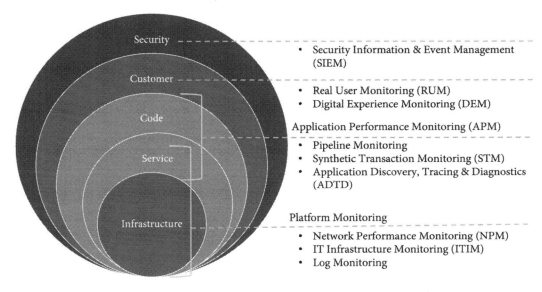

Figure 15.13 – The different layers of monitoring

All these layers should report their data to your SIEM system to perform analytics and use AI to detect anomalies. Many organizations collect data on different levels but forget to include it in the monitoring due to different responsibilities. To security harden your releases, you should consider the following:

- Include **all monitoring sources** and events in your SIEM solution.

- Monitor the **entire pipeline** including your agents and test environments. Include all processes and network activity.

- **Log deployment events** with the according version. If new processes are suddenly running or ports are opened after a deployment, you want to be able to associate these changes with this deployment to facilitate forensics.

- Collect **real-time application security data** and display it on the dashboard of your engineers. This could include **abnormal program termination**, **SQL injection** attempts, **Cross-site scripting (XSS)** attempts, **failed logins (brute force attacks)**, or **DDoS attacks**, but it depends a lot on your product. To detect SQL injection or XSS, you have to include extra logging before encoding user input if the input contains suspicious characters or elements.

The best way to create awareness is to see that the threat is real.

Case study

Until now, **Tailwind Gears** has paid an external company to perform **security reviews** of the architecture, help with **threat modelling** and a **risk analysis**, and perform security testing before major releases. They have never been breached and most of the investments so far went into network security. But now leveraging more and more cloud services, they've already been aware that they must do something to be able to **detect**, **respond**, and **recover**.

The IT department already started to use **Splunk** as their **SIEM** and **ITIM** solution and integrate more and more sources that feed data, but until now, the IT department could not be certain whether they would really detect an ongoing attack in real-time. Tailwind Gears decides to change the way they deal with security. They talk to their security partner, and they plan the first **red team / blue team** simulation. The scenario is an **inside attacker** to the web application of our DevOps pilot teams.

The simulation takes 3 days and the red team wins by finding two ways to compromise production:

- A **spear phishing** attack on a few developers in another team is successful and reveals the credentials of one of the developers. Using **BloodHound**, they find out that the developer has access to the former Jenkins server that now runs the GitHub Actions runner and has not yet been ported to the Kubernetes solution completely. The server does not have MFA enabled and **mimikatz** allows to capture the credentials of a test account. The test account has access to a test environment, and they can capture credentials of an admin account there that allows data extraction of the staging environment (that counts as production in the game).

- Since all developers have read access to all repositories, an analysis of the dependencies of the web application shows a dependency that is vulnerable to XSS and has not been patched yet. The component is a search control and allows the red team with the help of a frontend developer of another team to execute scripts in the context of other users. They open an issue in an internal GitHub repository and use the GitHub API to post a comment to the issue on each execution as proof.

The simulation results in many backlog items that will be addressed over the next weeks. Some things do not concern our DevOps teams, such as enabling MFA for all internal systems or regularly executing phishing simulations to create awareness among employees.

But many items also concern the teams. Tailwind Gears decides to bake security into the development process. This includes **secret scanning**, **dependency management** with Dependabot, and **code scanning**.

The team will also work together with the IT department to securely harden the release pipeline by moving the build server to Kubernetes, implementing **security logging** in the entire pipeline, and using **OpenID Connect** and a secure **Key Vault** for secret handling.

Everyone is looking forward to the next red team/blue team simulation in 3 months.

Summary

In this chapter, you've learned how to secure your release pipeline and deployments by scanning containers and IaC, ensuring consistency of code and configuration, and security-hardening the complete pipeline.

In the next chapter, we'll talk about the impact of your software architecture on your software delivery performance.

Further reading

These are the references from this chapter that you can also use to get more information on the topics:

- Kim G., Humble J., Debois P. & Willis J. (2016). *The DevOps Handbook: How to Create World-Class Agility, Reliability, and Security in Technology Organizations* (1st ed.). IT Revolution Press

- Forsgren N., Humble, J., & Kim, G. (2018). *Accelerate: The Science of Lean Software and DevOps: Building and Scaling High Performing Technology Organizations* (1st ed.) [E-book]. IT Revolution Press.

- Oladimeji S., Kerner S. M. (2021). *SolarWinds hack explained: Everything you need to know.* https://whatis.techtarget.com/feature/SolarWinds-hack-explained-Everything-you-need-to-know

- Sudhakar Ramakrishna (2021). *New Findings From Our Investigation of SUNBURST.* https://orangematter.solarwinds.com/2021/01/11/new-findings-from-our-investigation-of-sunburst/

- Crowdstrike blog (2021). *SUNSPOT: An Implant in the Build Process.* https://www.crowdstrike.com/blog/sunspot-malware-technical-analysis/

- Eckels S., Smith J. & Ballenthin W. (2020). *SUNBURST Additional Technical Details.* `https://www.mandiant.com/resources/sunburst-additional-technical-details`

- Souppaya M., Morello J., & Scarfone K. (2017). *Application Container Security Guide*: `https://doi.org/10.6028/NIST.SP.800-190`

- National Telecommunications and Information Administration (NTIA), *Software Bill of Materials*: `https://www.ntia.gov/sbom`

- Thomas Claburn (2018). *Check your repos... Crypto-coin-stealing code sneaks into fairly popular NPM lib (2m downloads per week)*: `https://www.theregister.com/2018/11/26/npm_repo_bitcoin_stealer/`

- Haymore A., Smart I., Gazdag V., Natesan D., & Fernick J. (2022). *10 real-world stories of how we've compromised CI/CD pipelines*: `https://research.nccgroup.com/2022/01/13/10-real-world-stories-of-how-weve-compromised-ci-cd-pipelines/`

- Rob Bos (2022). *Setup an internal GitHub Actions Marketplace*: `https://devopsjournal.io/blog/2021/10/14/GitHub-Actions-Internal-Marketplace.html`

Part 4: Software Architecture

Part 4 is about the correlation of your software architecture and the communication in your organization. You'll learn how to transform your monolith gradually to a loosely coupled, event-based architecture.

This part of the book comprises the following chapters:

- *Chapter 16, Loosely Coupled Architecture and Microservices*
- *Chapter 17, Empower Your Teams*

16

Loosely Coupled Architecture and Microservices

Interestingly, software architecture has a bigger impact on software delivery performance than the type of systems that you build. It doesn't matter if your product is a cloud service, embedded software that runs on manufactured hardware, a consumer app, an enterprise application, or even mainframe software. This has basically no impact on engineering performance if your architecture has certain characteristics (*Forsgren N., Humble, J., and Kim, G., 2018*). There are high and low performers for every system type. But the characteristics of architecture are clearly correlated with engineering velocity and make it one of the key accelerators.

In this chapter, I'll give you an overview of loosely coupled systems and how you can evolve your software and system design to achieve a high engineering velocity.

The following topics will be covered in this chapter:

- Loosely coupled systems
- Microservices
- Evolutionary design
- Event-based architecture

Loosely coupled systems

All developers that have worked at least once on a tightly coupled, monolithic application know the problems it induces. The communication overhead and the meetings needed to perform bigger changes. New bugs that occur after fixing a bug in another part of the application. Changes that break functionality from other developers. All these problems lead to fear of integrating and deploying and slow down developer velocity.

When designing your system and software, you should focus on the following characteristics:

- **Deployability**: Can each team release their application independent of other applications or teams?
- **Testability**: Can each team do most of their testing without requiring a test environment in which multiple independent solutions from other teams must be deployed together?

The team size here is a small **two-pizza team** (see *Chapter 17, Empower Your Teams*). If you design your systems for the deployability and testability of small teams, it will automatically lead to loosely coupled systems with well-defined interfaces.

Microservices

The most common architectural pattern for loosely coupled systems is the **microservices** pattern, *"an approach to developing a single application as a suite of small services, each running in its own process and communicating with lightweight mechanisms, often an HTTP resource API"* (*Lewis J. & Fowler M., 2014*).

Microservices evolved out of **Service-Oriented Architecture (SOA)** with some additional characteristics. Microservices have **decentralized data management** – meaning that every service completely owns its own data. Additionally, microservices favor lightweight messaging instead of complex protocols or central orchestration for interservice communication – **smart endpoints** and **dumb pipes**.

One important characteristic of microservices is often missed – they are built around business capabilities. This also defines how small a service should be. To define the scope of your services, you must understand the business domain. One microservice matches one **bounded context** in **domain-driven design** (*Eric Evans, 2003*).

Another characteristic is that microservices are completely and independently **deployable** and **testable**. That's the reason why they are associated with high engineering velocity.

Microservices have many advantages. They scale very well, as you can scale every service independently. They also allow each team to work with its own programming languages and data storage solution that best meets its needs. Most importantly, they allow teams in big and complex applications to move fast without disrupting other teams.

But these advantages come with a cost. Microservice-based applications are complex and hard to operate and troubleshoot.

There are many famous microservice-based solutions – for example, Netflix and Amazon. They run world-scale services and have an architecture that allows them to deploy thousands of times each day.

But there are also many companies that have tried to implement microservices and have failed. The number of greenfield projects that fail is especially high. The reason for this is often a lack of knowledge of the business domain and the wrong definition of the bounded context for each service, especially when the application is developed by an external company that has yet to learn the **ubiquitous language** of the domain. Another reason is that the complexity of operating the service is underestimated.

So, instead of implementing microservices, you should focus on the **deployability** and **testability** characteristics of your architecture and adjust the solution design to your needs. The needs are not constant and evolve over time – and so should your architecture.

Evolutionary design

The advantages and disadvantages of certain architectural styles shift for various reasons. One is the scale of your application. Another is the knowledge of your domain and your customers and the ability to operate at scale. Depending on these factors, different architectural styles are better suited for you (see *Figure 16.1*):

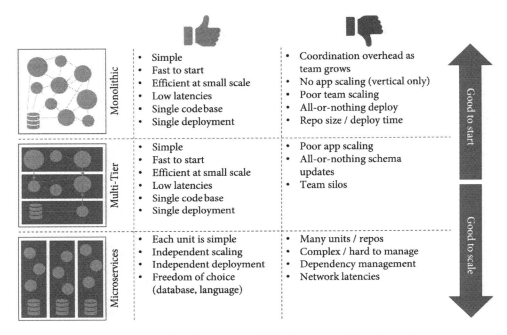

Figure 16.1 – The advantages and disadvantages shift with scale

Constantly adapting your architecture and system design to your current needs is called **evolutionary design**. To start a greenfield product, it's best to start with a monolithic approach and one team. This allows you to move fast without much overhead. If you scale up and learn more about the domain, you can start to modularize your application using the capabilities of your programming language. At one point, the complexity and scale will be so high that microservices help you to keep your product testable and deployable.

The question is this – how do you arrive at the architecture you need from the architecture you have? A complete rewrite is very expensive and risky. The better approach is to evolve your design. Martin Fowler calls this the **StranglerFigApplication** pattern (*Martin Fowler, 2004*). The strangler fig is a plant that seeds in the upper branches of a tree and gradually grows its roots downward over the tree until it roots in the soil. The supporting tree is strangled and dies at some point – leaving an organic structure that supports itself.

Instead of rewriting your application, you grow a new "strangler fig" application around it, letting it grow gradually until the old system is strangled and can be shut down.

Event-driven architecture

There are other architectural styles besides microservices, monolithic, and multi-tier applications – for example, **Event-Driven Architecture (EDA)**. EDA is a pattern around the publication, processing, and persistence of events. The backbone is a message broker – for example, **Apache Kafka** – and individual services or components can publish events (a **publisher**) or subscribe to events (a **subscriber**).

EDA can be a good fit with a microservices-based approach – but it can also be used with other architectural styles. It can help you to keep consistency in loosely coupled components or services, and it can scale perfectly horizontally due to the asynchronous nature of events and is therefore well suited for solutions that process big amounts of data in motion, such as IoT solutions that process sensor data in near real time.

Especially in cloud-native environments, EDA can help you to move fast and to build loosely coupled and global scalable solutions in a very short time.

One pattern that is often used with EDA is **event sourcing**. Instead of persisting entities, event sourcing captures all changes to the application state – including the entities – as a sequence of events (see *Martin Fowler, 2005*). To retrieve an entity, the application must replay all events to get to the latest state. Since events are immutable, this provides a perfect audit trail. You can think of the event stream as an immutable stream of facts that can be seen as the single source of truth. In addition to auditability, event sourcing has many benefits in scalability and testability.

Event sourcing is a suitable pattern if you need to capture intent, purpose, or reason for your data, when it's vital to avoid conflicting updates, and when you must keep a history and frequently roll back changes. Event sourcing works very well together with **Command and Query Responsibility Segregation (CQRS)** – a pattern that separates read and write operations.

But be aware that event sourcing is very complex, and modeling a domain in events does not come naturally to most developers. If the aforementioned criteria do not suit your product, then event sourcing is probably not a good pattern for you.

An architectural style that is more suitable for simple domains is the **Web-Queue-Worker**. It's a pattern mainly used with serverless PaaS components, and it consists of a web frontend that serves client requests and a worker that performs long-running tasks in the background. Frontend and backend are stateless and communicate using a message queue. The pattern is normally combined with other cloud services such as an identity provider, a database, a Redis cache, and a CDN. Web-Queue-Worker is a good pattern to get started with cloud-native applications.

Whatever architectural style you pick, keep it as simple as possible. It's better to start simple and evolve your design over time with increasing demands than to overengineer and end up with a complex solution that slows you down.

Summary

If you are adopting CI/CD and DevOps practices but you're not accelerating, then you should have a close look at your solution architecture as one of the key indicators for engineering velocity. Focus on the deployability and testability characteristics rather than on the architectural styles.

In this chapter, I gave you an overview of loosely coupled systems' evolutionary design, and I introduced some relevant architectural styles and patterns.

In the next chapter, we'll discuss the correlation between your organizational structure and your software architecture and how it all comes together in GitHub.

Further reading

These are the references from this chapter that you can also use to get more information on the topics:

- Forsgren N., Humble, J., and Kim, G. (2018). *Accelerate: The Science of Lean Software and DevOps: Building and Scaling High Performing Technology Organizations* (1st ed.) [E-book]. IT Revolution Press.

- Lewis J. and Fowler M. (2014). *Microservices*: https://martinfowler.com/articles/microservices.html.

- Eric Evans (2003). *Domain-Driven Design: Tackling Complexity in the Heart of Software*. Addison-Wesley Professional.

- Martin Fowler (2004). *StranglerFigApplication*: https://martinfowler.com/bliki/StranglerFigApplication.html.

- Michael T. Nygard (2017). *Release It!: Design and Deploy Production-Ready Software.* Pragmatic Programmers.

- Martin Fowler (2005). *Event Sourcing*: `https://martinfowler.com/eaaDev/EventSourcing.html`.

- Lucas Krause (2015). *Microservices: Patterns and Applications – Designing fine-grained services by applying patterns* [Kindle Edition].

17
Empower Your Teams

If my customers are not content with their architecture, I let them explain the organizational structure of their product and draw a diagram of it. If you compare this organizational chart with their architecture diagram, you always can find a lot of similarities. This correlation between the organizational structure and software architecture is called **Conway's law**.

In this chapter, you'll learn how you can leverage this correlation to improve your architecture, organization structure, and software delivery performance.

The following are the core topics in this chapter:

- Conway's law
- The two-pizza team
- Inverse Conway Maneuver
- Delivery cadence
- A mono- or multi-repo strategy

Conway's law

Conway's law goes back to an essay from 1968 (*Conway, Melvin, 1968*, p31):

> *"Organizations which design systems (...) are constrained to produce designs which are copies of the communication structure of the organizations."*

> *– Melvin E. Conway*

The law is not specific to software or system architecture but to the design of any system. Note that it is not referring to an organization's management structure but its communication structure. These might be the same thing – but in some cases, it's not. Normally, if the organizational chart does not match the software design, you can look for the communication flow, and it is different from the organizational chart.

If, for example, you have many small teams or individual developers that receive requirements from different customers or consultants, they will probably talk to each other without any organizational boundaries. The system they are working on will reflect that and consist of many modules with a high cohesion that reference each other – a so-called *spaghetti architecture*. Whereas teams that work together and receive their input through one communication channel – for example, a product owner – will build a system with a high cohesion in the modules that the team works on. But the parts of the system the other teams work on will have fewer references. To put it in the words of *Eric S. Raymond*, "*if three teams are working on a compiler, you'll get a three-pass compiler*" (see *Raymond, Eric S. 1996*, p124). *Figure 17.1* visualizes these two examples:

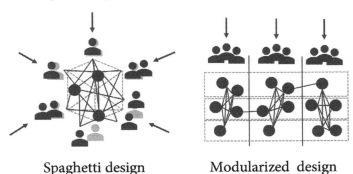

Spaghetti design   Modularized design

Figure 17.1 – Examples of the different software designs based on a communication structure

But what is the desired communication structure that will lead to a system design that helps teams to accelerate their engineering velocity?

The two-pizza team

One of the most discussed microservice-based architectures that allows thousands of deployments per day at a large scale is the architecture of **Amazon**. They use the **two-pizza rule** for their team setup (*Amazon, 2020*):

"We try to create teams that are no larger than can be fed by two pizzas."

– Jeff Bezos

But how many people exactly can you feed with two pizzas? In our user groups, we always calculate one party pizza for three to four people. That would make a team size of six to eight people. At Giordano's in the US, they use the 3/8 rule – the number of pizzas you order should be three times the number of people to feed divided by eight:

This would result in a maximum of 5 to 6 people in each team. So, the size of a two-pizza team is not very well defined – and I think it has nothing to do with the hunger of the team members. The rule just means that the team should be small.

The problem with big teams is that the number of links in the team grows rapidly with every team member added. You can calculate the number of links using the following formula:

Here, *n* is the number of people in the team. This means that a team with 6 members has 15 links between the members – whereas a team of 12 already has 66 links (see *Figure 17.2*):

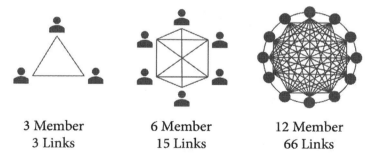

| 3 Member | 6 Member | 12 Member |
| 3 Links | 15 Links | 66 Links |

Figure 17.2 – The number of links between the members of a team

If people work in teams, they experience a positive synergy. The diversity and communication help to increase quality as well as the outcome. But if you add more people to the team, communication overhead and slower decision-making lead to a negative synergy (see *Figure 17.3*):

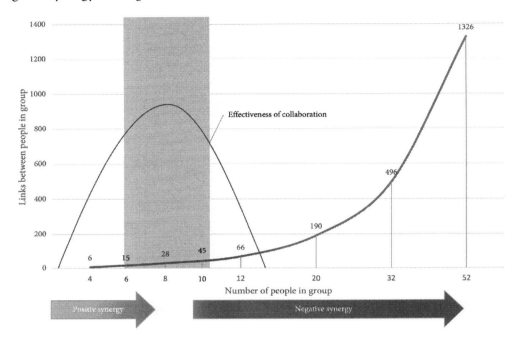

Figure 17.3 – Effectiveness of collaboration and team size

But what is the magic number – the optimum number of people for a team?

The US Navy Seals state that four is the optimal size for a combat team (*Willink, J. and Leif Babin, L., 2017*). They also rely on high-frequency communication in a complex environment. But the skills of a combat team are probably more linear than those of a cross-functional development team. So, there is no evidence that the number is also optimum for development teams.

In Scrum, **Miller's law** states that the magical number seven, plus or minus two (*Miller, G.A., 1956*), is used to define the recommended team size. Miller's law is an essay from 1956 on the limitations of our short memory that was associated with communication capabilities. But Miller's law was scientifically refuted, and the reason that Scrum still uses the numbers is that five to nine is simply a good team size in many circumstances – but without any scientific substantiation. There are also high-performance scrum teams with only 3 members – and others with 14 members.

There is a study from QSM analyzing 491 development projects. The study concludes that smaller teams have higher productivity, less development effort, and a better development schedule (*QSM, 2011*). The clusters of a team with 1.5 to 3 people, 3 to 5 people, and 5 to 7 people were close together. More than seven people led to a dramatic increase in development effort (see *Figure 17.4*):

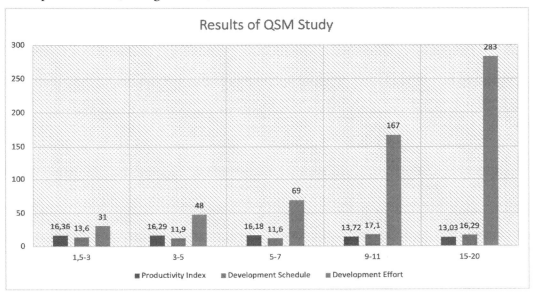

Figure 17.4 – A summary of the results of the QSM study

There are several reasons why smaller teams perform better than larger teams (see *Cohn M., 2009*, pp177–180):

- **Social loafing**: Social loafing is a phenomenon where persons tend to exert less effort to achieve a goal when they work in a group where individual performance cannot be measured (*Karau, S.J., and Williams, K.D., 1993*). Smaller groups tend to be less affected by social loafing.

- **Cohesion and ownership**: Smaller teams have more constructive interactions, and it is easier for the members to build feelings of trust, mutual ownership, and cohesiveness (*Robbins S., 2005*).

- **Coordination effort**: In a smaller team, there is less time spent on coordination. Simple things – such as coordinating a meeting – tend to be much more complex in larger teams.

- **More rewarding**: The contributions of an individual are more visible in smaller teams. This, and the better social cohesiveness, lead to a more rewarding environment if the team size is smaller (*Steiner, I.D., 1972*).

Of course, smaller teams have also some disadvantages. The biggest is the risk of **losing one or more team members**, which is much harder to be compensated for in smaller teams. Another disadvantage is **the lack of certain expert skills**. If you need deep expertise in five areas, it is nearly impossible to deliver it with a three-member team.

Looking at this data, the optimal size for a two-pizza team is somewhere between three and seven – balancing the advantages and disadvantages, depending on your environment.

Inverse Conway Maneuver

Now that we know the optimal size for our teams, we can perform something that is called the **Inverse Conway Maneuver** (*Forsgren N., Humble, J., and Kim, G., 2018*, page 102). If you evolve your organization structure to autonomous two-pizza teams, your architecture evolves into a more loosely coupled one.

But it's not just the team size! If you create your teams around functionalities, it will result in a layered or multi-tier architecture. If you put frontend developers and database specialists in teams, your architecture will decouple at these communication points (see *Figure 17.5*):

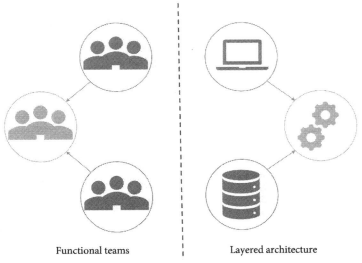

Functional teams   Layered architecture

Figure 17.5 – Functional teams lead to a layered architecture

To achieve a deployable and testable architecture that empowers the teams, you must create cross-functional teams responsible for business outcomes. This will lead to the desired architecture that helps you to move fast (see *Figure 17.6*):

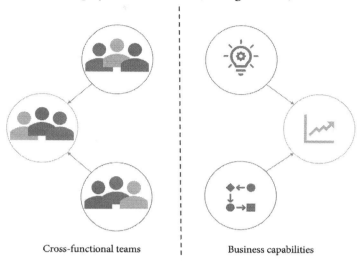

Cross-functional teams | Business capabilities

Figure 17.6 – Cross-functional teams aligned around business capabilities for fast value delivery

There are four types of team topologies that have a positive impact on system architecture and, therefore, software delivery performance (*Skelton M., and Pais M., 2019*):

- **Value stream-aligned**: This is the most important team topology – cross-functional teams that can deliver significant value to their customers without relying on other teams to do so. These teams need all required skills to deliver value – for example, UX, QA, DBA, and operational skills.

- **Platform teams**: Teams that build the platform that enables the value stream-aligned teams to deliver value by reducing complexity and simplifying the software delivery process.

- **Enabling teams**: Teams that enable other teams to take responsibility as part of an onboarding, transitional, or training phase.

- **Subsystem team**: This team type should only be created if absolutely necessary! If a subsystem is too complicated to be handled by stream-aligned teams or platform teams, it might be preferable to have a functional team that handles this subsystem.

It is important that each team has a clear responsibility and can deliver value without relying on other teams to finish certain tasks.

But to achieve the desired effect on performance, you have to limit how the teams interact to one of the following three **modes of interaction**:

- **Collaboration**: Two or more teams work closely together for a certain time and share the responsibility.

- **Self-service**: A team provides its value to another team as a service. The responsibilities are clearly separated, and the service can be consumed as easily and automated as possible.

- **Facilitating**: One team enables another team and helps them for a certain time to learn new things or develop new habits.

Building an effective team topology with good, well-defined communication and interaction has a huge influence – not only on the system architecture but also on the engineering velocity.

Delivery cadence

Even with cross-functional, autonomous teams, you'll still have some interdependencies and communication flow occurring between the teams. In the first chapters of this book, when I explained the flow of work and metrics, I focused on efficiency, flow, batch size, and a continuous delivery value. But you still need some cadence to control your flow. In Scrum, this is called **empirical process control**. After a certain time, you pause to **inspect** and **adopt** – not only what you deliver but also your process and team dynamics. This time span is called a **sprint** in Scrum. I don't like that term because it implies a fast pace, and development should have a constant, steady pace. You don't sprint if you want to run a marathon – and product development is a marathon and not a series of sprints (but a marathon does not match with the analogy of rugby, of course). But no matter what you call these intervals, they are important for continuous learning and adoption and team building. These intervals are also important to communicate – to stakeholders and other teams.

That's why these intervals should be aligned across all teams. They should determine the steady cadence and act as the heartbeat of the engineering organization.

The intervals should not be too long and not too short. A month would be the maximum and a minimum of 2 weeks for most companies. That does not mean that teams can't do smaller iterations or sprints. They can still do 1-week sprints; they just would align them with the global cadence. You can have a faster pace and align it to a slower cadence – but not vice versa (see *Figure 17.7*):

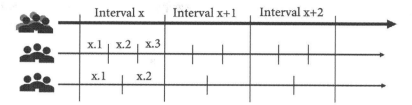

Figure 17.7 – Aligning faster iterations with the delivery cadence

In this case, *x* does not necessarily have to be measured in weeks. When defining the cadence, think about the **pulse of the entire organization**. If everything in your organization runs on a monthly basis, then a 3-week cadence would not be in sync with the rest of your company. In this case, defining a monthly cadence – or a fraction of it – is the better choice and causes less friction. If your company is publicly traded and uses the 4-4-5 calendar, a fiscal quarter might be your pulse. Have a look at the organization pulse and sync your sprint cadence with it so that the intervals are in harmony with the organization pulse (see *Figure 17.8*):

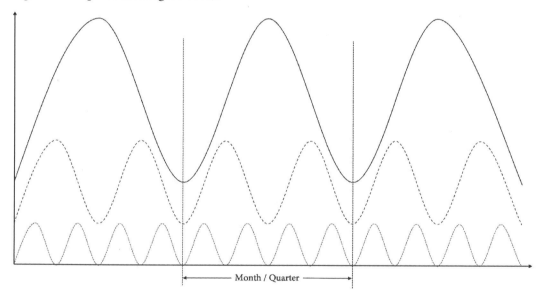

Figure 17.8 – Align your cadence to be in sync with the organization pulse

If your cadence is not in sync with your organization, it will generate friction. Meetings will conflict, and feedback and numbers might not be available when you need them. A consistent cadence in sync with your organizational pulse will help to smooth out flow and improve communication (*Reinertsen D., 2009*, pp176–78).

A mono- or multi-repo strategy

Besides team size and cadence, the way you structure your code has also an impact on your architecture if you want to perform the Inverse Conway Maneuver. There are two strategies:

- **A mono-repo strategy**: There is only one repository that contains all modules (or microservices) that are needed by an application.

- **A multi-repo strategy**: Each module or microservice lives in its own repository, and you must deploy multiple repositories to get a complete working application.

Both strategies have advantages and disadvantages. The biggest advantage of the mono-repo strategy is that it is easy to deploy and debug the entire application. But mono repos tend to get very large very fast, and that reduces the performance of Git. Also, deploying and testing different parts of the application independently becomes difficult with a growing repository. This leads to a tighter coupling of the architecture.

Working with large mono repositories

What does big repo mean in the context of Git? The repo of the Linux kernel is about 3 GB. It takes quite some time to clone, and the individual Git commands are slow – but still in an acceptable range. The Windows repository has about 300 GB – 100 times the Linux kernel. Performing certain Git actions on the Windows repository takes some time:

- `git clone`: About 12 hours

- `git checkout`: About 3 hours

- `git status`: About 8 minutes

- `git add` and `git commit`: About 3 minutes

That's why Microsoft maintains its own fork of the Git client (`https://github.com/microsoft/git`). This fork contains a lot of optimizations for large repositories. It includes the **scalar CLI** (`https://github.com/microsoft/git/blob/HEAD/contrib/scalar/docs/index.md`) that can be used to set advanced Git config settings, maintain the repository in the background, and help to reduce data sent across the network. These improvements reduce the time for the Git actions in the Windows repository enormously:

- `git clone`: 12 hours to 90 seconds

- `git checkout`: 3 hours to 30 seconds

- `git status`: 8 minutes to 3 seconds

Many of these optimizations are already part of the Git client now. You can use, for example, `git sparse-checkout` (https://git-scm.com/docs/git-sparse-checkout), which allows you to only download the parts of your repository that you need.

You only need the Microsoft fork if your repository is really huge; otherwise, you can probably optimize using the normal Git features.

Organizing your repos with topics and star lists

The biggest advantage of the multi-repo strategy is that you reduce the complexity of the individual repositories. Each repository can be maintained and deployed autonomously. The biggest disadvantage is that it is hard to build and test the entire application. But to get feedback from real users or to debug complex bugs, it is normally not enough to deploy an individual service or module – you need to update the entire application. This means coordinating multiple deployments across your repo boundaries.

If you choose the multi-repo strategy, you'll end up with many small repositories. A good naming convention can help to structure them. You can also use **topics** to organize your repos. Topics can be set at the top-right corner of your repo (see *Figure 17.9*).

About   ⚙

This is the companion repository for the book Accelerate DevOps with GitHub (2022). You can find all hands-on labs and other examples from the book here. Please reach out to me if something is broken.

🔗 wulfland.github.io/acceleratedevops/

`github` `devops`

📖 Readme

⚖ MIT License

☆ 3 stars

👁 0 watching

⑂ 6 forks

Figure 17.9 – You can set topics for your repositories for better discoverability

You can filter your repositories using the `topic:` keyword (see *Figure 17.10*):

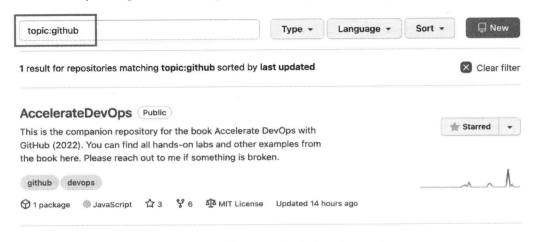

Figure 17.10 – Filter repositories based on topics

Another feature that you can use to organize large numbers of repositories is **star lists**. This is a personal feature and cannot be shared. In your GitHub profile, you can create lists and organize your starred repositories (see *Figure 17.11*):

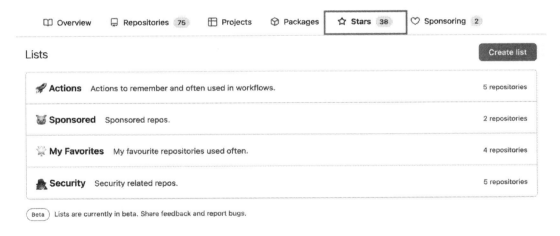

Figure 17.11 – Organize your starred repositories in lists

You can use these features like favorites in your browser, but they do not solve the problem of deploying, debugging, or testing your entire application.

If you are using Kubernetes for your microservices, you can use the **Bridge to Kubernetes** plugin (`https://marketplace.visualstudio.com/items?itemName=mindaro.mindaro`) in Visual Studio Code to debug a local service in the context of a production or test cluster (see *Medina A. M., 2021*). But if you rely on building and deploying all services at once, the best solution is to have a meta-repository that references all services as a submodule.

Using Git submodules to structure your code

You can use a meta-repository that contains all other repositories as submodules. This allows you to clone all repositories with one command:

```
$ git clone --recurse-submodules
```

Alternatively, to update the meta-repository if you already have it cloned, use this command:

```
$ git submodule update --init --recursive
```

The repository can contain the scripts or workflows to deploy the application as a whole.

You can use this meta-repository to do the release management and bundle the stable versions together. If you use branches for releases, then you can set your submodule to a certain branch and update it before you release the latest version:

```
$ git config -f .gitmodules submodule.<SUB>.branch main
$ git submodule update --remote
```

If you use tags for releases, then you can set each submodule to a specific version and commit this to your meta-repository:

```
$ cd <SUB>
$ git checkout <TAG>
$ cd ..
$ git add <SUB>
$ git commit -m "Update <SUB> to <TAG>"
$ git push
```

Other people can then pull the changes and update the submodules to the version corresponding to the tag:

```
$ git pull
$ git submodule update --init --recursive
```

Git submodules are a nice way to work in multi-repos and deploy independently while still being able to manage an application as a whole. But be aware that the more interdependencies you have, the more complex the maintenance of the meta-repos and keeping them in a deployable state will be.

What's the right strategy?

If the mono-repo strategy or the multi-repo strategy are better suited for your teams it tightly couples to *Chapter 16, Loosely Coupled Architecture and Microservices*, when we talked about **evolutionary design**. Mono-repos are good for small products and greenfield projects. With growing size and complexity, it's best to split microservices or modules up and move them to their own repos. But always have testability and deployability in mind – for the individual service/module and for the application as a whole.

Case study

After the first three successful sprints, more teams at **Tailwind Gears** are moved to a new platform. The first teams have been selected to own a product that is already independently testable and deployable. With the scrum master, product owner, and QA member, they are a little big for the two-pizza rule, but this will be addressed later. The teams to follow are way too big, and they work on big monolith applications with a lot of interdependencies. To perform the Inverse Conway Maneuver, all the teams come together and self-organize the next teams to be moved to the new platform. The constraints are as follows:

- No bigger than a two-pizza team
- Responsible for a business capability (a **bounded context**) that can be extracted using the `StranglerFigApplication` pattern and be tested and deployed autonomously

This helps to evolve the design of the applications. The new microservices are cloud-native and have their own cloud-native data store. They get integrated into the existing applications using an API and event-driven architecture. The microservices are moved to their own repositories on the new platform because they get deployed independently most of the time. Synchronization with the other teams is done using feature flags.

For embedded software, this does not work. The teams need a way to build and deploy the application as a whole. But they also want to deploy and test individual modules. That's why the teams decide to split the application into different repositories and have one meta-repository that includes the other repos as submodules. This allows the individual teams to deploy their module to test hardware at any time to test new features in real-world scenarios – but it keeps the product in state, where it can be released at any time.

When the first teams were moved to the new platform, they kept their existing **sprint cadence** of 3 weeks. Since the teams could work more or less autonomously, this was not a problem. With more teams coming to the new platform, the cadence gets aligned with the other teams. Tailwind Gears is a public traded company and used to do all its business reporting on a quarterly basis. They also report on a weekly basis and have a normalized 4-4-5 calendar. There are a lot of meetings at the end and beginning of each quarter that often collide with sprint meetings. The teams decide to adjust their cadence to this rhythm. The quarter consists of 13 weeks – but one week has the quarterly meeting, so this week is stripped from the sprint calendar. This week is also used for the quarterly big-room planning. The remaining 12 weeks are divided into 6 two-week sprints.

Summary

In this chapter, you've learned how to use the influence of your team structure and communication flow on your software and system architecture to perform the Inverse Conway Maneuver. This helps you to achieve a loosely coupled architecture of autonomously testable and deployable units that have a positive impact on your software delivery performance.

In the next chapters, we'll focus more on what to build and less on how to build it. You'll learn about lean product development and how to incorporate customer feedback in your work.

Further reading

These are the references from this chapter that you can also use to get more information on the topics:

- Conway, Melvin (1968). *How do committees invent*: http://www.melconway.com/Home/pdf/committees.pdf

- Raymond, Eric S. (1996). *The New Hacker's Dictionary* [3rd ed.]. MIT Press

- Amazon (2020): *Introduction to DevOps on AWS - Two-Pizza Teams*: https://docs.aws.amazon.com/whitepapers/latest/introduction-devops-aws/two-pizza-teams.html

- Willink, J. and Leif Babin, L. (2017). *Extreme Ownership: How U.S. Navy SEALs Lead and Win*. Macmillan

- Miller, G.A. (1956). *The magical number seven, plus or minus two: Some limits on our capacity for processing information*: `http://psychclassics.yorku.ca/Miller/`

- Cohn M. (2009). *Succeeding with Agile: Software Development Using Scrum*. Addison-Wesley

- QSM (2011). *Team Size Can Be the Key to a Successful Software Project*: `https://www.qsm.com/process_improvement_01.html`

- Karau, S. J. and Williams, K. D. (1993). *Social loafing: A meta-analytic review and theoretical integration. Journal of Personality and Social Psychology*, 65(4), 681–706. `https://doi.org/10.1037/0022-3514.65.4.681`

- Robbins S. (2005). *Essentials of organizational behavior*. Prentice Hall

- Steiner, I.D. (1972). *Group process and productivity*. Academic Press Inc.

- Forsgren N., Humble, J., and Kim, G. (2018). *Accelerate: The Science of Lean Software and DevOps: Building and Scaling High Performing Technology Organizations* (1st ed.) [E-book]. IT Revolution Press

- Skelton M. and Pais M. (2019). *Team Topologies: Organizing Business and Technology Teams for Fast Flow*. IT Revolution

- Reinertsen D. (2009). *The Principles of Product Development Flow: Second Generation Lean Product Development*. Celeritas Publishing

- Medina A. M. (2021). *Remote debugging on Kubernetes using VS Code*: `https://developers.redhat.com/articles/2021/12/13/remote-debugging-kubernetes-using-vs-code`

Part 5: Lean Product Management

In *Part 5*, you'll learn the importance of lean product management, how to integrate customer feedback into your flow of work, and how to combine hypothesis-driven development with OKR.

This part of the book comprises the following chapters:

18
Lean Product Development and Lean Startup

Until now, we have only focused on *how* you should build and deliver software and not on *what* you should build or how you can determine whether you are building the right thing. But **lean product development** practices have a great positive impact on software delivery performance, organizational performance, and organizational culture (*Forsgren N., Humble J., & Kim G., (2018), p. 129*). Therefore, many DevOps transformations start by analyzing the value streams and try to optimize product management alongside the engineering practices. But, in my opinion, this results in too many moving pieces, and it is also a chicken and egg problem. If you are not able to deliver frequently in small batch sizes, it is hard to apply lean product management practices.

In this chapter, we'll have a look into how you can apply lean product development and lean startup practices to build products that delight your end users. This chapter covers the following:

- Lean product development
- Incorporating customer feedback
- The **minimal viable product** (MVP)

- Enterprise portfolio management
- The Business Model Canvas

Lean product development

Building the right things is hard and often underestimated. You cannot just ask potential customers what they want. What people say they want, what they really want, and what they are willing to pay for, are three completely different things.

Lean product development was introduced by **Toyota** to address challenges in their product development approach, notably the lack of innovation, long development cycles, and many reproduction cycles (*Ward, Allen 2007 p. 3*).

Lean product development is built on cross-functional teams that take an incremental approach. The main characteristics are as follows:

- Work in **small batches**.
- Make the **flow of work** visible.
- Gather and implement **customer feedback**.
- **Team experimentation**.

As you can see, this completely aligns with what we've learned in *Part 1, Lean Management and Collaboration*. The new dimension is customer feedback and experimentation. But without the ability to work in small batches and a visible flow of work, it is not possible to experiment based on customer feedback.

Incorporating customer feedback

But how can you gather customer feedback and implement it as a learning into your product? Most importantly, you need the **autonomy** to do it. As long as your team still receives requirements to deliver, you are not able to learn from customer feedback and incorporate the feedback into your product. Besides that, you need people with the right skills in the team or you must train your engineers. **Product management** and **user experience design** are skills that are not present in most teams but are crucial to learning from customer feedback and interactions.

One way to gather customer feedback is by interviewing your customers or performing **guerrilla usability testing** (see *Chapter 12, Shift Left Testing for Increased Quality*). But, you must be very careful when interpreting the results. What people say and how they behave are normally two completely different things.

To really close the feedback loop and learn from customer behavior, you need the following:

- **Customer data** (not only interviews but also feedback, usage data, evaluations, and performance data, for example)

- The knowledge to interpret the data (**product management skills**)

- A scientific approach

The **lean startup** methodology moves product management away from intuition (alchemy) to a scientific approach, performing **hypothesis-driven experimentation** using a **build-measure-learn** loop (see *Ries, Eric 2011*):

- You formulate a **hypothesis** based upon an analysis of your current customer feedback/data:

```
We believe {customer segment},
wants {product / feature} because
{value proposition}
```

- To prove or disprove the hypothesis, the team conducts an **experiment**. The experiment will impact certain metrics.

- The team analyzes the metrics impacted by the experiment and learns from them, normally by formulating a new hypothesis.

Figure 18.1 shows the build-measure-learn loop used for hypothesis-driven experimentation:

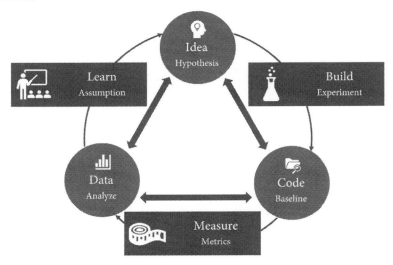

Figure 18.1 – Hypothesis-driven experimentation, the build-measure-learn loop

Practicing hypothesis-driven development is not easy. You need a lot of metrics and a good understanding of how your end users are using your application. Usage data alone is not enough. You must be able to combine this with performance metrics, error logs, security logs, and custom metrics to get the full picture of what is happening. How many people stopped using the application because it was too slow? How many people cannot log in? How many password resets are attacks and how many real users cannot log in? The more you experiment, the more you will find gaps in the knowledge of how your users are behaving. But, with every loop, you will learn and add more metrics and you will build an application that is better for your users. And, you will learn what features bring real value to your users and what is only waste that you can remove to make your product leaner.

Hypothesis-driven experimentation can perfectly be combined with **objectives and key results (OKRs)** – see *Chapter 1, Metrics That Matter*. OKRs give you the ability to align your autonomous teams to a greater vision by setting measurable key results on certain metrics, such as growth, engagement, or customer satisfaction.

The MVP

One of the most misused terms over the last years is the MVP. Everything that used to be a **proof of concept (PoC)** or a **spike** is now called an MVP. But an MVP is a version of a product that enables a full turn of the build-measure-learn loop with the minimum amount of effort (*Ries, Eric 2011* position 996).

A diagram I often see that resonates very well with the audience is this:

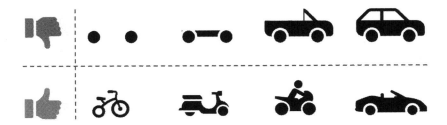

Figure 18.2 – Bad example of how to build an MVP

It shows that you should deliver with every iteration value by solving the problem domain – in this example, transportation. The problem is that this is not an MVP. This is agile delivery. But a bicycle does not allow you to test the value proposition of a sports car! Tesla could not have created an electrical bicycle to conduct an experiment on the success of an electric sports car.

If you test an MVP with your real customers, always keep in mind that it can destroy your reputation and that you might lose customers. An MVP cannot just have the bare minimum of functionality. It must also be reliable, user-friendly, and desirable:

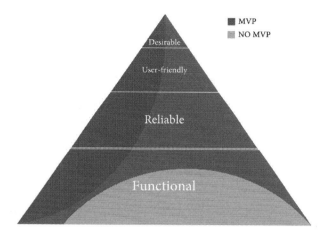

Figure 18.3 – An MVP must test all levels in the hierarchy of needs

Therefore, it is much easier to conduct experiments using an MVP if you have an existing product and customer base. For start-ups and new products, it is much harder, and you must include usability and reliability testing before putting your MVP out in the wild. If not, the experiment could go completely wrong. But even for existing products, when trying new features with your customers, make sure to make them reliable, user-friendly, and delightful!

Enterprise portfolio management

In a start-up, it is normally easy – at least in the beginning. But if you have multiple teams and multiple products, the question is, how can you ensure that cross-functional, autonomous teams pull in the same direction and take decisions that serve the long-term goals of your organization?

To practice lean product development, your company needs to move away from command-and-control processes to the **principles of mission** (*Humble J., Molesky J. & O'Reilly B. 2020*). This affects the portfolio management in your company:

- **Budgeting**: Instead of traditional budgeting for the next fiscal year, your management sets out high-level objectives across multiple perspectives and reviews them regularly. This steering can be done on multiple levels and allows the allocation of resources dynamically when needed.

- **Program management**: Instead of creating a detailed, upfront plan, your management specifies on a program level the measurable objectives for the next period. The teams then figure out for themselves how they can meet these objectives.

This can be perfectly combined with OKRs (see *Chapter 1, Metrics That Matter*).

But the principle of mission means that you need knowledge about product management and the market on all levels. It is important to understand that like each feature (see *Chapter 10, Feature Flags and the Feature Lifecycle*), each product has a lifecycle. New technology gets adopted by different groups of people. There are the **innovators** who just try everything, and there are **early adopters** or visionaries who try to stay ahead of the herd. Then, you have the big majority – around 70% in total. You can separate the majority into **early majority** (pragmatists) and **late majority** (conservatives). In the end, you also have the laggards or skeptics that only follow the trend, if there is no other option:

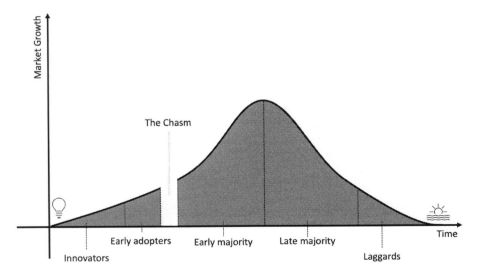

Figure 18.4 – The technology adoption lifecycle

An interesting thing here is the **chasm** – the logical divide between the early adopters and the early majority. The chasm is based upon the observation that many innovations struggle after they are not seen as a source of competitive advantage by the innovators but are not yet sufficiently established to be seen as safe by the early majority. Many products fail at exactly that point.

Once the early majority has started adopting the new technology, normally, other products and offerings enter the market. The market total is still growing, but the market changes as there are more competitors and the expectation of quality and price change:

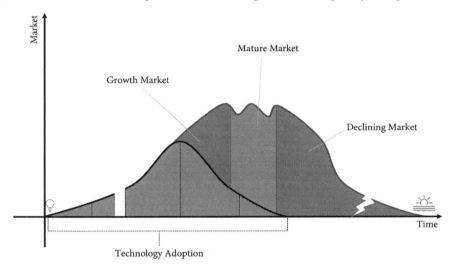

Figure 18.5 – Market maturity

It is important to understand where in this lifecycle a product is, as each stage requires a different strategy to be successful.

Start-ups begin with **exploration**. They search for new business models that align with the vision of the founder, deliver customer value, and can drive profitable growth. In this exploration phase, when a start-up has found a *problem/solution fit*, it tries to evaluate as fast as possible whether it also is a *product/market fit* by using an MVP.

Once the business model is found, the tactic changes to **exploitation**. The start-up exploits the business model by scaling up and driving down costs by improving efficiency.

Exploration and exploitation are completely different strategies that require different competencies, processes, risk management, and mindsets. Start-ups are normally good at exploration and bad at exploitation – enterprises are good at exploitation and bad at exploration.

It is important for all companies to find a balance between exploiting existing products and exploring new business models because, in the long run, you can only exist if you are able to manage both. That's the reason why so many enterprises now have **innovation** and **incubation hubs** to *mimic* start-ups to evaluate new business models.

To manage your portfolio, you can plot your products on a growth matrix. The matrix has four quadrants for growth and the importance of the products relative to the other investments:

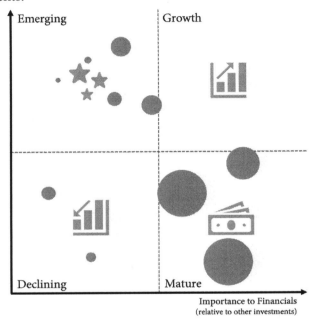

Figure 18.6 – The growth matrix for portfolio management

The size of the products can be the revenue or margin. You should always have enough products in the **emerging** quadrant that can be developed to the **growth** or **mature** quadrants because some will just **decline** without gaining relevance. The left side shows the products that you should explore, and the right side the ones you should exploit.

The matrix is very similar to the **growth-share matrix** from the **Boston Consulting Group (BCG)**. The framework was created by Alan Zakon – later CEO of BCG – in 1970. The growth-share matrix uses the market share instead of the financial importance on the *x* axis:

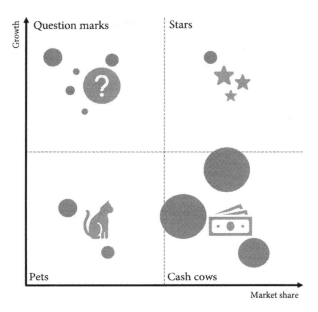

Figure 18.7 – The growth-share matrix

The matrix is suited if you have a clear view of the markets, but it works in the same way. The **question marks** are the products with high growth that must be explored and developed to **stars** or **cash cows**, which then get exploited. **Pets** are either failed experiments or declining cash cows. But, in either case, you should shut them down sooner or later.

The challenge for enterprises is to create products in the **stars** (or **growth**) quadrant without acquisitions. The reason is the market dynamic (*Figure 18.5*), and the way enterprises manage their portfolio. You can use the **three-horizon model** to manage an enterprise portfolio:

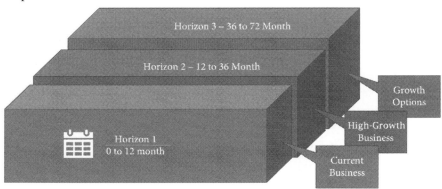

Figure 18.8 – The three-horizon model

The three horizons are as follows:

- **Horizon 1**: Generates today's cash flow

- **Horizon 2**: Today's revenue growth and tomorrow's cash flow

- **Horizon 3**: Options for future high-growth businesses

Horizon 1 is your mature products or cash cows. Investments in these will return results in the same year. **Horizon 2** are emerging products that have the potential to become new cash cows. They need a lot of investment but will not deliver the same level of results as the investments in Horizon 1. **Horizon 3** are the potential stars of the future, but with a big chance to fail.

The three horizons are completely different, and you need different strategies to be successful (*Humble J., Molesky J. & O'Reilly B. 2020*). But not only do you need different strategies, but often the new products will disrupt the market and take away share and revenue from existing business. Kodak invented the digital camera in 1975, but their business was built upon developing photographs and not on capturing memories, and the invention was turned down by management. Kodak filed for bankruptcy in 2012 – a year in which nearly every person had at least two digital cameras in their pocket at any time. A successful example is Amazon, where electronic books took away a lot from their classical business model of selling physical books, or a Microsoft cloud business that would lead to a decline in license sales for on-premises products.

With new products taking away market share and revenue from existing markets, it is important to steer the enterprise in a way that all people share the same goal of long-term success. If not, people will start to conspire against the new products to preserve their dominance inside the enterprise.

To balance the three horizons, you should have a transparent process of allocating the resources and the different strategies that apply. A common amount to invest in Horizon 3 is 10% – often quarterly, funded based upon validated learning. *Table 18.1* shows the different strategies and investments for the three horizons:

	Horizon 1	Horizon 2	Horizon 3
Goals	Maximize returns	Cross the chasm	Find product/market fits
Key metrics	Revenue, share, profitability, net promoter	Growth rate, new customers, target accounts, increasing efficiency	Brand perception, popularity, innovation score, active product usage
Strategy	Compete, exploit	Scale, accelerate	Innovate, explore
Investment	60% – 70%	20% - 30%	10%

Table 18.1 – The different strategies for the three horizons

But should you put the horizons in different business units? I believe not. This will just result in more competency and silos. A good company culture with a growth mindset and objectives that balance short and long-term goals allows you to be innovative on all levels and embrace innovation. But good product management is needed to visualize what products and features are in what phase of their lifecycle for all to understand the different strategies applied.

Improving your product management skills

Product management is a skill that is crucial to successful DevOps teams that want to practice lean product development. Many agile projects fail because the product owner is not able to drive the vision and make tough decisions that are often necessary. Product management is based upon three pillars:

- Understanding your customers
- Understanding your business
- Understanding your product

Understanding your customers

To build products that delight customers, it is necessary to have deep empathy for the persons that use the product. In software development, we use **personas** (fictional characters) to represent user segments that use our product since the 90s (*Goodwin, Kim (2009)*). Having specific characters in mind when designing a feature helps us to be more empathetic to the needs and limitations of our customers compared to just thinking of the customers as a big group with mixed characteristics.

But today, we can do more. We can gather data on how our customers are using our product. What personas (usability cluster) can we extract from that data? What are the most common use cases? What features aren't used? What use cases get terminated before they are complete? These are questions we should regularly answer by analyzing the data.

Understanding your business

To build successful products, your team does also have to understand the business. What is the market we are in and how big is our market share? Who are our competitors and what are their strengths and weaknesses?

Understanding the business is normally a completely new discipline for engineers. Traditionally, this was done on a different level and only a little information was passed to the engineers. Exercises such as the **Business Model Canvas** (*see the next section*) can help you foster these skills in your teams.

Understanding your product

Understanding the product is normally the strong capability of the engineering team. But understanding the product does not only mean that you know the feature but it also means you know how the product is operated, load-balanced, how the performance is, and how much technical debt you've accumulated.

Of course, you can add members to your team who are experienced product managers and user experience designers. But, as we discussed in the previous chapter, you should keep your teams small. The skills are needed for every feature you create and release, every experiment you conduct, and every decision you take. It is better to upskill your team and have, for example, user experience designers that can help your team if needed.

Business Model Canvas

To strengthen the product management skills of your engineers, you can perform an exercise to create a **Business Model Canvas** – a template for creating business models or documenting existing ones. The Business Model Canvas was developed by Alexander Osterwalder in 2005. You can download a free copy of the template here: `https://www.strategyzer.com/canvas/business-model-canvas`.

The Canvas is meant to be printed out on a large piece of paper and the team can brainstorm and jointly sketch or add post-it notes on it. It contains nine essential components for a business model:

- **Value proposition**: What problems are we going to solve? What needs are we satisfying?

- **Customer segments**: For whom are we creating value? Who are our most important customers?

- **Customer relationships**: What type of relationship does each of our customers expect from us?

- **Channels**: Through which channels do our customers want to be reached?

- **Key partners**: With whom do we have to create a partnership? Who are our key suppliers?

- **Key activities**: What activities will be required to fulfill our value proposition?

- **Key resources**: What resources – such as people, technology, and processes – does our value proposition require?

- **Cost structure**: What are the most important cost drivers for the business model? Are they fixed or variable?

- **Revenue streams**: For what value are the customers willing to pay? How much and how often?

The Canvas contains some more hints that help your team to create the business model, as you can see in the following screenshot:

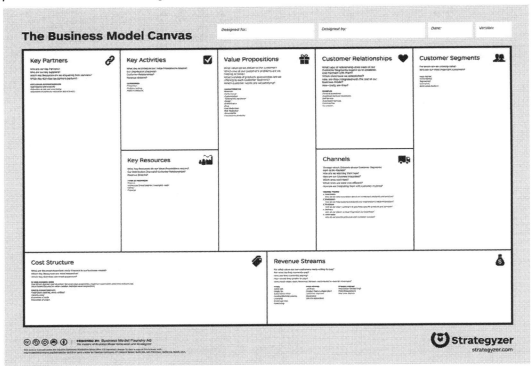

Figure 18.9 – The Business Model Canvas

By filling out all areas of the Canvas, you are considering any potential ideas in terms of the entire business model, and you are encouraged to think in a holistic manner about how all the elements fit together.

Summary

In this chapter, you've learned the importance of lean product management and how you can incorporate customer feedback into your flow of work. You have learned what an MVP is and how you can use hypothesis-driven development to build the right things.

In the next chapter, we'll have a closer look at how to perform A/B testing to conduct experiments.

Further reading

These are the references from this chapter that you can also use to get more information on the topics:

- Forsgren N., Humble, J., & Kim, G. (2018). *Accelerate: The Science of Lean Software and DevOps: Building and Scaling High Performing Technology Organizations* (1st ed.) [E-book]. IT Revolution Press

- Ward, Allen (2007). *Lean Product and Process Development.* Lean Enterprise Institute, US

- Ries, Eric (2011). *The Lean Startup: How Today's Entrepreneurs Use Continuous Innovation to Create Radically Successful Businesses* [Kindl Edition]. Currency

- Humble J., Molesky J. & O'Reilly B. (2015). *Lean Enterprise: How High Performance Organizations Innovate at Scale* [Kindle Edition]. O'Reilly Media

- Osterwalder, Alexander (2004). *The Business Model Ontology: A Proposition In A Design Science Approach*: `http://www.hec.unil.ch/aosterwa/PhD/Osterwalder_PhD_BM_Ontology.pdf`.

- Goodwin, Kim (2009). *Designing for the Digital Age - How to Create Human-Centered Products and Services.* Wiley

19
Experimentation and A|B Testing

In this chapter, we will discuss how you can evolve and continuously improve your products by conducting experiments to validate hypotheses through evidence-based DevOps practices, such as **A|B testing**. This is sometimes called **hypothesis-driven development** or just **experimentation**.

The following topics will be covered in this chapter:

- Conducting experiments with the scientific method
- Effective A|B testing with GrowthBook and Flagger
- Experimentation and OKR

Conducting experiments with the scientific method

Traditionally, requirements management was more guesswork than science. The closest that came to a scientific approach were interviews or market research in general. The problem with this approach is that you cannot ask people what they do not yet know. You can ask them what they want but not what they need, as they probably won't know that yet, especially in a market segment that gets disrupted.

The idea of hypothesis-driven development is to apply the **scientific method** to product management, an empirical method of acquiring evidence-based knowledge.

The scientific method is a process of experimentation used to explore observations and answer questions that aim to discover cause-and-effect relationships. It follows certain process steps (see *Figure 19.1*):

Figure 19.1 – The scientific method

We will look at the various steps in detail:

1. **Observation**: Observing reality using all five senses: smell, sight, sound, touch, and taste.

2. **Question**: Formulating a question based on observation and existing research or previous experiments.

3. **Hypothesis**: Stating a hypothesis based on knowledge obtained while formulating the question. The hypothesis is a prediction of what you think will occur based on observation and research. Hypotheses are often written in the *if … then …* form, for example: "*if* we modify this variable, *then* we expect this change to be observable."

4. **Experiment**: The experiment proves or disproves the hypothesis. In the experiment, you have different variables. **Independent variables** are the ones you change to trigger a result. **Dependent variables** are the things you measure and expect to change. In the experiment, you collect **qualitative data** through observations and **quantitative data** by measuring and collecting metrics.

Experiments also use control groups to prove that the variance is more than just chance. To test treatment with a drug, you must design an experiment in which a portion of the population – the **control group** – is left untreated and given a placebo, while the **experimental group** is treated with the potential drug (see *Figure 19.2*).

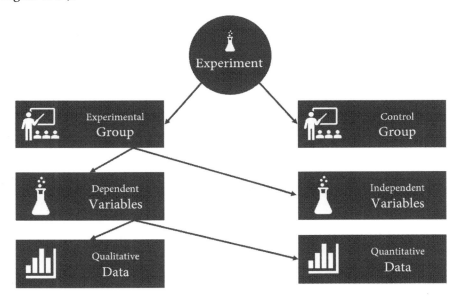

Figure 19.2 – Conducting a scientific experiment

To have a good experiment, you should only change *one variable at a time* while keeping all other variables the same. You should also *avoid bias*. No matter how hard you try, bias can sneak so easily into your observations and conclusions.

5. **Conclusion**: After the experiment, you analyze the results and compare the actual results to the expected ones. What have you learned from the experiment? Can you verify or refute your hypothesis? Is there a new hypothesis or new question to formulate? Or do you need more experiments to be sure?

6. **Results**: The final step is to share your results. Even if your hypothesis was refuted, it is still valuable learning.

The scientific method is an iterative, empirical method, but the steps do not necessarily occur in that order. At any point, you can modify your question and change your hypothesis – and observation is going on all the time. Instead of a clear cycle, the process diagram looks more like *Figure 19.3*:

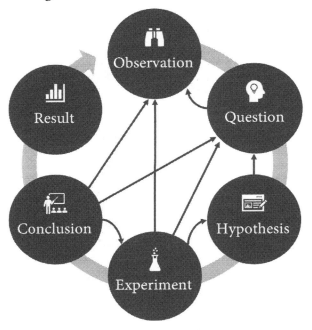

Figure 19.3 – There is no strict order of the steps in the process

The scientific approach is very important in our industry – not only for building the right things. You should also use the approach when hunting down bugs or production issues: formulate a hypothesis based on facts observed. Conduct an experiment by changing only one thing at a time, normally a configuration value. Perform a cross-check to ensure that there is no other system or variable interfering with your experiment. Make a conclusion and document your results before starting with the next hypothesis.

Let's have a look at how you can use the scientific method to evolve and continuously improve your software.

Observation – gathering and analyzing the data

You can watch people using your application for observation. We've talked in *Chapter 12, Shift Left Testing for Increased Quality*, about **usability testing** techniques, such as **hallway testing** or **guerrilla usability**. However, normally users are scattered across the world and it's easier to look at the data they produce than to interview them.

Data is the most important ingredient for **hypothesis-driven development**! The more you experiment, the more data you will collect over time.

When observing data, you should not only focus on the data points at hand. Ask yourself what the data does not tell you. If your goal was to increase the number of active users every month, you should not only focus your observation on the data about the current users. Check the data for failed login attempts. How many users would like to use your applications but are locked out and can't recover their password or second authentication factor? How many people do not come back after they need to verify their mail or mobile number? How many cancel the registration process and how long do they wait before doing so?

To answer these kinds of questions, you cannot simply look into your usage data. You have to combine data from all sources available (see *Figure 19.4*):

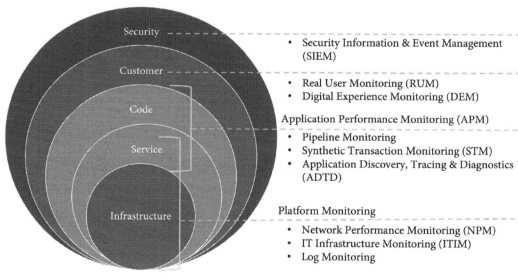

- Security
- Customer
- Code
- Service
- Infrastructure

- Security Information & Event Management (SIEM)

- Real User Monitoring (RUM)
- Digital Experience Monitoring (DEM)

Application Performance Monitoring (APM)
- Pipeline Monitoring
- Synthetic Transaction Monitoring (STM)
- Application Discovery, Tracing & Diagnostics (ADTD)

Platform Monitoring
- Network Performance Monitoring (NPM)
- IT Infrastructure Monitoring (ITIM)
- Log Monitoring

Figure 19.4 – Logging sources for gathering data

This quantitative data can then be combined with qualitative data, such as customer surveys, data from your customer service center, or any kind of analytics data. *Figure 19.5* shows the different data sources that you can use to gain insights and formulate the question:

Figure 19.5 – Data sources for observation

With these questions in mind, you can then start to formulate a hypothesis.

Formulating the hypothesis

The hypothesis is the prediction of what you think will occur based on your observation and research. Hypotheses can be written in a simple *if … then …* form: *If <we modify this variable>, then <we expect this change to be observable>.*

If we shorten our registration form by deleting fields such as phone number and mailing address, *then* the number of people canceling the registration process (*abandonment rate*) will decrease.

Since you will have many hypotheses on your backlog, it is common to have a fix form, similar to user stories, which includes the customer segment and the feature name. This makes your hypotheses more discoverable on a backlog:

We believe {customer segment}

want {feature}

because {value proposition}

This form also forces you to bring three aspects into your hypothesis:

- **Who**: for whom are we changing the application?
- **What**: what are we changing?
- **How**: how will this change impact the users?

These ingredients make up a good hypothesis:

We believe new users

want a shorter registration form with fewer input fields

because this allows them to test the application and gain confidence before revealing their personal data.

Note that focusing on the value proposition leads to a more abstract description of the **how** with a greater focus on the **why**. In marketing, you often find details like this in your hypothesis:

- What is the impact?
- By how much/how great it is?
- After what period of time?

This results in a one-to-one relationship between hypotheses and experiments. Especially when starting with experimentation, I think separating the experiment from the underlaying hypothesis helps. You will probably need multiple experiments before you finally can say with certainty whether the hypothesis was true or false.

Building the experiment

When defining your experiment, you should try to keep as many variables fixed as possible. The best thing is to look at your baseline data. How will weekends and vacations impact your data? How will political and macroeconomic trends impact your experiment?

Also, make sure that both your control group and your experimental group are big enough. If you only experiment on a small group, your results might not be representative. If your control group is too small, you might not have enough data to compare your results to, especially if there are other external factors that you did not foresee. A good experiment should contain the following information:

- What's the change?
- What's the expected impact?
- Who is the audience or the customer segment?
- How much change are we expecting?
- How long do we run the experiment?
- What is the baseline we compare the data to (a control group or historical data)?

Here is an example.

The new, *shorter registration form* (**what's the change**) will *reduce the abandonment rate of the registration form* (**impact**) for *50%* of our *new users* (**for whom**) by more than *15%* (**how much**) after *14 days* (**after how long**) compared to our control group (**baseline**).

With the experiment defined, you can start implementing and running it. If you develop with feature flags (see *Chapter 10, Feature Flags and the Feature Lifecycle*), this is as simple as writing a new feature. The only difference is that you do not turn the feature on for all users but for your experimentation group instead.

Validating the results

After the experiment, you analyze the results and compare the actual results to the expected ones. What have you learned from the experiment? Can you verify or falsify your hypothesis or do you need more experiments to be sure? Is there a new hypothesis or new question to formulate?

The retrospective study of the results is an important part. Do not skip it and just assume that the hypothesis is true or false because your metrics exceed a threshold. Analyze the data and check for unexpected influences, strays, and statistical outliers.

Learning from your hypotheses and experiments should lead to new ideas and complete the build-measure-learn loop (see *Figure 19.6*):

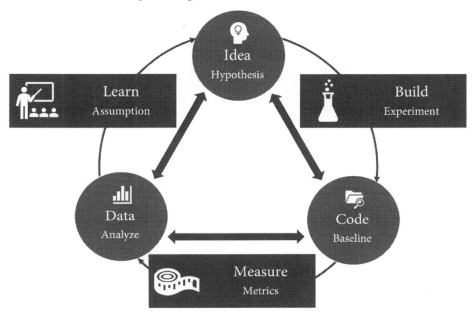

Figure 19.6 – Hypothesis-driven experimentation with the build-measure-learn loop

There are many tools available that can help you with effective A|B testing and experimentation.

Effective A|B testing with GrowthBook and Flagger

GitHub does not have the tooling to help you with A|B testing but there are many tools available on the market. The problem is that many of these tools have completely different scopes. Some are more like web experience tools, which you can use to build your website using a **content management system** (**CMS**) or to build A|B tests using a visual editor to create and test your variations (for example, **Optimizely** – see https://www.optimizely.com/). Some are more focused on marketing, landing pages, and campaign management, such as **HubSpot** (https://www.hubspot.com/). These tools are great but probably not the right choice for an engineering team.

A better solution is provided by the tools for doing feature flags, such as **LaunchDarkly**, **VWO**, or **Unleash**. I have covered these tools in *Chapter 10, Feature Flags and the Feature Lifecycle*, so I will not cover them again here. If you are using one of these solutions for feature flags, this is the first place you should look for a solution for A|B testing.

In this chapter, I will focus on **GrowthBook** and **Flagger**, two open source projects with a strong focus on experimentation, but with a completely different approach.

GrowthBook

GrowthBook (`https://github.com/growthbook/growthbook`) is a solution with a free and open core. It is also available as a SaaS and Enterprise plan. It provides an SDK for **React**, **JavaScript**, **PHP**, **Ruby**, **Python**, **Go**, and **Kotlin**.

The solution design of GrowthBook is completely containerized. If you want to try it out, you just have to clone the repository and then run the following:

```
docker-compose up -d
```

Once up, you can access the Growthbook on `http://localhost:3000`.

> **Running GrowthBook in GitHub Codespaces**
>
> If you want to try out GrowthBook, you can run it in GitHub Codespaces. For this to work, you have to configure `docker-compose.yml` to use the correct DNS names, since GrowthBook uses localhost to connect to its MongoDB. Set `APP_ORIGIN` under `environment` to your local address of port `3000` and `API_HOST` to your local address of port `3001` and make port `3001` visible.

Once connected, you can use it to serve feature flags or build experiments. To build experiments, you have to connect a data source to GrowthBook – for example, **BigQuery**, **Snowflake**, **Redshift**, or **Google Analytics**, among many others. There are predefined data schemas and you can also build your own. You then create metrics based on your data source. Metrics can be any of the following:

- **Binomial**: A simple yes or no conversation (for example, `Account Created`)

- **Count**: Multiple conversations per user (for example, `Page Visits`)

- **Duration**: How much time something takes on average (for example, `Time on Site`)

- **Revenue**: The revenue gained or lost on average (for example, `Revenue per User`)

To run an experiment, you would normally use your feature flags. You could also run an inline experiment directly with one of the SDKs. This is what an experiment would look like in JavaScript:

```javascript
const { value } = growthbook.run({
  key: "my-experiment",
  variations: ["red", "blue", "green"],
});
```

The experiment runs based on your defined metrics and the results look like they do in *Figure 19.7*:

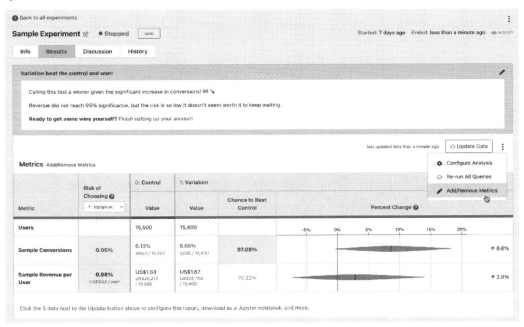

Figure 19.7 – The results of an experiment in GrowthBook

You can add and remove metrics to the experiment and also export it as a Jupyter notebook.

GrowthBook also comes with the Google Chrome extension **GrowthBook DevTools** for JavaScript and the React SDK, which allows you to directly interact with your feature flags in the browser. A visual editor is currently in beta.

GrowthBook is straightforward and also based on feature flags like the solutions introduced in *Chapter 10*.

Flagger

A completely different approach uses **Flagger** (`https://flagger.app/`). It's a delivery operator for **Kubernetes** and can be used with the **service mesh Istio**. Flagger is more often used for **canary releases** to Kubernetes clusters but it can also route traffic on HTTP match conditions.

You could create an experiment for all users with an `insider` cookie for 20 minutes, like so:

```
analysis:
  # schedule interval (default 60s)
  interval: 1m
  # total number of iterations
  iterations: 20
  # max number of failed metric checks before rollback
  threshold: 2
  # canary match condition
  match:
    - headers:
        cookie:
          regex: "^(.*?;)?(type=insider)(;.*)?$"
```

You can combine Flagger with metrics from **Prometheus, Datadog, Dynatrace,** among many others. I'm not going to go into more detail here. See the Flagger documentation (`https://docs.flagger.app/`) for more information. There is also a good tutorial from Stefan Prodan: *GitOps recipe for Progressive Delivery with Flux v2, Flagger and Istio* (see `https://github.com/stefanprodan/gitops-istio`).

A solution with Flagger and Istio brings great flexibility but it is also quite complex and not suited to beginners. If you are already on Kubernetes and Istio and perform canary releases, then Flagger might be a powerful framework for you.

As you can see, there are many solutions out there that can help you run experiments and A|B tests. From CMS- and campaign-focused tools to Kubernetes operators, there is a wide range of solutions that have completely different approaches. The best solution for you depends on a lot of things – mostly your existing toolchain, pricing, and support. I think it is more important to focus on the process and data analytics. Serving two versions of your application should not be the challenge – making sense of your data probably is.

Experimentation and OKR

In *Chapter 1, Metrics That Matter*, I introduced you to **Objectives and Key Results (OKRs)** as a framework to define and track objectives and their outcomes in a transparent way. OKRs help organizations achieve high alignment on strategic goals while keeping a maximum level of autonomy for the individual teams.

Engineering teams are an expensive resource and a lot of stakeholders are requesting things from them all the time: testers submitting bugs, customers requesting new features, and management wanting to catch up with the competition and make promises to important customers. How should a team ever find the freedom to conduct experiments? And what experiments would be the best to start with?

OKRs can give you the ability to have a strong alignment with higher-level goals by simultaneously preserving the autonomy to decide *what* to build and *how* to build it.

Let's assume your company wants to be the market leader with a market share of 75% and it will need a constant growth rate of newly registered users to achieve that. The **key result** for your team is a growth rate of 20% each month. This will then set the priority for your team. Of course, there will be other things to do, but the priority will be the OKR. The team probably first investigates how many people come to the registration page in the first place and from what referral. How many people click on the **Register Now** button? How many finish the dialog? At what point do they not come back? And at that point, they are automatically starting to formulate hypotheses and can run experiments to prove them.

OKRs are also good for cross-team collaboration, as teams probably have OKRs with high synergy effects, as they are aligned to higher-level goals. In this example, the team probably wants to talk with marketing, as they will have similar OKRs. They might have their own ideas for experiments to help drive the engagement rate for the landing pages that lead to your registration site.

OKRs are a great tool to grant people the freedom to experiment by ensuring alignment with other teams and higher-level goals.

Summary

Experimentation, A|B testing, and hypothesis-driven development are difficult topics as they require a high level of maturity in many areas:

- **Management**: Your teams need the autonomy to decide on their own *what* to build and *how* to build it.

- **Culture**: You need a culture of trust where people are not afraid to fail.

- **Cross-team collaboration**: Your teams must be able to work interdisciplinarily, as experimentation often requires the collaboration of different departments.

- **Technical capabilities**: You must be able to release changes in a very short time to production and target individual customer segments.

- **Insights**: You must have strong analytics capabilities and combine data and metrics from different sources.

If you are not there yet, don't worry. Many teams I work with are not. Just keep on improving your capabilities and check that your metrics show results. DevOps is a journey and not a goal, and you must take it one step at a time.

In this chapter, you've learned the basics of experimentation, A|B testing, and hypothesis-driven development, and I introduced some tools that can help you build solutions for it.

In the next chapter, you will learn the basics of GitHub – hosting options, pricing, and how you can integrate it into your existing toolchain and your enterprise.

Further reading

These are the references and links from this chapter that you can also use to get more information on the topics:

- *The Scientific method*: https://en.wikipedia.org/wiki/Scientific_method

- *Ring-based deployments*: https://docs.microsoft.com/en-us/azure/devops/migrate/phase-rollout-with-rings

- *Optimizely*: https://www.optimizely.com/

- *Hubspot*: https://www.hubspot.com/

- *GrowthBook*: https://github.com/growthbook/growthbook

- *Flagger*: https://flagger.app/

- Stefan Prodan: *GitOps recipe for progressive delivery with Flux v2, Flagger, and Istio*: https://github.com/stefanprodan/gitops-istio

Part 6: GitHub for your Enterprise

In *Part 6*, you'll learn about the different hosting and pricing options of GitHub, how you can migrate to GitHub from other platforms, and best practices for structuring your teams and products inside GitHub Enterprise.

This part of the book comprises the following chapters:

20
GitHub – The Home for All Developers

In this chapter, I'll explain some of the basics of the GitHub platform. You'll learn about the different hosting options, pricing, and how you can integrate it into your existing toolchain.

The key topics are as follows:

- Hosting options and pricing
- GitHub Connect
- Hands-on – create your account on GitHub.com
- Enterprise Security
- GitHub Learning Lab

Hosting options and pricing

GitHub has many different licenses and hosting options. It is important to understand them to make the right choice for your enterprise.

Hosting options

GitHub (`https://github.com`) is hosted in data centers in the United States. You can sign up on GitHub for free and you'll get unlimited private and public repositories for free. Many of the features in GitHub are free for open source projects but not for private repositories.

For enterprises, you have different options to host GitHub (see *Figure 20.1*):

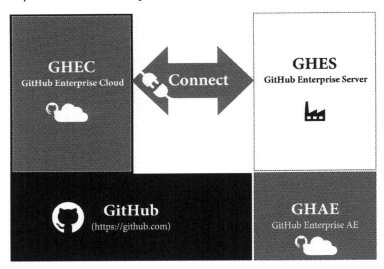

Figure 20.1 – Hosting options for GitHub Enterprise

GitHub Enterprise Cloud

GitHub Enterprise Cloud (**GHEC**) is a SaaS offering from GitHub and is completely hosted by GitHub in their cloud infrastructure in the United States. You can apply additional security and support single sign-on for your users. GHEC allows you to host private and public repositories so that you can host open source projects in the context of your enterprise.

GHEC is guaranteeing you an **SLA** of *99.9%* monthly uptime, meaning a maximum downtime of 45 minutes per month.

GitHub Enterprise Server

GitHub Enterprise Server (**GHES**) is a system that you can host wherever you want. You can host it in your own data center or in a cloud environment such as Azure or AWS. You can use GitHub Connect to connect to `GitHub.com` – this allows you to share licenses and make use of open source resources on your server.

GHES is based on the same source as GHEC, so eventually, all features will come to the server a few months later. But there are some things provided in the cloud that you must take care of on GHES for yourself, for example, the runners in GitHub Actions. In the cloud you can leverage GitHub hosted runners; on GHES, you must build your own solution using self-hosted runners.

There are also managed services that offer to host GHES for you – for example, in an Azure data center in your region. This way, you have full data residency and don't have to manage the servers by yourself. Some also include offering to host managed GitHub Actions runners.

GitHub Enterprise AE

GitHub is building a service called **GitHub Enterprise AE** (**GHAE**). It is currently in private beta for customers with more than 500 seats and there is not yet a date when the service will be available publicly.

GHAE is a completely isolated, managed offering from GitHub in a Microsoft Azure region of your choice. This gives you full data residency and compliance.

For customers that need data residency and compliance, this will be a good option in the future, but for now, it is not clear when it will be available, what the pricing will be, and what the minimum number of seats will be.

GitHub Connect

The power of GitHub lies in its community and the value the community provides. To be able to leverage this on the server, you can connect your server to GitHub using **GitHub Connect**. You can activate each feature individually, as you can see in *Figure 20.2*:

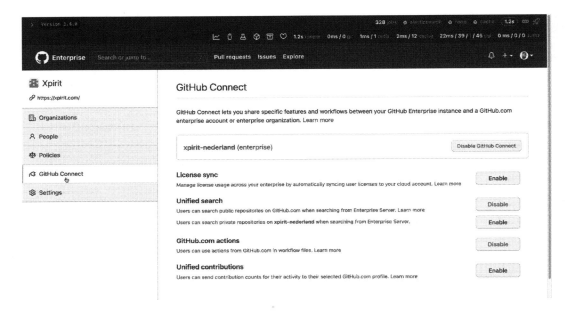

Figure 20.2 – Configure GitHub Connect on GHES

The following is a list of the features:

- **License sync**: Manage license usage across your enterprise on multiple servers or organizations. This helps to ensure that one user only consumes one license, no matter where they sign in.

- **Unified search**: One option is to allow searching on the server and getting results for public repositories from GitHub.com. Additionally, you can allow searching on the server and finding private repositories that belong to your enterprise (of course, only when the user has access to the repositories).

- **GitHub.com actions**: To load public actions in workflows, you must enable this option. Without this, you must fork all actions to your server and reference them from there. You can still configure at the organization level what actions are allowed.

- **Unified contributions**: Without this option, users' contributions on the server will not show up in their public profile. No sensitive data is exposed with this option. Only the number of contributions – such as commits, issues, discussions, or pull requests – are sent to GitHub.com.

Pricing

The cost of GitHub is billed monthly per user, and it is built upon three different tiers, **Free**, **Team**, and **Enterprise** (see *Figure 20.3*):

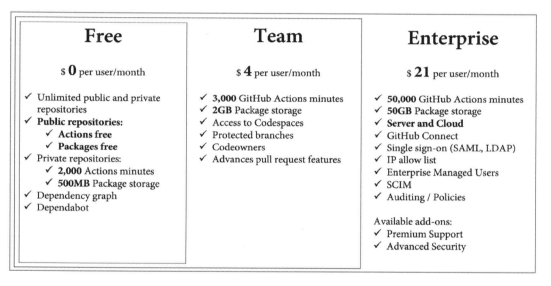

Figure 20.3 – Overview of GitHub pricing tiers

Public repositories – and therefore open source – are **free** and contain a lot of features for free, such as Actions, Packages, and many security features. Private repositories are free with limited functionality and 2,000 Action minutes and 500 MB of storage. The pricing for Actions was covered in depth in *Chapter 7, Running Your Workflows*.

If you really want to collaborate with GitHub in private repositories, you need at least the **Team** license. It includes **protected branches**, **code owners**, and other advanced pull request features. And you get access to **Codespaces**, but you must pay for them separately (see *Chapter 13, Shift Left Security and DevSecOps*, for the pricing of Codespaces). The team tier contains 3,000 Action minutes and 2 GB of storage for packages.

Free and Team are only available on GitHub.com. If you need GHEC, GHES, or GHAE, you must buy the GitHub **Enterprise** license. This license contains all the Enterprise features, such as single sign-on, user management, auditing, and policies, and it comes with 50,000 Action minutes and 50 GB of storage for packages. It also gives you the option to purchase additional add-ons such as **Advanced Security** or **Premium Support**.

Licenses are bought in blocks of 10 and can be paid monthly or yearly. If you want to use GitHub Advances Security or Premium Support, you must talk to the GitHub Sales team or a GitHub partner. They can give you a quote for that.

There are certain things that are paid on a per-use basis in addition to the license tiers, such as the following:

- Actions
- Packages
- Codespaces
- Marketplace pay-per-use apps

You can configure spending limits on the organization or enterprise level.

Hands-on – create your account on GitHub.com

Until now, I just assumed that you already have a GitHub account. With over 70 million users, chances are high that you do. If you have one, just skip this section and continue with **enterprise security**.

Signing up for GitHub is straightforward. It is designed like a wizard that looks like a console. The steps to create a new account are as follows:

1. Visit https://github.com and click on **Sign up**.
2. Enter your email address and click **Continue** or press *Enter*, as in *Figure 20.4*:

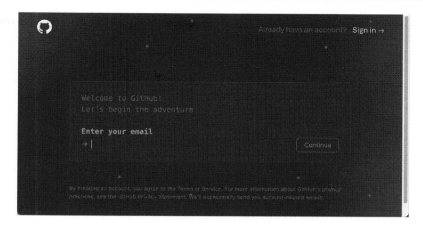

Figure 20.4 – Enter your email address

3. Enter a strong password and click **Continue**.

4. Enter a username. The username must be unique. GitHub will tell you whether your name is available or not, as in *Figure 20.5*:

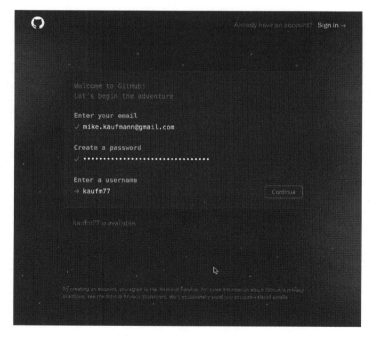

Figure 20.5 – Create a password and pick a unique username

Click **Continue** if you found a unique username.

5. Now, you can opt in or out of email communication. Type y for *yes* or n for *no*, then click **Continue** or press *Enter*.

6. Solve the captcha by clicking on the specified part of the image. Note that the captcha might appear in the preferred language of your browser (see *Figure 20.6*):

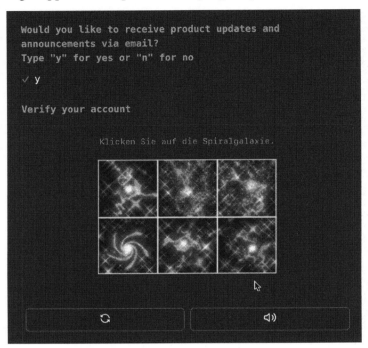

Figure 20.6 – Email communication and captcha

7. Now, check your email account. You should have received a code that you can paste into the following fields (see *Figure 20.7*):

Figure 20.7 – Enter the code that was sent to your email address

8. The next dialogs are to personalize your experience. You can skip them if you want.

9. You can choose a free 30-day trial of GitHub Enterprise. This should give you enough time to try out all the features.

After you have successfully created your account, there are some steps you should do right away:

1. Go to `https://github.com/settings/security` and check **Enable two-factor authentication** to secure your account.

2. Fill in your profile at `https://github.com/settings/profile` and pick a good avatar.

3. Select the theme of your choice at `https://github.com/settings/appearance`. You can choose a single light or dark theme, or you can choose to sync the theme with your system.

4. Choose how to deal with your email address at `https://github.com/settings/emails`. You can choose to keep your email address private. GitHub will then use a special email address when performing web-based Git operations. The address has the following format: `<user-id>+<user-name>@users.noreply.github.com`. You have to configure this address locally if you want to block command-line pushes that contain your real email address:

```
$ git config --global user.email <email address>
```

Your GitHub account is now ready, and you can start creating repositories or contributing to open source projects.

Enterprise security

As an enterprise, you can use **SAML single sign-on (SSO)** with your **identity provider (IdP)** to protect your GitHub Enterprise resources. SSO can be configured in GHEC at the enterprise and organization levels. In GHES, it can only be configured for the entire server.

SAML SSO can be configured with every IdP that supports SAML – but not all support the **System for Cross-domain Identity Management (SCIM)**. These are compatible: **Azure AD (AAD)**, Okta, and OneLogin.

SAML authentication

Configuring SAML SSO in GitHub is straightforward. You can find the corresponding settings in the enterprise or organization settings under **Authentication security** (`/settings/security`) | **SAML single sign-on**. Here, you can find the consumer URL you will need to configure your IdP (see *Figure 20.8*):

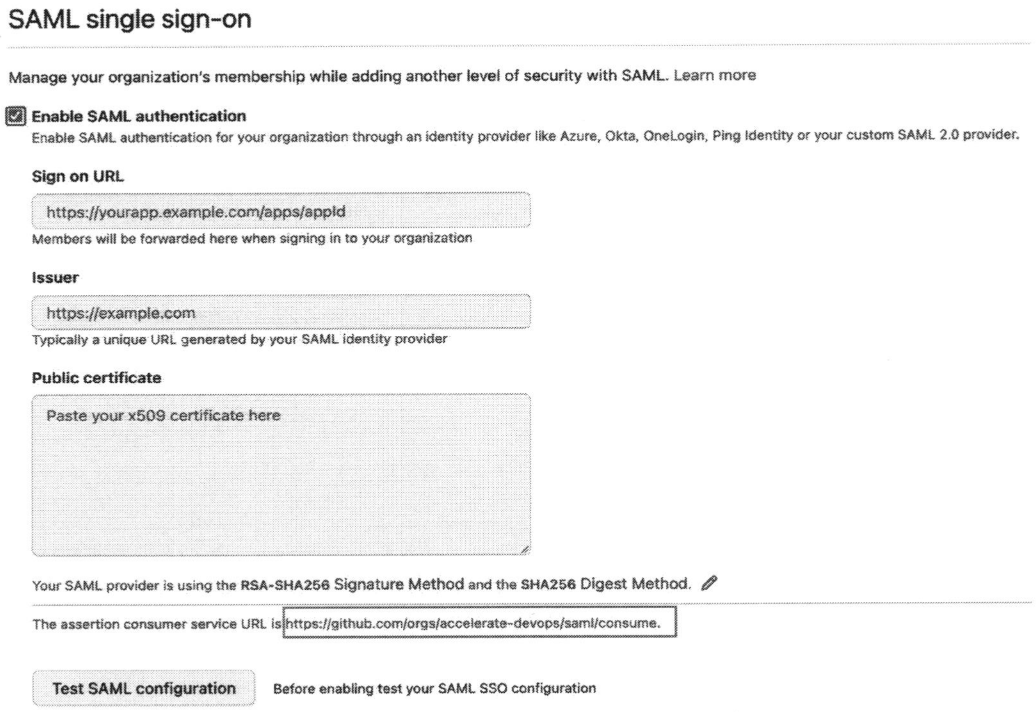

SAML single sign-on

Manage your organization's membership while adding another level of security with SAML. Learn more

☑ **Enable SAML authentication**
Enable SAML authentication for your organization through an identity provider like Azure, Okta, OneLogin, Ping Identity or your custom SAML 2.0 provider.

Sign on URL

> https://yourapp.example.com/apps/appId

Members will be forwarded here when signing in to your organization

Issuer

> https://example.com

Typically a unique URL generated by your SAML identity provider

Public certificate

> Paste your x509 certificate here

Your SAML provider is using the **RSA-SHA256** Signature Method and the **SHA256** Digest Method. ✎

The assertion consumer service URL is https://github.com/orgs/accelerate-devops/saml/consume.

Test SAML configuration   Before enabling test your SAML SSO configuration

Figure 20.8 – Configure SAML SSO in GitHub

The values for the fields must be configured in your IdP. Check their documentation for more information. In AAD, for example, you can find detailed instructions here: `https://docs.microsoft.com/en-us/azure/active-directory/saas-apps/github-tutorial`. You have to create a new Enterprise application in AAD. You can search the templates for GitHub and pick the corresponding one (for enterprise, organization, or server). See *Figure 20.9* for the currently available templates:

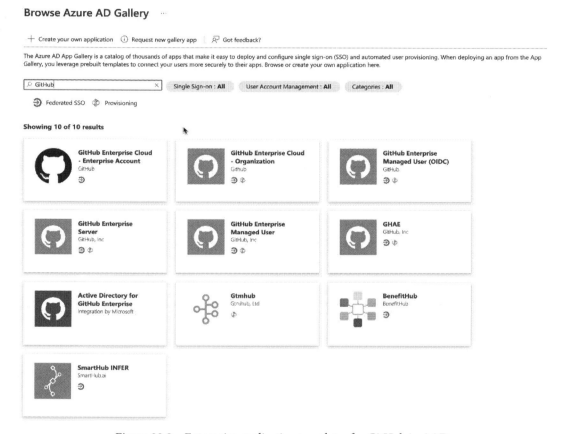

Figure 20.9 – Enterprise application templates for GitHub in AAD

Assign users or groups to the application that you want to have access to GitHub. The important configuration happens in **Set up single sign on** (see *Figure 20.10*):

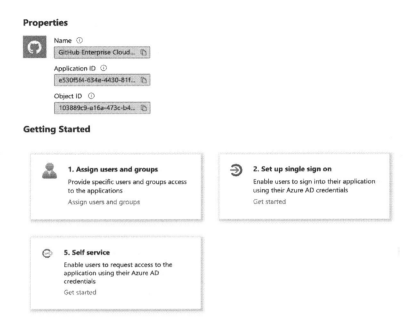

Figure 20.10 – Configuring your Enterprise application

Use the organization or enterprise URL as the identifier. You can use the first part of the URL you have seen in *Figure 20.8*, only without /saml/consume. Use this URL as **Entity ID**. Add /saml/consume for **Reply URL** and /sso for **Sign on URL**. The result should look like *Figure 20.11*:

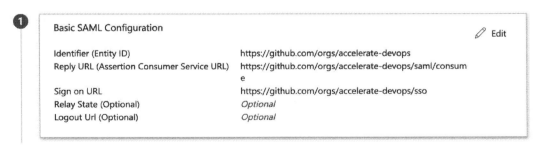

Figure 20.11 – Basic SAML configuration in AAD Enterprise application

The attributes and claims can be used to adjust the mappings for the fields in AAD. The default settings should work if your AAD was not customized (see *Figure 20.12*):

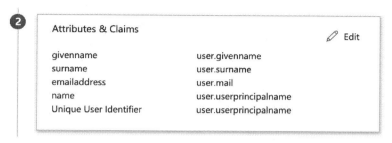

Figure 20.12 – Configure the attributes and claims for the SAML token

Download the **Base64** certificate used to sign the SAML token (see *Figure 20.13*):

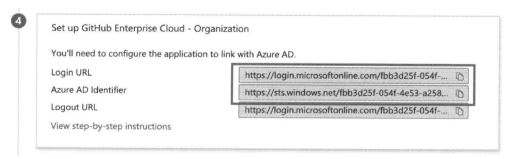

Figure 20.13 – Download the SAML signing certificate

Copy the **Login URL** and **Azure AD Identifier** URLs (see *Figure 20.14*):

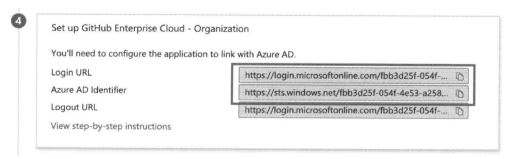

Figure 20.14 – Get Login URL and Azure AD Identifier

You can now head back to GitHub and fill in the data. Then, paste the **Login URL** information into the **Sign on URL** field and the **Azure AD Identifier** URL into the **Issuer** field. Open the certificate in a text editor and paste the content in the **Public certificate** field. The result looks like *Figure 20.15*:

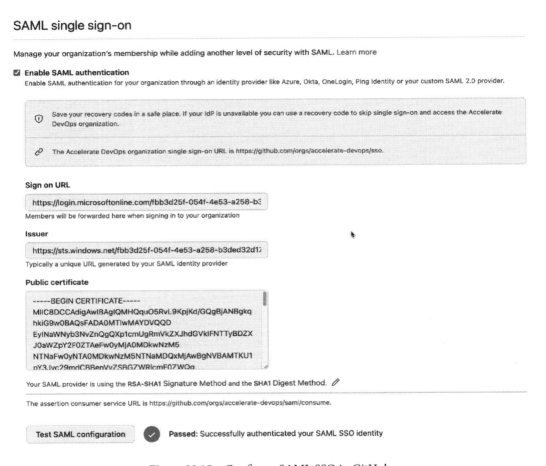

Figure 20.15 – Configure SAML SSO in GitHub

Click **Test SAML configuration** and log in with your AAD credentials. If everything was successful, you can check **Require SAML authentication** to enforce the access with SAML. GitHub will then check which users have not been granted access through the IdP and remove them after your confirmation.

Note that only authorized PAT tokens and SSH keys can access content that is protected by SSO. Each user must go to their PAT tokens/SSH keys and authorize them as in the example in *Figure 20.16*:

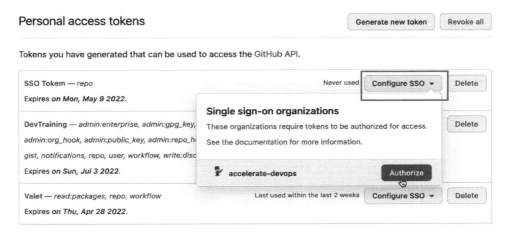

Figure 20.16 – Authorize a PAT token for SSO protected organizations

Of course, the configuration for every IdP is different, and the values vary slightly depending on whether you configure an enterprise, an organization, or a server. But with the documentation of your IdP, the setup should be straightforward.

SCIM

If you enable SAML SSO, users will not be automatically deprovisioned when you deactivate a user in your IdP. You can implement **SCIM** in GHEC to automatically add, manage, and remove access based on the information of your IdP.

SCIM is an API endpoint (see `https://docs.github.com/en/enterprise-cloud@latest/rest/reference/scim`) that is used by your IdP to manage the users in GitHub. Compatible IdPs are, for example, **Azure AD**, **Okta**, and **OneLogin**. To configure SCIM, you must follow the documentation of your IdP if they are compatible. Here is the tutorial for AAD: `https://docs.microsoft.com/en-us/azure/active-directory/saas-apps/github-provisioning-tutorial`.

> **Disable Third-Party Access Restrictions**
>
> Note that you have to disable third-party access restrictions in the settings of your organization before authorizing your IdP. You can do this under **Settings | Third-party access | Disable access restrictions**.

Automatic team synchronization

If you use SAML SSO on GHEC, you can set up **team synchronization** to automatically sync team membership with your IdP. Currently, team synchronization only supports **AAD** and **Okta**.

You can enable team synchronization in the settings of your organization under **Authentication security** (`/settings/security`). There, you can then see how many teams are synchronized and jump to the filtered audit log to see all relevant events (see *Figure 20.17*):

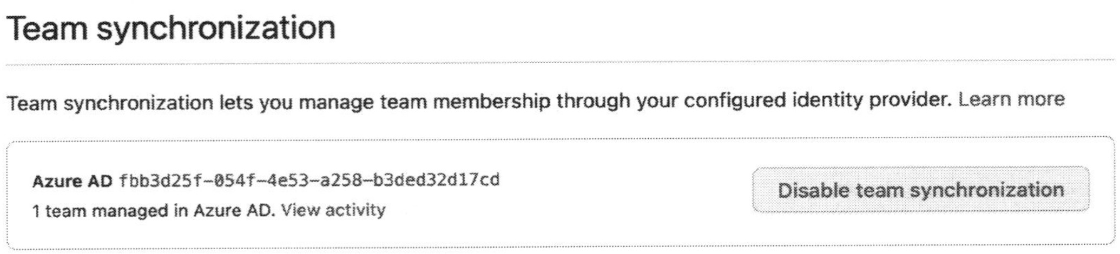

Team synchronization

Team synchronization lets you manage team membership through your configured identity provider. Learn more

Azure AD fbb3d25f–054f–4e53–a258–b3ded32d17cd
1 team managed in Azure AD. View activity

Disable team synchronization

Figure 20.17 – Enabling team synchronization for an organization

Once enabled, you can create new teams and select one or more groups from your IdP that get synchronized with your team, as you can see in *Figure 20.18*:

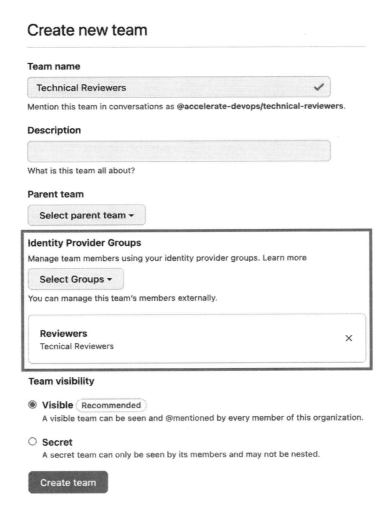

Figure 20.18 – Creating teams with automatic synchronization

You can add these teams inside other teams (**Parent team**), but you cannot sync nested groups to GitHub.

Enterprise Managed Users

In GHEC, even if you set up SAML SSO for your enterprise or organization, every user still needs a user account on GitHub.com. The GitHub user account is basically the identity of the user, and the SAML authorization is the access granted to certain Enterprise resources. The user could contribute to open source and other organizations using their identity, and must authenticate using SSO to access Enterprise resources. But many organizations don't want that. They want complete control over the identity of their users. The solution for that is **Enterprise Managed Users** (**EMU**). With EMU, the identity of users gets completely managed in the IdP. A new user gets created if a user logs in for the first time using the identity from the IdP. This user cannot contribute to open source or be added as an outside collaborator to other repositories. Also, the contributions only count to the profile of that user.

EMU gives your enterprise a lot of control over the identities, but it comes with a lot of restrictions, as shown in the following examples:

- Users cannot **collaborate** on, **star**, **watch**, or **fork** repositories outside of the enterprise. They cannot create issues or pull requests, **push code**, comment, or add reactions to these repositories.

- Users are only visible to other members of the same enterprise, and they cannot follow other users outside of the enterprise.

- They cannot install **GitHub Apps** on their user accounts.

- Users can only create **private** and **internal** repositories.

These restrictions make a lot of things difficult. One of the main benefits of GitHub is its integration of open source repositories. But if EMU allows you to use the cloud instead of a server instance, it might be worth giving it a shot.

Currently, EMU-supported IdPs are **AAD** and **Okta**.

If you want to try EMU, you must contact GitHub's sales team and they will create a new enterprise for you.

To learn more about EMU, see `https://docs.github.com/en/enterprise-cloud@latest/admin/identity-and-access-management/managing-iam-with-enterprise-managed-users/about-enterprise-managed-users`.

Authentication with GHES

On the server, things work differently. You can configure SSO for **SAML**, **LDAP**, or **CAS**. The configuration is straightforward and not so different from GHEC. Users do not need a `GitHub.com` account; they can sign in directly to the server using the IdP, similar to EMU. But if GitHub Connect is configured, users can connect their GitHub account in **User Settings | GitHub Connect** and share the number of contributions with their public GitHub profile. This way, they can connect multiple corporate identities to their GitHub profile if they choose to do so.

The Audit API

GHEC, as well as GHES, supports audit logging. The log contains log entries for all security-relevant events. Each audit log entry shows applicable information about an event, such as the following:

- The enterprise or organization an action was performed in
- The user (`actor`) who performed the action
- The user affected by the action
- Which repository an action was performed in
- The action that was performed
- Which country the action took place in
- The date and time the action occurred

Figure 20.19 shows a sample audit log in GHEC at the enterprise level. You can search and filter the audit log. You can pick predefined filters and click on the title elements of the log entries to create a filter statement:

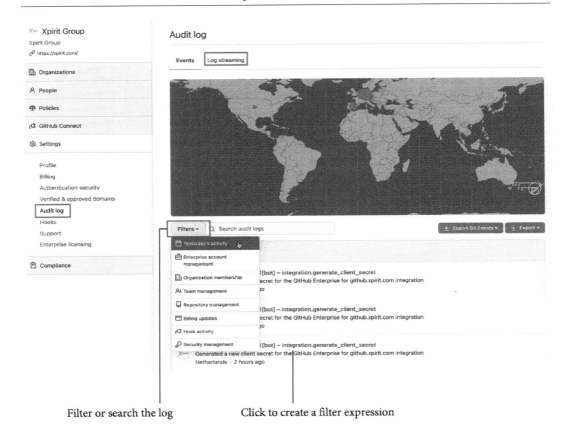

Figure 20.19 – The audit log of a GHEC instance

On GHEC, you can enable log streaming and configure automatic streaming of all events to one of the following targets:

- Amazon S3
- Azure Blob storage
- Azure Event Hubs
- Google Cloud Storage
- Splunk

You can forward the events with Azure Event Hubs to other tools such as Log Analytics or Sentinel.

You can also access the audit log using the audit log API. You can query the audit log using GraphQL or the REST API. The following example shows how you could retrieve all events for a specific date using the REST API:

```
$ curl -H "Authorization: token TOKEN" \
--request GET \
"https://api.github.com/enterprises/name/audit-
log?phrase=created:2022-01-01&page=1&per_page=100"
```

For more information about querying audit logs using the API, see https://docs.github.com/en/enterprise-cloud@latest/admin/monitoring-activity-in-your-enterprise/reviewing-audit-logs-for-your-enterprise/using-the-audit-log-api-for-your-enterprise.

GitHub Learning Lab

One of the big advantages of GitHub is that most developers already know how it works. This means less time for training and onboarding. But, of course, there are still developers that are new to GitHub. GitHub offers the GitHub Learning Lab (https://lab.github.com/) for free. It contains many learning paths that use GitHub issues and a bot to provide you with a hands-on experience to learn GitHub.

There are also many free learning paths available on Microsoft Learn if you prefer this way of learning. Just go to Microsoft Learn and filter by product, GitHub: https://docs.microsoft.com/en-us/learn/browse/?products=github.

Summary

In this chapter, you learned about the different pricing and hosting options for GitHub. You learned about enterprise security and how you can integrate GitHub into your enterprise.

In the next chapter, I'll show you how you can migrate from your existing source control system or DevOps solution to GitHub.

Further reading

Use the following links to get more information on the topics:

- *Pricing*: `https://github.com/pricing`
- *GitHub AE*: `https://docs.github.com/en/github-ae@latest/admin/overview/about-github-ae`
- *SCIM*: `https://docs.github.com/en/enterprise-cloud@latest/rest/reference/scim`
- *Enterprise Managed Users*: `https://docs.github.com/en/enterprise-cloud@latest/admin/identity-and-access-management/managing-iam-with-enterprise-managed-users/about-enterprise-managed-users`
- *Audit logs*: `https://docs.github.com/en/enterprise-cloud@latest/admin/monitoring-activity-in-your-enterprise/reviewing-audit-logs-for-your-enterprise/about-the-audit-log-for-your-enterprise`
- *GitHub Learning Lab*: `https://lab.github.com`
- *Microsoft Learn*: `https://docs.microsoft.com/en-us/learn`

21
Migrating to GitHub

If you are not a start-up, then you always have existing tools and processes that must be considered when moving to a new platform. In this chapter, we will discuss different strategies related to migrating to GitHub from different platforms.

In this chapter, we will cover the following:

- Picking the right migration strategy
- Achieving compliance with low-fidelity migrations
- Synchronizing requirements for a smooth transition
- Migrating from Azure DevOps with the GitHub Enterprise Importer
- Migrating pipelines using Valet

Picking the right migration strategy

When migrating to a new platform, you have different options:

- **High-fidelity migration**: You try to migrate as much as possible to the new platform.
- **Clean cut-over migration**: You only migrate the bare minimum that is necessary to start working on the new platform.

High-fidelity migrations to complex platforms have different problems. The main problem is that there is not a 1-to-1 mapping of all entities and that things just work differently on different platforms. By migrating everything over, you influence the way people use the new system. The data is optimized for the old system using old processes. Also, the time, costs, and complexity involved in a high-fidelity migration are not linear. The more you try to get to 100% fidelity, the more complex and expensive it gets, and 100% is normally not achievable at all (see *Figure 21.1*).

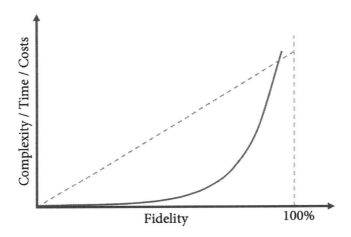

Figure 21.1 – Complexity, time, and costs for different levels of fidelity

Clean cut-over migrations are optimal if you want to achieve a change in behavior and use the new platform optimally. In the case study in this book, I assume a clean cut-over migration: the teams start on the new platform and only move over what is absolutely necessary.

The reality is somewhere in between these two extremes. If you want to accelerate software delivery, you start with a clean cut-over migration, but to scale in your enterprise and drive adoption, you provide some migration paths and tooling for the teams to move over fast. And there will be some dormant projects/products that you may want to archive for later reactivation. Keep all the old systems running or just migrate them over.

Achieving compliance with low-fidelity migrations

One concern that many customers have is **end-to-end traceability** for **compliance** reasons. In many highly-regulated industries, you have to provide end-to-end traceability for all requirements and final functional tests. The problem with low-fidelity migration is that you will get a cut in that traceability chain.

But that does not mean that the only solution is high-fidelity migration. You can still do a clean cut-over and keep the old systems in read-only mode running for as long as necessary. In the new system, you must achieve end-to-end traceability anyway. To stay compliant, you need a mapping of the old system identifiers to the new system for the requirements that span both systems.

In the case of an audit, you can provide reports from both systems – both the old and the new. For some requirements, you might have to look at both reports, but that will still provide valid traceability if you have identifiers that allow mapping between the systems.

The inconvenience of keeping the old system running is normally far less than trying to perform a high-fidelity migration, but this depends on many things, such as the licenses of the old system.

Synchronizing requirements for a smooth transition

One option that is interesting in this context, especially for big enterprises with many different tools, is the synchronization of requirements across different platforms with a product like **Tasktop** (`https://www.tasktop.com/`). Tasktop has connectors to many products like Jira, Salesforce, ServiceNow, IBM Rational, IBM DOORS, Polarion ALM, Azure DevOps, and many more. Synchronizing requirements and work items between tools enables multiple use cases:

- Work in both tools – the old and the new – at the same time during a migration period. This gives you more time for the migration and allows you to move over one team after the other while maintaining full traceability.

- Give different roles and teams the freedom to work using the tools they prefer. Your project managers prefer Jira, the architects IBM Rational, operations ServiceNow, and your developers want to switch to GitHub? You can enable these kinds of workflows by synching data between these tools.

Especially in complex environments where you have a large product that multiple teams work on simultaneously, synchronizing requirements and work items can help you to optimize migration.

Migrating your code

The easiest thing to do when moving to GitHub is migrating your code, especially when the code is already stored in another Git repository. Just clone the repository using `--bare` to make sure the repository is in a clean state:

```
$ git clone --bare <URL to old system>
```

Then push the code to the repository:

```
$ git push --mirror <URL to new repository>
```

If the repository already contains code, you must add the `--force` parameter to override. You can also use the GitHub CLI to create a repository on the fly when pushing an existing one:

```
$ gh repo create <NAME> --private --source <local path>
```

Since in Git the author information is matched using an email address, you just have to create user accounts in GitHub for all users and assign them the email address used in your previous Git system. The authors will then be resolved correctly.

You can also import code using the **GitHub Importer**. Besides Git, the following repository types are supported:

- **Subversion**
- **Mercurial**
- **Team Foundation Version Control (TFVC)**

The GitHub Importer takes the URL to the source system and creates a new repository. Files larger than 100 MB can be excluded or added to the Git **Large File Storage (LFS)**.

To import a repository using the GitHub Importer, click the plus next to your profile picture and select **Import repository** (see *Figure 21.2*):

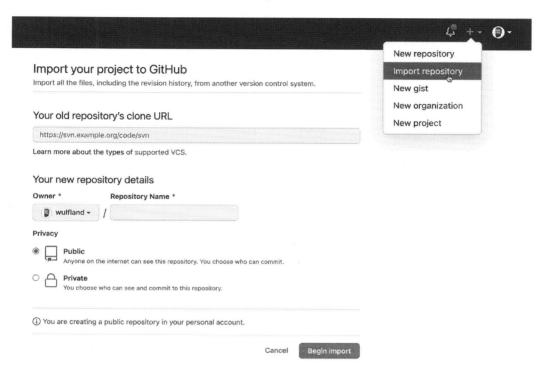

Figure 21.2 – Importing a repository

If you migrate from **Subversion**, you can use **git-svn** (https://git-scm.com/docs/git-svn) to sync your changes between a Git and a Subversion repository:

```
$ git svn <command>
```

If you migrate from **Azure DevOps/Team Foundation Server**, the best way is to migrate to Git from **TFVC** first, and then migrate to GitHub. There is also a tool similar to git-svn: **git-tfs** (https://github.com/git-tfs/git-tfs). This allows you also to sync changes between Git and TFVC or directly migrate to GitHub:

```
$ git tfs <command>
```

> **Note**
>
> Git is optimized for short-lived branches – TFVC isn't. You should not just migrate your code and all branches over. Use the chance for a clean cut-over and start with a new branching model. Migrating code to Git can be a first step to keeping parts of your history, but you should adjust your branching model after the migration.

Migrating your code to GitHub is not the challenge. There are many tools that can help you. The challenge is to get from an older branching model to a new one that is optimized for your new platform and offers accelerated software delivery performance (see *Chapter 11, Trunk-Based Development*).

The challenge lies in the things that are not directly stored in Git: pull requests, linked work items, and pipelines. These need more attention than just the Git repository itself.

Migrating from Azure DevOps or GitHub

If you migrate from GitHub to GitHub or from Azure DevOps to GitHub, you can use the **GitHub Enterprise Importer** (**GEI**) (see `https://github.com/github/gh-gei`). It is an extension for the GitHub CLI and can be installed using `extension install`:

```
$ gh extension install github/gh-gei
$ gh gei --help
```

You can set the **Personal Access Tokens** (**PAT**) as environment variables to authenticate to the source and target system:

```
$ export ADO_PAT=<personal access token>
$ export GH_SOURCE_PAT=<personal access token>
$ export GH_PAT=<personal access token>
```

You could also pass them to `generate-script` using `--github-source-pat` and `--ado-pat` parameters.

To create the migration script, execute one of the following commands depending on whether you want to migrate from GitHub or Azure DevOps:

```
$ gh gei generate-script --ado-source-org <source> --github-
target-org <target>
$ gh gei generate-script --github-source-org <source> --github-
target-org <target>
```

This will generate a PowerShell script `migrate.ps1` that can be used for the actual migration. The script will call `gh gei migrate-repo` for all team projects found in Azure DevOps or GitHub organization. This will queue the actual migration. It then gets the status by executing `gh gei wait-for-migration --migration-id` with the output of the previous command.

GEI currently supports the following:

- **Azure DevOps (ADO)**
- **GitHub Enterprise Server (GHES)** 3.4.1+
- GitHub Enterprise Cloud

For Azure DevOps, the following items will be migrated:

- Git source
- Pull requests
- User history for pull requests
- Work item links on pull requests
- Attachments on pull requests
- Branch protections for the repository

For GitHub Enterprise Server and Cloud, the following items are migrated additionally:

- Issues
- Milestones
- Wikis
- Project boards at the repository level
- GitHub Actions workflows (secrets and workflow run history not included)
- Commit comments
- Active webhooks
- Repository settings
- Branch protections

- GitHub Pages settings
- User history for the above data

See `https://docs.github.com/en/early-access/github/migrating-with-github-enterprise-importer` for more information. Note that GEI is still in beta and might change frequently.

If you are using GitHub Enterprise Server, you can also use `ghe-migrator` to import data, either from another server instance, or from GitHub Enterprise Cloud. See `https://docs.github.com/en/enterprise-server@3.4/admin/user-management/migrating-data-to-and-from-your-enterprise/about-migrations` for more information on data export and import on GitHub Enterprise Server.

Migrating your pipelines

To migrate your pipelines to GitHub Actions, you can use a tool called **Valet**. It supports the following sources:

- Azure DevOps (Classic pipelines, YAML pipelines, and releases)
- Jenkins
- Travis CI
- Circle CI
- GitLab CI

Valet is a Ruby-based command-line tool that gets installed using Docker.

> **Note**
> Valet is still in private beta at the time of writing and is still subject to change. Valet is not intended to be a 100% effective solution that can migrate everything! It is extensible and you will have to write your own transformers and probably still need to do some manual steps after the migration.

The distribution of Valet happens by pulling down a container image and using the two scripts `valet` and `valet-update` to interact with it:

```
$ docker pull ghcr.io/valet-customers/valet-cli
```

You have to authenticate to ghcr.io once you have access to the private beta using your username and a PAT token with read:packages access:

```
$ docker login ghcr.io -u <USERNAME>
```

The best way is to install Valet as a GitHub CLI extension, but you still need Docker running on your machine and you have to be authenticated to the registry. To install Valet as a GitHub CLI extension, execute the following command:

```
$ gh extension install github/gh-valet
```

You can now easily update Valet using gh valet update.

Valet is configured using environment variables. The easiest way to do this is to set these in a file called .env.local in the folder that you are using Valet in. This, for example, is the configuration for migrating pipelines from Azure to GitHub Enterprise Cloud:

```
GITHUB_ACCESS_TOKEN=<GitHub PAT>
GITHUB_INSTANCE_URL=https://github.com

AZURE_DEVOPS_PROJECT=<project name>
AZURE_DEVOPS_ORGANIZATION=<org name>
AZURE_DEVOPS_INSTANCE_URL=https://dev.azure.com/<org>
```

Valet has three modes:

- gh valet audit will analyze the source download information about all pipelines supported. It will create an audit summary report (Markdown) with all the pipelines, build steps, and environments found. You can use an audit to plan your migrations.

- gh valet dry-run will convert the pipelines to a GitHub Actions workflow file and output the YAML file.

- gh valet migrate will convert the pipeline to a GitHub Actions workflow file and create a pull request in the target GitHub repository containing the changes to the workflow file.

- gh valet forecast forecasts the usage of GitHub Actions based on historical pipeline utilization.

To run an audit using the previous configuration and create a report, just run the following command:

```
$ gh valet audit azure-devops --output-dir .
```

This will generate an `audit_summary.md` report and three files for every supported pipeline: a `.config.json` file containing the configuration, a `.source.yml` file containing the source pipeline converted to YAML, and a `.yml` file containing the transformed GitHub Actions workflow that will later be migrated. To execute the migration for one pipeline, run `valet migrate`:

```
$ valet migrate azure-devops pipeline \
    --target-url https://github.com/<org>/<repo-name> \
    --pipeline-id <definition-id>
```

Remember that this is a best-effort migration! Not everything can be migrated. For example, the following elements cannot be migrated:

- Secrets
- Service connections
- Unknown tasks
- Self-hosted runners
- Variables from Key Vault

You can write your own transformers for pipeline steps, either for unknown steps or to override existing behavior from Valet. Create a new Ruby file (`.rb`) and add a function in the following format:

```
transform "taskname" do |item|
end
```

For Azure DevOps tasks, the name includes the version number. To see what the item object contains, you can output it to the console using `puts item`.

Here is a sample transformer that would override the DotNetCoreCLI task version
2 and replace it with a run step on Bash that uses the globstar syntax to iterate all
.csproj files and execute the command using the arguments from the source pipeline:

```
transform "DotNetCoreCLI@2" do |item|
  if(item["command"].nil?)
    item["command"] = "build"
  end


  {
    shell: "bash",
    run: "shopt -s globstar; for f in ./**/*.csproj; do dotnet
#{ item['command']} $f #{item['arguments'] } ; done"
  }
end
```

To use your custom transformers, you can use the --custom-transformers
parameter. You can specify individual transformers or entire directories if you have many
transformers:

```
$ valet migrate azure-devops pipeline \
    --target-url https://github.com/<org>/<repo-name> \
    --pipeline-id <definition-id> \
    --custom-transformers plugin/*
```

Each workflow system is different! Make sure to spend time analyzing how you want your
pipelines to be transformed to optimize for the new platform instead of just trying to
migrate everything over. If you've figured that out, then Valet will be a great tool that can
help you to transition your teams faster to GitHub.

Summary

GitHub is a complex, fast-growing ecosystem that is challenging for any kind of migration. When migrating, make sure to focus on optimizing for productivity on the new platform rather than on migrating everything over and then letting your teams deal with the mess. Depending on the size of your organization and the source platforms, your migration story might look completely different.

In this chapter, you've learned about the different tools from GitHub and partners that can help you facilitate your migration.

In the next chapter, we'll talk about organizing your teams and repositories for optimal collaboration.

Further reading

These are the links from this chapter that you can use to get more information on the topics discussed:

- *GitHub Importer*: `https://docs.github.com/en/get-started/importing-your-projects-to-github/importing-source-code-to-github/importing-a-repository-with-github-importer`
- *GitHub Enterprise Importer CLI*: `https://github.com/github/gh-gei` and `https://docs.github.com/en/early-access/github/migrating-with-github-enterprise-importer`
- *GitHub Enterprise Server Importer*: `https://docs.github.com/en/enterprise-server@3.4/admin/user-management/migrating-data-to-and-from-your-enterprise/about-migrations`
- *ghe-migrator*: `https://docs.github.com/en/enterprise-server@3.4/admin/user-management/migrating-data-to-and-from-your-enterprise/about-migrations`
- *Tasktop*: `https://www.tasktop.com/`
- *git-svn*: `https://git-scm.com/docs/git-svn`
- *git-tfs*: `https://github.com/git-tfs/git-tfs`

22
Organizing Your Teams

In this chapter, you'll learn about the best practices for structuring your repositories and teams into organizations and enterprises to foster collaboration and facilitate administration.

In this chapter, we will cover the following topics:

- GitHub scopes and namespaces
- Structuring GitHub teams
- Role-based access
- Custom roles
- Outside collaborators

GitHub scopes and namespaces

The main entities in GitHub are repositories. A repository can be created for a user or an organization. The URL of the repository will be in the following format:

```
https://github.com/<username>/<repository>
https://github.com/<organization>/<repository>
```

For GitHub Enterprise Server, you must replace `https://github.com` with the URL of your server. A user and organization name on a platform must be unique since they provide a namespace. The name of a repository must be unique in that namespace.

GitHub enterprises

In GitHub, an enterprise is a container for multiple organizations. Enterprises are not namespaces – the organization names must still be unique. Enterprises have a URL slug that is used to refer to the enterprise. The URL to your enterprise will look like this:

```
https://github.com/enterprises/<enterprise-slug>
```

If you own an organization that is paid by invoice, then you can upgrade to an enterprise under **Settings | Billing and plans**. Otherwise, you must contact GitHub sales.

A GitHub enterprise has three roles:

- **Owner**: Has full administrative rights to the enterprise but not to organizations
- **Members**: Members or outside collaborators with access to at least one organization
- **Billing Managers**: Can only view and manage billing information

There are some settings you can configure at the enterprise level for all organizations, such as **SAML authentication**, **SSH Certificate Authorities**, or an **IP allow list**. There are also some enterprise-level webhooks and you can access the audit log for the entire enterprise. Audit log streaming to cloud storage, Splunk, or Azure Event Hubs is only available at the enterprise level, but most of the settings are around **billing** and **licensing**.

You can also set policies for many of the settings that can be configured at the organization level. If a policy has been set, the owner of the organization cannot change the settings. If a policy hasn't been defined, the setting can be configured by the owners of the organizations.

GitHub organizations

The main way to manage your repositories and teams is by using organizations. They can also exist without an enterprise, and you can move them between different enterprises. Organizations are not meant to be given out as a self-service for your teams to organize themselves. Some companies have more than 2,000 organizations – and this is a big problem, especially for managing integrations. GitHub Apps, for example, can only be configured at the organization level – not at the enterprise level. If you want to configure integration with your Jira instance, then you must do this for all organizations. You cannot configure this at the enterprise level.

One organization should be enough for most customers. If your company has different legal entities that must be separate, then this might be a reason to have multiple organizations. Another reason would be if you want to separate open and inner source. However, you should not have one organization for all departments or divisions. It is better to use teams for that.

An organization has the following roles:

- **Owner**: Has full access to teams, settings, and repositories
- **Members**: Can see members and non-secret teams, as well as create repositories
- **Outside Collaborators**: These are not members of the organization but they have access to one or more repositories

Organizations have projects, packages, teams, and repositories. You can configure many settings for repositories. If you don't configure these settings at the organization level, these settings can be set at the repository level.

The main way to structure your organization is by using teams. We'll look at these in the next section.

Structuring GitHub teams

Teams are not just the more convenient way to grant permissions to repositories that allow faster on- and off-boarding. They can also be used to share knowledge and notify certain groups of changes.

Teams have discussions, and you can see their repositories and projects. Teams can have one of the following two visibilities:

- **Visible**: A visible team can be seen and mentioned by every member of this organization
- **Secret**: A secret team can only be seen by its members and may not be nested

A team exists in the namespace of an organization. This means that the name of the team must be unique inside the organization. You can mention a team or add it as a code owner using the following syntax:

```
@<organization>/<team-name>
```

You can use teams to reflect your company or group's structure with cascading access permissions and mentions by nesting them. You can do this by specifying a parent team when creating a new team. This makes the new team a child team. Child teams can also be parent teams – this way, you can create a deep hierarchy. Teams inherit permissions and notifications from their parent teams, but not the other way around.

By nesting teams, you can create the structure of your company. You could create a team for all employees, each division, each department, and each product team (**vertical teams**). You can also use teams for **horizontal teams** – interest groups such as communities of practices (see *Figure 22.1*):

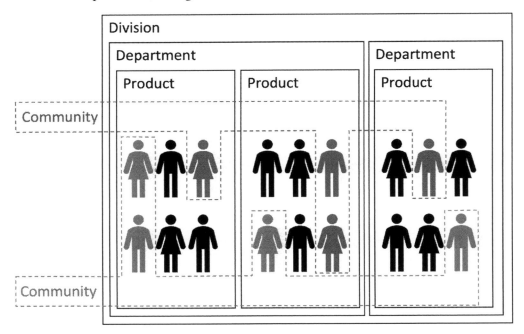

Figure 22.1 – Structuring your organizations using teams

This allows you to share knowledge and ownership across your value stream teams. You can also nest horizontal teams if this fits your community structure.

Nested teams can be expanded in the **Teams** tab of an organization (see *Figure 22.2*):

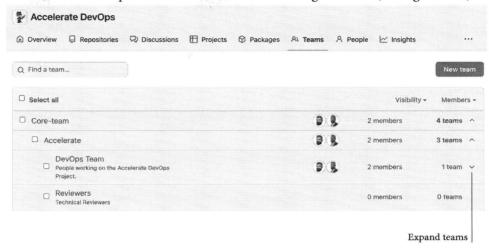

Figure 22.2 – Nested teams in the Teams tab of an organization

Teams have pages for discussions. Organization members can create and participate in discussions with the team, but the team can also have private discussions that are not visible to the rest of the organization (see *Figure 22.3*):

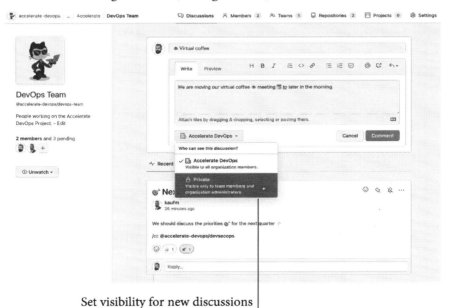

Figure 22.3 – Team pages with discussion

Teams can be mentioned and assigned as reviewers and code owners. It is a very powerful tool for structuring your organization simplistically. But try to keep it simple and use names that people can easily understand. You don't want to build a bureaucratic monster! Keep it simple.

Role-based access

At the repository level, you can grant role-based access to teams or individual people. You can use one of the following default roles:

- **Read**: Read and clone repositories. Open and comment on issues and pull requests.

- **Triage**: Read permissions, plus manage issues and pull requests.

- **Write**: Triage permissions, plus read, clone, and push to repositories.

- **Maintain**: Write permissions, plus manage issues, pull requests, and configure some repository settings.

- **Admin**: Full access to repositories, including sensitive and destructive actions.

Note that the **read** role can do more than just read! It can open and comment on issues and pull requests. **Triage** and **maintain** are typical roles in open source projects. They are not so commonly used in enterprise scenarios.

You can set a base permission for an organization to read, write, or admin. This will grant all members the corresponding permission to all repositories. Outside collaborators do not inherit the base permission (see `https://docs.github.com/en/organizations/managing-access-to-your-organizations-repositories/setting-base-permissions-for-an-organization` for more information).

Custom roles

You can define custom roles in the organization settings under **Repository roles** (`/settings/roles`). Click **Create a role** and specify a name and description for the new role. Then, select a default role to inherit the permissions from and add permissions to it (see *Figure 22.4*):

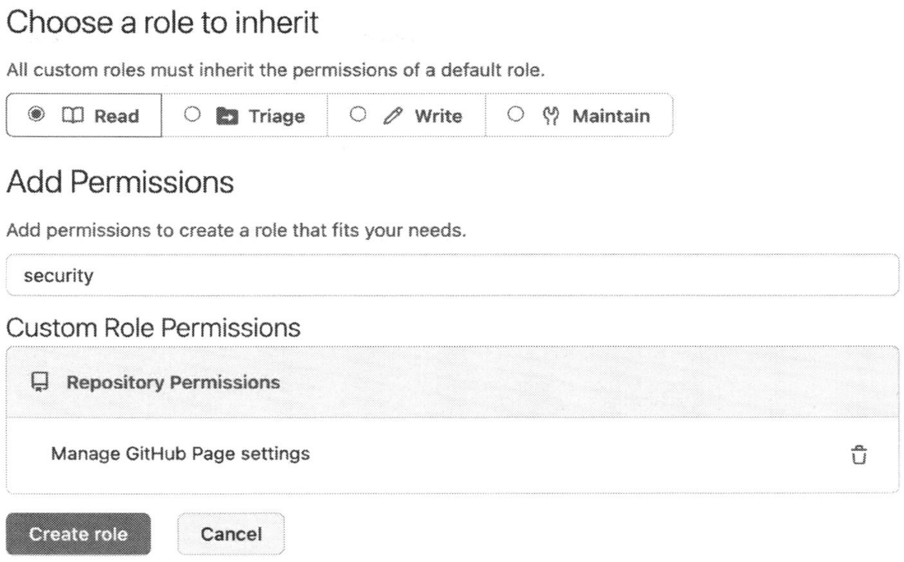

Choose a role to inherit

All custom roles must inherit the permissions of a default role.

| ◉ 📖 **Read** | ○ 🗂 **Triage** | ○ ✏️ **Write** | ○ 👷 **Maintain** |

Add Permissions

Add permissions to create a role that fits your needs.

> security

Custom Role Permissions

🖥 **Repository Permissions**	
Manage GitHub Page settings	🗑

[Create role]   [Cancel]

Figure 22.4 – Creating custom roles in GitHub

The permissions are categorized. So, if you type `security` in the search box, the list will show you all the available permission related to security.

Permissions are available in the following categories:

- Discussions
- Issue
- Pull request
- Repository
- Security

Note that not everything is configurable. For example, there are no specific permissions for GitHub Packages at the time of writing.

If a person is given different levels of access, the higher permissions always override the lower ones. If a person has been given multiple roles, a warning will appear on GitHub next to the person with **Mixed roles**.

And again: try not to go too crazy with custom roles. Keep it as simple as possible.

Outside collaborators

An **outside collaborator** is a person who is not a member of your organization but has access to one or more of your organization's repositories.

> **Note**
> Adding an outside collaborator to a private repository will consume one of your paid licenses!

Outside collaborators are not **members** of your organization. They don't see internal repositories and they do not inherit base permissions.

You can't invite outside collaborators at the organization level – you can only invite members to your organization and then convert them into outside collaborators, (see *Figure 22.5*):

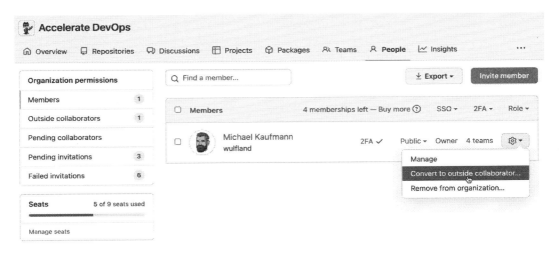

Figure 22.5 – Converting members into outside collaborators

As a repository administrator, if you **Add people** under **Settings | Collaborators and teams**, if they already belong to the organization, they will be automatically added as members. If not, they will be added as outside collaborators.

Outside collaborators are a great way to easily collaborate with partners and customers without requiring them to be part of your organization. But keep in mind that this does not work if you use **Enterprise Managed Users**. And if you have **SAML Single Sign On** enabled, outside collaborators will bypass that. That's why organization owners can prevent repository administrators from inviting outside collaborators to repositories in the settings of the organization.

Summary

In this chapter, you learned about the best practices for structuring organizations, repositories, and teams in your enterprise. We talked about nesting teams, using teams for interest groups, role-based access, and outside collaborators.

In the last chapter, we'll put all the pieces of this book together and guide you through the process of using GitHub to transform your enterprise and use it to accelerate DevOps in your organization.

Further reading

Please refer to the following links and further GitHub documentation to learn more about the topics that were covered in this chapter:

- *About teams*: `https://docs.github.com/en/organizations/organizing-members-into-teams/about-teams`

- *Base permissions*: `https://docs.github.com/en/organizations/managing-access-to-your-organizations-repositories/setting-base-permissions-for-an-organization`

- *Custom roles*: `https://docs.github.com/en/enterprise-cloud@latest/organizations/managing-peoples-access-to-your-organization-with-roles/managing-custom-repository-roles-for-an-organization`

- *Outside collaborators*: `https://docs.github.com/en/organizations/managing-access-to-your-organizations-repositories/adding-outside-collaborators-to-repositories-in-your-organization`

- *Managing access to your repository*: `https://docs.github.com/en/repositories/managing-your-repositorys-settings-and-features/managing-repository-settings/managing-teams-and-people-with-access-to-your-repository#inviting-a-team-or-person`

23
Transform Your Enterprise

In this last chapter, we'll talk about enterprise transformation. I'll explain how you can put all the pieces explained in this book together to transform your enterprise into one with an engineering culture with increased developer velocity.

We will cover the following topics:

- Why many transformations fail
- Starting with WHY?
- Data-driven transformation

Why many transformations fail

Software is at the heart of every product and service in every industry – from the customer experience to supply chain management (see *Chapter 1, Metrics That Matter*). This means a lot of enterprises must transform to become digital high-performance companies, but many of these transformations fail. Roles are renamed, management levels are restructured, and hosting is renamed to private cloud, but often the culture and performance do not change. There are many reasons why transformations fail and I want to give you some examples here.

Assuming your company or industry is special

Many customers that I meet believe that they are completely special, but they are not. And, I'm sorry to say, it's probable that neither is your company or industry. At least, not when it comes to digital transformation. Could your product kill people if it has a defect? So could cars, airplanes, trucks, medical devices, and so on. And the same is true for all of the parts that are produced for these products. They are nothing special. Must you comply with certain standards? Do you create military products? Are you publicly traded? Do you work for governments? Whatever you think makes your company special, chances are there are many companies that face the same challenges that you do and the same rules apply to them as to you when it comes to your DevOps transformation.

If you look at the studies mentioned in *Chapter 1*, you'll find that they apply to all companies: from small start-ups to big enterprises and from cutting-edge internet companies to highly regulated industries, such as finance, healthcare, and government (*Forsgren N., Humble, J., & Kim, G., 2018*, p. 22).

But this is actually a good thing. This means a lot of the problems you're probably facing during your own transformation have already been solved by others. You can learn from their failures and don't have to experience them yourself.

Having no sense of urgency

The biggest blocker to change is complacency. If people in your business are complacent, they will tend to resist change and keep on doing *business as usual*.

You must establish a true sense of urgency for people to address critical things now. Urgency in this case does not mean pressure from management that creates anxiety. True urgency should drive people to change with a deep determination to win – not with anxiety about losing (*John P. Kotter 2008*).

Without a sense of true urgency, people will resist change and are more likely to keep up their old behaviors. Note that a sense of urgency might arise for completely different reasons at distinct levels of your organization. Management might feel pressure from the market and the lack of agility to react with frequent releases. Engineers might feel the pressure of technical debt and the problem of attracting and retaining talent because of old processes and tools. It is important to align these stories to a common root course using a clear vision. Only if you manage to align the different senses of urgency into a single force that drives in the same direction can you ensure that the different forces will not neutralize themselves

Having no clear vision

It is easy to replace tools, processes, and roles, but it is hard to change behavior, culture, and stories. Without a clear vision, the transformation will not yield the desired results.

If I hear customers saying *we are not Microsoft or Google* or *we are not a cutting-edge internet company*, it tells me that they are missing a clear vision. If your vision clearly states that you want to become the digital leader in your industry or change from a product company to a service company, people will not dare to say things that contradict it.

A good vision to drive change is a clear and compelling statement of where all your transformation leads (*John P. Kotter 2012*).

I believe it is worth noting that DevOps transformations are not always driven by upper management. I know many companies where the DevOps transformation is driven by individual departments or even teams. Nevertheless, the same rules apply – you need a clear vision for the teams in your team or department and to establish a sense of urgency to ensure that the transformation is successful.

Letting obstacles block your progress

When you start a transformation, many obstacles will block your transformation. Good examples that I often experience are certain regulations in certain industries. Many regulations, such as ISO26262 or GxP, propose the **V-Model** for software engineering. The V-Model is based upon the **waterfall model**, so it contradicts basically everything we have learned in many years of DevOps research. If you insist on keeping the waterfall model, your DevOps transformation will most likely fail, but this is due to your internal interpretations of the regulations. If you have a closer look at them, you'll realize that they just insist on best practices. If your practices are superior to the recommended ones, you can justify that and still pass an audit.

Most obstacles you'll encounter are caused by your organization, for example, your organizational structure, tight job categories, processes, or trench warfare between the working council and management. Don't permit these obstacles to block your transformation.

Not getting help

Consultants have a bad reputation in many companies, mostly because of bad experiences. I helped a customer once with digitalizing their product. The customer was used to doing everything in line with the waterfall method and I introduced Scrum and CI/CD to them. We did some training and used agile development successfully over the next couple of years. After two years, management paid an expensive consultant firm to introduce Scrum. They basically had the same slides and told the same story that I had told everyone two years earlier. This kind of consultancy leads to a bad reputation.

But if you want to learn a new sport, you don't just buy the equipment and watch some videos on YouTube. You join a club or find yourself a coach that will guide you. Sports are not just about knowledge and tools – they are about building skills. And without an experienced coach, it is hard or impossible to succeed in certain sports.

The same is true for building new skills and capabilities in your business. There is no shame in getting help from someone more experienced that can guide you through the change. The odds are high that help will be cheap based on what you save in time and effort, never mind the costs of failure.

Starting with WHY?

For a transformation to succeed, you need a clear vision and a sense of urgency. The vision should be precise, compelling, short, and should inspire people to follow it. To communicate the vision, you can follow the *Golden Circle* (*Simon Sinek 2011, p.38*) and communicate from the inside to the outside (see *Figure 23.1*):

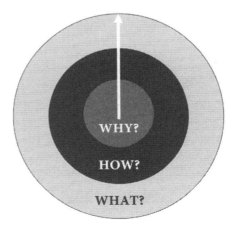

Figure 23.1 – Communicating a vision should start with WHY?

Let us see in more detail:

- **WHY?**: The reason why your company will undertake the transformation. This gives it a purpose and establishes a sense of urgency. Why should anyone care?

- **HOW?**: How are you going to succeed in the transformation process?

- **WHAT?**: The actual thing that you want to transform. What are you doing or making?

A purpose-driven mission

Don't underestimate the power of vision! If you are a manufacturer of combustion engine cars, transformation to electrical cars will not come easy. There will be resistance. People will be afraid to lose the power of their jobs.

To succeed, you need a clear vision and to communicate the *WHY?* – like the Volkswagen Group in its *goTOzero* mission statement in 2019, which concentrated on four main fields of action: climate change, resources, air quality, and environmental compliance.

By 2050, the entire **Volkswagen Group** wants to become balance sheet CO_2-neutral. By 2025, the company plans to reduce the carbon footprint of its fleet by 30 percent over its entire life cycle compared to 2015 (*Volkswagen 2019*).

This perfectly explains the WHY?, establishes urgency, and fits into their overall updated vision *to make this world a mobile, sustainable place with access to all the citizens.*

Equally, **Mercedes-Benz** stated in their *Ambition 2039* statement from 2019 that they aim to have a carbon-neutral car fleet and production over the next 20 years (*Mercedes-Benz Group Media 2019*).

And it is the same when you transform a product company into a software or services company. Even if you only transform from a waterfall organization to a DevOps organization, people will be afraid of the change and there will be resistance if you cannot paint a picture of a desirable future and explain *why* you have to undertake the transformation.

Establishing an engineering culture

Having a purpose-driven vision will help you to establish an **engineering culture** during your transformation: an inclusive and secure organizational culture that fosters talent and is driven by sharing and equality (*de Vries, M., & van Osnabrugge, R. 2022*).

This is a culture where people feel safe to speak up when they feel something is wrong, a culture where people feel safe to experiment and be creative without fear, and a culture where everyone feels welcome and safe – independent of heritage, gender, or religion.

The culture of an organization is a set of shared assumptions that guides behaviors within the organization (*Ravasi, D., & Schultz, M. 2006*). That's why it is hard to change it. Creating PowerPoint slides with values and mission statements might affect the culture but maybe not in the way management intends to do so.

As an engineer, you might ask yourself why the organization's culture matters to you. Isn't that a task for management? However, the culture is the result of the assumptions and the behaviors of every single person in the system – and that means that every single person can change it. As an engineer, you should be aware of your culture and you should speak up if you see that something is wrong. Start doing the right things and telling the right stories.

Culture is best ingrained into corporate behavior using little quotes and principles that have a deeper meaning. They are easy to remember and encourage people to do the right things. Here are some examples you will often hear in companies with great engineering cultures:

- *Ask forgiveness, not permission*: Encourage people to do the right thing, even if it is against current rules or processes.

- *You build it, you run it*: Establish end-to-end responsibility and ownership for the things built.

- *Fail early, fail fast, fail often (or fail fast, roll forward)*: Try to fail early and fast instead of making everything 100% bullet-proof.

- *Embrace failure*: Encourage people to experiment and take risks and ensure blameless learnings from failure. *Take responsibility and don't blame others.*

- *Collaborate, don't compete* or *work together not against*: Foster collaboration – across organizational boundaries and also with customers and partners.

- *Go fix*: Encourage people to take ownership and fix things instead of just complaining, but you have to ensure that innovation is not suppressed. Make sure people are also empowered to really fix the things they complain about.

- *Treat servers like cattle, not like pets*: Encourage people to *automate everything*.

- *If it hurts, do it more often*: Motivate people to practice things that are hard to build up the skills to accomplish. This phrase is often used in relation to releasing or testing applications.

These are just a few examples. More stories and sayings will arise when you transform your culture and establish DevOps.

A great engineering culture is not just the responsibility of management. They have to let it happen and provide the vision but the best culture is then created by the engineers themselves during the transformation.

Data-driven transformation

If you want your transformation to succeed, it is critical to measure the right metrics and to prove that the transformation really yields better results than the old system. That's why, in *Chapter 1*, *Metrics That Matter*, I introduced the data points you can collect to know what to optimize first and to achieve small wins that will help you keep everyone motivated to continue with the DevOps transformation. Measuring the right data should always be the start. Optimizing something that is not a constraint is a waste of resources and can even have a negative impact. Let's take adding caching to your application without proof that the operation was slowing down the system in the first place or of how much faster it can be when caching certain data, as an example. Caching introduces complexity and is a source of errors. So, maybe you did not optimize the system at all but made it worse by working based on assumptions. The same is true for your DevOps practices.

The Theory of Constraints

The **Theory of Constraints** (**TOC**) is based on systems theory and assumes that the throughput of a system would be infinite if it weren't for limiting constraints. The TOC tries to maximize the throughput for a system with its current constraints or to optimize the system by reducing these constraints.

A typical example to explain the theory is a freeway (*Small World 2016*). Let's assume we have a freeway with five lanes but with two construction sites that limit the capacity of two lanes (see *Figure 23.2*):

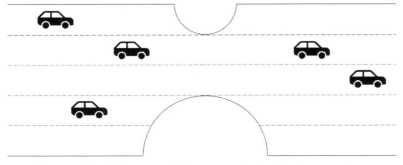

Figure 23.2 – A freeway with fewer cars, limited by its constraints

The traffic flows through the constraints but this only works up to a certain throughput. If there are too many cars, they will start interacting and slowing each other down, resulting in a traffic jam (see *Figure 23.3*):

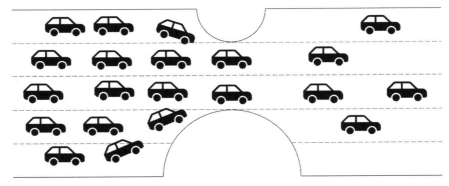

Figure 23.3 – If the throughput is too high, it grinds the traffic to a halt

To optimize the traffic for a maximal flow, you have to limit the traffic to the capacity of the biggest constraint (see *Figure 23.4*):

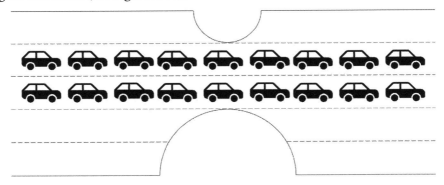

Figure 23.4 – The maximum flow equals the capacity of the constraint

Optimizing anything else other than the biggest constraint will not result in any improvement. Many cities have tried to add lanes before and after a tunnel with basically no improvement of the flow or any reduction of traffic jams. The same is true for your value streams – optimizing anything but the biggest constraint will not result in any improvement.

Eliminating bottlenecks

The TOC provides five focus steps for eliminating constraints (see *Figure 23.5*):

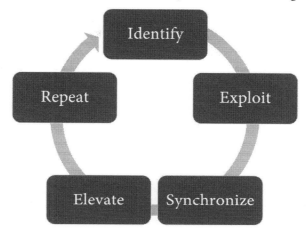

Figure 23.5 – The five focus steps for identifying and eliminating constraints

More details of the five steps are as follows:

- **Identify**: Identify the constraint that limits your current throughput
- **Exploit**: Make improvements to the throughput of the constraint
- **Synchronize**: Review and subordinate the other activities in the system and make sure they are aligned and support the constraint in an optimal way
- **Elevate**: Try to eliminate the constraint and work on the root cause of the problem
- **Repeat**: Continuously improve the system by identifying the next constraint that is limiting your current throughput

Systematically eliminating bottlenecks in your flow of work is the key to a successful DevOps transformation!

DevOps is a journey of continuous improvement

DevOps is a journey of continuously pushing the boundaries of software delivery performance further by eliminating bottlenecks. In the kickoff to their own DevOps transformation, Microsoft showed some videos of some pit stops from different areas: from Indianapolis in 1950 with 67 seconds to Melbourne in 2013 with about 2.96 seconds. It is a great metaphor for DevOps, continuously improving performance with automation and optimized processes.

DevOps is the union of people, process, and products to enable continuous delivery of value to our end users (Donovan Brown 2015).

It is an engineering culture of research, development, collaboration, learning, and ownership, and it only works if you enact all aspects together. You cannot just pick one aspect of DevOps and implement it without the others.

You can only improve a system that is about flow if you know the biggest bottleneck and work on that. Trying to optimize other things will not yield any results and is a waste of time and resources. That's why it is so important to perform a data-driven transformation and measure the right metrics to continuously monitor whether your improvements really yield the expected results. Identify one bottleneck, exploit it, improve it, and repeat.

Optimizing for value stream-aligned teams

I have not talked about any **DevOps team topologies** (*Matthew Skelton 2013*) in this book. I see them used often in more IT-driven transformations and it is commonplace to start your transformation journey aligning to one of the topologies and then switching to another model later after achieving a higher DevOps maturity (*Martyn Coupland 2022, p27*). Instead, I focused on **value stream-aligned** teams (see *Chapter 17, Empower Your Teams*).

Your DevOps journey should start with them and optimize everything to enable them to deliver value. This will automatically lead to **developer-first thinking** (developers being the engineers delivering the value here). If you practice a data-driven transformation and optimize for value by eliminating bottlenecks, topologies such as platform teams or enabling teams will arise. There is no need to plan this upfront. A DevOps organization should be a self-improving system, so once you get to that point, the rest will fall into place nicely.

A successful data-driven DevOps transformation has three major phases (as visualized in *Figure 23.6*):

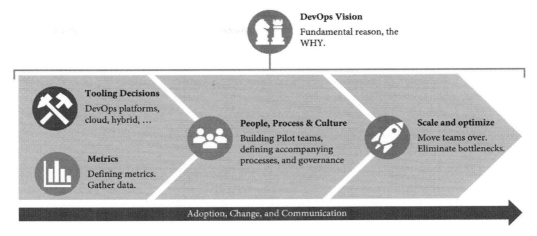

Figure 23.6 – The phases of data-driven DevOps transformation

More details of the phases are as follows:

- **Metrics**: Start by defining metrics and gathering data (see *Chapter 1, Metrics That Matter*).

- **Tooling decisions**: You will have to make some basic tooling decisions. In this book, I assume **GitHub** is the DevOps platform, but there will be more decisions to make regarding cloud usage and alignment to current governance processes.

- **People, process, and culture**: Carefully pick your pilot teams and bring them to the new platform by transforming their way of working to **lean management** and **higher collaboration**. Teach and enable them to adopt **engineering DevOps practices** such as automation and trunk-based development and enable them to **release** frequently **with confidence**. The metrics should improve rapidly. These are the quick wins you need to keep everyone motivated.

- **Scale and optimize**: With the pilot teams successful, you can start to scale by creating more teams that work on the new platform with the new processes and tools. This is also the time when you start optimizing more capabilities, such as **software architecture** and **lean product management** techniques. Take one bottleneck at a time, always observing whether the metrics confirm the desired results.

  Since DevOps is a journey and not a goal, this phase basically never ends. You may adjust the metrics after some time, you will optimize team size and autonomy, but the optimization does not end. The results just get smaller and smaller as you are already on a higher level.

- **DevOps vision**: The heart of the transformation throughout all phases is a strong vision that explains the *WHY?* and establishes a sense of urgency. Ensure that you have a good communication and change management strategy in place. There is resistance to any change and you have to address fear and communicate the *WHY?*, *HOW?*, and *WHAT?* of the process and the many success stories you gather along the way to motivate everyone to move forward.

Summary

To remain competitive, companies cannot just solve a customer's problem. They need to deliver products and services that delight their customers and they must be able to engage with the market and respond fast to changing demands. This makes every company today a software company. If your company will not be able to transform, it will probably be out of business in a few years.

Many transformations fail but many are successful and these companies prove that even big enterprises or companies in highly regulated environments are able to transform and adopt DevOps.

With GitHub, you have one of the best products on the market, which is loved by more than 73 million developers worldwide, by all big open source communities, and by more than 84% of the Fortune 500 companies. This means less training, quicker onboarding, and high developer satisfaction, which leads to better talent attraction and retention. But the open source communities also provide you with building blocks for your applications, for tooling, for your pipeline, and they will also power the templates for your process templates. Leveraging the power of the community will help you to accelerate and GitHub gives you the opportunity to pay the community back by contributing yourself or by sponsoring the projects that you rely on.

I hope this book helps as a practical guide to a successful DevOps transformation using the power of GitHub. There is nothing more rewarding for me than seeing engineers having fun working on solving real engineering problems in a DevOps culture, instead of fighting bugs in production or estimating requirements they think are stupid.

Further reading

These are the references from this chapter that you can also use to get more information on the relevant topics:

- Simon Sinek (2011), *Start With Why – How Great Leaders Inspire Everyone to Take Action*, Penguin

- Simon Sinek (2019), *The Infinite Game*, Penguin

- Nadella, S., Shaw, G. & Nichols, J. T. (2017), *Hit Refresh: The Quest to Rediscover Microsoft's Soul and Imagine a Better Future for Everyone*, Harper Business

- Srivastava S., Trehan K., Wagle D. & Wang J. (April 2020). *Developer Velocity: How software excellence fuels business performance.* https://www.mckinsey.com/industries/technology-media-and-telecommunications/our-insights/developer-velocity-how-software-excellence-fuels-business-performance

- Forsgren N., Humble, J., & Kim, G. (2018). *Accelerate: The Science of Lean Software and DevOps: Building and Scaling High Performing Technology Organizations* (1st ed.) [E-book]. IT Revolution Press.

- John P. Kotter (2008), *A Sense of Urgency*, Harvard Business Review Press

- John P. Kotter (2012), *Leading Change*, Harvard Business Review Press

- Volkswagen (2019): *Volkswagen with New Corporate Mission Statement Environment "goTOzero"*: https://www.volkswagenag.com/en/news/2019/07/goTOzero.html

- Mercedes-Benz Group Media (2019): *"Ambition2039": Our path to sustainable mobility*: https://group-media.mercedes-benz.com/marsMediaSite/ko/en/43348842

- *Theory of constraints*: https://www.leanproduction.com/theory-of-constraints

- Small World (2016): *Theory of constraints – Drum-Buffer-Rope*: https://www.smallworldsocial.com/theory-of-constraints-104-balance-flow-not-capacity/

- de Vries, M., & van Osnabrugge, R. (2022): *Together we build an Engineering Culture.* XPRT Magazine #12: https://xpirit.com/together-we-build-an-engineering-culture/

- Ravasi, D., & Schultz, M. (2006). *Responding to organizational identity threats: Exploring the role of organizational culture.* Academy of Management Journal.

- Donovan Brown (2015): *What is DevOps?* https://www.donovanbrown.com/post/what-is-devops

- Matthew Skelton (2013): *What Team Structure is Right for DevOps to Flourish?* https://web.devopstopologies.com/

- Martyn Coupland (2022): *DevOps Adoption Strategies: Principles, Processes, Tools, and Trends*, Packt

Index

Packt.com

Subscribe to our online digital library for full access to over 7,000 books and videos, as well as industry leading tools to help you plan your personal development and advance your career. For more information, please visit our website.

Why subscribe?

- Spend less time learning and more time coding with practical eBooks and Videos from over 4,000 industry professionals
- Improve your learning with Skill Plans built especially for you
- Get a free eBook or video every month
- Fully searchable for easy access to vital information
- Copy and paste, print, and bookmark content

Did you know that Packt offers eBook versions of every book published, with PDF and ePub files available? You can upgrade to the eBook version at packt.com and as a print book customer, you are entitled to a discount on the eBook copy. Get in touch with us at customercare@packtpub.com for more details.

At www.packt.com, you can also read a collection of free technical articles, sign up for a range of free newsletters, and receive exclusive discounts and offers on Packt books and eBooks.

Other Books You May Enjoy

If you enjoyed this book, you may be interested in these other books by Packt:

Learning DevOps - Second Edition

Mikael Krief

ISBN: 9781801818964

- Understand the basics of infrastructure as code patterns and practices
- Get an overview of Git command and Git flow
- Install and write Packer, Terraform, and Ansible code for provisioning and configuring cloud infrastructure based on Azure examples
- Use Vagrant to create a local development environment
- Containerize applications with Docker and Kubernetes
- Apply DevSecOps for testing compliance and securing DevOps infrastructure
- Build DevOps CI/CD pipelines with Jenkins, Azure Pipelines, and GitLab CI
- Explore blue-green deployment and DevOps practices for open sources projects

Go for DevOps

John Doak, David Justice

ISBN: 9781801818896

- Understand the basic structure of the Go language to begin your DevOps journey
- Interact with filesystems to read or stream data
- Communicate with remote services via REST and gRPC
- Explore writing tools that can be used in the DevOps environment
- Develop command-line operational software in Go
- Work with popular frameworks to deploy production software
- Create GitHub actions that streamline your CI/CD process
- Write a ChatOps application with Slack to simplify production visibility

Packt is searching for authors like you

If you're interested in becoming an author for Packt, please visit `authors.packtpub.com` and apply today. We have worked with thousands of developers and tech professionals, just like you, to help them share their insight with the global tech community. You can make a general application, apply for a specific hot topic that we are recruiting an author for, or submit your own idea.

Share Your Thoughts

Now you've finished *Accelerate DevOps with GitHub*, we'd love to hear your thoughts! Scan the QR code below to go straight to the Amazon review page for this book and share your feedback or leave a review on the site that you purchased it from.

`https://packt.link/r/1801813353`

Your review is important to us and the tech community and will help us make sure we're delivering excellent quality content.

Printed in Great Britain
by Amazon

85710833R00307